SONS AGAINST FATHERS

Sons against Fathers

STUDIES IN
RUSSIAN RADICALISM AND
REVOLUTION

E. LAMPERT

OXFORD
AT THE CLARENDON PRESS

Oxford University Press, Ely House, London W. 1

GLASGOW NEW YORK TORONTO MELBOURNE WELLINGTON
CAPE TOWN SALISBURY IBADAN NAIROBI DAR ES SALAAM LUSAKA ADDIS ABABA
BOMBAY CALCUTTA MADRAS KARACHI LAHORE DACCA
KUALA LUMPUR SINGAPORE HONG KONG TOKYO

© *Oxford University Press 1965*

FIRST PUBLISHED 1965
REPRINTED LITHOGRAPHICALLY IN GREAT BRITAIN
FROM CORRECTED SHEETS OF THE FIRST EDITION
AT THE UNIVERSITY PRESS, OXFORD
BY VIVIAN RIDLER
PRINTER TO THE UNIVERSITY
1971

PREFACE

THIS book, originally planned as part of a larger work, is concerned with Russian radical and revolutionary thought in the eighteen-sixties, and its theme is the interplay of persons, ideas, and events. A historical section is combined with studies of three characters who both expressed and helped to shape a crucial period in Russian revolutionary history. As the events peculiar to the time resulted in a far-reaching transformation of men and society, it seemed necessary to give a fairly detailed account of the historical background. I felt justified, however, in keeping this in a separate section. The social, economic, and political developments described in it are shown to have produced new tensions and conflicts in Russian life, new ways of thinking and acting, and they are the essential evidence which guided me in the interpretation of the characters. But to weave this evidence into the story of the life and thought of the characters themselves would have tended to produce a too widely spread and featureless picture and lessen the interest in what they are, as distinct from what they are for. I hope the method adopted does not affect unduly the intended and underlying unity of the book.

Long and in part detailed though the historical account is, I do not claim that it is either exhaustive or exclusive. I did not concern myself with mere facts, whatever these may be. My chief aim was to look at the historical situation as it presented itself to radical contemporaries in Russia and to convey something of their own historical experience. The evidence from outside which I was able to find in support of this experience served to strengthen the conviction that to see events as their contemporaries—to be precise, their most awakened contemporaries—see them is a necessary element of a genuine historical view. But, at the same time, no student of history can avoid being involved in his own times in terms of the past, or at least in the past in terms of his own experience.

I am grateful to Cressida Ridley for her textual criticisms of some sections of the book; to John Simmons for letting me take

advantage of his unique bibliographical knowledge; and to
Patrick Thompson for his translation of the poems on pp. 123–4.
I also wish to record my general indebtedness to the many,
mainly Soviet, writers and scholars who have done much to
initiate and promote the study of my subject and whose names
and works are cited in the footnotes. To avoid wearying the
reader by their profusion and occasional elaborate length,
the footnotes have been banished from the text to the end of
the book.

   Finally, I owe a debt of gratitude to the Delegates of the
Oxford University Press for their interest in this work and to
the Press Readers for their assistance and patience in dealing
with my inaptness in typographical matters.

E. L.

Oxford 1964

NOTE

ALL dates prior to 1918 are given in the Old Style, which was twelve days behind the western Gregorian calendar in the nineteenth century and thirteen days in the twentieth century.

The English titles of untranslated or generally unknown Russian books, periodicals, and newspapers are printed in roman characters with quotation marks when cited on their own or before the transliterated and italicized Russian titles (in parentheses), and without quotation marks when they follow (in parentheses) the Russian titles: for instance, 'Annals of the Fatherland', or 'Contemporary' (*Sovremennik*), and *Russkoe slovo* (Russian Word). All other titles, English and foreign, are italicized in the usual way.

CONTENTS

LIST OF PLATES

I

REVOLUTION FROM ABOVE

1. *Alexander the Liberator*

SOCIETY, it has been claimed, can achieve well-being and equilibrium only in those periods in which conservative forces are strong enough to establish and maintain a control over the fissiparous tendencies of men. It is debatable whether recorded history provides any justification for this claim, but something akin to such a situation characterizes the period in Russian history which began with the suppression of the Decembrist rising in 1825 and ended with the death of Nicholas I thirty years later. The Tsar achieved relative equilibrium, though certainly not well-being, by turning Russia into a vast, drab, military barrack in which, as the young Speransky, Alexander I's adviser, had put it, there were only two classes, 'the slaves of the autocrat and the slaves of the landowners', and of whom he said 'the former are free merely by comparison with the latter; in actual fact there are no free men in Russia except beggars and philosophers'. But though Nicholas was the most rigid of autocrats, his régime was not an efficient monolithic system, and his proverbial terror was unable to penetrate with requisite vigour and consistency the whole Russian Empire. The patriarchal and religious feelings, real or imaginary, of the Russian people which were called to the aid of loyalty were as inadequate as were the official 'projects for the introduction of unanimity' and the arbitrary police measures to support the social structure. The long attempt to create order broke down through its own top-heavy bureaucratic weight, exposing in the disaster of the Crimean War the political and economic hollowness of the system.

When Alexander II came to the throne in 1855 he was faced with a crisis which called for fundamental changes and which was to give his reign a crucial position in Russian history. Indeed, no other moment between Peter the Great and Lenin

—not even the period of revolutionary events at the beginning of the twentieth century—was more pregnant with possibilities of development or more burdened with tensions and ambiguities than Alexander's reign. The Tsar himself was only dimly conscious of the situation, nor did he question his predecessor's autocratic and bureaucratic assumptions. Yet he hesitated to accept in its entirety the basic belief of the tsarist system which had been so clearly enunciated by his father's Minister of Education Uvarov: 'Political religion', Uvarov wrote, 'has its dogmas, eternal like those of Christianity. With us they are autocracy and serfdom. Why touch them when, fortunately for Russia, they have been preserved by a powerful hand?'

Alexander's mere uncertainty, when contrasted with the record of his predecessors, perhaps entitles him to the label 'Tsar Liberator' or 'Great Reformer' which historical textbooks have awarded him. As a man and a statesman, however, he was in no way equipped to be either a liberator or a reformer; and since he was an autocrat holding the reins of power his personal character had a direct bearing on the social and political development that took place during his reign.

Alexander was gentle, indulgent, and even humane up to a point. These traits distinguished him favourably from his iron-fisted, square-souled father, and perhaps less favourably from his great technocratic forbear Peter I, and they have moved his official biographers to paeans of praise.[1] But the gentleness concealed not only an immense capacity for lachrymose sentimentality (Alexander had a habit of weeping profusely in public) and splenetic peevishness, but also an overwhelming indolence of will, a lack of direction or even of conviction. There were occasions on which he intervened directly in the course of events, notably in connexion with the series of measures which culminated in the emancipation of the serfs; but he had neither the strength nor the determination to make such intervention fruitful, and, as will be seen, the emancipation, too, proved a failure. Here as elsewhere he showed a remarkable tendency to drift from an original enunciation of high principles, through various stages of compromise (often by choosing ministers and advisers whose views and policies were so opposed as to cancel each other out) to ultimate betrayal. This is the substance of the charge levelled against him by Herzen and other critics.

The successor of Nicholas [Herzen wrote] received an onerous heritage: a futile and inglorious war, shattered finances, universal peculation, discontent, distrust and expectancy. He was standing, as in the fairy-tale, at the parting of three ways: to grant the gentry real rights and to try to achieve with their help the *lunar* freedom of representative government; to free the peasants with land and initiate a new era of popular and economic emancipation; or else, instead of either, to continue to suppress every manifestation of life until the muscles burst, both of the suppressor and the suppressed. Which road, then, did our fairy-prince take?

He took all three. . . .

This precarious, uncertain posture of a man only half-awake is the hallmark of the new reign. There is something face-less, disabled, flimsy about it: hence the concessions to all and the traps for all.[2]

Some of the more bigoted representatives of the dominant reaction (Katkov, the Metropolitan Philaret, Panin, Pobedonostsev, P. A. Shuvalov, Dimitry Tolstoy) believed that the Tsar was losing control over the country by defying tradition, by capitulating to the enemies of autocracy or aristocracy. In point of fact, his failures were due largely to infirmity of purpose. For whenever Alexander made concessions to greater freedom he hastily withdrew, surrendering to his own or to his advisers' haunting fear that to give way is to endanger the principles of autocracy and to produce a nucleus of social disorder. The resulting sense of insecurity undermined all confidence between government and people and imposed on the latter a double standard of morality. From it, too, sprang the element of tragedy which characterizes the personal fate of Alexander. The first attempt on his life in 1866 was followed by many others which became more desperate as his reign became more deceitful and oppressive, until its course was brutally terminated by his assassination in 1881. 'What have these wretches against me?' he cried. 'Why do they hunt me down like a wild beast?' Alexander's tendency to take the line of least resistance was accompanied by a curious, pathetic, dreamy, and resentful kind of courage. He believed that his life and work were in the hands of God, and that no human agency could avail once divine aid

was inscrutably withdrawn, yet he himself consistently rein-
forced divine resources by most prosaic and sinister means.

All this may seem to have turned the activity of the Government during Alexander's reign into mere make-believe and
shadow-play. And it is not surprising that, as the evidence of
what actually happened accumulates, the historian's account
of the reality behind the myth gives the impression of obloquy.[3]
None the less, though the historian is concerned with the things
that men actually do, he cannot ignore the things they profess to
do. The Holy Roman Empire may not have been either holy, or
Roman, or an empire, but it was intended to be these things,
and the intention is as much a part of history as is its failure.

The intention—whether deliberate or imposed by circumstances—as well as the failure of Alexander's rule did not therefore produce another round of changes which changed nothing.
They clearly served as a catalyst, which touched off many
issues, reshaped patterns of loyalty and, generally, revealed
the face of Russia in all its complexity. The effect was psychological as well as political and economic. The change impressed
a characteristic ethos on the period, roughly speaking, between
1856 (when Alexander first raised the question of the abolition
of serfdom) and 1866 (when the first attempt on the Tsar's life
was made)—'the sixties', according to the mythology of divisions in Russian history, which managed, as often before and
after, to concentrate centuries of western European social and
cultural development into years, and years into days.

After the dull uniformity imposed by the system of Nicholas I
Russia suddenly started to throb with life. There ensued a
genuine 'thaw'—one of many in Russian history which, as
often as not, were followed by a new frost. 'Whoever was not
alive in Russia in 1856', wrote Tolstoy, 'does not know what
life is.' The new era was proclaimed in turgid tones in Turgenev's novel *On the Eve* (1860), and Chernyshevsky, in ironic
vein, recalled in his novel *Prologue* (1868) that 'the whole of
educated Petersburg revelled in its bright new spring'. People
began to breathe, to speak, and even to travel more freely.
Indeed, writers during the first years of Alexander's reign
enjoyed a greater freedom than ever before or since (until the
revolution of 1905). The reforms or rumours of reform stimulated a burgeoning of public opinion on social questions that,

for a while, made discussion almost a government necessity. The current of radicalism, held back by the advance of reaction during the preceding thirty years, came flooding in. Writers, thinkers, journalists, though still deprived of direct political activity, began to crystallize into distinct groups with radical, liberal, or reactionary allegiances. Despite the persisting if more wayward and easily gullible censorship, they employed an increasing number of books, papers, and magazines as their mouthpieces. Herzen's *Kolokol* (Bell), with its motto *Vivos voco*, and Chernyshevsky's *Sovremennik* (Contemporary) cried out for 'the liberation of the people' and they became the acknowledged conscience of Russia. These expressions of a new mood coincided with great economic changes, with the rise of new social patterns and even with changes in social habits, especially among those sections of society in which traditional values were being worn down under the pressure of new interests.

2. *The Liberators and the Liberated*

In this new climate, many problems, above all that of serfdom, began to cry more urgently for solution. Already in the eighteenth century it had deeply disturbed all those who were seriously concerned about the state of Russian society; now it became the touchstone of moral and social survival.

From time to time issues arise which are discussed and fought out once and for all, and whose importance goes beyond their immediate relevance, for they make men look at reality from a different angle. The fundamental equality of men was such an issue: it echoed the voice of outraged human nature but also gave evidence of a new social and historical experience. It was a product of the French Revolution, and it was decided then for all men and for all time whatever betrayals and falsifications there may have followed in subsequent history. Ironically, Alexander II became the instrument whereby an important truth of the French Revolution was belatedly (that is, seventy-two years after serfdom was abolished in France but four years before slavery was abolished in America) applied in Russia. To some extent, this provides support for the opinion of some students of the period who call the sixties 'our short-lived eighteenth century' (Trotsky). Alexander's attempt, therefore, half-hearted though it was, to bring the problem of slavery into the open, itself amounted to a kind of revolution which produced qualitative changes in the character and direction of Russian historical development, and which also served to make, for a time at least, the fate of the peasant the chief human and social preoccupation of Russian thinkers.

The peasants finally lost their freedom to the landowners (and from them to the State) in the course of the seventeenth century, although they did not thereby become, strictly speaking, slaves (*kholopy*), as from time immemorial any pauper could become by being sold to his fellow man. What the great Russian reformers—Peter I and Catherine II—did was in the main to consolidate and finally to exploit the disfranchisement of the seventeenth century. By then and until the emancipation the peasantry represented a distinct class virtually without legal status 'in obligation' to the State and to the gentry (*obyazannye krestyane*, as they were defined by a law of 1842).[4] To discharge their 'obligation' the peasants had to pay their owner, in addition to state taxes, annual dues in money or in kind (*obrok*, quitrent), predominantly in less fertile regions, or to work on his land (*barshchina, corvée*), particularly in fertile regions, or both together. As members of the village community they held periodically redistributable or fixed inheritable strips of arable land (*zemelnye nadely*), the size of which was in inverse proportion to its fertility. These they cultivated for themselves when not performing tasks for their master who required anything between three and seven days' work in the week (the Emperors Paul and Alexander I forbade the landowner to make his serfs work on Sundays, but the practice continued until the emancipation). Many of their landless equals were household servants (*dvorovye*), broadly regarded by their owners as chattels; others worked compulsorily or for hire in industrial establishments; yet others represented a completely dispossessed rural proletariat working on the master's land for a monthly payment in kind (*mesyach-niki*). The landowners had the power to sell their peasants, to remove them to other places, to deprive them of land by turning them into household serfs or into *mesyachniki*, to make them work without reward, to arrange their marriages against their wishes, to send them at any time to the army or to Siberia, without accusing them of any offence, and to flog them.[5]

Until the system of serfdom began to show unmistakable economic disadvantages it was maintained by the State as something essential to the preservation of the prerogatives and the dominant position of the gentry, which the Tsar himself described as 'the mainstay of the throne'—an attitude differing only by the absence of wit from Catherine the Great's magnificent rebuke of the French Revolution: 'Je suis aristocrate, c'est mon métier.' But the dominant position of the gentry was throughout endangered by unforeseen opposition on the part of the peasants, who often failed to live up to the accepted notion of a dark but loyal and conservative bulwark against disorder, and whose decisive part in Russian history sprang from no qualities of leadership, but from their ability to say 'no' in the last resort. As an English historian of Russia put it, their resistance took two extreme forms: either flight from oppression or fight against oppression. In these as in other respects the Russian peasant had little in common with the freeholder of the western European type, and his capacity for escape was safeguarded by his status as rebel, nomad, pedlar, and roving craftsman. In Russia, he embodied the perennial conflict between the individual (in his own right or as a member of the community) and the State—a conflict which alternately wavered between the sublime and the ridiculous, leading from time to time to a total denial of all state power and authority.

Peasant revolts had been a recurrent phenomenon since the very beginning of the seventeenth century. Bolotnikov (†1608), Stenka Razin (†1671), Bulavin (1660–1708), Pugachev (1742–75) are familiar and almost legendary names of peasant rebels. Resistance naturally became weaker as the State became more efficient, and its methods of suppression improved; or rather the revolts became smaller but more frequent. The situation grew particularly alarming during the reign of Nicholas I (when according to incomplete data, 674 peasant risings occurred in various parts in Russia), intensified in the crucial years following the Emancipation Edict, and, after a relative lull in the last quarter of the century, new and violent risings preceded and accompanied the revolution of 1905.

Under the conditions of the prevailing censorship, it was not possible to examine, discuss, or even mention publicly these revolutionary occurrences, but ever since the thirties of the last century details of outbreaks were recorded in the archives of the secret police, that is, the Third Section of His Majesty's Own Chancery, and of the Ministry of the Interior. The threat was in some ways more disturbing than the provocative liberalism of the gentry—the 'harmless innuendoes' (*bezvredney zlorechya*) as Nicholas I himself described it—which in any case were easily supervised by the Argus of the Third Section. Herzen, Bakunin, and the other dangerous radicals were abroad, but 'the unthinking, unrelenting revolt' (*bunt bessmyslennyi i bezposhchadnyi*) of the serfs threatened ominously and unpredictably on the horizon.

It is not easy to form an accurate picture of revolutionary feelings among the peasantry before the emancipation. The archives provide some illuminating material but it does not clearly indicate the temper of the peasants. This is better conveyed in the memoirs and correspondence of those who had experience of rural life. The evidence of the Slavophils may be regarded as particularly revealing, for they cannot be accused of any radical bias, in spite of their belief that the gentry separated the people from the Tsar. Samarin was quite outspoken about the prevailing revolutionary mood among the peasants, and the prominent conservative historian Pogodin wrote during the Crimean war that

> we are not afraid of Mirabeau, but we are frightened by Emelka Pugachev; Ledru-Rollin and his communists will find no sympathizers over here, but any village will goggle at Nikita Pustosvyat. No one will side with Mazzini, but Stenka Razin has only to say the word! . . . That's where our revolution is lurking, that is where our danger lies. . . . And even now are not thirty landowners killed every year—vicarious victims of the right to tyranny over others? All these, you see, are local revolutions which only lack co-ordination to acquire a special significance.[6]

One should not conclude, however, that the peasants who ran away or resisted were the majority. Most of them were resigned, working and eating their bread in the sweat of their brow—bread which, to judge from the secret reports of some harassed provincial governors, sometimes consisted of little but chaff and straw. As usual, slavery served to stultify the mind and make men into the obedient victims of the system that enslaved them. A few individual peasants succeeded in buying their freedom, despite the enormous redemption fees, or made the best of their enslavement by giving good service, by managing their master's affairs, by playing in their orchestras and theatres. Some even contrived to become rich themselves, and in turn exploited servile labour (e.g. the famous peasant factory 'owners' of Ivanovo in the province of Vladimir who paid their master—Count Sheremetev—20,000 roubles in annual dues).

In the face of mounting disaffection the Government for a time came to doubt the effectiveness of the stick, a policy which led to such desperate straits during the Crimean war. The defeat in the war was economic and financial as well as military.[7] It was in the interests of the Government and the governing class alike to bring into being new productive forces, and serfdom undoubtedly impeded the task. Not only Russian industry but agriculture too, which in the seventeenth and eighteenth centuries relied on a servile village population, was now clamouring for free, cheap, and mobile labour.[8] Some historians are satisfied that this provides the only adequate explanation of the reforms initiated by Alexander II: they maintain that the reforms accorded with the 'logic' of social and historical development, or were a simple function of the movement of grain-prices (Pokrovsky); that the changes would have happened without any pressure from above or from below had the Russian gentry been capable of interpreting its own interests at the time, and that the impoverishment produced by the reforms among a few landowners did not affect the final result, namely the survival and even the revival of the Russian gentry in its transition from feudalism to capitalism.

This at once involves us in the argument of those who believe in an historical inevitability which remorselessly unfolds, moving all things and all men in a predestined direction towards inescapable ends. In addition, the voice of the surly *advocatus diaboli* whispers in our ear that man's alleged benevolence is camouflaged self-interest, and that he means 'cash' when he says 'truth'. It is doubtful whether an honest historian can avoid being in some measure an *advocatus diaboli*, although there is no reason why he should regard the economic nexus as the only source of motivation which enables men to dissimulate truth and to make shadows parade as substance. But appeals to historical necessity may suggest single-track lines of cause and effect which belie the complexity of history. History is the product not of logic but of people. They provide the variability, which is absent from foreordained schemes, the contrasts between intention and achievement, effort and failure, hope and disappointment, decision and policy. Indeed, the 'logic' itself, the fortunes and misfortunes of history, come into existence as a result of acts by human beings. And yet, it is difficult to see the human impress on the consequences of such acts. History abounds in apparently irreducible conflicts between freedom and necessity: it is the realm of man's actions and responsibilities, and yet it pursues no recognizable human end. Man is maimed by it and perishes in it. It is a record of man's achievements, but also of deeds which themselves add to the limitation of his freedom, of aims which once realized recoil upon him and illusions which turn into hard, compulsive reality. No objection of 'determinism' can, therefore, be raised against an historical explanation that detects a peculiar logic, a grim momentum of its own in the course and consequences of human action.

In any case it is now no longer possible to adopt the position of the traditional Russian historians who attribute the abolition of serfdom to Alexander's generous impulses towards the common good and to his charitable disposition: these may have been real enough but they never moved him to do anything to prejudice a system that so manifestly equated its own conservation with moral worth. Nor can it be ascribed to the upsurge of a social conscience which led the gentry to devote themselves to improving the lot of the peasants. In fact they acted not so much from the fullness of their hearts as from the emptiness of their pockets: they were prepared to let the peasant go so that they might retain his labour and his land, or as much of it as possible for their own purposes.

Nevertheless, there *was* pressure from above, and it is important to analyse its incentives and effects in order to understand the state of Russian society in the eighteen-sixties. In his manifesto on the conclusion of the Peace of Paris in 1856 Alexander II had promised the Russian people an opportunity of 'enjoying the fruits of their labour'. Soon afterwards, in a famous speech to the representatives of the gentry of Moscow, he said, echoing Radishchev and Herzen, that 'it is better to abolish serfdom from above than to wait until it begins to abolish itself from below'.

Gentlemen [he announced in a characteristically ambiguous passage], I have heard that rumours are being circulated among you that I intend to abolish serfdom: this is unjust, and you may convey this to all and sundry. But unfortunately a hostile feeling between the peasants and their landowners does exist, and for this reason there have already been some cases of insubordination to the landowners. I am convinced that sooner or later we must do this [?]. I think that you agree with me: consequently it is much better . . .', &c.[9]

The first reaction to the Tsar's initiative, however, was one of consternation, and even those of the gentry who favoured reforms dreaded, as Samarin admitted in a candid moment, 'the premature action by the government as well as the anger of the people', whilst others suggested that 'the whole problem has been invented by people who have no immovable property: scholars, theoreticians and sons of the clergy' (Muraviev). Indeed, it is clear from the documents which cover the intricate process of preparation for the final settlement, that a mixture of fear and uneasiness, avowed and unavowed, filled the minds of the gentry.[10] They knew that the reform would be a gamble, but hoped that it might be a gamble that would pay rich dividends. The fear, as will be seen, soon spread to the Government, which, when it came to the point of practical decision, never questioned the overriding interests of the gentry. Yet the Government, the Minister of the Interior Lanskoy and his assistant Milyutin, together with such outspoken advocates of emancipation as the Tsar's brother and aunt, was itself the spearhead of reform.

The manner in which the details of the settlement were worked is familiar. After repeated reminders and exhortations by the Government, the gentry of the various provinces formed committees for the preparation of projects of emancipation.[11] The projects were forwarded to a central committee sitting in St. Petersburg, composed for the most part of officials, whose duty it was to compare them and to elaborate a final scheme ('Statutes', *polozheniya*) which was submitted for approval to the State Council (*Gosudarstennyi Soviet*), the Tsar's supreme advisory legislative organ. It was then confirmed by the Tsar himself, and an edict (*manifest*) based on it was published by imperial command.

The story of the provincial committees is very instructive, for it shows both the tragic lack of solidarity with the people whom the gentry set out to liberate and the astonishing disparity between what the gentry professed to do and what in effect they did. It is also characteristic of the incalculable régime of Alexander II, whose every measure seeped away into the sands of ineffectiveness and prevarication.

It would be quite wrong to imagine that no one was actuated by conviction, that all the committees consisted of greedy proprietors driven by sheer economic compulsion. There was a natural spate of talk and argument; there were tensions not only between the committees and the Government, but also between the various committees and between members within the committees. There were 'liberal' and 'conservative' trends. The very fact that such an important issue had been brought into the open and freely discussed produced an intellectual ferment. This ferment affected many sections of society, which, class-ridden though it may have been, shared a common sense of urgency and a new awareness. It is more elusive and imponderable than the ostensible material transactions, but no less important for that. Yet with all this, even the most cautious student cannot escape the crude and disconcerting fact that the old social pattern reasserted itself, posing as acutely as ever the question of the effect of social determination on the character of man's ideas and behaviour.

'In the past, as a rule, two parties contended in our provinces', Saltykov-Shchedrin wrote in 'Satires in Prose' (*Satiry v proze*) of his own observation as an active member of the provincial bureaucracy:

the party of the retiring Marshal of the nobility and that of his successor. Both parties were exclusively concerned with eating and drinking their respective patrons out of house and home and creating an uproar during the elections. . . . Their struggles had no political significance whatsoever: it was all a matter of who would out-gorge whom. . . . To-day . . . everybody talks. At times it seems the world is going to drown in a flood of words, groans and clamour. . . . We now have reactionaries, we have red liberals and moderate liberals; we even have people who agree with all three and hope somehow to wriggle through somewhere in the middle. . . . We now have two main parties: reactionaries and liberals (naturally, moderate ones). It is hard to judge what the reactionaries want or what the liberals seek. But if one insists on definitions, this is as good a guess as any other: the former is reactionarily liberal and the other is liberally reactionary.

A less satirical examination will show that the divergencies in the recommendations made by the provincial committees were due as much to the different economic conditions in the various regions as to the politics of the committee members.

Not a single peasant took part in the proceedings and none was consulted about his prospective freedom. The peasantry in each region was ostensibly represented by two delegates. These were appointed by the provincial Governor, the highest local functionary of the Government, and were drawn from the ranks of the land-owning gentry, as were the chairmen of the committees (provincial marshals of the nobility) and the other delegates elected by the county assemblies of the gentry (*uezdnye dvoryanskie sobraniya*). The fact that the work of the committees was accompanied by an orgy of *Te Deums*, gala dinners with toasts to Alexander and speeches in honour of 'the glorious Russian gentry', by splendid balls reverberating with music played by serf-orchestras—all this was a poor preparation for what one speaker chose to call 'our supreme sacrifice on the altar of the common good'. The mass of self-congratulatory and patriotic speeches pronounced by the delegates in the course of these activities leaves a painful impression; and the enlightened liberal Kavelin was no less responsible for such monuments of insincerity than were parochial nonentities from Kherson.

On the whole, and apart from a handful of disgruntled diehards or impoverished landowners living on a few dozen 'souls' for whom almost any change would spell complete ruin, the gentry felt confident that whatever happened, and despite all anxieties, the system would continue to operate on their behalf; and they were supported in this by the Tsar himself, who, while not prepared to make any political concessions to the gentry, solemnly announced in 1859 and again in 1861 his resolve to defend their economic interests. In the circumstances it is not surprising that not one of the 1,377 members of the local committees, whatever *nobilière* prejudices they may have harboured, stood up for the old order in its entirety or even ventured to express openly extreme reactionary attitudes, i.e. that the serf ought not personally to be made free. The eighteenth- or early nineteenth-century notion that 'souls' could be easily and profitably exchanged for pedigree dogs was certainly considered to be a preposterous and uneconomic anachronism. What the gentry needed was real profits from their estates, or as Samarin put it: 'the gentry came to realize the need of concerning themselves more closely with their affairs, of increasing their incomes'.

The less progressive regarded such profits as being dependent on the retention of as much land as possible and on the perpetuation in some form or other of the *corvée*. They relied on a 'natural' agricultural economy which would, in the words of Kiselev, 'work by itself' unaided by any central authority. These ideas dominated some of the most important committees (for example, those of St. Petersburg and Moscow), and one of their principal and ablest spokesmen was Yuri Samarin, a convinced opponent of serfdom and an equally convinced advocate of the *corvée*. He, together with other Slavophil or near-Slavophil members of the gentry of central Russia, was intensely suspicious of anything that might serve to strengthen the differentiation and industrialization of Russian society, because such tendencies uprooted the peasantry, destroyed primitive simplicity, and snapped the 'organic' ties of tradition, deference, and obligation. The system of quitrents (*obrok*), as distinct from the *corvée* (*barshchina*), in Samarin's view, caused the stratification of peasant society by introducing the quasi-capitalist relations of a money economy.[12] The maintenance of 'organic' relations between landowner and peasant (including police supervision by the former over the latter) would somehow preserve the Russian soul from being corrupted by the disruptive, constricting, and formalizing spirit so powerful in the *bourgeois* society of western Europe. A closer examination of the facts, however, shows that paternalistically-minded Russian landowners had very little natural affinity with the people whom they ruled, even when well intentioned. They could build up estates, as Khomyakov, Samarin's friend and teacher, did so successfully at the price of, to use his own words, 'implacable taxation and compulsive labour' (*neumolimye podati i povinnosti*), but they were unable to create an organic society, whatever this may mean. No one, perhaps, felt this more acutely and painfully than Leo Tolstoy, who was determined to 'establish human relations with the peasants', but had to admit (in his Diary and in *Landlord's Morning*) the unsurmountable estrangement and lack of understanding between the landowners and 'the people'.

The more progressive committees (Tver, Kaluga, Kharkov), which were in the minority, insisted on removing feudal restrictions in agricultural development and on the need for capital investment in farming. Many of them were absentee landlords or benevolent agriculturalists, who were willing to surrender land in return for large compensation which was based not so much on the value of the land as on the value of the services of the peasants living on the land, or their ability to pay rents. But most landowners were unanimous in regarding the emancipation as a measure which would turn the peasant into a labourer, either in agriculture or industry, without giving him any title to any portion of the land as absolute property. While the peasant expressed his attitude in the often-quoted saying 'I belong to you, but the land belongs to me', his master's answer ran roughly: 'when you no longer belong to me the land given to you to live upon will no longer be yours either'.

Throughout these deliberations the question of the quality of the land was as important in influencing the recommendations of the committees as that of its quantity. Not surprisingly, those landowners whose estates lay within the rich belt of the black earth (the provinces of Voronezh, Tambov, Kursk, Orlov, Poltava, Ekaterinoslav, Kherson, Tavrida, and parts of Ryazan and Simbirsk) tended to advocate (with some exceptions) emancipation of the serfs without land. Their land had suffered little erosion, cultivation was cheap, and little capital was required. 'Our valuable commodity', Prince Cherkassky, a member of the Samarin group declared, 'must not be alienated.' These landowners did not even object to granting the peasants complete personal freedom without compensation, as long as they (the landowners) could keep all the land or receive high premiums for those portions of the land which had hitherto been used by the peasants; whilst landowners from poor or industrial regions expected to be indemnified above all for the loss of valuable free labour.[13]

The mentality of the gentry from the rich provinces is obliquely illustrated by a correspondent of Pogodin: 'One could easily provide them [the peasants] with a silver rouble', he wrote, 'fuddle them with vodka and add to this a cheerful farewell *Te Deum*. . . . [The experts] have reckoned—and it appears to be perfectly true—that the cultivation of the land by hired men is incomparably more profitable, for such men must only be fed while working and after that farewell, begone! But if they belong to you, you have to feed them all the year round, the whole scum (*vsyu svoloch*), the old with all the others.' But such a view seems to be too uninhibitedly cynical to be taken quite seriously. As often as not the arguments approximated those of the respectable middle class in England which opposed the Factory Acts, because they interfered with 'freedom of labour', and devoted itself to the idea of self-help and Christian benevolence.

One of the most active and interesting figures in the progressive group was Unkovsky, Marshal of the nobility and chairman of the Tver committee.[14] For him the question of the emancipation of the peasants was only one aspect of the political and economic liberation of Russia as a whole and he resolutely opposed what he called the 'vast system of malfeasance which is raised in Russia to the dignity of state government'. He represented a new type of Russian landowner, a far cry not only from the crowd of philistine provincials, whether arrogant or indolent, but also from the enlightened Slavophil proprietors who were prominent in the preparation of the land reform. *Der Ritter ist Landwirt* (or just plain *Wirtschafter*) *geworden*: not for him a sacred earth, endowing life with some magic quality of truth. It would, indeed, have been more than fanciful to attribute such properties to the eroded, impoverished soil of Tver tilled by a peasantry living on the brink of starvation, forever battling against famine and drought. But Tver was a commercial centre and the seat of an important textile industry, and the gentry of the province could increase its prosperity by helping to rationalize industry as well as agriculture, and by employing a cheap labour force for the purpose. This, Unkovsky believed, would also improve ('in the long run') the lot of the peasants, although, in the appalling labour conditions of Russian factories in the second half of the nineteenth century, the proletarianization of the peasants, in Tver or elsewhere, made, in fact, little if any difference to their incurable misery. Nevertheless, although eventually he gave in completely to officialdom, in the sixties Unkovsky displayed a courage which was rare among contemporary landowners and conspicuously so among the sycophantic upholders of the monarchy. Moreover, it was combined with a public spirit and sense of duty unlucky for their owner, for he was put under police surveillance and exiled for a brief term to the remote provinces. He fought on two fronts: against government tutelage (in spite of supporting State compensation for any losses the gentry might suffer in letting the peasants go); and against what he called the 'illusory freedom of the peasants', i.e. freedom without land, advocated by 'our feudal proprietors' intent on perpetuating a 'smug, muddleheaded', 'domineering and ludicrous' squirearchical order.

Unkovsky and his liberal group preferred a free peasantry as more conducive to the development of efficient and profitable agriculture. But, involved though they were in the new social and economic inevitabilities, they found it hard to adapt themselves to *bourgeois* habits of life and thought. Until the end of the century, and in some cases later still, they managed to maintain, as did the Decembrists and the radicals during Catherine II's reign, a sense of relative freedom from the pressure of time and events which forces men busily and greedily through social development. This was true of many members of the idealistically educated 'middle gentry' which Turgenev and Tolstoy made so recognizable and endearing in their novels, and which even Saltykov-Shchedrin's gloomy picture does not altogether succeed in deposing. They may have been lazy and improvident, or sensual and self-indulgent, but they were relatively free from the weight of envy, tuft-hunting, and personal imperialism. And yet, even Unkovsky oscillated between the idea of a gentry exercising a natural power over a loyal peasantry and that of the 'absolute rights of private property', irrespective of the social origin of the owner. He reflected in some degree the temper of a growing acquisitive *bourgeois* society in Russia in the sixties; and this was forcibly expressed by the Tver gentry on the occasion of its first assembly after the Emancipation Act, when it renounced 'all the privileges of its estate', but not its claims to redemption payments by the peasants.

At the end of 1859 the work of the committees was completed
to the accompaniment of *Te Deums* before wonder-working icons
and speeches in honour of the gentry and the Emperor, in
which, as far as recorded evidence goes, not a word was uttered
about the peasant whose fate the committees had been deciding.
Only the members for Tver presented their chairman Unkovsky
with a golden cup, bearing the engraved picture of a bare-
headed, bowing peasant, holding a tray with the traditional
bread and salt as 'a token of gratitude for freedom and land'.
'The Kharkov committee had finished its task in a Christian
manner: it was wound up today with prayers and supplications
on behalf of its Monarch.' The prayers were followed by a gala
dinner and dance for the local gentry.

According to the original plan, a meeting was to follow
between the representatives of the gentry and the Government
agencies. For the gentry it was an awkward moment, for almost
until the eve of the Revolution they recoiled fastidiously from
collaboration with the bureaucracy. This was certainly true of
relations with the representatives of the Central Government in
the provinces, where any self-respecting and reasonably enlightened member of the gentry would, except of necessity,
refrain from hobnobbing with provincial Governors, even
though, to quote a member of the Senate (Y. Soloviev), 'the
landowners expected to see in Governors men of dignified
presence, wealth and amiability, ready to carry out the wishes
of the gentry, especially of those among them who had influence'.
But this was also true to some extent of relations with highly
placed functionaries in the capital, whom they tended to regard
as upstarts. Any disdain here was, however, rather misplaced,
since most of these functionaries themselves were members of
the gentry or of the aristocracy. At any rate the central committee, which dealt with the drafting of the emancipation
statutes, to be more precise, the editorial commissions which
prepared the work of the committee, contained a formidable
contingent of wealthy landowners, some of whom (Prince
Paskevich and Count P. P. Shuvalov) were avowed opponents
of land reform. Others (Samarin and Prince Cherkassky)
favoured the reform but could scarcely be regarded as agents of
the bureaucracy. The chairman, General Rostovtsev, it is true,
was a commoner of considerable common sense, loyalty, and

very little tact or cultivation, but he died at the beginning of
1860 when he was succeeded by the Minister of Justice, Count
Panin. And Panin, for whom reaction was not merely a policy
but a state of mind, behaved like authority incarnate, whip in
hand. He confessed on a famous occasion that 'as a wealthy
landowner I consider the matter of emancipation to be a
private, family affair of the landowners'.[15]

Russian bureaucracy, a creation of Peter the Great, reshaped
in accordance with more modern requirements by Alexander I
and expanded to vast proportions by Nicholas I, was a well-
known *bête noire* and laughing-stock of Russian literature and
political thought. Its members lived in a self-contained, inflated
world of their own and they were obsequiously dependent on
the authority of the tsars; inevitably, they were out of touch
with the peasants no less than with the liberal section of the
educated minority. The system tended to produce, as all
bureaucracies do, a uniform type and to discourage every form
of originality and experiment. The Governors in the provinces
and the administrators in the Central Government were predominantly stable-minded, safe, and at times unscrupulous men
who were obsessed with the satisfactoriness of things as they are.
Senator Dimitry Khrushchev, however, whose compilation of
documents concerning the land reform has been mentioned
above, reckoned that, in the late fifties, 24 of the 45 Governors
ought to have been dismissed out of hand: of these 12 were
well-known 'crooks' (*moshenniki*), and 12 were of doubtful
honesty and complete ineptitude; of the remaining 21, 10 could
be tolerated *faute de mieux*, 9 were fairly good men, and only 2
could be regarded as exemplary. Such outstanding men as
Prince Mikhail Vorontsov, Governor of New Russia, were
almost an anomaly. Ministers, as a rule, had no brains and
when, exceptionally, they surpassed the traditional standards of
ministerial intelligence they found themselves in serious trouble.
On the other hand, Government servants in high but secondary
positions were often men of extraordinary ability and energy,
and at least one member of the peasant commissions, Nicholas
Milyutin, assistant Minister of the Interior, belonged to this
class.

Milyutin was an outstanding figure in Russian governmental
history, for he represented, at any rate in his public personality,

the aloof impartial administrator, combining immense knowledge, bureaucratic skill, dignity, and sincere conviction. Unlike Rostovtsev, who conscientiously carried out his duty in the
preparation of the reform as he would have carried out any
other imperial command, Milyutin did so out of a feeling of
implicit confidence in the cause. Alexander both listened to him
and distrusted him; people near to the Tsar considered him a
'crypto-red' or a Jacobin, and the gentry openly charged him
with 'communism'. Later he became the darling of the liberals.
In fact only one of these charges seems to stick. Milyutin was a
kind of monarchistic Jacobin. He believed in the need 'to raise
the oppressed mass of the people and to put them on their feet',
but he relied on the unlimited power of the tsarist state to fulfil
the task, unimpeded, amongst other things, by the demands of
the gentry. As the Marxist historian Pokrovsky put it, 'in the
last resort Milyutin wished to substitute State slavery for feudal
dependence'. 'He dreamt of classless State power, dispassionate
and as inexorable as fate.' He disliked the gentry and, having
during the course of his long bureaucratic career in the economic department of the Ministry of the Interior become familiar
with a good measure of what he called 'the infamies of the
landowners' (*pomeshchich'i bezobraziya*), this was perhaps not
surprising, although he was realistic enough to see that he
could not altogether circumvent them. Nor is it surprising that
the gentry in turn detested him.[16]

Milyutin was not alone in his opposition to the gentry.
Lanskoy, his superior at the Ministry of the Interior, a man of
much less ability and character, was equally outspoken. In a
famous memorandum to Alexander on the state of the peasant
question (*Vzglyad na polozhenie krestyanskogo voprosa v nastoyashchee
vremya*) he expressed his fear that the gentry might prove a
formidable obstacle to the Government's plans and depicted
the provincial committees as gangs of stupid and ignorant reactionaries intent on deceiving the Government in their own
interest. Alexander vacillated, and with characteristic timidity
gave in to the campaign against the 'first-born of the Russian
land'. He was frightened not only by the rebelliousness of the
peasants but also by the unexpected urge to independence
among the gentry, whose 'constitutional desires' he described
as 'vulgar imitations of foreign pamphleteers, issuing from

complete ignorance of our native customs and from extreme immaturity of thought'.

It should be noted that the expectation of imminent land reform produced a momentary decrease in peasant risings, and, for a while, the Government itself felt driven to defend the interests of the peasants—not on account of any mystical links between the Tsar and 'the people' but in order to offset the treasonably oligarchic leanings of the gentry. The situation presented a certain analogy to the old alliance between the Crown and the Commons against the aristocracy in England. To achieve its purpose and to reinforce its position, the Government assumed the role of benefactor and advocated small land-holdings vested in a free but obedient peasantry, although events showed, as they ordinarily do in such cases, that the views of the benefactor and the views of the beneficiaries regarding the value of benefaction are apt to differ. For the first time since the Decembrist rising unmistakable friction appeared in the governing classes—friction which would have been inconceivable in the framework of the imposed uniformity of Nicholas I's system and which gained strength intermittently throughout the reign of Alexander and his successors, particularly in connexion with the *zemstvo* or local government activities.

Against this background the first encounter between the spokesmen of the provincial committees and members of the Government did not augur well, especially as the former represented mainly the black earth regions. Rumours current among the landowners that 'bureaucratic intrigues' might prevent an understanding between the Crown and the gentry, that the gentry had been double-crossed turned out to be correct in some measure. As one group of landowners complained, 'we found ourselves in a humiliating, indeed a ridiculous, position'. The humiliations, admittedly, exceeded all limits, even if it be taken into account that many of the noble delegates behaved arrogantly and tactlessly. They were forced to hang about in ante-chambers; they were forbidden to enter into consultation among themselves or even to meet in groups; they were not invited to discuss anything and their main role was to report on local conditions.[17]

However, it is something of an anti-climax to discover that

this conflict, with its promising dramatic implications, turned out to be no more than a storm in a tea cup. Lanskoy and Milyutin notwithstanding, Alexander's entourage, known in enlightened circles as 'the aristocratic camarilla', soon realized that the gentry were not seditious *sans-culottes* but belonged to their own stock, and were part of the same order. 'Do you really believe we will let you finish this business?' one member of a provincial committee (Count Bobrinsky) remarked to Milyutin; '. . . less than a month will pass before you are kicked out (*v trubu vyletete*) and we shall be in your shoes.' Events, and above all the Act of Emancipation itself, proved Bobrinsky right. Soon Alexander solemnly reaffirmed that he considered himself first and foremost a member of the gentry and that, in his own words, 'everything that could be done to protect the profits of the landowners has been done', even though he continued to resist the notion of limiting his absolute political power.

There ensued, it is true, a few wrangles about the ways and means of diminishing the extent of the land allotted to the peasants; but when Panin succeeded Rostovtsev harmony between the gentry and the Government was re-established, and was followed by dinners with amicable speeches from both sides about the sacred and inviolable rights of private property. Even Milyutin and Kavelin deferred to the gentry: they agreed that the landowners ought to be compensated not only for the land on which the serfs lived, but also for the serfs themselves 'according to the locally current prices' (Kavelin). And it was Kavelin who wrote that 'class distinctions . . . are a phenomenon common to all mankind from the beginning of the world to our own days. . . . It is clear that the inequality of classes is established not by circumstances but by the very nature of man and of human society.' It is regrettable, Kavelin continued, that people 'devise libertarian theories of equality which fill history with tears and blood, and unreservedly deny all inequality, which . . . is the basic law of human society'. And he concluded that the land reform will free Russian society from 'dreamy theories of equality, from repugnant envy and hatred towards the upper classes and from the ensuing social revolution'.[18]

The drafting commissions, the central committee and finally

the State Council, all of which had the task of formulating and revising the principles and methods of the land reform, progressively made modifications in favour of the landowners. The only conclusion to be drawn from the emancipation statutes themselves is that they represent in the last analysis a charter not for the peasants but for the landowners, and in particular for those whose estates lay in the black-earth belt or other fertile regions and who constituted the majority.[19] The statutes reflected, moreover, all the ambiguities of Alexander's uncertain policy. In one sense, they put an end to the degradation of the peasant in Russia by raising him in the scale of humanity. The peasant became theoretically accountable to law alone. He could not be bought or sold any more, but could himself buy, sell, and own property, even though restrictions of property rights were involved in his membership of the village community, which theoretically precluded the possibility of disposing land-holdings on a private basis. He was delivered from the power of the master to make him work without paying him a wage; and, in theory, it was conceded that he could not be free unless he had means of subsistence. On the face of it, all this seemed to challenge the principle of slavery. But, having ceased to be a 'subject' of the landowner, he became to all intents and purposes what he was in the sixteenth century: a natural tax-paying beast of burden in human shape, or 'working cattle' (*rabochy skot*), to use the term by which the Nizhny Novgorod provincial committee chose to define its landless peasants. The reform failed to solve the problem that ought to have been solved, as indeed was admitted both in the famous 'Tver resolution' of 1862 and, before that, by Milyutin himself, one of the principal architects of the emancipation: 'I am convinced', he wrote, 'that at present people are unable not only to carry out the task which lies before them but even to understand it.' Even much later, an official commission under the ex-Minister of the Interior Valuev acknowledged, in a memorandum of 1873, that the position of the vast majority of the peasants 'remains [after the emancipation] either the same or has considerably deteriorated'. The peasant was left subject to a system of enforced contracts which proved a no less fatal source of bondage than his previous condition. Instead of receiving what he considered to be his freedom, he had merely been provoked to demand it. There is scarcely a more striking example in Russian history of the dominant role of the economic factor in the enslavement of man than this substitution of economic dependence for legal compulsion. It is not surprising that Marxist historians should find this period such a fruitful subject.

As the Government was chiefly concerned with the interests of the landowners (and where industry was involved, with those of the *entrepreneurs*) it was unable, without indemnifying the landowners, to transfer to the peasants the land to which hitherto they themselves had been assigned; but it was also afraid to deprive the peasants of their hereditary cottages, gardens, and fields, to give them merely the freedom of the birds. It therefore hit on an unfortunate expedient: while pretending to liberate him, it declared the serf 'temporarily obliged' to continue his *corvée* up to three days a week (which in fact was the law if not the practice since the end of the eighteenth century) or his payments for two years in the first instance, until the area of the land allotted to him and the obligations towards the landowner had been defined. The payments were to continue thereafter until he had redeemed the value of the allotted land (homesteads and fields) on which he had been working for generations and which he regarded as his by right. In other words, he remained as before subject to his landowner and continued to carry out his usual 'obligations'. With the Government continually reassessing the peasant's debt, the redemption payments, made to the State, which in turn compensated the landowner, would have continued until the middle of the twentieth century, had not more catastrophic events intervened and defeated the ill-conceived programme.

The serfs for their part, unlettered and unversed in the mysteries of economics though they were, had a traditional attitude towards liberation which led them to expect it to take much the same course in Russia as in Prussia, in Poland, in Hungary, and in Austria generally. They considered their 'obligation' temporary and diminishing while there was no diminution in the land set apart for their use. The *corvée* and forced payments could and indeed should be abolished, while the peasant land remained undiminished. All they knew was that the land belonged to them and that they belonged, although they knew they ought not to belong, to their master, or, in religious terms, that the land was God's and the right of using it belonged to him who tilled it. Ownership consisted, in their view, not in the mere fact of holding the land but in working it: they saw in toil the source of their warrant and title.

In fact, the land allocated to the peasants by the Emancipation Act, though varying in size from district to district, turned out in general to be smaller than the land they held before the reform. The statutes not only assured the landowner of the inviolability of his right to the whole land but also enabled him to 'portion off' for himself from one- to two-fifths of the land (*otrezki*) previously occupied by the peasants, who, not unnaturally, regarded this as sheer confiscation. In addition, the surveying was carried out in such a way that the peasants were invariably assigned land of inferior quality, and as often as not they found themselves deprived of the necessary appendages (forests, meadows, water rights, &c.). The value of redemption payments exceeded the real value of the land by as much as 50 to 75 per cent. Furthermore, the income derivable from the allotted land could not suffice to meet their new imposed financial obligations, so that they had to work for the landowner in order to fulfil them. *De facto* therefore, if not *de jure*, the peasant was paying not only for the land but also for his individual freedom and for the loss of servile labour sustained by the master.[20] Indeed, some left-wing historians maintained that a trap had been laid, that a cunning trick had been played upon the peasants. But a careful study of the work of the provincial committees and drafting commissions shows that this was by no means universal. The disparity between what the landowners professed to do and what in fact they did was real enough. Yet many of them also openly sought and got compensation for the loss of services as well as for the land, even though the Government resisted an open discussion of this aspect of the measure.

Apart from the disastrous moral effect which all this produced on the peasantry, it led to economic disaster, for arrears in redemption payments accumulated regularly, and this brought about the ruin of peasant farming and the pauperization and proletarianization of rural life. Even the Peasant's Bank, founded in the middle of the eighties and designed to give credit to those who wanted to take up more land, failed to arrest the process, and in fact stimulated it. The exaction of 'obligations' was treated on a par with State taxes, and although arrears were occasionally written off (at coronations, for example), they were punishable with confiscation of property and/or flogging, and the peasant was liable to forced labour. It is true that the revolution of 1905 compelled the Government to cancel the debt altogether, but by that time it had collected from the peasants (excluding State and Crown peasants) 1·9 milliard roubles in redemption dues and interest which, taking into account the devaluation of the rouble in the course of these forty-four years, exceeded the market value of the land nearly three times over.

For the peasant, the injustice of this colossal operation was self-evident, and it is not surprising that, contrary to Kavelin's prognosis, the scheme should have proved a fertile ground for a savage class struggle. But apart from being morally unacceptable, the operation failed in practice, for it was like the nursery rhyme which is found in some version in all languages and which begins 'Butcher, butcher, kill the ox . . .'. If the butcher prepares to kill the ox, the ox proceeds to some operation which leads to some other operation, and so on, and the great object is eventually attained. Thus if the peasant had passed from the *corvée* to money payments, as formerly he would have been only too glad to do; if he had then paid his dues regularly; if, moreover, he had made overtures for the redemption of his house and garden and afterwards agreed to purchase his allotment (that is, if he had done what he regarded as manifestly unjust), then the State would have helped him, he would have become a freeholder with half a century in which to wipe off his debt (artificially inflated), while the landowner would have gained by the reform even more than was already the case.[21]

As for these greater gains, one must admit that the landed gentry did not benefit from the emancipation as much as it could have done or had hoped to do. Even large-scale farming in Russia remained relatively backward (except among a minority) and most landowners failed, at any rate until much later in the century, to invest money in agricultural improvements. Considerable sums received in compensation went back to the Government in settlement of outstanding mortgage loans, and a great deal was said to have been spent then and there, or in the newly accessible capitals and resorts of western Europe, on more pleasurable pursuits. The growing practice of leasing land to the peasants may have transformed the landlords, as is sometimes claimed, into 'agrarian capitalists' or even 'land usurers', but this by itself could not contribute to the improvement of agriculture which alone would have effectively served the interests of the gentry so sedulously upheld by the architects of the land reform.

Economically as well as administratively, the peasants continued to be treated, as before the emancipation, on a collective basis, i.e. in terms of village communities, not of individuals or full citizens. Whatever intrinsic social and moral merits the communal system may have (and the question was one of the most hotly debated in nineteenth-century Russia), both the Government and the majority of the landowners had an undoubted vested interest in its preservation, although the influential Slavophil section brought forward the familiar esoteric reasons in its favour. According to Rostovtsev, whose views on the matter were generally accepted in the drafting commissions, the village community (*obshchina* and its administrative organ the *mir*) was to serve as 'a necessary substitute for the strong authority of the landowners'; and 'without the community the landowners will never obtain the payments and services owing to them and the Government will not collect taxes'. To ensure the due exercise of such authority and the prompt fulfilment of all obligations, the village communities, amongst other provisions, were put under the new jurisdiction of a *volost'* (district), dominated by 'arbitrators' (*mirovye posredniki*) drawn from the local gentry. These arbitrators did not wield power in their own individual right as landowners previously used to do, but as legalized representatives of the landowning 'estate' as a whole. As such, their influence proved more pervasive than the private arbitrariness of feudal relations, and from time to time they even showed a bold front to the more reactionary and feudalistic of their fellow landowners, as well as to Government officialdom. Engelhardt, a well-known Russian agriculturalist and populist writer, whose essays 'From the Village' (*Iz derevni*) provide important source material for the study of rural life in Russia after the emancipation, gives evidence of the relent-less ubiquity of 'arbitrators'.[22] Their activities neutralized to a great extent the new rudimentary forms of peasant self-govern-ment, designed to carry out some of the administrative functions formerly vested in the landowners.

The arbitrator is everything [Engelhardt writes]: the opening of schools, the closing of pot-houses, the collection of donations—all spring from the arbitrator. Should the arbitrator so decide, the peasants will proclaim their intention to have in every district not only a school but a university. Should the arbitrator so decide, a resolution will be adopted that the peasants of a certain district, recognizing the advantage of horticulture, have decided to contri-bute so many kopeks per head to some society in Haarlem for the cultivation of hyacinth bulbs. Should the arbitrator so decide, the peasants of any village will drink vodka in one pot-house and close down another.

In consequence, the peasants viewed the arbitrator with horror just as they abhorred the whole economic and adminis-trative system, ostensibly new but, to them at least, indistin-guishable from the old.[23] Deceived in their hopes, they responded to the reform with a new and almost unprecedented wave of mass rebellions. But before dealing with this tragic outcome of Alexander II's liberating activity, it is important to say some-thing of the Emancipation Edict itself and of its reception by the urban population.

The statutes were promulgated on 19 February 1861 (old style), but the 'revolution from above' was announced in a separate edict, published in all the newspapers, proclaimed in all the churches, displayed on the walls of the capitals and pro-vincial towns, and made known in all the villages. In manner and matter the edict is a curious document. It was written by the Metropolitan Philaret, the most outstanding figure in the hierarchy of the Russian Orthodox Church in the nineteenth century, who deprecated emancipation in any form on reli-gious grounds, but who succeeded in proving to his own satis-faction that, for the moment at any rate, reasons of state coincided with the intention of God. Unlike the matter-of-fact *Amtssprache* of the statutes, the edict is written in the vein of pulpit oratory, of that politico-religious rhetoric used from time immemorial by rulers to persuade their subjects that they ought to obey them. It is noteworthy that the edict avoids the term 'emancipation' (*osvobozhdenie*): this dangerous expression yields to the hollow euphemism 'amelioration in the conditions of the peasants' or 'new organization of the peasants' way of life'. The document abounds in reminders of Gospel precepts and duties of allegiance, and in unrelieved demonstrations of self-righteousness that must have jarred on the most sympathetic and loyal reader. Tolstoy, in a letter to Herzen, wrote of the edict that 'the *muzhiks* won't understand a word of it; and we shan't believe a word of it'.

Elaborate preparations were made to turn the emancipation into a great national occasion, and from the very beginning a rich mythology began to surround it. On 28 February Pogodin wrote about the impending Act in the St. Petersburg paper 'The Northern Bee' (*Severnaya pchela*): 'Is there in the history of Europe—nay, of the world—an event, purer, loftier, nobler than this one, an event equal to or comparable with this one? Find it, show it to me! Russian people! Russian people! On your knees! Thank God for this sublime, incomparable happiness vouchsafed to us all, for this glorious page which embellishes our native history!'

On the appointed day [Pogodin prophesied] the peasants will array themselves in their *kaftans*, anoint their locks with *kvas* and go out with their wives and children in their Sunday clothes to worship God. From the church the peasants will walk in procession to their landowners, offer them bread and salt, and bowing deeply they will say: 'thank you, your honour, for the bounty which you have dispensed to us, our fathers and our forefathers; may your mercy not abandon us in the future, while we shall for ever be your servants and labourers'.

Another writer, the conservative journalist Ermolov, expatiated on the 'raptures' which the reform evoked 'in the best Russians', on the 'palpitation of the noblest Russian hearts' and on the 'beautiful fruits of poetic genius' that will emerge 'from the newly gained popular freedom'.

These forecasts cannot be assessed apart from the simultaneous arrangements made by the Government behind the scenes. As early as 1858 Alexander expressed to Lanskoy his fear that 'when the new statute is put into operation the people will realize that their expectation, i.e. freedom as they understand it, has not been fulfilled: might this not be a moment of disappointment?' To prevent a revolutionary explosion, a meeting of the central committee for the drafting of the statutes in January 1859 decided, in the presence of the Tsar, to send 'trusted persons' to various parts of the country 'to superintend the preservation of public order while the statutes . . . are carried out'. They were to be given 'full powers to act in certain cases in the name of the Sovereign'. Later, on the eve of the proclamation, Alexander ordered 'the dispatch to every province of a major-general or aides-de-camp from the escort of His Imperial Majesty' whose duty it would be 'to co-operate with the provincial Governors to maintain peace and order'.[24] At the same time an urgent 're-deployment of troops' was carried out throughout the country to assist the authorities in the quelling of possible peasant disturbances. These arrangements could not be completed before 19 February which, amongst other things, caused the publication of the edict to be delayed until 5 March. In short, the Government viewed the inauguration of its reform as a kind of military operation. This moved Herzen to biting diatribes against 'liberation by the lash' (*vsekaemoe osvobozhdenie*) by the 'janissaries of the "Liberator"' (*oprichniki 'Osvoboditelya'*), by 'blood-thirsty aides-de-camp' and 'improvised hangmen'. Herzen's strong reaction, and particularly the even more uncompromising attitude adopted by his allies or successors inside Russia—the men with whom the main bulk of this book is concerned—can be better appreciated if we examine more closely the prevailing atmosphere in the country at this time.

Although many eye-witnesses have left valuable records of the fateful days before and after 19 February, they are mainly in the form of political memoirs written years after the event, with the inevitable rationalizations—whether favourable or unfavourable to the Government—which writing after the event involves.[25] But there exists an important contemporary document which conveys the prevailing mood, and tells with directness and candour what actually happened and how people reacted. The document, unpublished and by its very nature unpublishable before the Revolution, was seized and kept in the archives of the Third Section, and is entitled 'Notes of a Contemporary on 1861' (*Zapiski sovremennika o 1861 g.*).[26] The author, Erast Pertsov, was a prosperous landowner and wine merchant, a gossip and a wit with an inquisitive disposition, some literary skill, and a considerable gift for observation. He seems to have had wide connexions among government officials, members of the nobility, generals, factory owners, and merchants. Moreover, he had a habit of rubbing shoulders with 'the people': 'assuming', as he says, 'a democratic exterior', he made a special point of mixing with the crowd of the newly liberated serf population of the capital. He expresses fairly strong disapproval of Herzen's political views and shows a certain affection for the reigning monarch, despite some scathing remarks about Alexander's 'empty-headedness' and excessive preoccupation with hunting and 'divorce' (a reference, perhaps, to one of Alexander's later, more serious *liaisons*, with Princess Ekaterina Dolgorukaya, which resulted in his final estrangement from the Empress Mariya Alexandrovna—a stiff and bigoted woman whose excessive religious piety was either the effect or the contributory cause of her husband's love-affairs). But Pertsov flays the mass of flatulent sycophancy about the Tsar in which 'aristocrats, merchants, officials and soldiers vie with one another'. For him, the greatest 'scoundrels' are the generals responsible for the implementation of the peasant statutes and for the protection of 'the exalted person of the Emperor himself'.[27] 'These brave soldiers', Pertsov says in one of his milder moments, 'wear military uniforms, but they have never smelt powder' and 'moral fresh air stinks in their nostrils'. 'They have seen all their service round ink-pots, at their desks, engaged in military campaigns against common sense, enlightenment and Russian orthography.'

Pertsov tells us how on the eve of 19 February members of the Government 'felt a cold shiver down their spines like that before sunrise' and took hurried, furtive measures to meet the expected peasant rebellion. Apart from the virtual mobilization of the army and the police, workshops received special orders for flogging-rods which were urgently dispatched in unprecedented quantities to various parts of the capital and its surroundings. Factory owners in the St. Petersburg region were given instructions by the police to make special increases in working hours so that workers should be too fatigued 'to contemplate any dangerous action'. There is a harrowing account, confirmed in some respects by other sources, of the scene in the Winter Palace on that fateful night and of the pale, frightened, restless figure of the Emperor;[28] of the extreme secrecy that was observed in the printing of the edict, and of the precautions that were taken to prevent its untimely revelation.[29] We are also told how, immediately after the proclamation, the authorities ordered all merchants to thank Alexander for the newly gained freedom and how factory owners, with the help of the police, rounded up workers, serfs until yesterday but now free, in front of the Palace to express their feelings of loyalty to the Tsar.

A house porter (*dvornik*), Pertsov reports, summoned by the police to receive instructions about informing against tenants, was asked by an unknown stranger why he went to the police and replied: 'It's about freedom (*za voley*) . . . it seems freedom has been granted, and that's certain, because they don't allow one to talk about it'—a remark that throws more light on the Russian peasant's attitude to those in power than volumes of sociological inquiry. The porter was subsequently given 230 strokes 'for spreading malicious rumours'. A mysterious 'she' became the accepted synonym for 'freedom' among the ordinary people. 'Why, it's to-day . . . so to speak . . . that "she" . . . what your honour just mentioned has been brought out . . .', a cab-driver observed reluctantly to Pertsov on the day of promulgation but before the publication of the edict. Unluckily, someone overheard the remark: the driver was taken to the police station and 'got such a beating as God forbid'. Such scenes occurred daily.

The generals and aides-de-camp, charged with supervising the implementation of the statute, were provided with augmented travelling allowances and huge trunks filled with copies of the edict and firearms for personal use 'at their own discretion' and 'with a view to moral persuasion and inducement of mental compliance'. 'The cowardice of the bureaucrats saw incipient rebellion in every poor peasant girl standing alone in the steppe.'

In the main, Pertsov could see nothing but apathy among the people in the capital. Their answers were evasive: 'I'm not literate, I haven't read the thing; but I guess—people said so yesterday—that for the house serfs (*dvorovye*) there will be

freedom in two years, but for the peasants there won't be any
for some time.' Or: 'I went to the Liturgy, some sort of hand-
bill was read out, but I couldn't hear much: they say we shall
still have to wait for "her", and now there's nothing special
(*a teper' tolko tak*). . . .' Or: 'Of course, I started reading it, but
couldn't make anything out (*v tolk nichego ne vzyal*); why, it's all
written for the masters (*dlya gospod*), not for us. . . .' 'Don't know
if people are telling the truth, but it seems there isn't any freedom after all: it's put off.' 'That is all I could hear on 5 March
from the sealed lips of the people', Pertsov concludes.

One landowner announced: 'A mountain has brought forth
a mouse'; whilst a highly placed official, on being informed of
the people's silence, exclaimed: 'Damn it! are those Scythians
still alive, or are they dead historically?'

Meanwhile, the Emperor, 'in a happy mood after his panic
of the night before', was showing himself to his people and drove
about all day long in a *troika* on the Nevsky with his whole
family, escorted by strong military guards. 'The people'
stopped, removed their hats, made the sign of the cross and
went on in silence.

The police continued to summon house-porters for new
instructions as to how they should conduct themselves when
His Majesty passed before the houses in their charge: they
were to go out into the street and shout 'hurrah!' In addition,
they were ordered to perambulate in the evening along their
respective streets and wherever they saw a concourse of people
similarly shout 'hurrah!', thereby 'inciting others to expressions
of grateful feeling'. 'But', writes Pertsov, 'since the people
have long lost the habit of public self-expression the democratic designs of the police failed completely. Only the very
best-intentioned and frightened porters shouted "hurrah!".'

The St. Petersburg papers and other official sources contain
accounts of a famous occasion on which the peasant workers of
a large iron-foundry in the St. Petersburg district are said to
have come out *en masse* for a spontaneous presentation to the
Tsar of bread and salt ('on a golden tray'!) in gratitude for
freedom. Pertsov was an eye-witness of what actually happened,
and his version is supported by other independent evidence.[30]
Anyone familiar with the political conditions of nineteenth-
century Russia must have known that no 'spontaneous mass

manifestation' of any kind was conceivable in the presence of the Tsar: if it had taken place it would have resulted in immediate mass arrests and beatings. In fact, the initiative came from the Tsar himself, and elaborate preparations were made by Ignatiev, the Governor-General of St. Petersburg, and by the director of the factory (Vassily Poletika, a figure of some notoriety among Russian nineteenth-century industrialists) to stage a demonstration.

Poletika invited other industrialists to join him and composed an address, which one worker was to recite to the Tsar and which all the workers were to sign. Most of them were, of course, illiterate and on signing the document as best they could they implored their master not to trick them, for they believed this was some sort of trap to get them into trouble ('Batyushka, ne podvedi ty nas pod chto nibud' khudoe, ne pogubi!'). Having allayed their fears, Poletika proceeded with his reluctant demonstrators to the Nevsky Monastery, where they happened to find 'a chance assembly of clergy' arrayed in festal vestments. 'The peasants waited for hours in the slushy March snow. First of all the Court police appeared. They pushed and shouted: "Where are you hiding, you ass? Come forward so that you can be seen": for many of the demonstrators got lost among the crowd of ordinary citizens attracted by the unusual spectacle. Someone was heard saying: "If only to-day they would stop beating the *muzhiks*! After all, they have come here to thank the Sovereign".' When the Tsar appeared Pertsov heard shouts of 'hurrah!', and the bread and salt on the golden tray were duly presented, to which Alexander replied: 'I thank you for not having forgotten me', and then added the well-known phrase: 'For better or for worse you have been set free: it is not my deed, but the gentry's, your masters. Pray God that everything may end happily!' When the crowd dispersed Pertsov asked a few demonstrators why they had come: 'If the masters command, how can you not go?' they replied.

Poletika's example was followed by others. 'The excesses of fulsome loyalists', Pertsov continues, 'have an infectious quality in Russia. They spread from person to person at lightning speed, increasing in the process both as regards the volume of degradation of human dignity and the number of those who degrade themselves. Others succeeded in assembling not only *muzhiks* but also peasant women and children from various villages. Boys carried the bread and salt, and girls presented flowers to the Empress.' 'I am told', Pertsov overheard someone remark in a well-known St. Petersburg salon, 'that it was almost impossible to look without laughter at these muzhikoid white negresses (*muzhikoobraznykh belykh negretyanok*) who drove for the first time in their lives along the Nevsky Prospect in hired coaches, solemnly holding before them exquisite outlandish flowers whose names they had never even heard.'

Such, according to Pertsov, were 'the mechanics of the first backstage puppet mysteries'. But the tragicomic masquerade was repeated endlessly—with variants—during this eventful time. The capital swarmed with police orders to shout 'hurrah!' whenever the Emperor appeared or was rumoured to be about to appear on the horizon. Pertsov says that in the end all this assumed such a manifestly meretricious and farcical character that Alexander, to his honour, put an end to the bustle. And when fawning newspaper editors projected a series of banquets in honour of the emancipation the Tsar declined to participate, although Pertsov suggests that this was due to the excessively protracted and exhausting nature of such manifestations, which 'took him away from hunting and divorces'. To compensate for their frustrated desire to express their 'servility and boot-licking' (*kholopstvo i nogolizanie*) the patriotic editors proceeded to give vent to it with renewed effort and zeal in their respective papers, which Alexander is known to have seldom or never read.

The evidence shows that the situation in Moscow did not differ from that in the capital, even though Pogodin wrote in *S.-Peterburgskie novosti* (St. Petersburg News), in his customary grandiloquent manner, of 'unheard-of raptures among the inhabitants of Moscow at the proclamation of the manifesto'. Tuchkov, Governor-General of Moscow, gave a more sober account in an official telegram to the Emperor which contained the crucial phrase: 'having taken the necessary measures, peace and order in the city have not been disturbed'.[31] And Lanskoy reported to Alexander about a major anticlimax: '. . . a circumstance', he wrote, 'has struck everybody by its ominous significance. Everybody expected that the drink-shops would

be besieged from joy. . . . Tax-farmers ordered a double supply
of spirits for several months. There is, however, not only no
increase in drunkenness but consumption of drink has actually
decreased . . ., despite the fact that the manifesto was published
on the last day before Lent (*maslenitsy*).'

II

REVOLUTION FROM BELOW

1. *Peasant Revolts*

MOST ex-serfs in the larger towns and cities immediately after the emancipation would seem to have borne their lot with bovine patience. The authorities were near at hand, and the people thought first of avoiding falling foul of their superiors or, sometimes, of how to cheat them without being found out, with the result that only those who cheated skilfully, with sufficient cunning and flattery, chiefly those engaged in trade, were able to improve their lot. The most unfortunate were the *dvorovye*, house serfs: hordes of such people (some 80,000 in Moscow alone) previously encamped in and around the house, receiving no wages and conditioned to an unnatural, servile, and useless existence, were thrown into the rudimentary làbour market. A noble lady complained that twelve of her Russian women servants could not do the work of one French chamber-maid: but now one had to pay for their services—very little, it is true—and one had to feed as well as pay them. Most of their previous owners preferred, therefore, to let them go, although some kept them as trusted servants or even friends, while the more avaricious exacted all they could, especially in the two year interim period between 1861 and 1863. The unemployed and unemployable house servants were joined by an army of jobless peasants from the villages, also hard hit by the emancipation. The demand for labour in factories and industry was growing, but not fast enough to absorb the flood of new labour. Thus an underpaid urban proletariat came into being.

The reaction in the country, however, was different. After the Emancipation Edict Russia went through a phase of abortive peasant rebellions, a nineteenth-century *jacquerie*, which proved Tocqueville's contention that the most dangerous moment for a bad government is when it begins to reform itself. 'The political situation in the country is tense in the extreme',

the Head of the Third Section reported to the Tsar. The tradition of the proverbial docility of the Russian peasant proved
unreliable, and the contradictions in his character, oscillating
between tenacious independence and compliance, savagery and
humanity were revealed. Inasmuch as the revolutionary movement was directed against the gentry, it opposed not any specific
feudal privileges, as in late eighteenth-century France, but the
principle of the monopoly of landed property, guaranteed by
the Act of Emancipation and enabling the gentry to exploit not
so much the land as their title to the land, and the peasant's
need of that land.

The peasant began to say plainly and despairingly that he
was being merely beguiled by unreal and insubstantial visions.
Discontent prevailed everywhere and became contagious, resulting in a spontaneous wave of uprisings that involved nearly
the whole of central Russia, the Middle Volga region (where it
assumed a particularly serious character), Lithuania, White
Russia, the Ukraine, New Russia, the European Ural region,
and other parts of the country not traditionally associated
with active opposition. The movement spread from villages in
estates belonging to individual landowners to State and Crown
peasants. Between 1861 and 1863 over 2,000 uprisings took
place; and, during the first year following the emancipation,
revolts occurred in 1,176 estates. The peasants rejected the
edict and the statutes, often on the grounds that they were
spurious documents which, as one group of peasants put it,
'will make the lot of the *muzhik* harder than before, and in two
years time the landowners will have ruined us altogether'; they
demanded 'true freedom' (*nastoyashchuyu volyu*); they seized
their masters' land; they set fire to his property; they refused
to carry out their 'obligations' to the landowners, leaving the
land unsown or the crops rotting, so that agricultural production
dropped. Some landowners were ruined, others were singled
out for indiscriminate revenge as a reprisal for pent-up feelings
of grievance.[32]

According to the generally accepted view, the uprisings, like
their numerous predecessors, were directed against the gentry
and the 'servants of the Tsar', not against the Tsar himself, and
Stenka Razin's appeal 'to stand firm for our Sovereign Lord
and to get rid of the traitors' (i.e. landowners and Government

officials) is said to have been as relevant in the eighteen-sixties as it was in the sixteen-seventies. It is true that the revolts after the emancipation, all unarmed, except for occasional pitch-forks and cudgels, had no political programme. It is also true that the remoteness of the Tsar tended to create an attitude of vague veneration among the peasantry. This may even have had its share of a rather fragile mysticism, which ob-viously did not apply to the landowners, the representatives of the Church and local officials of whose habitual injustice they had direct experience. Indeed, the Central Government, though never fostering the disaffection of the peasants *vis-à-vis* the landowners, from time to time expressed misplaced fears lest any bond of sympathy and mutual interest should be established between the gentry and the peasants.[33]

Nevertheless, the peasants' devotion to the Tsar, whose solicitude for 'the people' was allegedly frustrated by his cun-ning advisers, was not as uncritical as some accounts make out. Only the most crushed and submissive peasants continued to entertain hopes of a merciful allotment of land by the boun-teous Tsar. Whenever the peasants were able to learn the true state of affairs, their loyalty turned into intense resentment. Whenever village communities had had occasion to send messengers (*khodoki*) to the Tsar to complain of their misery—a frequent, though quite useless practice, involving nothing but expense and humiliation—the peasants afterwards reacted to any rumours of the Tsar's mercy with unconcealed anger. Even Samarin agreed (in a letter of 22 April 1861) that for the peasants

edicts, uniforms, civil servants, decrees, Governor-Generals, priests with crosses, imperial commands, are nothing but falsehood, fraud and forgery. The people submit to these things as they submit to hard frosts, to blizzards, to drought; but they believe in nothing, acknowledge nothing, give in to no one. Admittedly, an image of the remote Tsar floats before their eyes, but it is not the Tsar who lives in St. Petersburg, who appoints Governors, issues decrees and moves armies: it is a wholly different, primeval, half mythical Tsar who might rise suddenly from nowhere in the shape of a drunken deacon or a peasant soldier on permanent leave.

Many peasants declared: 'it would have been better for him [the Tsar] not to promise freedom if he can't command the landowners'; or they stated openly that 'the root of evil is in the Sovereign', realizing that they would have to rely on their own actions and not on superior benevolence.

As has been noted, the Government was fully prepared for the disturbances, which were crushed with appalling severity. Punitive expeditions were dispatched; there were mass executions, floggings, deportations to forced labour in Siberia and, exceptionally, wholesale razing of villages. Detailed news of this reached Herzen in London. 'The poor, poor peasants!', he wrote. 'People in Europe do not suspect what suppression by Major-Generals and aides-de-camp means. . . . The government of progress and liberal ideas, supported by bayonets and Pogodin's articles, has tasted Polish blood and now goes downhill: blood is slippery.'[34]

A striking incident occurred in the village of Bezdna, on the estate of Count Musin-Pushkin, involving parts of the Kazan, Samara, and Simbirsk provinces, where the memory of Pugachev was still alive. It caused a sensation among the Russian public: even the Government, which ordinarily suppressed the news of such revolutionary occurrences, felt obliged to give its own version of the incident (in the *St. Petersburg Gazette* of 19 May 1861), in view of reports that had reached the foreign press as well as Herzen's *Bell*. An account of what happened will help to explain the deep impression which such incidents produced on radical opinion.

The edict had been read in Simbirsk on 9 March which was market day, and handbills with extracts from the statutes had been distributed among the peasants. The news spread with great rapidity throughout the whole district. The people assembled, and having consulted with each other, decided that the declared provisions of the statutes were 'rubbish' (*pustyaki*). The frightened local authorities then prohibited the reading of the edict by private persons, and it was entrusted to priests and officials. Unhappily this served only to increase the peasants' suspicions and to encourage rumours. A quiet, stubborn, religious peasant called Anton Petrov in Bezdna became the focal point of these secret discussions. Within a few days, his fellow peasants made of him 'a prophet of new freedom': people came from far and wide to hear his views on the edict, and the prophet of Bezdna, in turn, sent out messengers to explain the nature of

true freedom. The peasants ceased to carry out their 'obligations' and proceeded to divide up the landowners' forests. All
the local authorities were removed from office, and when
General Count Apraksin arrived on the scene with a punitive
expedition 'virtual independence had already been established'.
Petrov encouraged the peasants to take the land and 'promised
freedom to thirty-four provinces'. When Apraksin issued an
order for the arrest of Petrov the people refused to hand him
over. By this time some 5,000 peasants had assembled in Bezdna
to defend their leader. A permanent watch was kept over
Petrov's cottage. Old people, women, and children were
evacuated to neighbouring villages, although everybody seemed
convinced that the soldiers would not dare to shoot, or 'at most
three salvoes', and nobody would be hurt.

On 12 April Apraksin again appeared in the village accompanied by 250 Cossacks. The peasants delegated two old men
to appear before the General with the traditional bread and
salt and explain the peasants' point of view, but the General
refused to enter into any negotiations and announced through
a priest in full liturgical vestments, attended by soldiers and
two officers, that he would give orders to open fire if the peasants
did not disperse. He then appeared in person and again demanded that Petrov should be handed over immediately. The
peasants, of whom none were armed,[35] stood in silence, and
when Apraksin began to curse them they shouted repeatedly in
chorus 'freedom', whereupon he gave the order to fire.

Thousands and thousands of peasants [an eye-witness reported]
clustered in a dense crowd around Petrov's cottage, on carts, on
fences, on the roofs of neighbouring cottages, forming an immense
sea of human heads, all turned towards the soldiers. The first three
salvoes left the crowd unmoved. The peasants continued to shout
'freedom!' and only covered their faces with their hands. From
Petrov's cottage someone cried: 'they want to frighten you, don't
disperse!', 'stand fast!', 'they won't shoot more than three times'.
But the salvoes did not stop, more and more of the peasants were
mown down and at last the crowd was seized with panic. A terrible
commotion ensued. In the general uproar, among the wailings,
howls, stampede and smoke a cossack was heard to shout: 'they are
turning' (obkhodyat) and the firing became continuous. Until the
shooting stopped the peasants rushed about wildly, falling over
each other and collapsing in pools of blood; others scattered into

neighbouring gardens and fields and poured into village side streets. At last Anton Petrov came out of the cottage, wearing a long shirt over his coat, as do the sectarians before prayer, with a copy of the emancipation statutes held above his head, and repeating in a quiet voice: 'the true freedom, the true freedom'. He was instantly arrested and sent to prison in Spassk.

According to the first official report sent in by Apraksin, there were 57 killed and 77 wounded. In fact, the number of killed and wounded was nearer 500, which is not surprising in view of the dense crowd and the intense firing. Apraksin was heard to remark angrily: 'Ugh, how many of them! . . . Never mind, we'll report fewer, it's usually done.' 'After the "combat" the General put two cannons in front of the village hall and proceeded to try the terrified peasants. He forced them to kneel for hours and swore at them.'

By imperial command, Petrov was brought before a military tribunal and shot in Bezdna itself a week after the event, in the presence of his fellow-peasants who had been forced to attend the execution. This appears to have had almost as terrible an effect on the peasants as the original shooting, and even some of the soldiers ran away. 'The twelve shots', the *Bell* reported, 'were so badly aimed that they did not penetrate Petrov's gaunt frame: he was finished off point-blank.'

The local gentry organized a dinner in honour of and in gratitude to Apraksin, with speeches which it would be otiose to repeat.[36]

At the same time, however, a few members of the Kazan intelligentsia, chiefly students of the university and theological Academy, were bold enough to arrange a requiem 'for God's servants who died for freedom and love of their country'. The requiem was celebrated by two young student-priests from the Academy. After the service Shchapov, a well-known populist historian and a professor at Kazan University, gave an address, copies of which were later clandestinely distributed throughout the town and which an official report described as 'insolent and highly unfavourable to the established authorities'. Alexander was intensely annoyed, especially because of the unprecedented and embarrassing religious context in which the demonstration occurred and himself wrote that 'Shchapov must be arrested without fail and the two monks committed to monastic imprisonment in Solovetsk'. The command was carried out, sixteen students were, in addition, expelled from the university, and Apraksin received the order of St. Vladimir 'for outstanding civil and military service': 'I cannot but approve of Count Apraksin's actions' was Alexander's verdict on the affair.

Only Herzen's *Bell* could freely comment on what happened in Bezdna and elsewhere throughout Russia:

Welcome, 'Northern Colossus', 'Giant obedient to the Tsar', yet not as obedient as of yore! [he apostrophized the peasantry in one of his most passionate articles]. Greetings to you: the time is ripe! Yours was a mighty slumber, but now awake in your might! Stretch yourself to your full stature, breathe in the fresh morning air, and blow away this flock of owls, crows, vampires, Putyatins, Muravievs, Ignatievs and other fetid feathered creatures! *You* awake: it is time that *they* retired. They are a creeping tribe that fear the light of day, holy woodlice; they are insects without wings but with insatiable appetites. Blow, Giant, leave no trace of them but the never to be forgotten stains of Polish and peasant blood!

Lord, how pitiful and comic is this redoubtable government! Where is its sergeant-majordom, its roisterer's frame and husky military voice? . . . It does not look as it looked in the good old days, soldier! Its strength is waning, its uniform hangs loose, and its helmet is falling over its eyes. . . .

Listen [Herzen continued, addressing himself now to the students who had been expelled from universities as a result of measures taken by the Minister of Education, Admiral Putyatin], listen, since darkness does not prevent you from hearing! From all parts of our vast land, from the Don to the Urals, from the Volga to the Dnieper, you hear the groans . . . in increasing volume. This is the first roar of the waves threatening storm after a wearisome and ominous calm: go among the people! Go to the people! That is your place, you outcasts of learning![37]

The Tsar was not entirely unaffected by the spreading opposition. What weighed upon him was that his good intentions were not appreciated. He accused the peasants of ingratitude; he searched for scapegoats; he followed the familiar course of ascribing unworthy motives and refusing to regard disturbing facts as anything but subversive, which indeed in a sense they were. And he showed increasing signs of irritability and resentment, which made him more and more inclined toward his most unbending advisers. From Alexander's point of view the fate of the peasants had been settled once and for all: 'Rumours reach me', he said in an address to a group of peasant elders in Poltava on 16 August 1861, 'that you expect some other freedom. There will be no other freedom, except the one I have granted you! Carry out what the law and the statutes demand of you! Exert yourselves and toil! Be obedient to the landowners!'

Nevertheless, the spirit of reform was still at work in the administration. Reforms, or preparations for reforms, followed each other in rapid succession: the financial reform of 1862, the university charter of 1863, the school law of 1864, the *zemstvo* or local government statute of 1865, the conscription law of 1874. Yet it is astonishing how little was altered by all these apparently promising measures designed by the bureaucratic machine. It was evident that attempts to apply advanced ideas to the social and political structure of the Russian State could not succeed, because in the long run it proved impossible to rationalize or liberalize the autocracy without destroying its foundations. As a result, the projects of reform were subjected at each and every stage to modifications which served to uphold the paramount economic and political interests of the established order. And it is significant that they failed to produce the slightest impression on those sections of public opinion which were concerned with the most urgent human problem confronting contemporary Russian society: the melancholy fate of the peasant, who was least impressed of all.

The financial reform brought about important technical improvements (such as the stabilization of the rouble, the introduction of proper budgets, and the centralization of all Government accounts in the Ministry of Finance) and ushered in a wave of foreign investment, company promotion, stock-exchange operations, and all the other varieties of the money-making game first invented in England. It did nothing to mitigate what one Russian economist (Khodsky) called the 'self-defeating over-optimism' of Russian financial policies or check their chronic bureaucratization. According to a Russian Minister of Finance (Greig), the latter made the Russian Government and financial administration 'a colossus with feet of clay': it was among the most costly in the world, and it was based, as before, on a system of taxation whose burden was borne almost exclusively by the peasants.[38]

The university charter, which in theory granted relative autonomy to the universities, was in practice effectively nullified by the appointment of Count Dimitry Tolstoy—an unrelenting enemy of academic as of any other freedom—as Minister of Education. Tolstoy was determined to suppress every manifestation of nonconformity in university life and teaching and he continued with remarkable success and consistency the system of student-baiting well established in Russia.[39]

The school law, which, amongst other things, abolished discrimination against the lower 'estates', proved 'too liberal' for Tolstoy. It was duly emasculated in accordance with the principle enunciated by Tolstoy himself that advanced education should be reserved 'for the upper class, which decides the fate of the nation and chooses its future course'; and that all subjects (such as literature, history, and geography) which provided occasion for teachers 'to indulge in generalizations are not only useless but often positively harmful', and should give way to divinity, Church Slavonic, and the classical languages.[40]

The *zemstvo* statute, the most important measure after the land reform, was responsible for the creation of a useful instrument of local administration and a means for the promotion of rural education and welfare. But it was doomed to failure as a charter of self-government. Its professed aim (explicitly abjured in 1884 as undermining 'the traditional class structure of Russia' and as 'endangering the very existence of the national State') was to unite 'all estates' (*vsesoslovnoe zemstvo*). But this aim was belied from the start by the preponderant role of the gentry within the *zemstvo*—a preponderance that was quite out of proportion to their number and to their financial obligations. Representation, in fact, reduced itself to the principle 'to him that hath shall be given, and from him that hath not shall be taken away'. An additional source of frustration was the iron-handed control which the Government, jealous of its own creation and intent on denying anybody the right to political articulation, exercised over all *zemstvo* activities. From the political point of view, the statute gave Russia an imitation of the old Austrian 'constitution', with the role of *Reichsrat* omitted: like the provincial diets of Austria the *zemstva* met, thanked the Emperor for allowing them to meet, sometimes went so far as to present 'postulates' or 'most and entirely loyal addresses to

his Majesty' which were or were not replied to, and broke up.[41]
It is this that made the later Russian Finance Minister Witte
observe that the *zemstvo* institutions 'failed to meet the requirements of self-government' and evoked Lenin's caustic remark
about 'the fifth wheel on the coach of Russian state administration'.

The most esoteric measure was the quite unobjectionable
legal reform, which appeared to insert into Russian jurispru-
dence the principles of the supremacy of the law, the independence of the courts and the equality of all before the law. In
fact, it in no way contravened the pragmatic basis of traditional
Russian legal assumptions, namely, that the law was an emanation and an instrument of the Tsar's will, even though the
reform aimed at making that will less capricious and more
regular. It belied in every way what Alexander I is made to
reply to a General in Tolstoy's *War and Peace*: 'I cannot,
General, I cannot because the law is stronger than me.' And
when Count Pahlen, an enemy of the reform, became Minister
of Justice he saw to it that no legal abstractions should interfere
with 'the power of the executive (guaranteed by the provisions
of the 1864 statute) to take measures . . . to prevent [political]
crimes and illegal activities'.[42]

The censorship law (to be more precise, 'provisional rules' of
censorship) did to some extent substitute legal for administrative
measures in dealing with literary and journalistic deviations,
and replaced preliminary censorship by a system of 'warnings'
and by the eventual seizure of books and periodicals *after*
publication. But the history of publishing during the reign of
Alexander II and his successors continued to bear out Talley-
rand's opinion that the gift of the word is given to man in order
that he may conceal his thoughts. It is of some interest that,
officially, the authorities claimed that the press was completely
independent, on the grounds that Russia was free of the party
system, unlike the 'so-called constitutional States', where the
press was not 'an expression of public conscience' but a tool of
sectional interests. Censorship was interpreted as a means of
protection of public safety. According to Katkov, 'what is not
contrary to the law and institutions of the country, what does
not offend public morality, what is not deceit and incitement
to violence—can be and is expressed in the press with absolute
independence'.[43]

Only the later reform of the army, the work of one of the ablest and most humane Russian soldiers, General Dimitry Milyutin, brother of the Assistant Minister of the Interior, appears to have been almost wholly admirable. By introducing universal military service, with some justified and some un-justified exemptions, and in particular by humanizing the entire system, it turned the Russian army, at any rate until Milyutin's successor, Vannovsky, managed to undo much of his predecessor's work, from a penal establishment into one of the most enlightened institutions of nineteenth-century Euro-pean military history.[44]

The Act of 1874 was the last reforming measure of Alexander's reign. The stubborn reaction, which became official policy in 1866, lasted, with a few short intermissions, until the end of the Romanovs. A renewed persecution of the intelligentsia and university students started as early as 1861, with the arrest of the poet Mikhail Mikhailov, charged with the authorship of secret revolutionary proclamations. This was followed in 1862 by the suppression of the only two radical journals, *Sovre-mennik* (Contemporary) and *Russkoe slovo* (Russian Word), and the closing of all voluntary institutions and clubs for the further-ance of education among the people. 1862 also marked the arrest of the leading radicals Chernyshevsky and Pisarev. Measures were taken to restrict the number of student admis-sions to the universities. All printing houses were put under the direct control of the Ministry of the Interior; all public lectures, conferences, and meetings not authorized by the same Ministry and by the Third Section were forbidden; and a special per-manent commission was instituted for the investigation of 'means whereby ill-intentioned persons weaken the confidence in, and respect for, the Government among the people'.

No wonder Herzen wrote, in a mood of despairing sarcasm:

Where are the free institutions upside down, the revolution wrong side out, the absolutists bottom side up, the ministerial dema-gogues? . . . Nicholas, so it seems, has been buried alive and is now rising again from the damp earth in his formal tightly-buttoned shroud. The Council of State, archdeacon Panin, saint Annenkov of Petersburg, saint Paul Gagarin and Philaret the Flogger are all assembled to intone the triumphant paschal song: 'Nicholas is risen!' 'In truth, he is risen', we reply to all those dead men who

have not died. Your way is clear, but it is the way that leads not
from the grave but into it. . . .[45]

2. The New Classes

To speculate on the might-have-beens of history and to
theorize about what might have happened or how the old
order could have survived had the reforms been different, or had
some Russian minds been less unruly and less outraged by them,
is a vain undertaking. The only conclusion justified by the
evidence is that Alexander's reforming activity was a kind of
retrenchment, a re-making, an enlargement, and elaboration
of what was essentially the same, that it did not cure the sickness of Russian society, but was itself largely a symptom of its
disease. But meanwhile, whatever the nature and the immediate
effect of the reforms, they and the forces that were indirectly
stimulated by them produced, as has already been noted, a new
atmosphere in the country. It was an atmosphere not so much
of release as of expansion and differentiation, as though some
central and unifying power that held the body politic together
had lost its impetus—a change which cannot be isolated by a
recapitulation of mere facts but which was clearly felt by contemporaries. The change owed much to the fact that autocracy of
the absolute variety would have to be made of sterner stuff than
Alexander's brand of it if it was to achieve the solid uniformity
of his father's régime. Hard as Alexander tried to consolidate
the autocratic structure in the changed conditions—by giving
support to the oppressive policies of his more stiff-necked
ministers, by encouraging ruthless police measures, by his own
sullen retreats before new ideas and commitments, and by his
very inconsistencies—he failed to arrest the centrifugal tendencies and, indeed, provoked clandestine opposition.

In one sphere the marked tendency to differentiate and to
expand was abrupt and immediately evident; for during the
period between 1861 and 1914 Russian society began to concern itself on a large scale with the problems of what is called
conventionally the industrial revolution. Industrial development in Russia started in the early eighteenth century. It owed
almost everything to State initiative; it largely served the requirements of the State; and it was, of course, sustained by servile

labour. Private industrial undertakings played a relatively minor if growing role even in the first half of the nineteenth century, and continued to depend in a great measure on the State, on State subsidies, State orders, and State tariffs. The needs of the vast majority of the population for manufactured goods were largely supplied by serf craftsmen, many of whom organized themselves into *artels*, i.e. into permanent or seasonal co-operatives with no legal status, producing domestic ware or selling their collective labour outside their villages (as carpenters, woodcutters, packers, &c.). Although Nicholas I lent a certain amount of support to individual merchants and factory owners, particularly textile manufacturers, their activities were greatly handicapped by the preponderant right of the gentry to own serfs, the limited supply of free labour, the primitive communications, and by the product of all these—a low level of internal consumption.[46]

The reforms removed these impediments. Industry, trade, and railway construction made rapid strides, and *pari passu* there came into existence a new commercial and industrial class, whose emergence was a source of bewilderment, incredulity, or disappointment to all those to whom Russia appeared exempt from the rigours and conflicts of social development. It consisted, in the first place, of old-fashioned merchants turned commercial *entrepreneurs*—wholesale dealers, grain-brokers, millowners, sugar-refiners, textile manufacturers, and even individual profit-making peasants (*kulaks*). With the increasing need and opportunity for foreign trade, they made a valuable contribution to the government policy of compulsory exportation, of wheat and other commodities, with famine often raging in the neighbourhood of the exporting regions. They had no reason to be dissatisfied with the reforms, and, in fact, accepted them almost unreservedly. They had economic but no cultural ambitions, although towards the end of the century some of them became munificent patrons of art and literature. They were stuffy, narrow-minded, ostentatious, and extravagant.

The symptoms of the breaking up of rural society, where the old, 'organic' order was supposed to survive best, was a source of particular anxiety and the occasion of a great deal of debate. Even leading articles in such semi-official organs as the St.

Petersburg *Golos* (Voice), edited by Kraevsky, were full of references to this new development. Differentiation in the village was stimulated above all by the fact that the new and heavy financial demands set the peasants plotting, and that the most well-to-do section of a peasant minority began to prosper at the price of the pauperization of the majority. The plots originally assigned differed in size and, while the better-off peasants purchased land from the landowners, peasants who were unable to subsist on their diminished land became hired labourers. With the natural increase in rural population, this led to a steady outflow of peasants to the towns and to the new industrial and transport regions which neither passport difficulties nor ties with the village could arrest. All these factors contributed to the disintegration of village life and increased economic contrasts. They also made it increasingly difficult to apply the statistics of averages to the distribution of wealth in the village. Engelhardt wrote in the seventies that 'the ideals of the *kulak* are reigning supreme in the villages'.

It is true that in repartitional peasant communities, where the periodic redistribution of land among the members tended to preserve an egalitarian system, there was less differentiation: hence the populist belief in the non-capitalist ways of Russia. Yet even here, the richer, 'solid' peasants were in the ascendant; and, as is well known, it is to them that Stolypin, who enacted the agrarian reform under Nicholas II, looked for support. They fostered unfair repartition; they exerted their influence by making the peasant community (*mir*) omit repartition altogether for decades at a time; and they even forced the communities by devious means to sell them repartitional land or to buy land on their behalf with the covert or overt permission of the authorities. All this prompted some historians to make the claim, perhaps with exaggeration, that it was the peasant minority and not the city *bourgeoisie* which carried out the '*bourgeois* revolution' in Russia, and that this constituted the fundamental difference between the Russian '*bourgeois* revolution' and those of western Europe.[47]

But the new post-emancipation class also comprised a *bourgeoisie* in the strict sense of the term—bankers, railway promoters, heavy industrialists, managers, administrators, many of whom were of gentry origin. They were more self-conscious and articulate in pursuing their social and economic experiment. They sought to create an institutional mould into which their energy and self-assertion could be poured. They relied on the support of the more progressive elements of the bureaucracy with whom they were closely associated. Like the contemporary Victorians in England, they prized respectability, deportment, cultivation, and character-building. One of the most typical representatives of this class was the immensely capable and energetic Sergey Witte. He had risen from a junior post in a provincial railway administration to become eventually in turn Minister of Transport, of Commerce, of Finance, of Industry and Labour, and President of the Council of Ministers in 1905.

As well as the emerging middle class, the industrial and commercial revolution gave rise to a rural and urban prole-tariat. So far as the peasants were concerned, in either case— whether the economy was free or servile—they footed the bill. But it was, of course, the 'free' system which was better adapted to the development of capitalism. As has been noted, the land reform owed a great deal to the landowner's preference for the work of a free but landless rural population. The new industrial *entrepreneur* was even more axious to have at his disposal land-less, cowed, and unorganized cottars, who were more mobile and more manageable than the 'solid' peasants, tied as these were to their own or their master's land and to the village community. Since many of the factories and mines lay in country districts, unskilled workers, and even skilled ones, maintained their ties with the rural peasantry from which they were drawn, and 'fluidity of labour' or seasonal labour (*otkhozhie promysly*) remained a persistent feature of the industrial system. But an analysis of the statistics for temporary and permanent employment of male workers (about half and half in 1884) suggests that the 'link with the land' has been greatly over-estimated and that it decreased rapidly with the growth of industry and commerce.[48]

On the other hand, for the reasons already given, the eman-cipation resulted in so much redundancy in agricultural districts that the 'reserve army' of labour available for industry was twice the size (about five million) of the 'field army' (about two and a half million). In these circumstances the employer regarded himself, and the village proletarians in search of labour regarded him, as a benefactor in that he agreed to pay any wages at all. As time went on, these did not increase, as happened to some extent in contemporary western European industrial communities, but consistently fell, except where great skill was at a premium. The Russian workers during the first years after the emancipation were, in fact, the most down-trodden, exploitable, and unresisting members of the peasantry.[49]

The conditions in which they worked beggar description. In nineteenth-century England, in a relatively open society with parliamentary institutions, the process of proletarianization was cruel enough. In Russia it was unspeakably brutal. The basis of the whole system of industrial employment was, or rather remained as under serfdom, the prison camp.[50] With this went the familiar phenomenon, not of course peculiar to Russia alone, that any suggestion of improvement in the conditions of the workers (there were no actual proposals until 1882, when a modest and ineffective beginning was made with factory inspection) met with strong resistance from private employers and their supporters in the Government.[51]

Russia was well on the way to becoming that social spectacle of modern history at large which projects and embodies man's avarice, greed, and lust of power, his obsessions with meaningless words, his worship of meaningless values, and all the other insanities. It may be useful to recall that insanity consists above all in not recognizing facts, in making wishes father thoughts. In accordance with this, official and semi-official Russian opinion proceeded to deny or explain away the reality of any social antagonisms and even the very existence of a proletariat in Russia. The Government's attitude was most explicitly stated in a long memorandum—a kind of official *Trostbuch*—on the socialist movement of the seventies and eighties in Russia, compiled by General Shebeko, Assistant Minister of the Interior under Count Dimitry Tolstoy:

Russia [he wrote] is the most unfavourable soil for the development of socialism and anarchism, for organizing strikes, for raising general questions concerning the organization of labour, or for propagating revolutionary ideas. Happily neither paupers nor proletarians exist in Russia. Russia occupies an enormous territory, containing sufficient wealth to guarantee the means of existence for an incomparably greater number of people. For this reason, the Russian people have not lent their ear to the far-off dreams and chimeras of the socialists. The impudent agitators have forgotten to take into account the historic allegiance of the Russian people to the Monarch, who occupies the next place after God in the popular mind. The Russian people can rightly see in the future bright, quiet and happy vistas, without fear of social crises and upheavals. Strong in the faith of her ancestors, conscious of national power and united in her tender love for the Monarch, far removed from strife and storm, . . . peaceful yet firm in international relations, Russia can serenely and confidently await the great destiny which Providence has in store for her.

None the less, the document describes in great detail the activities of 'a small group of people who try to sow dissension', but who can be and are being easily eliminated, while the people know 'that all they need is provided by the Government'.[52]

The liberal and conservative Russian press, *Vestnik Evropy* (The Messenger of Europe), *S.-Peterburgskie vedomosti* (St. Petersburg Gazette), *Moskovskie vedomosti* (Moscow Gazette), and many others, were unanimous in regarding the whole question of the workers' welfare as 'an economic fantasy generated by the principle of crude envy', a matter of 'unbridled passions', 'senseless and immoral', 'encroaching on the sacred principle of private property' ('The Messenger of Europe'). When, occasionally, abuses were admitted, notably in the liberal press, these were attributed to the vanishing survivals of pre-Reform conditions, or to bureaucratic elements obstructing the smooth running of the emerging healthy competitive order. 'It is not difficult', states the 'St. Petersburg Gazette', 'to convince oneself that our society is not susceptible of any danger from "social movements" in the western sense, that there is not a trace of class enmity between the Russian proprietors and the labourers, and that we must only strive to avoid fostering it artificially by means of favouring the one group at the expense of the other.'

Such leading public men as Katkov and Pobedonostsev even refused to discuss the matter on the grounds that in Russia 'the problem of the proletariat and of the monopoly of capital has no relevance'. The conservative 'Moscow Gazette' charged 'antinational parties in the outlying districts of the country' (presumably Poland) with inciting public disorder 'by means of the bogy of the workers' problem'. It admits the existence of 'certain misunderstandings between workers and proprietors' but attributes them to 'purely extraneous reasons', whose extraneousness is not defined, but which are said 'to impede the normal development of free labour'.

The moderate populists adopted a different but comparable attitude. They assumed a fundamental dissimilarity in social and economic development between western Europe and Russia. 'Owing to the village community, which has been lost in the west but has fortunately been preserved in Russia', wrote the populist *Nedelya* (Week), 'our worker is a landholder; he can, therefore, profit from a considerable portion of his labour without the intervention of the employer—a situation which is out of the question in the west. This puts a completely different meaning on the question and makes factory work or domestic manufacture in Russia closely dependent on land tenure.'[53] Nevertheless, the populists believed that the obligations attendant on the emancipation statutes (redemption payments, poll-taxes, land-taxes, quitrents, and other services) wiped out most of the advantages, in particular the supposed independence *vis-à-vis* their employer, that peasant workers were expected to derive from their landholdings. Short of a radical change, few populists during the sixties or even the seventies expected the Government or the landowners to abolish these onerous obligations and by so doing vindicate the populist belief.

Others, for example Tkachev, went still further and admitted the existence of conflicts *within* the village community, and foresaw its ensuing gradual disintegration. Of this, as has been seen, there was abundant evidence even then, and, in the view of many populists, only a revolution could arrest it. It is, indeed, one of the most important if rarely discussed achievements of populist thought to have shown the illusory character of Russian Government policy which adhered to the belief in the 'natural harmony of classes'. 'Class struggle' may have become a myth and a slogan, but this gives no ground for assuming that conflicts of interest and ambition between human beings or groups of human beings are illusory. And all the evidence goes to show that Russia was in no way exempt from this human or inhuman condition.[54]

3. *Divisions and Loyalties*

(a) *Conservative Russia*

The rise of industrialism, of new classes, and new forms and relationships in production formed only one aspect of a larger movement of spiritual and psychological change, in which philosophical thought, religion, and literature played their part. The reforms accomplished for Russia what the French Revolution accomplished for France and, by implication, for western Europe as a whole. Against the avowed wishes of the Tsars, who persisted in ruling the Empire as a paternalistic landowner might administer his estates, they unwittingly substituted the nineteenth-century conception of society as a battleground of conflicting forces for the idea of a harmonious mechanism, constructed and operated by an all-wise providence. The latter idea had already been shaken in Russia by Peter the Great, whose whirlwind energy brought about the agonizing but largely superficial transformation of feudal patriarchal Russia; it was, similarly, challenged by the Decembrists and the lonely rebels of the 'remarkable decade' of the eighteen-forties. But now society as a whole was breaking up and exposing deep-seated divisions and dilemmas.

There were still no parties and hardly any political organizations: only movements and individuals. Side by side with the new economic processes, the key to this period lies in the development of ideas and of men who fill the crowded canvas, each embodying a different strain of temperament and working out the concepts of the new situation.[55]

One can distinguish, roughly speaking, three groups of people and of opinion: the conservative, the liberal, and the radical, although each of these groups shades into the next, is criss-crossed by other allegiances, or shows signs of internal division.

However much the governing, conservative class in Russia lived in fear of violent revolution from within or of revolutionary influence from without, it lacked the intellectual resources to formulate its beliefs, as Burke did for the English, or de Maistre for the French aristocracy to refute the ideals of the French Revolution. It is true that Ivan Aksakov, Katkov, and even Pobedonostsev have been variously suggested as claimants to the title of a Russian Burke, but, so far as the last two are concerned, this is certainly unfair to the real Burke, except, perhaps, that they shared his opposition to the intrusion of rational principles into political life and his contempt for 'starry-eyed idealism'. The so-called 'official nationalism' with its tripartite formula 'Orthodoxy, Autocracy, Nationality', designed as a motto for the régime of Nicholas I, continued to be extolled in official pronouncements and in the conservative press. But it had no recognizable intellectual, moral, or cultural content, and nothing to rely on except the armed security of the State. Intelligence is scattered by the gods in sundry and unexpected places, and it is sometimes found beneath a monarch's crown. But few monarchs had so little respect for intellect, or were so alarmingly sterile in intellectual and cultural respects as the last four Romanovs. Statesmanship for them and their direct supporters consisted in waging wars or making peace abroad, and politics in keeping power at home. Ideas were regarded at best as useful weapons of political warfare, but mostly as subversive doctrines which constitute a menace to stability, whilst the available intelligent men were employed as tools to be thrown away when their usefulness became blunted, or their intelligence too obvious and explicit.

Pogodin and Shevyrev continued to preach that, in the words of Benckendorff's famous statement to Chaadaev (made in French), 'Russia's past is admirable, her present more than magnificent, as for the future, it is beyond the grasp of the most daring imagination'. They were now joined by the extremely influential and able political journalist Katkov, who, after 1862, under the impact of the growing revolutionary movement and of the Polish rising of 1863, was spurred into extreme reaction and had won the deserved title of 'dictator of the Russian press'. They were also aided by such men as Katkov's biographer Nikolai Lyubimov, by the historian Ustryalov, by the popular writers Boleslav Markievicz and Dimitry Averkiev, and above all by the triumvirs of Russian reaction at its most sinister, Pobedonostsev, Dimitry Tolstoy, and Prince Vladimir Meshchersky. For them, in any case for Pobedonostsev, the only thing wrong with economic and political oppression was that there was not enough of it. Pogodin's misty, extravagant nationalism became transformed in their hands into unashamed jingoism, into tribal, religious chauvinism, and into anti-Semitism. They expressed a widespread and officially fostered fear or distrust of public opinion, although they paid occasional lip-service to it. They disliked controversy and never asked or admitted questions when it was known that the answers might be unpleasant. They were authoritarian and claimed divine sanction for the existing social and political order, although, on the whole, they had little patience with unprofitable mystic rhapsodizing about the eternal destiny of Russia. From time to time they gave voice to a strong suspicion of 'the needy (*nedostatochnye*) and unprovided (*neobezpechennye*) elements of society'. The conservative press, official and semi-official reports, memoranda, and correspondence abounded in moralizings, favourite slogans and phrases, such as 'sacred autocracy', 'Christ-loving Sovereign' (and Army), 'moral preparation', 'inviolability of religious beliefs' linked with 'thrift and affluence', 'loss of traditional submissiveness among the lower estates', 'dangerous thoughts and utterances unheard of among the simple people only a few years ago', and so on. The latter crimes were habitually attributed to unworthy motives, and it was held that every enemy of the existing order was either dishonest or deranged.[56]

There is every reason to believe that some spokesmen of official conservatism were sincere, upright, and loyal men. One is content to call others good on much less exigent terms than these. What turned them into evil-doers (which Pobedonostsev, Dimitry Tolstoy, and Meshchersky undoubtedly were) was not their individual qualities, but slavery to their own beliefs—the whole hierarchy of the existing order on which they depended, with which they identified themselves and for the maintenance of which all means and sanctions were brought into play. Thus they embodied all the atavistic prejudices that disfigured the social and spiritual scene in Russia until the end of the monarchy. They were conservative, but only one part of conservative, Russia, atrophied Russia, lacking moral and intellectual reflexes and lashing out, at haphazard, from an inability or an unwillingness to recognize the real sources of frustration.

The other conservative Russia was represented by two more or less distinct but interdependent groups: the Slavophils and the *pochvenniki* (i.e. those who believed in the soil, men of the soil, from *pochva*, soil or ground).

The fate of the earlier Slavophils does not come within the scope of this study. Khomyakov, the brothers Kireevsky, and Konstantin Aksakov did not survive the emancipation. Their influential followers and allies included Ivan Aksakov (1823–86), Alexander Koshelev (1806–83), editor of the most important Slavophil journal, *Russkaya beseda* (Russian Conversation), Yury Samarin (1819–76), Prince Vladimir Cherkassky (1824–78), and Alexander Hilferding (1831–72).[57] They continued to uphold the essential Slavophil creed, and on the whole lost none of the natural decency and enthusiasm which characterized their more distinguished predecessors. But they were less idealistic, less generous, and less given to the comforts of patriarchal affection and romantic nostalgia, although they continued to regard everything that divided the Russian people as sinful, and aimed at preserving links with the unruffled, contented way of life of the landed gentry of central Russia. The basic Slavophil notion that it is possible for a nation's social life and culture to exist as a pure entity, evolving according to a pattern laid down by a divinely conceived national genius, that departures from this pattern are accompanied by undesirable social changes and are the result of insidiously corrupting influences from outside—this notion became increasingly a device for diverting attention from internal sources of conflict and change. Khomyakov had still been a cultivated European, with no contempt for humanity as a whole and one who, at times, was even capable of seeing both sides of a question. He and his fellow-Slavophils were at least dimly aware of some of the difficulties inherent in relating their myths to the realities of history, and their obscurity and diffuseness are largely to be found in those parts of their doctrines which descend from the imaginative to the moral and social worlds. Their successors knew nothing of such difficulties, and they readily and uninhibitedly used the Slavophil mythology as a substitute for secular purposes. They could no longer even take advantage of the original Slavophil claim to have redressed the balance *vis-à-vis* the Westerners and to have striven for the recognition of a largely unfamiliar and for the most part unwelcome point of view.

Ivan Aksakov, it is true, with Samarin and Koshelev, defended the right of free speech. But they also displayed most of the narrow political and nationalistic prejudices that distinguished contemporary official conservatism. This became particularly marked in the case of Aksakov when he reached the height of his political influence. The background was provided by the movement for the liberation of the Balkan Slavs, which stimulated the diffusion of Great Russian nationalism and panslavism—'the Slavophilism without any fantasy, but also without any shame' as Vladimir Soloviev described it. Unlike many other Russians, Aksakov turned panslavist not because he 'felt the urge to do something in order to escape intolerable apathy and boredom' (Pypin), but from deep and passionate conviction. Russia's policy in the Balkans was for him 'the fulfilment of our sacred mission'—a messianic pursuit which neither the Russian Foreign Ministry nor even the Tsar shared, but which they knew how to make use of until it became evident that Russian interests were better served by renouncing further adventures in the Balkans. Aksakov was heart-broken and pathetic when finding himself betrayed by the gods of his own creation.

The process which made the Slavophils the tame mouthpieces of reaction can be further examined in Aksakov's career as a journalist. He began his editorship of the 'Day' with a daring plea for freedom. When informed of the dissatisfaction this produced among his aristocratic protectors, Aksakov wrote to a highly placed Lady (Countess Bludova) that his paper 'attacks materialism but it also attacks whenever possible the Holy Synod, together with Count Tolstoy, Prince Urusov, Askochensky, Barkov, and the rest. They are worse, they have brought greater evil than the materialists. . . . I am horrified at the suggestion of alignment with the Petersburg government, with the Court, and so on. I am going my own way. . . . No one will succeed in making me a *Hofpoet* or *Hofpublizist*.'[58]

But soon Aksakov's voice became all but indistinguishable from the official press as far as the main issues of the day were concerned, such as the Government's treatment of the peasant question, its repressive measures against the universities and the radical intelligentsia, the oppression in Poland and Russia's policy in the Balkans and in the East. The 'Day' ceased publication mainly because it had become redundant, as Aksakov himself frankly admitted. Its successors, the newspapers 'Moscow' and 'Russia', existed only as long as they reflected the government line.

A similar development may be observed in regard to the Jewish question in Russia. Outside ecclesiastical circles there was little anti-Semitism before Nicholas I. The Jews suffered a number of disabilities, but the traditional policy of the tsarist Government was one of assimilation, pursued, it is true, under Nicholas I by rather odious means and, on the whole, opposed by the Jewish communities themselves. But anti-Semitic ideas and practices became increasingly prominent in the latter half of the nineteenth century, and the *epigoni* of Slavophilism had a conspicuous share in this development. Khomyakov had not a trace of anti-Semitism in him. Ivan Kireevsky disliked the Jews but did not dwell on the matter. Samarin, as can be seen from his correspondence, was undoubtedly an anti-Semite, and Aksakov's newspapers 'Moscow' and 'Russia' show him in the role of an overt Jew-baiter, one of the first in Russia to propagate the old nightmare of the Hidden Jewish Hand—the diabolical plotter of destruction against Christianity and Holy Russia. He did not actually foster Jewish pogroms, which became a constant feature during and after the reign of Alexander III, but he did everything to justify them or to explain them away. To this extent a direct link came to be established between Slavophilism and the 'Union of the Russian People', which, together with the 'Black Hundred', were the principal unofficial government agencies for Jewish pogroms.[59]

It may be said that no single group of any consequence in Russian history has ever found itself, consciously and unconsciously, in such an invidious position as did the Slavophils in the second half of the nineteenth century. They recoiled instinctively from 'official' Russia; they traditionally regarded all political power and all State machinery as fundamentally malignant growths on the body politic; they believed, instead, in the family, in the natural, spontaneous laws of social evolution, in the organic tsardom and in the inevitable conflict between centralization and freedom. But they never succeeded in explaining why families or natural evolution or organic tsardoms should be less likely than secular States to encroach on the freedom of their subject members. This fundamental obscurity involved the Slavophils in a kind of chain of social reactions at the end of which they found themselves sitting with the pillars of the bureaucracy on important government committees, deciding the fate of the peasants, of local government, and of Poland (Koshelev, Samarin, Cherkassky), becoming harsh civil governors (Cherkassky), advocating military dictatorship in Poland (Samarin) and the flogging of peasants in Russia (Cherkassky, Samarin), in fact, promoting, in the approving words of Cherkassky, 'the interests of the Government by means of moderate concessions made in time and with the appearance [*sic*] of sincere good-will'.[60]

A new and more interesting version of Slavophilism was *pochvennichestvo*, the chief exponents of which were Apollon Grigoriev (1822–64), Dostoevsky, and the philosopher and critic Nikolai Strakhov (1828–96). Their principal organ was at first *Moskvityanin* (The Muscovite), where Grigoriev, the dramatist Ostrovsky, and their friends were known as 'the young Muscovites', and later the St. Petersburg *Vremya* (Time), revived after its suppression in 1863 as *Epokha* (Epoch) under the editorship of Fyodor Dostoevsky and his brother Mikhail.

Grigoriev, who called himself the last of the romantics, is one of the most remarkable and impassioned figures among the men of the sixties and, in a period poor in poetry, a poet of notable power who exercised a considerable influence on the Russian symbolists. His work, no less than his life, suffered from his failure to extricate himself from the consequence of his debts (as a result of which he spent the last years of his life in a debtor's prison), from habitual indolence and wild debauchery. But this was counterveiled by a wonderful sensibility and imagination, and by an integrity which made him unacceptable to the editors for whom he tried to work throughout his chequered literary career. Only Dostoevsky, who used him as a prototype for one of his own favourite characters, Dimitry Karamazov, seemed to have been able to understand and appreciate him.[61]

The main preoccupation of the *pochvenniki*, and of Grigoriev especially, was literary rather than social and political. They postulated a kind of impersonal, undifferentiated *Volksgeist* which finds its outlet through some writers, such as Ostrovsky and, rather more intricately, Pushkin. Only those who express spontaneously the primitive soil, who advocate man's complete and unquestioned harmony with the pattern of life into which he is born deserve the name of true artists. What gave importance to the life of individuals and communities was their 'telluric' weight. The soil was the only sure and sacred value. Those who abandoned it joined automatically the class of useless people who sow death and destruction. By a somewhat un-expected analogy with the opposing school of radical literary criticism, literature existed for the *pochvenniki* not to delight the reader or even to portray life but to establish communion. Their positive heroes (Pushkin's Belkin, Lermontov's Maksim Maksimych, Dostoevsky's Myshkin, Shatov, and above all the weird, mysterious figure of the crippled idiot Marya Timofeevna in *The Possessed*) were the accepting, the humiliated, and offended, at one with the earth and with God, rather than those who are independent, conscious, and sophisticated. The 'meek' (*krotkie*) and the 'predatory' (*khishchnye*) constitute the 'paradoxes of organic criticism': that is the title of Grigoriev's main critical work.

As with the Slavophils, words like 'organic', 'nature', 'earth', came to have a mystical significance on which much of the *pochvennik* argument depends. Anything which led to separation from the sacred bosom of the earth was a modern sin: the individualistic self-reliant western European, the uprooted in-dustrial worker, the *déclassé* of the radical intelligentsia are, therefore, the fallen men, guilty of hate of the Great Mother and of Russia. Whether from an exaggerated pride in being humble or from mere failure to digest their history, the *pochvenniki*, no less, perhaps more than the Slavophils, were perpetually being Russian, always trying to define Russia, always proving that one is right to be what one is, and reconstituting their national personality. But unlike the Slavophils, they thought in psycho-logical rather than historical terms, and they lacked the Slavo-phil facility for developing broad and synthetic views of history. It is Dostoevsky and Grigoriev who are largely responsible for the discovery of the 'Russian soul'—that curious, unreasonable and yet not entirely preposterous facet of the Slavophil convic-tion that salvation, spiritual as well as temporal, comes from Russia.

Russia, for the *pochvenniki*, meant in the first place the 'simple people': its sufferings and resignation, its 'meekness', wisdom, and eccentricity; its life of unremitting labour through the seasons of the year, its beliefs, customs, celebrations, and super-stitions. When Grigoriev spoke of Russian culture he meant the world of Ostrovsky's dramas, with their domestic tyranny, their brutal and bullying fathers, mothers, uncles, and aunts side by side with the helplessness and innocence of the provincial Russian Mélisandes; or it meant breathlessly speeding troikas and intoxicating gipsy choruses; or, again, it meant the culture that produced or reflected folk-lore, the culture of picturesque, exuberant village pageantry, of peasant artisans and peasant clergy, which Leskov described and praised but did not live by.[62] It was a Russia remote from official conservatism, from bureaucracy, from liberalism, or even from populism, but it, too, provided a refuge for those who were unable or unwilling to see that the real peasants increasingly preferred survival and vodka.

The *pochvenniki*, however, were beset by many contradictions that remained quite alien to the psychologically and sociologically much more coherent attitude of the Slavophils. They saw, indeed, man's home in the world of organic nature, but they themselves and their literary heroes were convincing only because they suffered the pangs of separation, of estrangement, the Bitter Sea. Neither Dostoevsky's compassion for stricken, prodigal humanity, nor the lonely Promethean, 'predatory' hero by whom Grigoriev was fearfully attracted despite himself, nor even Strakhov's more detached philosophical commendation of man's desire 'to break out of the totality of things and sever his links with the world' are really compatible with the ideal of mute bucolic values.[63] In fact, the *pochvenniki* reflected all the spiritual and social conflicts of post-Reform Russia and exhibited many features of the uprooted, refractory rebellious intelligentsia, which evoked their greatest disapproval, but which, none the less, Dostoevsky himself extolled in the image of the 'Russian Wanderer'.

Dostoevsky, it is true, believed that the Word of God was given flesh in Russia rather than Palestine, but, at the same time, he admitted that his *inamorata* was far from being without blemish, and to be Russian for him meant moral and intellectual crucifixion. He dwelt heavily on evil and the tragic fate of man in defiance not only of the radical 'optimists', but of all the accepted divine and human sanctions for the more atrocious dispensations of history. He was a traditionalist who believed in revolution, or, on the contrary, a revolutionary who sought a foothold in tradition among the uncertainties and anxieties of revolutionary experience. These ambiguities had, undoubtedly, a political aspect, but they were due not so much to lack of courage to indict the country he loved, as to a characteristic inability to combine two or more disparate sides of his nature and faith in what could only be a fictitious whole. When he tried to do so (as, for example, in the articles he contributed to 'Time' and 'Epoch', and to the extreme reactionary 'Citizen', or even in the later *Diary of a Writer*) he fell far below either what he intended or what he thought he had achieved. It has been often and rightly said that in the discrepancies which occur between his novels and his *pochvennik* journalism it is usually the latter that rings false.

The beliefs of the *pochvenniki* were a means of understanding all and forgiving all of a kind which as often as not turns into a suit of the familiar emperor's new clothes with which people seek to cover an all-too evident nakedness. They represented too much of what was smug, stifling, and pretentious, and from them there arose the ruling philosophy of self-satisfied nationalism and the graven idols of the established order in Russia. Indeed, few ideas lent themselves so easily to exploitation by reaction and were so much at the mercy of an oppressive social and political climate as were the ideas of the Slavophils and *pochvenniki*, particularly during the reigns of the last two Romanovs. Dostoevsky has much to answer in this regard; and his colossal stature does not altogether exculpate him. But during the sixties his views and those of his way of thinking produced little impression either on official conservative opinion or on the general reading public.

Two other names must be mentioned in this examination of types of conservatism: Nikolai Danilevsky (1822–95) and Konstantin Leontiev (1831–91). Danilevsky's importance today lies in his anticipation of Spengler's notion of successive cultures as national personifications, and of the cyclic or biological view of history which he swallowed whole and expounded in a book entitled 'Russia and Europe'.[64] His scheme claimed to show that the succession, which had led up to the decadent Germano-Roman or European civilization, was about to be crowned by the rise of a Russo-Slavonic culture which was to be the last word in human development. The notion of neatly recurrent patterns in history found some response among Russian as well as other thinkers before and after Danilevsky and stimulated an interesting discussion among later Russian historiographers. But his main thesis belongs to the fabulous world of the fairy-tale and does not deserve serious consideration.

Nevertheless, Danilevsky unconsciously demonstrated the hollowness of the Slavophil belief in the superiority of Russian and Slav culture over that of 'Europe', when it is shorn of its religious and ideological trappings. His book set forth the inevitability of a 'historical' conflict between the Slavs and western Europe which, in his view, was to end in the final 'decline of the West'. It is significant that Danilevsky's *Russia and Europe* appeared in the same year (1869) as the much discussed 'A View of the Eastern Question' (*Mnenie o vostochnom voprose*) of his friend, the political journalist General Rostislav Fadeev, in which the latter postulated an armed conflict between the Slavs and western Europe as a necessary condition for the fulfilment of Russia's historical destiny. Fadeev's articulate, would-be Slavophil fellow-generals—Dragomirov, Chernyaev, Skobelev, and others—who played a distinguished part in Russia's military expansion in the Balkans, in Central Asia and the Far East during the reign of Alexander II, went so far as to claim for Russia the possession of a special, inherently Russian doctrine of military strategy and tactics, which they believed to be a guarantee of Russia's invincibility. Their hero, however, was not the impassive, enigmatic Kutuzov who defended Russia against Napoleon but opposed the crossing of the Russian frontier in pursuit of the enemy with the aim of 'saving Europe', but the dynamic, aggressive Suvorov who led the Russian army into conquest of Poland and helped to bring about Poland's dismemberment in the eighteenth century.

The name of Danilevsky is frequently found side by side with that of Leontiev, who can be mentioned here only in passing since, like Leskov's, his main work belongs to a later period. But Leontiev's idea of culture owed a great deal to Danilevsky's biological interpretation of history, and, as in the case of the Slavophils and *pochvenniki*, his great and irreverent genius spent itself in the service of authority, tradition, and reaction. Nevertheless, Leontiev was very much an outsider and a source of embarrassment to his conservative allies and sponsors. He had

a muscular, intransigent mind which was as much in revolt
against patriarchal Muscovite Slavophilism and Dostoevsky's
God-bearing Russian nationalism as it was against the ideals of
perfectible evolutionary man and 'collective democratic
mediocrity', or any other ideological subservience. 'Good God!
Am I a patriot?' Leontiev exclaimed. 'Do I despise or love my
country? I tremble to reply. It seems to me that I love it like a
mother, yet despise it as one despises a sot or a mawkish fool.'
His world was formed of sin and inexorable necessity, and anything that suggested hope or love was for him like a temptation
of the fool's paradise. At the same time he found the world
around him a place of endless drama and fascination, with its
failures, its goodness and its no less precious wickedness. He was a
tortured pagan born too late, who finished his life as a monk,
in a mood of Kierkegaardian 'dread of faith', and presaged the
celebrated 'return' of a section of the Russian intelligentsia to
the Orthodox Church.[65]

(b) The Church

No picture of conservative Russia would be complete without
an outline of the role of the Church. The importance of the
subject will, moreover, become clear if it is borne in mind that
many of the leading members of the radical intelligentsia of the
sixties were sons of the clergy, who spent their early years in a
milieu where Orthodoxy was as much a fact as were climate
and history.

The relations which prevailed between the Church and the
State in Russia are familiar. Their character was not peculiar
to Russia, for in one form or another it has embarrassed all the
Churches throughout their recorded history: 'es ist eine alte
Geschichte, doch bleibt sie immer neu.' In nineteenth-century
Russia these relations rapidly entangled the Church with
reaction and its official trinity 'Orthodoxy, Autocracy, Nationality'. Such was the undisputed fact, more unfortunate indeed
as a historical comment on the nature of the Church or the
nature of man than unbelievers would have us believe. It is not
my task, however, to discuss what the 'inner truth' of the Church
might mean against the background of this state of affairs. I am
concerned mainly with the reasons that made people react to
the Church in the way they did, rather than with any attempt

to shroud the Church's acknowledged or unacknowledged frailties in the mystery of its transcendental infallibility.

A recent historian of Russian thought, Zenkovsky, has presented Russia's intellectual development after Peter the Great as a gradual polarization towards either the religious and ecclesiastical tradition of Orthodoxy, on the one hand, or, on the other, radicalisms of various descriptions. The radicals, according to Zenkovsky, while retaining a utopian affection for the 'kingdom of God on earth', had abandoned the Church at their peril and disastrously fallen under the spell of secularist or materialist or 'immanentist' deviations.[66]

This interpretation, advanced by other scholars as well as by Zenkovsky, is based on a patent misapprehension. In point of fact, it was the Church which surrendered to secularism, relying as it increasingly did on material power and on the existing social order, and determined as it was by the heavy weight of external circumstances. To be a member of the Church called for a strong measure of those very qualities which make for secularization, for man's submission to society with its delusions and pretences, while dissension and defection from the Church expressed an attitude of spiritual independence and fidelity to truth. Secularization was not so much a falling away from the Church as a process within the Church. Nor was it merely imposed on the Church from without by a powerful bureaucratic State; for, by the nineteenth century at any rate, submission and conformity were already flowing in its veins and informing its utterance. 'I am so sickened by the flat panegyrics delivered to me in every town . . .', Alexander I wrote to the Procurator of the Holy Synod in 1817, 'that I have decided to prohibit the practice by a decree of the Holy Synod.' But the practice, with its innumerable possibilities, was renewed towards the end of Alexander I's reign and continued with unabated zest until the Revolution. It was not even a case of mere voluntary abdication from moral authority, no mere withdrawal into a cloistered ecclesiastical activity—an attitude that might be legitimately adopted within a secular irreligious or anti-religious society, where the Church delivers its message by its mere existence, rather than by attempts to enforce recognition of itself. The Russian Church lived in a professedly Christian society in which it occupied an important and recognized position. It did not, admittedly, seek to rule in its own right, as did the Roman Church in *its* claim to and assumption of temporal authority, but it sought to rule through the power of the existing order. And it preached a distinct social and political gospel—that on which the existing order was firmly imprinted.

This gospel consisted, roughly speaking, in a public defence of social inequality, on the grounds that our Lord had said that the poor will be always with us, that God made some men high and others lowly and ordered their estate, and that the more misery or tribulation there is, the less one's chance of falling into the damnable error of pride and thereby forfeiting one's salvation. Side by side with this no effort was spared in supporting the political order and in discouraging everything in the world around that made for doubt, struggle, or unflinching search for truth.[67] Most of the major issues of the sixties were seen by the Church in this light.

In so doing, the Church showed no grasp of events in the rapidly changing society, except as a possible threat to its own status and to the whole established order. No abuse was exposed and no one inclined to question the principles of that order, much less to encourage others to do so. Relying on time-honoured myths, habits, and blind consent, the Church, though not static, seemed to move like a slow, ponderous dinosaur. Only in its immensely rich liturgical life did it bring relief.

The attitude of Philaret, Metropolitan of Moscow, to serfdom has already been mentioned. This distinguished prelate, who, as Herzen put it, 'combined the mitre of a bishop with the shoulder-tabs of a *gendarme*', defended 'the justice of the servile estate' (*spravedlivost' krepostnogo sostoyaniya*) with the help of biblical texts. When the abolition of serfdom became a matter of urgent concern the Church invariably supported the extreme anti-abolitionist wing. Philaret's objections to the liberation of the peasants with land were expressed in the following rhetorical question: 'Will not the landowners find themselves restricted in their property rights and economic circumstances if land is allotted to the peasants? And will this not affect unfavourably the warmth of their support for the Government?' He also defended the retention of flogging for the peasants: in a memorandum ('The Christian Attitude to Corporal Punishment') addressed to Dimitry Tolstoy he insisted that 'Christianity in no way condemns this measure of severity [towards the peasant]'.[68]

Similar views were expressed by the celebrated theologian and ecclesiastical historian, Metropolitan Makary Bulgakov (1816–82), by Bishop Theophan Govorov (1815–94), and Archpriest John Sergiev (1829–1908), two leading Christian moralists, and by many others, including the famous *startsy* or elders of the monastic hermitages, whose piety and spirituality were otherwise unimpeachable.[69] They all shared a remarkable denseness about human relationships and the release of man from his burdens, from slavery, ignorance, the subjection of women, economic exploitation, and intellectual obscurantism. These things tended to be publicly and privately endorsed precisely by those who, presumably, had received a spiritual illumination that should have revealed the nature of evil. Part of the explanation lay, no doubt, in the inclination—somewhat paradoxical in a Church which claimed and enjoyed unqualified political and social prestige—to discount the importance of worldly affairs and to stress love and unselfishness as individual qualities. But there was no equal emphasis on justice in human relations, or indeed any clear realization of what evil was and what part it played in history and in society.

On the eve of Emancipation the Church, supported by the police, was brought into a state of 'fighting readiness', and Philaret, followed by the diocesan bishops throughout Russia, issued 'directions' (*nastavleniya*) in anticipation of peasant disturbances. Every parish priest was instructed, under the threat of severe penalties, to explain 'the biblical notion of freedom', i.e. that 'true freedom consists in complete submission to divine and civil authority'. The scrupulous observance of these directions exposed the unfortunate priests on occasion to savage reprisals by the peasants, who accused them of concealing the 'true freedom'. The Synod was deluged by urgent requests from diocesan bishops 'to protect the village clergy from the dangerous conflict with the landowners' peasants'.[70]

The attitude of the peasants was all the more surprising because, on the whole, the Church had deep roots in the country-side, not easily pulled up by the greatest provocations. But the authorities could by no means always rely on this; and, apart from the manifestations of rebelliousness previously referred to, there was a continual loss of the most intensely religious elements of the peasantry from the Church to dissent. According to later estimates, the number of religious dissenters in the middle of the nineteenth century approached ten million. Some of them were attracted by visions of a better and freer life or by the teachings of messianic prophets, or by the wild emotional indulgences of the *khlysty* (flaggelants) and the manichaean *skoptsy* (castrates); others were sober evangelicals (*shtundisty, molokane, dukhobory*), whose moral behaviour was entirely unobjectionable; still others preserved tenuous links with the Orthodox Church, but followed their own ways and pursued their own spiritual ideals. The life and thought of these numerous dissenters are of inestimable value for the study of Russia. They were the epitome of Russia in search of God, truth and justice, dedicated, courageous, untrammelled, and sometimes exasperatingly stubborn. All sectarians (including the Old Believers) were subjected to continuous persecution and discrimination by Church and State, although antisectarian measures could not always be fully enforced because the movement was largely clandestine. The Church's attempts to deal constructively with the situation by sending specially trained missionaries where dissent (itself debarred, of course, from all missionary activity or propaganda) was known to be most widespread makes a painful story of crude and ineffective spiritual and physical intimidation—a story, in fact, in which bad means prevented the achievement of bad ends.[71]

While under Alexander I, or, more precisely, until the closing years of his reign, a tolerant spirit prevailed towards dissenters and non-Orthodox Christians in general, a vigorous campaign against freedom of conscience characterized all the subsequent reigns, with a brief intermission during the early years of Alexander II's rule. The campaign acquired an increasingly political complexion and culminated, under Alexander III, in a systematic crushing of all self-expression, religious, cultural, and even linguistic, on the part of national minorities within the Empire. The underlying principle was that all Russians, including Ukrainians, must belong to the Orthodox Church, and that all servants of the Government, including school and university teachers, must be practising, communicant members of that Church. At the same time, the permission hitherto given

to non-Russians, notably Poles, to practise their religion began
to be withdrawn, and any attempt to convert an Orthodox to
non-Orthodox beliefs and practices became an offence punishable with imprisonment or exile to Siberia. Next to Dimitry
Tolstoy and Pobedonostsev—the *éminences grises* of the last three
Romanovs—the leading role in this expanding movement of
religious and national intolerance belonged to the Church,
which thereby seemed finally to have abrogated all moral
authority and forfeited its spiritual and intellectual influence.
'Freedom of conscience', a prominent hierarch (Antony Khrapo-
vitsky) announced, 'is a senseless notion.'

It would be wrong to conclude that the Church was entirely
barren of intellectual activity. The theological seminaries, it is
true, tended to generate an atmosphere in which anyone who
was mentally alert soon began gasping for air; and there was
hardly a single human group in Russia which was more humourless and stodgy than were the seminarists and most of their
tutors. The curriculum in seminaries was poor in intellectual
content, or what there was impressed mainly by its crabbed,
dogmatic, unimaginative nature.[72] Still, it provided a certain
mental training, especially in the classical languages, and anyone who was suitably endowed by nature and had survived
the enforced mental constipation could proceed to one of the
four theological Academies at Kiev, Moscow, St. Petersburg, or
Kazan. Here academic standards were incomparably higher,
higher even in some respects than in the universities. Indeed,
the Academies made a noteworthy contribution to learning in
Russia and some of the greatest Russian scholars were trained,
and a few subsequently taught, in them. The fields in which
they distinguished themselves most were history, secular and
ecclesiastical (the names of Klyuchevsky, Bolotov, and Golubinsky are known even outside Russia), archaeology, liturgio-
logy, and, with less originality, metaphysics. But ecclesiastical
censorship proved an even greater handicap than the political
kind. The eminent historian Sergei Soloviev complained that
'the more talented teachers of the Moscow theological Academy
were martyrs . . . Philaret saw to it that they, their lectures and
their writings were drained of all living thought, until the men
turned into mummies.'[73]

Each of the four Academies published its own journal, and

these are notable for industrious researches, presented, as a rule, in a competent but heavy and undistinguished form, which still provide valuable material for the specialists. But critical biblical studies were discouraged, since the Church traditionally found the Bible an embarrassing document. The fine arts were entirely ignored, no secular literature being admitted, and aesthetic sensibility smothered in order to produce well-trained philistines, weak in psychological interest and insight. These tendencies, characteristic of the clerical milieu as a whole, were in some cases shared by those sections of the new intelligentsia which had clerical origins.[74]

The main charges adduced against Russian theology by Florovsky, the author of the most important work on the history of Russian theological thought, are that it failed to recapture the original spirit of Orthodoxy, that it suffered either from scholastic intellectual habits or was unduly addicted to cerebrations derived from hazy Teutonic sources. This legitimate criticism may also explain a certain clumsiness, prolixity, and flat-footedness which, despite the rarified subject-matter, characterized most of the speculative work produced by the graduates of the theological Academies. What Florovsky does not mention is their complete barrenness in the moral and social sciences. Partly because of ecclesiastical and political censorship, but mainly from natural inhibition, academic theological and philosophical thought failed entirely wherever exploration of the real world and of man was involved. The little that was done in this field may have been comforting to the experts—most of all to those who wished to see what faith does to the faithful—but it was profoundly inapplicable to the real human situation and unsuited to the doubts and complexities of the nineteenth century. Admittedly, by the eighteen-sixties there already existed a certain body of Christian apologetic literature (such as the review *Vera i razum*—'Faith and Reason—' published in Kharkov), though this was full of ponderous platitudes, crudities, question-begging use of scientific terms imperfectly understood and borrowed from theories already out-moded and superseded. There was Yurkevich's attempt at coming to grips with Chernyshevsky (about which more will be said later). What the Church needed, and what in the nature of things it seemed incapable of producing, however, was not an apologist or even a religious philosopher to conduct skirmishes, but compassionate minds who could respond to and ponder on the real condition of man and society. A few did so, but their fate was a sad one indeed.

A striking and tragic case in point is that of Alexander (archimandrite Fyodor) Bukharev (1824–71). After the usual education—church school, seminary, and theological Academy —Bukharev became a monk and a professor of Christian doctrine at the theological Academy of Kazan. A man of great sensibility, he found himself at odds with his environment, and this led to his early resignation. Soon afterwards (in 1860) he published a collection of essays entitled *O pravoslavii v otnoshenii k sovremennosti* (On Orthodoxy in Relation to Contemporary Life), in which he tried to discuss artlessly and sincerely a number of problems which were unfamiliar and challenging to the traditional attitudes of the Russian Orthodox Church. This marked the beginning of a long series of ordeals: his writings were forbidden and he was charged with apostasy, for, in the words of his chief detractor, 'everyone who is active on behalf of Orthodoxy and stretches out his hand to modern civilization is a coward, a renegade and a traitor'. In the end, Bukharev was forced to abandon his monastic habit and his priesthood but remained a loyal member of the Church. He was prohibited from residing in the two capitals, or in any other town where he was known as a monk; he was deprived of his degrees, of civic rights, and all means of subsistence. He died, destitute, at the age of 47. His case reveals the agony of divided and, in the circumstances, irreconcilable loyalties, the torture that they inflict on the spirit and an extraordinary moral integrity. In the majority of similar cases people felt themselves so much beyond the pale as to have no choice left except total repudiation of the Church and all it stood for.[75]

(c) *Liberal Russia*

The initial difficulty in discussing liberalism in Russia is one of definition. It has become customary to speak of that vague group of people who from the sixties onwards occupied a middle position between the revolutionaries and the supporters of tsarist bureaucracy as the Russian liberals. They were said to represent so-called *obshchestvo* or *obshchestvennost''*, i.e. something like social or public spirit—an attitude of fairly broad-minded, melioristic, socially conscious benevolence which eschews the influences that are likely to disturb—whether through government arbitrariness or through revolutionary impatience—the progressive political and economic development of society.

The definition, valid as far as it goes, does not go far enough to cover the considerable variety of attitudes and convictions which go by the name of Russian liberalism. In addition, it is chronologically misleading, for it may be applied to certain trends which were in evidence some hundred years earlier, during the reign of Catherine II, who liked to pose as a liberal, or to the activities of the young Alexander I and his entourage, or to the reforming schemes of tsarist bureaucracy under Speransky and to the views of the moderate Decembrists.

There is, perhaps, no better way of assessing liberal ideas in Russia than by comparing them with the growth of liberalism in western Europe after the break-up of the medieval order (though less in Germany and Austria, where the scene presents certain analogies with Russia). At the cost of considerable simplifications, it may be said that in the West liberal trends were deeply linked with individualism, even if the latter by no means always proved a safeguard for the concrete human person. Some of the most important elements of European history—the early scientific discoveries, humanism, the Reformation, the idealist and Cartesian philosophy, the French Enlightenment, political radicalism, and *laissez-faire* economics—coincide with the development of liberalism, and they all denoted a trend from the collective to the individual, from defined patterns of spiritual, social, and political life to individual self-expression. Admittedly, the trend, more easily detectable in some of its stages, grew more complex and ambiguous, particularly with the movement which issued from Rousseau, the French Revolution, and romanticism. But until at any rate the twentieth century it was never completely reversed. Even the important differences due to the background of Whig respectability in English and of Jacobin revolution in French liberalism proved undecisive: they both arrived at the belief that progress was to be achieved by the working of the free market and individual economic enterprise. The trend impressed itself in particular on the image of the State, which was denied claims to interfere in man's free activity, its sole function being to guarantee the necessary conditions in which such activity could take place. Indeed, the State itself, the whole organization of law and order, was widely held to be the result of a contract, real or imaginary, between consenting individuals who 'join into and make one society of citizens' (Locke), to be more precise, property-owning citizens, whose initiative, enrichment, and expansion became a determining factor in the social history of western Europe.

In Russia, the opposite was largely the case. The individual, unless he was prepared to question the whole structure of society, tended to express himself within a defined framework, and social development was shaped throughout not by the influences of individual men, but by impersonal forces, traditions, and patterns of life. In so far as the individual had any distinct place in society, this was inferred from a divinely ordained, hierarchically constituted harmony in which each God-given capacity would fulfil a necessary function in relation to the rest and in which all would be subordinated to a supreme authority.[76] The State, in consequence, assumed divine character and power bestowed on certain fortunate or, as the Slavophils believed, unfortunate persons and their heirs, and rebellion against it was held to be not only treason but sacrilege. There were no 'citizens' but merely 'subjects', sharing in government only to the extent to which *it* was dependent on their capacities for production and military defence, and submissive to its rule because there were no recognized means of resisting it, or because it gave support to their own vested interests (such as the Crown's virtual surrender of control over the peasants to the landowners). The whole social edifice was consciously and unchallengeably based on this hierarchical conception, according to which the system of government and of social life in general devolved, making man, both individually and in association with others, not an agent but part instrument, and part recipient. All political and economic activity was thus subordinated to the Crown; all initiative was taken under the tutelage of the Crown; all changes were imposed from the centre. Russian liberalism came into being and developed in accordance with this conception.

No history can, admittedly, be a piecemeal process of extraneous national developments: it is constantly upset and thrown out of gear by the interaction of ideas and attitudes peculiar to different societies. To this extent Russian liberalism was, for good or ill, undoubtedly subject to influences from western Europe, as can be seen, for instance, in the popularity of French, and particularly English, liberal ideas during the reigns of Alexander I and Alexander II. But this did not shape the specific character of Russian liberalism, and the majority of Russian liberals thought not in terms of the individual exercising his rights and privileges but, on the contrary, in terms of the given hierarchal structure of society, in which social activity issued from and depended on centralized authority. Liberalism in Russia was, therefore, first and foremost, a form of ministration to and co-operation with the Government. The unhesitating endorsement by Russian liberal opinion of Poland's obliteration—such an important event in the sixties—was a natural and tragic consequence of this state of affairs.

Alexander II's career and, in particular, the ironic story of his reforms provide sufficient evidence for assessing the workings and effects of liberal trends within the framework of traditional tsarist institutions. Alexander himself, his brother Constantine, his aunt Helena, his Ministers Lanskoy, Valuev, and Loris-Melikov, and his assistant Ministers Rostovtsev and Milyutin were in a sense all liberals; yet, as has been seen, their liberal activity, far from liberating anybody, merely created or mirrored the conditions which made liberation an increasingly insistent and desperate problem. They were, in their various ways, and in different degrees, representative of what has come to be known as 'conservative liberalism', whose main acknowledged or unacknowledged achievement was to safeguard, reinforce, and camouflage the fabric of the existing order. Led by Alexander II, they could all have endorsed unreservedly his father's statement while cross-examining the Decembrist Dimitry Zavalishin: 'What do you want a revolution for? I am your revolution.'

Conservative liberalism has been studied and defended by many Russian writers in the nineteenth century, but no other work assimilates its doctrines more skilfully than a recent German book, *Geschichte des Liberalismus in Rußland*, by Victor Leontovich, which has been acclaimed in the West as a new departure in the study of Russian political history.[77] It is remarkable, both for the light it throws on the development of

Government liberal theory and practice in Russia and for being itself a belated example of such liberalism. The author displays considerable scholarship, yet there is something profoundly anachronistic about the book. The underlying conviction is that Russia was never confronted with a choice between reaction and revolution and that but for the disrupting influences and activities of the revolutionaries and radicals she would have, by the mere passage of time, emerged, and indeed was emerging, into a *Rechtsstaat* on a solid constitutional basis.

The book is well documented and claims to be a history: in fact it is a lawyer's book, dealing not with concrete historical situations and experiences but with legal abstractions, with long-term intellectual schemes and the manœuvres of bureaucratic committees. Life has been folded and put away. Instead there stretch decades and centuries of peaceable, if not pleasurable, 'objective' administrative evolution towards the liberal goal. An analogy can be seen in the metahistorical Hegelian Idea which gives an aura of perfection to the most outrageous realities and which, if accepted, would justify every internal tyranny so long as the ultimate progress is kept in view and the desirable end pursued. Neither the disabilities of the peasants brought about by the land reform nor the conditions of poverty and destitution among the liberated serfs; neither Stolypin's change of the election law in view of securing a *Duma* subservient to the Government, nor his advocacy of flogging as 'a matter of principle'; neither the intensified pursuit of nationalism under Nicholas II, nor the maintenance of public peace and security by an increasing use of the knout and the gallows: none of these things could have, 'in the long run', impeded the constitutional progress, the orderly, patient, inevitable march towards final liberation, which, as so often with inevitabilities, was never happening.[78]

Leontovich's book represents, in fact, the attitude of a group of ideologues of Russian administrative liberalism who were active in the sixties of the last century: the economist Ivan Babst and Vladimir Bezobrazov; the editor of the 'Moscow Gazette' and later of the 'St. Petersburg Gazette', Valentin Korsh; the editor of the 'Government Messenger (*Pravitelstvennyi vestnik*), Pyotr Kapnist; the jurist Boris Chicherin, and others to all of whom Herzen referred bitterly as 'the Muscovite constables of science

and sheriffs of enlightenment'. They have, admittedly, stimulated a certain amount of reflection on economic and political
matters, and they were themselves symptomatic of the changed
conditions in which such reflection had become possible. But,
above all, they relied on the schemes and measures devised by
the imperial bureaucracy, because they were sure of the
emperor's 'august concern for the well-being of the Russian
people'. They were not so sure what this meant in concrete
human and social terms, what were the real conditions of life
among the people while the insubstantial plans of administrative benevolence were coming to fruition. Nor did they realize
what despair and intense indignation these plans provoked.

The only arresting figure among these conservative liberals
was Boris Chicherin (1828–1904), and he deserves more than a
passing mention. There was something of the Roman of the
the late empire about him, with a touch, perhaps, of the
Bismarckian iron hand, of the ruler sitting at his desk while the
walls crumble and the barbarians break in. He was completely
unperturbed (except for occasional contemptuous misgivings
about peasant uprisings), unbending, and self-assured. In his
philosophy, a mixture of Hegelian teleology and Whig rationalism, everyone conducts himself according to rule, the uncertainties of human behaviour vanish and everything moves gradually
towards infinite improvement. He was a confirmed Westerner,
and his intellectual development illustrates as well as any the
fate of Westernism in the latter part of the nineteenth century.

What gives importance to Chicherin in the present context is
that for him freedom existed only within the traditional framework of strong authority, and any enlargement of freedom
which weakened this framework was bound to bring misfortune
and inefficiency. Although he was an admirer of Speransky, he
did not share Speransky's intention of limiting autocracy,
however uncertain this intention may in fact have been. He
visualized the State as a sentient person endowed with unique
characteristics, uplifted over its subjects and pursuing aims
which made it an ennobling force that aroused man to the
fulfilment of his highest ideals. 'To avoid this'—'irritating the
Government by immoderate demands'—, Chicherin stated on
accepting office as Mayor of Moscow, 'to await with confidence
the decision of the supreme authority, and to show ourselves

worthy of our high calling by working in a measured way for the public good—this, in my view, should be our attitude.'

He believed, it is true, in the steady pressure of economic laws, and in the creation of markets which would in time lead the Government towards granting constitutional elbow-room for the property-accumulating individual, and, by bringing the peasants under capitalism, detribalize and 'only temporarily' pauperize them. In this spirit, he welcomed the statutes of 1861 as 'the greatest monument of Russian legislation'. For Chicherin, as for the majority of Russian liberals, Alexander's reforms signified a triumph and a vindication of western ideas in Russian social development. Even the strong support they lent to Russia's hegemony in the East and in the Balkans was based on the notion that since 1861 she was the spearhead of western European civilization in these parts of the world. This was, no doubt, an unexpected outcome of the original position of the Westerners, and a somewhat ironical comment on it. A practical justification for it may be found only in the fact that 'revolution from above' was a current phenomenon in some of the central European autocracies, and that gradualism was common to certain types of liberal theory and practice in western Europe. In Chicherin's opinion, the secret of success lay in avoiding anything excessive, in sitting tight, in preventing the disintegration of traditional authority. It is not surprising, therefore, to find him extending the hand of friendship to Pobedonostsev, even though he did not share his religious rationalizations of unlimited autocracy. And, although he quarrelled with Katkov on minor matters, he welcomed his advocacy of firm control by the Government and the gentry over the political (the *zemstvo* in particular) and economic life of the country.[79]

The ideas of conservative liberalism were on the whole confined to a small and isolated circle of political and economic thinkers and newspaper editors, but they had at least one tenet in common with a larger number of people to be found in government circles, among the emerging commercial and industrial *haute bourgeoisie*, and even among certain sections of the progressive intelligentsia, namely, that radicalism was a social peril which halted the growth of liberal institutions or even that anarchy must follow its victory. It is a recurrent sentiment in the diary of Dimitry Milyutin, Alexander II's enlightened

Minister of War: 'I can understand one kind of revolution', he wrote: 'the kind that is accomplished calmly, considerately, in the heads of men capable of understanding properly the needs of the people. But . . . no violent, popular revolution can lead to the betterment of society, because it only destroys without building anything. . . . One cannot achieve success in the public weal without reasonableness.'[80]

It is well known that during the so-called 'white terror', which reigned in Russia after Karakozov's attempt on the life of Alexander II in 1866, but which, in fact, started almost immediately after the emancipation, nearly every cross-examination of political prisoners by the officers of the Third Section began or finished with warnings that 'progressive haste' will be met with extreme penalties (e.g. Mikhailov's cross-examination before his trial and deportation to Siberia in 1861). The liberal papers in the sixties were full of warnings about 'the undermining of foundations' (*podkapyvanie osnov*) and 'the need to keep watch and ward', which reflected a widespread distaste not only in Government circles, but among industrialists and landowners, for every kind of extreme measure. Some literally-minded landowners took the warnings so seriously that, long after the original wave of peasant risings, they erected high fences and dug deep ditches round their estates, bought supplies of arms and ammunition, and set up a day and night patrol around their mansions.

But the landowners, too, were not unaffected by liberal influences, although their contribution to the ideological debate was nugatory. The *zemstvo* or local government statute of 1864 was preceded and accompanied by a great deal of discussion and even agitation among the land-owning gentry. For many of these the Emancipation Act could only be made effective by the curbing of bureaucracy, if not of autocracy. Some, like Mikhail Bezobrazov, Count Orlov-Davydov, or Shidlovsky, had vague oligarchic aspirations and aimed at an elected assembly which should represent the 'first estate' and share in the exercise of central political power. Others, like Unkovsky and his group, thought in terms of an assembly of elected representatives from all estates with no defined claims of independent jurisdiction, except in local affairs. Others still, like Koshelev and Aksakov, advocated a Muscovite assembly, with the Tsar and the people reunited in one happy family divorced from the iniquities of bureaucratic Petersburg. The controversy aroused by these views in the late fifties and early sixties marked a period of 'senseless dreams', soon to be followed by one of 'small deeds'.[81]

The general political atmosphere at the time, the revolutionary mood of the peasantry, the fears as well as the hopes of the gentry, disposed the latter to expect more from the *zemstvo* institutions than was justified. Their enthusiasm soon yielded to disappointment and even to loss of interest, as was indicated by the chronically empty chambers of the *zemstvo* assemblies, which as often as not were attended only when the landowners' immediate interests were at stake. Not until the eighties did the *zemstva* become centres of real if fruitless opposition; and this was in no small measure due to the influx of professional people —doctors, teachers, engineers, agriculturalists—who were employed by the *zemstva* and drawn chiefly from the ranks of the *raznochintsy* ('the outsiders')—and from the uprooted sections of the gentry. But even later the *zemstva* were unable to make themselves felt as a political force of any importance, though not for any lack of trying. In the meantime, their political activity amounted to no more than a mixture of irritated conformity with and mild displeasure at bureaucratic interference. The view that at the very outset a real contest ensued between the *zemstvo* and the Government in which democracy vanquished autocracy is quite untenable.[82] And the accusations levelled by the Russian diehards at the 'liberalizing gentry' (*liberalnichayu-shchie dvoryane*) to the effect that they were inciting to revolution can only be described as a scapegoat hunt. Not one of these liberal noblemen, not even the courageous Unkovsky nor Petrunkevich, ever dreamt of calling in question the structure of the autocratic order. They merely made 'entirely loyal' requests or 'humble petitions'; they asked for indulgence so as 'to be able to resist the forces of disruption more effectively', and for concessions, from which the peasant with his known legal and economic disabilities profited least of all. There is ample evidence in the letters of Chicherin, Samarin, the brothers Milyutin, and other correspondence and published writings that the liberal gentry and Government alike regarded such concessions as serving to strengthen the existing order, which, in fact, was far removed from providing that creative momentum

for the life of Russian society which some of the gentry
expected of it. 'Official Russia', Herzen wrote, 'naturally groups
itself into a Government and an opposition, so that some servants
of the Government represent . . . a liberal, others a conservative
element . . . and both remain in office, receiving ranks and
orders.'[83]

The main liberal group, however, consisted not of enlightened
traditionalists, skilful statesmen, tough-minded jurists and
journalists, or advocates of local government, all relying on
more or less progressive principles for their success and the
success of the autocracy which they served: though equally
complaisant, it was more high-minded, more impartial and
perceptive. It found its most effective voice in Konstantin
Kavelin (1818–85), and its most serious and intelligent organs
were the 'Messenger of Europe' and, until it passed into other
hands, the 'Annals of the Fatherland'.[84]

There is scarcely an event, a social milieu, or intellectual
issue in mid-nineteenth-century Russia in which at some point
or other one does not come upon the name of Kavelin. In his
youth he was close to the Slavophils, later he became a pupil of
Belinsky and a confirmed Westerner, and took part at the side
of Herzen and Granovsky in the original contest between these
two schools of thought. Through his aristocratic family connexions he was drawn into court circles and became a tutor of
the Tsarevich, infusing into him, so it is claimed, the 'lofty
principles of prudent, enlightened liberalism'. Alexander, and
even more Alexander's aunt Helena and brother Constantine,
had a great regard and affection for him. Later, as has already
been noted, he took an active part in the preparatory work for
the emancipation, and was equally prominent in the reorganiza-
tion of higher education which led to the abortive university
charter of 1863. In addition, his was one of the most brilliant
if not unperturbed academic careers in the disturbed conditions
of nineteenth-century Russia.

Prudence was Kavelin's chief characteristic. He was a man of
great intelligence and of infinite precaution, invariably acting
so as to avoid upsetting the equilibrium. But he was quite free
from dogmatism, xenophobia, and narrowness of mind, and his
dislike of mere convention, his sceptical attitude to received
ideas, and his advocacy of intellectual freedom made him

appear bolder than many of his educated contemporaries. Few if any Russians have ever shown such an un-Russian ability and willingness to admit both sides of any question. There was in this an attractive absence of arrogance, a flexibility of mind which he shared with Ivan Turgenev. And, like Turgenev, his taste for compromise enabled him to adjust himself with miraculous ease. Had he lived at another time and in another society, he would have been the ideal member of a political coalition. In Russia, in the sixties, he was uneasily, or one should say easily, poised between orthodoxy and radicalism—a position that had its dramatic moments, especially when he came up against the passionate imagination and the fiery, sardonic, and subtle mind of such a *révolté* as Herzen.[85] Kavelin took refuge in the love of the gradual, in the enlightened belief that change with commotion is reprehensible, that, while conditions should be promoted in which the good life can be lived, this would defeat its purpose in the absence of a judicious respect for order and stability.

I have already mentioned Kavelin's attitude to some of the important issues which had a bearing on the abolition of serfdom. His extensive memorandum on the peasant question contains a thoughtful and patient analysis of Russia's economic position: he was concerned not so much with exposing the iniquities of serfdom as with persuading the authorities that the servile system was above all contrary to the interests of the State itself, that it was responsible for economic stagnation, waste, and arrested industrial and cultural development. At the same time, he insisted that the solution of the problem should be approached 'imperceptibly', 'gently', 'gradually', on the basis of justice and 'in the light of state interests'.[86]

I would have considered myself dishonourable [he wrote to Herzen] if I had advised the landlord, the priest, the *muzhik*, the officer, the student to hasten the decay of the rotten traditional social forms. No! I will shout at the top of my voice [which is known to have been soft and chirping]: step cautiously, warily, do not pour oil on the flames, do not take a naked candle into a powder-magazine! Let turbulent thoughts calm down, let things crystallize! If we don't live to see it—what does it matter? We shall gain the gratitude of the coming generations. Every new undertaking involves effort, great effort: have patience![87]

Kavelin's instinctive aversion against the urge to interrupt the normal course of events, which assails those more readily inflamed by love, faith, or anger, was very deep indeed. He even took fright at any move towards constitutionalism in Russia. 'This playing at a constitution', he wrote to Herzen some two months before the above letter, 'frightens me so much that I cannot think of anything else. These gentry will only incite the *muzhiki*: they will persuade them by their pseudo-liberal frivolity that they, the gentry, are really plotting against the Tsar, and then the row will start. This is nearer and more likely than it may seem. Our historical fate is very much like that of France. God forbid that the results should also be alike. But, for all I know, this is just what the gentry will bring about—by their unreasonableness . . ., or their doctrinaire attitude, or their immaturity.' Curiously, Kavelin borrowed arguments from Marx as an antidote to revolutionary propaganda. 'These words alone', he wrote apropos of the notion of the 'natural historical process of social development' contained in the preface to volume I of *Capital*, 'should suffice for those who can take heed: but there are very few such people. Marx did not speak merely of "historical process", but deemed it necessary to add "natural historical process", that is, a process in which all transitions from one form to the other take place not by force but of their own accord.'[88]

But, of course, Kavelin was no Marxist: he was an enlightened liberal with a strong respect for the established order. In some ways he was nearer to certain forms of western European liberalism than any of his Russian contemporaries. If the distinction between the two great branches of European liberalism be taken as a guide—the pragmatic type that rests on historical empiricism and the type which by means of *a priori* or of scientific reasoning aims at achieving universal patterns—he, unlike Chicherin, would have to be regarded as, roughly, belonging to the first branch. Like many spokesmen of modern liberal political theory, Kavelin recoiled from all forms of ideology, from utopian and messianic ideas, and looked forward to a world, no less utopian, of universal tolerance, where every radical solution is regarded as equally unnecessary. And this is consistent with the distinctly anti-metaphysical, anti-idealist, relativistic position he adopted in philosophy.[89]

(d) Radical Russia

It is one of the most bitter ironies of Russian history that the 19th of February 1861, which should have been the climax of the nineteenth century, the day awaited by conscience-stricken Russia ever since Novikov and Radishchev—'the great day of reconciliation', as Dostoevsky called it, between the Tsar and 'the people'—in fact opened an impassable gulf between them and was the signal for the final rupture between the Government and the intelligentsia. Faced with the substitution of one kind of bondage for another, the intelligentsia resumed its militant role on a more serious scale.

But the intelligentsia was no longer what it had been in 1825 or 1835. It differed in mood, in conviction, in social status and composition. It still included a few army officers and a few members of the gentry, but they had been largely displaced or absorbed by the *raznochintsy*, the *déclassés* of Russian society. These had existed earlier, but mainly as isolated individuals— Belinsky was their most outstanding representative—and they had hardly been aware of their social identity. They began to attract public attention only in the latter half of the forties. As servants of society, whether in central or local government, they were more energetic and more effective, if less cultivated, than their noble fellow-countrymen; but they were also more energetic, more formidable as opponents of society. In this capacity they emerged for the first time in connexion with the Petrashevsky affair. It is of some interest that a secret report about the Petrashevsky circle (of which more will be said in the section on Chernyshevsky) lists with unconcealed dismay among the members of the circle 'officers of the Guards and secretaries of the Foreign Ministry side by side with students who have never graduated, artists of no importance, tradesmen, petty towns-people and even tobacconists . . . but most of all teachers, students, and scribblers of every sort'. Similar descriptions are used in official reports with reference to most of the accused in the famous political trials of the sixties and seventies, and it is persons of this kind who formed the bulk of the radical in-telligentsia.[90]

They represented a new type of man who may be defined as an intellectual, politician, and conspirator rolled into one, but first and foremost as a man who says 'no' to the existing order. Being a radical meant a way of life, in which intellectual activity was not something special or separate, for its practice involved the whole of a man's thought and attitude. As before, a book, an article, a secret proclamation was a form of action, possibly a violent one, with serious consequences for author and reader alike. But the situation of the new radical rendered him more rootless, more mobile than his predecessors of the forties. Alike by conviction and origin he had no feeling for his milieu and was not part of it, although the paradox of his situation is that he was concerned with social problems almost to the exclusion of everything else. He inherited nothing, not even his personality, which he had, as it were, to create anew. He detested conventions and hierarchies, the careers and rights of literary men, and all the stuffy pomposity of life. Everything in his condition led him to sunder the secure, comforting bonds of custom and familiarity, to cut himself off from the group in which he grew up. But he did not pride himself on his lack of roots, like the pathological 'outsiders' of our time: his passion for freedom was on behalf of others; it was vicarious and self-sacrificing. His tendency to prickliness when confronted with examples of entrenched superiority, or contempt for what he considered to be mere airs and graces rarely sprang from private resentment. He had no wish to find a niche for himself in the prevailing class structure, even though he believed that important truths were revealed to him and that he had a mission to teach those truths to society. To be more accurate, he was bent on creating a new society, not on gate-crashing, ideologically or convivially, the old one, which he believed to be doomed.

Nor did he wish to insinuate himself into 'the people', even when he professed populist ideals and, by his devotion to 'the people', appeared to express a need for acceptance by and unity with it. Contrary to the constant refrain of the contemporary official Russian press, he was not an alien intruder who 'came to us from the west and therefore belongs exclusively to that milieu which exists in estrangement from the people' (Katkov). No one really believed this, and least of all Alexander II (to whom Katkov submitted the view) and the Third Section of the Tsar's Own Chancery. As happens in all countries where democratic practice has no roots, the Russian intelligentsia, admittedly, considered itself to be representative of the 'true people' and the bearer of a mission on its behalf. But there is little evidence in the two radical journals of the sixties, the 'Contemporary' and the 'Russian Word', of idealized or idolized peasants. Chernyshevsky, Dobrolyubov, Mikhailov, Tkachev, Shchedrin, or their younger contemporaries Nikolai and Gleb Uspensky, even while relying on him as the real force behind the revolution, saw the peasant as he was, in all the degradation and obscurity to which he had been reduced through centuries of oppression and ignorance; they did not see him, in the manner of sentimental philanthropists, as an embodiment of truth and perfection.[91]

The radical intelligentsia was estranged indeed, yet not from the people but from the cultural environment, in which 'the people' had no part. Hitherto culture had been an aristocratic privilege in Russia. In a sense, it always is so, for culture presupposes qualitative selection and personal originality. The vision of truth and beauty, artistic inspiration and creativity are unique, unrepeatable experiences incompatible with subservience to the crowd, which in any case is not in the habit of setting great store by spiritual culture. But neither can culture be confined to the few; and the instinct that drives people into isolated cultural *élites* engaged in mutual veneration is a herd instinct as deleterious to culture as dilution in the crowd, and often more comic. A sense of service and human solidarity is a more aristocratic feeling than the consciousness of one's privileged position. The radical intelligentsia in Russia believed that culture could not survive without such a sense of service and solidarity, and that Russian culture was suffering from deeprooted social alienation.

It cannot be denied that even Pushkin was not universal, not woven into the imaginative life of the people as were, for instance, Corneille and Racine in France or, even more, Shakespeare in England. Until the Revolution Russian literature evoked no response from the people and provided no common ground for taste. Only folk-lore and the semi-vernacular liturgy could have claimed 'popularity', but, with notable exceptions, they had no influence on Russian literature. The alienation of Russian culture goes far towards explaining the rejection of culture by the men of the sixties. Everything that had hitherto provided the cultural framework had, in their eyes, ceased to serve a human purpose. One must begin anew, without the ancient myths, without divine or social sanctions. Man had no longer any place, not only in society, but in the entire ancient universe of discourse.

This attitude might have condemned the radical intelligentsia to sterility or killed their imagination, but they were saved by an awareness of human values, of historical momentum, as well as by social responsibility. Their greatest virtue was their ability to judge in terms of human integrity, their vision of man acting from the centre of his being and spurred by his sense of solidarity with other human beings, rather than conditioned by his position in society. They discovered a break-through to the human person and a new sense of human dignity. With all their limitations, this enabled them to achieve remarkable moral independence—in their attitude to life and people, in their habits, actions, and principles of conduct. Even those traits, which, on the purely private level, were often little more than fads, became in public a proclamation or assertion of freedom, of love of truth and nobility. This ethos continues to animate the post-revolutionary Russian intelligentsia.

By the time the new radicals became articulate the fires of philosophical speculation that had made the forties intellectually so exciting had already burnt low. They cared little for metaphysical disputes and were prone to puncture idealism. They laughed at every kind of soulfulness, at the marvellous, the recondite, and the precious. They aimed deliberately at cultural and social democratization. In every possible way—in their manners, their speech, letters, even in their jokes and abuse—they wished to prove that men were not rarefied spirits, but made of flesh and blood, racked by physical needs and crudely engaged in the brutal conflict of life. Their insatiable appetite for facts and disillusionment with theory made them put their trust in the results of scientific knowledge and enlightened self-interest. Despite the formidable obstructions of the censorship, this gave a considerable stimulus to the study of science in Russia. Most of the great Russian scientists (Sechenov, Mechnikov, Kovalevskaya, Pavlov, Timiryazev, and others), who made an important contribution to the scientific heritage of mankind, were typical representatives of the new intelligentsia. The actual knowledge of science among the rank and file, however, was not extensive: what they possessed in a considerable measure was the characteristic Russian quality of absorbing generalizations before acquiring the practical background. They were anxious to defend not so much a given scientific discipline as the scientific outlook. It will be seen later that their own disregard for material advancement and self-interest gave this attitude a significance beyond its immediate context.

Still, the confidence in science and enlightenment was sufficiently pronounced to suggest that the radical sixties were the Russian equivalent of the western European Enlightenment in the eighteenth century.[92] Yet nobody seems to have noticed the curious and significant reversal of the western European sequence of events in which the Enlightenment, with its rationalist attack on religion, its cult of happiness and self-interest, its belief in scientific benevolence *preceded* romanticism. The Russian 'Enlightenment' was a decade of declining and disenchanted romanticism. Indeed, it was scarcely an Enlightenment at all, for it lacked its contentment, its harmoniousness, and sense of civilized values. There was small concern for civilization, but a great deal for salvation. No one in the radical sixties would have appreciated or enjoyed Voltairian success or Diderot's sweetness, reason, and light; no one had that eighteenth-century curiosity and charm, that delicacy and sensuality. The whole tenor was non-erotic and austere. The Russian counterpart to the tidy, sophisticated rationalism, conqueror over the violence of more barbarous times, was anger and turmoil that combined to challenge the actual world and to seek a just and truthful one.

It would be more accurate to say that the new intelligentsia reflected a period of incipient social and industrial transformation, in which 'organic personality' could not survive. Despite the populist ideas, there was something essentially megalopolitan about it: it consisted of St. Petersburg men who had experienced exile and for whom the things of beauty and intellectual enjoyment were absent. But they were not all of a piece, as their contemporary and future detractors maintained. To see them as part of a movement must not deprive them of individuality: each had his own nuances which contested their

supposedly uniform tone and nature. Under a mask of toughness, they were sensitive men, as deeply wounded by the sufferings of their fellows as their conscience-stricken predecessors of
the gentry. While retaining the fundamental moral and social
attitudes of the 'remarkable decade', however, they were
sterner and more exacting. An atmosphere of monumental
sobriety surrounded them, making them suspicious and often
incapable of the paradoxes and flashes of insight in which such
great rebuking geniuses as Herzen delighted.

Herzen's relations with the new intelligentsia throw much
light on the men of the sixties. In a bitter moment, he charged
them with collective migraine, with letting the struggle, common
to them all, sour and embitter their lives, and accused them of
lacking the good humour to admit this. He shared their search
for the truth beneath the accepted insincerities of the world, but
he recoiled from their strenuous, argumentative behaviour and
from their austerity which, in his view, gave them a self-conscious if not puritanical air. On occasion, he found them gauche
and comic. And, no doubt, compared with the coruscating
genius of Herzen, or even Belinsky and Bakunin, they lacked
the imaginative power and eloquence to do justice to the tragic
times in which they lived. Life to them was not so much tragic
as outrageous. Everything dramatic or romantic, everything
that intoxicated was rejected out of hand. Their language
was dry, as can be seen from the waspish but stimulating pages
of the 'Contemporary' and the 'Russian Word'.

Following the coinage of Turgenev, it has become customary
to call them 'sons' or 'children' (he also suggested the nickname
'snakes' and 'rattle-snakes'); but curiously enough, they were
if anything prematurely disciplined and old. They were called
'sons' because their habit, at times a compulsion, of identifying
ideas with individuals led to brash and discourteous behaviour;
because some, like Dobrolyubov and Pisarev, slammed doors
and struck angry or cynical attitudes, while others, like Antonovich and Zaitsev, attacked their opponents too fiercely, ruth-
lessly, and unfairly. But the wisest and oldest amongst them,
such as Chernyshevsky, were perfectly aware that their own
ideas and aims had been formed by contact with their predecessors. Indeed, at first sight the nature of the attack on the
older revolutionary intelligentsia might appear surprising:

few if any ideological differences divided these radical 'fathers' from the 'sons'. Their only recognizable crime, apart from occasional temperamental incompatibility, was to have engaged in 'utopian' enterprises, to have dreamt, in fact to have done what 'sons' normally do before they become 'fathers'. But this attack, too, was a form of refusal to disguise the realities of the surrounding world, with its vanishing values and new insecurities.

What Herzen called the 'callous trickery', by which the reforms in Russia were defeated or invalidated, gave rise to the conviction of promises dissolved into thin air, of a great betrayal and, inevitably, to a conflict where all would be staked. The demands of the future seemed now more difficult but also more urgent and demanding. Instead of vague hopes and possibilities, the radicals saw before them a clearly marked field of revolution, with its 'axes', its hard materials, instruments, implacabilities. Tradition, as has been seen, had no meaning for them, because they believed that they were living in a period when all known paths had been trodden, when all values had to be rethought and a new code of moral and social relations worked out from scratch. Hence their scepticism of half-measures and their impatience; hence also their outspoken anti-liberalism, for in the conditions of post-Reform Russia liberalism was a euphemism for avoiding the real issue of the human situation, a form of self-satisfied, soothing cant.

Each generation has its gestures of revolt. But the hostility that animated the Russian 'sons' was much more profound than anything to be explained merely by the conditioned reflexes of problem children, of rebels without a cause. They were rebels because they felt man's inhumanity to man; because they found themselves driven into a world where there were only two choices, and any other choice than the one they made was, to them, a betrayal of humanity. They became the incarnation of human decency in one of the least attractive periods of Russian history. They were the conscience of Russia.

To be the conscience of anyone or anything is unrewarding both for those who have it and for those who have none: it is absolutist; it is everything or nothing; it is conducive to quarrels; it abuses whatever it cannot praise; it prevents anybody having any fun; above all, it is explosive.

Fearless consistency [Herzen wrote in an article entitled 'Young and Old Russia'] is a characteristic trait of the Russian genius. Nothing cherished has been bequeathed to us by history; we do not possess those esteemed respectabilities, which hamper the western European but which he holds so dear. In face of servitude . . ., of estrangement from our fellow men, of separation from the people, of inability to act, we were left with but one consolation, a true consolation—in the bareness of denial, in logical relentlessness. We uttered with a strange relish those extreme, *ultimate* words which the lips of our mentors scarcely whispered in fear and trembling. Yes, we uttered them aloud, and we felt better, in expectation of the storm that they were to rouse. We had nothing to lose.[93]

There were, of course, plenty of Russians in the sixties who felt none of this 'ultimate' discomfort: all those who from conviction, complacency or vested interest, identified themselves with things as they were. And they were intent on displacing all those who chose to defy these things. The conflict that ensued is not surprising. What surprises is that it should have been the defiers, in the face of formidable odds, who were able to give the whole period its peculiar character and significance, and even to impress their attitude on subsequent decades. It is they, rather than the liberals, who provided the main inspiration and driving force for political thinking in Russia. Indeed, a myth has grown up to the effect that it was the radical intelligentsia, rather than the conservatives or liberals, who had a sense of being official, who were the intellectual Establishment. The value of this contention cannot be judged without reference to the characteristic way in which the Government met the radical challenge: a large-scale prison programme was initiated in the early sixties after repeated complaints by the police about the acute shortage of accommodation for the rapidly increasing number of political prisoners and the 'tightly packed (*bitkom nabitye*) cells of the Peter and Paul Fortress'.

If, nevertheless, the radicals succeeded, they did so because they served as a sparking plug for the accumulated social and moral energy, whose importance was recognized by the very means which the Government devised in order to combat it. One might say that in default of these men others would have emerged. Their genius fitted with the needs of the time. Whether as guides, as exponents, or merely as the conscience of the age, they are unthinkable outside the sixties. We cannot separate Chernyshevsky from the sixties or the sixties from Chernyshevsky, although he left behind him a living moral and political tradition. To some it is a puzzle how the radicals managed to make such a little go such a long way. They were neither philosophers in any technical sense, nor, in comparison with their predecessors and successors, original thinkers; they were neither artists nor politicians. If they had the effect they had, this was due partly to the obliquity and confusion of the other side, partly, again, to the relevance of their moral and social challenge.

Posterity has been less indulgent. Outside Soviet Russia few nowadays seem to take them seriously or study them sympathetically. Their dethronement began at the turn of the century and was announced in a book entitled *Vekhi* (The Landmarks), published in 1909, which was a powerful indictment of the whole spirit of the Russian intelligentsia, and in which seven authors, themselves members of the intelligentsia, chose to ignore or to make light of the ice-blue flame that burnt in its eyes. We may deplore the authors' trivial and uncompassionate view of the human predicament and the frivolity of their historical imagination; but then every period of Russian history, and none more than the sixties, bears witness to Russia as a country of desperate oppositions and absolute alternatives. 'Russia', Herzen observed, 'will never be a *juste milieu*.'

III

NIKOLAI CHERNYSHEVSKY
1828–1889

1. *Saint and Revolutionary*

CHERNYSHEVSKY'S life was one of the most cheerless imaginable. But his childhood was far from unhappy. He was born into the family of a parish priest on 12 June 1828 in Saratov, a town on the lower Volga, lying midway between European and Asiatic Russia, in a territory traditionally associated with peasant revolts. His parents were kindly, unselfish people and, though narrow in outlook, comparatively well educated. Before the local theological seminary, Chernyshevsky received the rudiments of his education from his father, whose extensive library contained the works of such unexpected authors as Radishchev, Herzen, George Sand, and Dickens. Chernyshevsky himself recalls a way of life which, for all its restrictions and lack of variety, was not unpleasant. It was a way, too, which did much to influence his own character, by its sobriety and self-discipline. When he broke away from his environment his memories were quite without resentment: there was even an endearing but unsentimental glow about them, although he criticized the stifling atmosphere of ingrown ecclesiastical orthodoxy and patriarchal family habits, and disapproved of his teachers and the theological disciplines of his day. The recollections of a number of people who knew his family or were his fellow seminarists show us an odd, lonely child, shy, intelligent, aspiring, almost immune from contact with other children until he went to the seminary at the age of 14, and possessed by a passion for books.[1] His whole upbringing appears to have been calculated to produce a mature mind on a foundation of underdeveloped emotions. At the age of 11 he was encouraged to write a treatise entitled 'Natural History' (*Estestvennaya istoriya*), which contained three parts: 'On Man and His

Senses', 'On Animals in General', and 'On Birds of the Marshes'.
When he left the seminary at the age of 16 he had well over 200
essays to his credit, all of which remain unpublished. To judge
from the published extracts, their quantity is not matched by
their readability, but more than a hundred of these were written
in German, French, Latin, Greek, Arabic, Persian, Tartar, and
Hebrew.

What is strange is that this phenomenon of precocious erudi-
tion should have become the symbol of Russia in revolt. It is
surprising, too, that neither his devout and kindly father, nor
his teachers, nor the whole pattern of religious life, with its
round of services and liturgical functions, in all of which he
participated conscientiously, seem to have impressed Chernyshevsky's mind with the possibility of real religious experience.
And when later he finally broke with the Church he appears to
have been more acutely conscious, at the time and afterwards,
of the hurt that this break was causing to the feelings of his
parents than of any wrench that the decision may have meant
for himself. The religious vacuum was filled by a growing sense
of the illiberal and dismal in his environment. There was, it is
true, little that could be considered dismal in the life of his
family, but beyond that lay the harsh and primitive world of a
mid-nineteenth-century country town. Personal acquaintance
with this and 'the life of the masses', as Chernyshevsky himself
says, formed his views of history and society. To the dismay
of his mentors, and despite what appeared to be a perfectly
secluded life, he was given to 'dangerous thoughts' about the
injustices which he could not help seeing around him, and to
which even his harmless father fell a victim. After much thought,
Chernyshevsky decided not to pursue the natural course of all
young men in his position, namely, to become a priest or to
proceed to a theological Academy—a decision which, in the
forties was fraught with considerable difficulties. He left Saratov
for the capital in 1846 in the company of his mother, and,
after a number of attempts, was finally accepted for matricula-
tion at the University of St. Petersburg.

Secular higher education, as has already been noted, was
beset by many restrictions, and few students from the lower
classes found their way into the universities, particularly in the
capital. An official rescript of 1845 laid down that 'the excessive

influx into higher and secondary schools of young men born in the lower strata of society is unnecessary, indeed a useless luxury and . . . tends to drive them away from their natural surroundings, without benefit either to themselves or to the State'. When Shirinsky-Shikhmatov became Minister of Education in 1849 conditions became even more difficult, and he did away with the little academic freedom that had remained under his predecessor Uvarov. Professors, as Governor General Bibikov decreed, were to be allowed 'to meet among themselves, but only to play cards', and students were to be treated 'with indulgence for drunkenness, but a soldier's uniform awaits any one who is known for his free thinking'. Academic standards were at their lowest and only the most neutral subjects, such as philology, archaeology, and the natural sciences, could be taught in relative freedom. These changes coincided with Chernyshevsky's student career. Only a small minority of university teachers tried to hold their own. Among these were the literary historian Pletnev, the celebrated mathematician Lobachevsky, the surgeon and educator Pirogov, and the now forgotten economist Poroshin, who exercised a considerable influence on his pupils and was responsible for the clandestine spread of Fourierist ideas in the university. Around them was a small group of students keenly interested in social and political questions, although on the whole they lacked that intellectual exuberance and versatility which characterized Herzen's student days in Moscow some fifteen years earlier.

In his first year, Chernyshevsky was completely absorbed in his work, studying Slavonic philology and literature. He attended all the prescribed lectures assiduously, went regularly to church, kept all the fasts, and even read the Bible. He was still a pattern of behaviour, rather prim, retiring, orderly in his ways and distressed by noise and agitation. Yet even as a seminarist he had a vague feeling that some 'hard destiny was dogging [his] footsteps' and forcing him out of every 'refuge from life'. His real contact with political issues, however, did not begin until, in his second year, he joined the informal political and literary circle of Irinarkh Vvedensky, known as the originator of nihilism in Russia, but more remarkable for his excellent translations of Dickens. This circle, as well as an almost simultaneous contact with members of the allied

Petrashevsky group, gave Chernyshevsky his first external political stimulus.[2]

He quickly made a reputation for himself as a man of uncommon intellectual gifts and learning: a provincial genius, of a kind thrown up by the sixties in unexpected places. His fellow students were particularly impressed by what one of them (Kostomarov) called his ability 'to draw extreme conclusions'. He appealed by his tendency to radicalism, despite a seeming diffidence, by his distaste for compromise and a passionate fidelity to truth. At first he spoke little in the company of his circle of friends, but when he did so he appeared to have considerable authority, even though the views he expressed were already 'in the air'. Meanwhile, he continued to work and read, pursuing whatever subject he had in hand with a pertinacity that never left loose ends, but concentrating increasingly on social, political, and economic questions. Already in 1848 he entered in his Diary that he had become 'a partisan of socialists and communists and extreme republicans—decidedly a *Montagnard*'. Among his fellow students he acquired the nickname Saint-Just. He is described as of medium height, well built but slight, with a good but not overpowering forehead, compressed lips, and weak but lively eyes behind steel-rimmed spectacles. He still kept all the rough mannerisms of the typical seminarist, but all his friends speak of his courtesy and quiet charm.

In 1850 Chernyshevsky finished the university course and, after a short spell of teaching at the St. Petersburg Cadet Corps, he gave in to the insistent requests of his parents, and in particular of his mother, and returned reluctantly to Saratov, where he became a teacher of literature at the local Secondary School (*gimnaziya*). He remained in Saratov only two years, but, though biographers tend to neglect this period, it occupies an important place in Chernyshevsky's development. It was then that for the first time he was moved to declare openly his revolutionary attitude, or what was regarded as such by people around him. It also marked an important change in his personal life.

Very soon it became evident that Chernyshevsky possessed extraordinary gifts as a teacher, which did not fail to surprise those who knew him as a young man of timid disposition. Moreover, he was not only a good teacher, but a new type of teacher,

almost unknown in the Russia of his time. The complete sub-
ordination of the schools to the State (through the provincial
Governor Generals), the dependence of teachers on detailed
instructions about what and how to teach (in particular, on the
need to detect tokens of divine providence in all things and to
emphasize 'the display of moderation and self-control' in historical situations and literary trends), the strict censorship of text
books, and the equally strict regimentation of children in and
out of school were all designed to produce complaisant servants
of the State or reliable champions of received ideas; and they
effectively guarded the young against any contact with social
and moral problems. Chernyshevsky was one of the first to
defy these educational principles and practices and, within a
year, the whole spirit of the school and the relations between
teachers and pupils underwent a change. His lessons, literary
seminars, and personal attitude to individual pupils aimed at
provoking the children to think for themselves and awakening
their sense of moral, social, and cultural values. The already
mentioned liberal historian Nikolai Kostomarov, who spent a
term of political exile in Saratov at the beginning of the fifties
but who had little sympathy with Chernyshevsky's views,
recalls in his autobiography that 'the Saratov school was completely refashioned by him [Chernyshevsky]; and he achieved
this with such ingenuity that neither the Headmaster nor the
Inspector [Censor], who represented a wholly different outlook, were able to control him'. 'He became the idol of the
young.'[3] Above all he influenced the school by his superb
moral and personal example.

His influence, not only on the boys but on the whole teaching staff
was enormous [writes one of his ex-pupils]. His mind, his wide
knowledge, his remarkable ability to lay open before his class-room
audience the inner world of a literary work, his warm-heartedness,
humanity and wonderful simplicity in human relations . . . drew
the children to him and established unforgettable links with the
young teacher. He seemed to experience personally what he was
teaching us. . . . The habitual cruelty of the teachers came to an
end: they stopped beating the boys, and even the school Censor
applied the birch less frequently. 'He is ashamed because of Nikolai
Gavrilovich', we used to say. And we were right. . . . It was sufficient for Nikolai Gavrilovich to make known his cordial relations

with the helpless assistant teacher of Russian who could not control his class to make the children stop tormenting him. And how did he achieve this? Merely by walking arm in arm with the unfortunate teacher along the corridors during 'long break' in full view of the boys and talking to him in a friendly manner. . . . No other admonition was necessary.

To sum up my own and my contemporaries' school recollections of Nikolai Gavrilovich, I can say that during his brief career as a teacher he breathed new life into a dry and soulless scholastic system, and even succeeded in forming a small group of like-minded teachers. In addition, he served, without any cant and ostentation, as a lofty ideal to his pupils—by his powerful mind, by his extensive and profound knowledge and by his humanity. . . .[4]

According to another contemporary, the Headmaster took fright when he realized the extent and influence of Chernyshevsky's pedagogical innovations: 'What liberties Chernyshevsky allows himself in my school! He speaks to his pupils of the harmfulness of serfdom. It's sheer free-thinking, Voltairianism! I shall finish up in Kamchatka because of him.'[5] Chernyshevsky himself was not unaware of the risks he took. 'I do and say things here, in class, which smell of penal servitude', he noted in his Diary on 21 February 1851, although the explanation given in a letter to Mikhailov at about the same time is harmless enough: 'my concern here', he wrote, 'is to help in the development of those young men who have themselves not yet succeeded in resembling decent human beings.' Somewhat later (14 March 1853), he again noted in his Diary: '. . . had an unpleasant talk with the Headmaster who, in his opinion, had acted honourably in not reporting me to Kazan.'

The Headmaster's and Chernyshevsky's apprehensions were justified. Rumours about the latter's influence had reached the Ministry of Education and the school was black-listed as an unrealiable educational establishment. This, however, had no immediate effect on Chernyshevsky, for soon afterwards he left Saratov. But the school episode was revived much later in unexpected circumstances. It was discovered that Karakozov had been a pupil in Saratov at the time when Chernyshevsky taught there (although there is no evidence that he was actually taught by Chernyshevsky), and it was mooted that Chernyshevsky should be held responsible for incitement to the assassination

of Alexander II. The scheme proved too far-fetched or superfluous since, in any case, Chernyshevsky was already in Siberia.
But the Minister of Education, Tolstoy, paid a special visit to
Saratov in 1866, as part of an intensified campaign to eradicate
Chernyshevsky's influence in Russia. 'It must be regretted', he
told the assembled teachers, 'that in the past your staff comprised certain individuals who should not have embarked on a
teaching career. They took upon themselves this great responsibility not for the benefit of the young but to their detriment,
for the propagation of destructive ideas, the effect of which, as
we now know from experience, was the mental and moral
corruption of some people who have become the unfortunate
victims of this propaganda.'[6]

The Saratov period in the life of Chernyshevsky had another,
less public, but in the end more significant side. Evidence of this
can be found partly in his Diary (particularly the section
entitled 'The Diary of my relations with her who now constitutes my happiness', i.e. with Olga Sokratovna Vasilieva),
partly in his equally revealing correspondence.

Chernyshevsky was assiduous in keeping a Diary between
1848 and 1853, although entries become increasingly sporadic
towards the end. It was, of course, never intended for publication, and its writer may be forgiven for making the reader lose
his patience long before the end of this tiresomely prolix and
graceless document, some of which reads like the minutes of a
committee meeting. There are also many cryptic and almost
unintelligible passages, written with a view to the censors, in
case the document should come into their hands. None the less,
it is of surpassing interest, not as a literary work but as a human
document and a description of the raw material out of which
were formed Chernyshevsky's characteristic attitudes. It has
great candour and simplicity, despite its all-pervading dis-
cursiveness. Hardly any sense of humour is displayed anywhere,
although there is an occasional glint of irony, which Chernyshevsky always kept up his sleeve for poking fun at human
habits, and more frequently at ideas with which he disagreed.
In general, he shows extreme tolerance of behaviour and much
less tolerance of ideas. But one has to look hard to find a dis-
creditable emotion, a hint of malice or of meanness, even when
he is at his most mordant and severe.

Chernyshevsky complains at length about his timidity and a sense of unworthiness, although he combined this with visions of himself in the role of a benefactor of mankind who, amongst other things, was to do away with poverty by means of a *perpetuum mobile*. He speaks of a tendency to 'Hamletism'. He is afraid of being a 'milksop' (*tryapka*), just when he ought to be resolute and firm. He says that he is made for obedience and submission, and is unable to reconcile this with his love of freedom. Yet almost in the same breath he claims to be capable of 'the boldest, maddest, most desperate acts', and writes that if a peasant revolution should occur, he was sure to be in the thick of it: 'neither filth, nor drunken peasants, not even slaughter, will frighten me.' Seldom or never does he confess to being baffled by an intellectual problem. But this did not prevent him from writing to Dobrolyubov, for whom he had an excessively self-effacing affection, that 'we assume roles in life which surpass man's natural powers, we wish to become angels, Christs, &c. We end by discovering our inadequacy; we lose our bearings but climb again, like a singer who tries to sing an aria in too high a key: his voice begins to rattle, to squeak and finally loses pitch.'[7]

The tendency to self-criticism, however, though both detailed and persistent, was coupled in Chernyshevsky with a remarkable absence of psychological insight into himself. Perhaps he was too cerebral and too desperately in earnest. In this respect, it is curious how little individuality emerges from what, on the whole, is a very introspective Diary, or indeed from his correspondence, although the facts are all there.[8] And when he speaks of other people, of poetry, or of love, the effect is usually the same. Even when he fell deeply and recklessly in love he set down in disconcertingly solemn periods, point by point (1., 2., 3., a., b., c.) the 'validity' or otherwise of his feelings, or tried to persuade himself and others that he was not in love with his future wife but 'merely respected her'. These grave reflections showed an emotional adolescence, a childish gaucherie of the heart, which owed a great deal to his upbringing. But it also reflected the characteristic temper of the *raznochintsy*, their instinctive resistance to emotional luxuries and impatience with the incommensurable in human behaviour. When compared with Herzen's combination of unflinching search for truth with

adult but joyful pleasure in the human scene and a keen eye
for the uncertainties of behaviour, Chernyshevsky seems merely
determined to tell the truth—about himself or about other
people and things—even at the cost of ignoring man as he is
recognizable in real life with all its complexities.

Chernyshevsky's anti-emotionalism deceived many into
imagining that he wished to abolish emotion, or that he himself lacked all sensibility. In point of fact, his somewhat dry,
saturnine mind concealed a tender heart. He hated to hurt the
feelings of others. He showed warmth and affection towards
the most unexpected people (including Vsevolod Kostomarov
who denounced him to the secret police). 'No outside observer
would have guessed', wrote Chernyshevsky's fellow prisoner
Nikolaev, 'that the controlled and calm exterior . . . concealed
a deep love of other men, purity and tenderness of heart,
combined with stormy passions.'[9] The Diary shows that
Chernyshevsky's self-criticism and his worries about his own
inadequacy were a compensation for a passionate temperament
and, since he was very reserved, a kind of alternative to intimacy. He was no amorist, but the story of his relations with
Olga Sokratovna, both before and after his marriage to her,
is one of the most remarkable love-stories of all times—through
its qualities of feeling, affection, and generosity. Indeed, a
great deal in Chernyshevsky can be understood only in the
light of this relationship: in a way, it provided the principle of
vitality in his work and almost took the place of spiritual life.

Olga Sokratovna Vasilieva, the daughter of a successful
provincial doctor who prided himself on having 'a real General'
among his patients, was a famous Saratov beauty. There is an
accurate if not very sympathetic description of her by Chernyshevsky's niece, Vera Pypina, which is largely corroborated by
other people who knew her and by the published correspondence.[10] According to Pypina, Olga Sokratovna was a woman
of great if rather gaudy charm, with an abundant zest for life
and a heart of ice. She had no inhibitions, a frisky girlish wit,
and a tendency to hysteria. Her darting, masterful nature
attracted a swarm of men and she exploited the situation, both
before and after marriage, with all the determination and
seductiveness at her disposal. Her main interests in life—apart
from adoring young and not so young men (whom she made

sit at her feet and bark like dogs)—were horses, carriages, dachas, *vaudevilles*, and any frippery available in Saratov, and later provided in greater abundance by Chernyshevsky in St. Petersburg. When her beauty began to fade, and with it the capacity to arouse admiration, she was left with little to occupy her but restless peregrinations from one Caucasian holiday resort to another, with recollections of her past conquests, whining complaints, self-pity, and the use of her temper. The Pypin family, which, after Chernyshevsky's deportation, was largely responsible for subsidizing her gorgeous living as well as for the education of her sons (who had little liking for her), were pathetic and patient victims of her whims. There was absolutely nothing in common between her and Chernyshevsky, who, none the less, spoke of his Dulcinea as 'a woman of genius', predicted her future as 'a Russian Madame de Staël', and devised plans for their collaboration in the writing of an 'encyclopaedia of civilization'. Needless to say, Olga Sokratovna had no taste for encyclopaedias and was frankly bored by her fiancé's or husband's pursuits and interests, although, from time to time, she knew how to play the part of a cloyingly understanding wife. 'What have we in common?' she asked, and then owned with characteristic outspokenness that 'the things which occupy him make me yawn.'[11]

Still, she was prepared 'to include [Chernyshevsky] among her suitors', and eventually agreed to marry him for no more subtle a reason than that he was, as she rightly believed, 'completely at her mercy': 'I wish to have a husband who is my obedient servant', she said to him on one occasion, while he assured her solemnly that 'when I ask for advice I want to receive a command'. He was also the only one among her admirers who took her at more than her face value. There is no evidence that Olga Sokratovna married him because of any material advantage or because she was in love with him (there is evidence to the contrary). That she should have craved for more active and less discursive lovers than Chernyshevsky is not surprising; what is surprising is that she was so calculating about it. 'No sooner was Olga Sokratovna married', writes Pypina, 'than she began to breathe freely. If previously she had met with few hindrances in life, now nobody at all repressed her, and least of all her immeasurably loving husband.'[12]

Chernyshevsky was indeed ecstatically in love with his wife. His profession of love as recorded in the Diary reads like Pascal's amulet: 'In the year 1853, on the 28th of March, at 9 o'clock 50 minutes in the morning—Love, Happiness, Joy. . . .' But, at the same time, his enduring devotion to her approached silliness, or saintliness. Actually it was composed in part of both, according to the way in which one looks at it. It was comic, but it had an undertone of sadness and loneliness. Sometimes he appeared almost like a conventional Pagliacci-clown, the jester with immortal longings and a broken heart, or, more appositely, like a formidable myopic savant, an illustrious bookworm with the feelings of a pure-souled adolescent lover.

Chernyshevsky's protracted love fantasy was not, however, entirely undisturbed even before Olga Sokratovna became his wife. He was increasingly conscious of his revolutionary calling. He told her repeatedly that he had no right to marry because he did not know if he would remain in freedom, because, as he said with remarkable prescience, he 'might be arrested at any time—God knows for how long'. He told her frankly that he could not change his views. Moreover, he was not blind to his fiancée's reputed paramours. 'I am prepared for everything', he noted sadly in his Dairy, 'I shall endure everything . . . I shall suffer, but love and be silent.' And again:

I shall not retreat, I shall not demur. . . . If only she will be my wife. . . . I know her, I love her! Away with doubts! I am sure of my happiness with her. I have now but one worry: money, money, money!—so that she may live in complete contentment. There will be money. . . . And she will be happy with me. And I shall be happy with her happiness.

Yes, you will be happy, as you deserve to be!

Yes, you will be happy, you who have given me so much happiness.[13]

To Chernyshevsky's warnings that he could not change his views Olga Sokratovna replied 'Why not?' His declarations of love left her fairly cold. The only thing which attracted her attention was, according to Pypina, Chernyshevsky's 'frequent disquisitions on the need to allow woman the same freedom of inclination as that enjoyed by man. He resented every kind of inequality.' 'To straighten a stick which has been bent for too

PLATE I

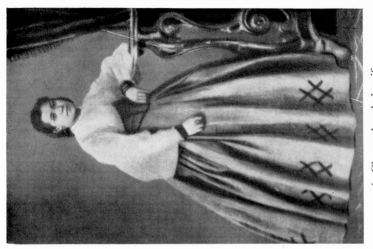

b. Chernyshevsky's wife

a. Chernyshevsky, aged 31

long in one direction', Chernyshevsky said, 'it is necessary to bend it the other way. . . . Woman is put below man, and, in my view, every decent man is in duty bound to put his wife above himself. Such temporary disparity is essential for the sake of the equality to come.' Being an almost insufferably doting monogynist, Chernyshevsky himself felt no instinctive need for any 'freedom, lest it should appear that he preaches it for his own advantage'.[14]

The idea that women were full members of society and must live by exercising choice deserves special attention, because it represented an attitude which governed personal relations among the *raznochintsy* and which was widely and hotly debated in the sixties. It shared many features with the movement for the emancipation of women all over Europe. But in Russia it instantly acquired an extreme character. Its adherents were concerned not only with the establishment of new social forms for old feelings and desires, but with what they claimed to be a change in the feelings and desires themselves.

The discussion began with a series of articles on the question of woman in the 'Contemporary' by a close friend of Chernyshevsky's, the already mentioned revolutionary poet Mikhailov.[15] These caused an avalanche of polemical literature, the appearance of which was made easier by the temporary régime of liberalization in the latter half of the fifties. Hardly any newspaper or periodical failed to discuss 'woman', including such unlikely journals as the *Morskoy sbornik* (Naval Miscellany) and the previously noted Slavophil 'Russian Conversation'. It gave rise to the first Russian woman's magazine—*Rassvet* (Dawn) 'a scientific, literary and artistic periodical for young ladies'—in which Pisarev made his journalistic début.

Chernyshevsky took little part in the controversy, but his great bad novel *What Is to Be Done?*, written in prison in 1862, proclaimed persuasively the attitude of the new generation, and it was, in turn, taken as a pattern for behaviour. The novel as imaginative literature will be discussed elsewhere, but a brief outline of its plot will show what this pattern was. It is the story of an ordinary but high-minded man (Lopukhov), who by means of a fictitious marriage to an equally high-minded girl (Vera Pavlovna), who dreams of perfect communal living, saves her from parental despotism. The fiction turns, not surprisingly, into reality, but subsequently Vera Pavlovna falls in love with another man (Kirsanov), a friend of her husband. Lopukhov stands aside and the new lovers unite. The author, so it seemed, pleaded for the duty of men to share their ladies with a number of people, according to arrangements designed by the ladies themselves to meet the demands of as many parties as possible, in the most satisfactory and reasonable manner. No 'sacrifice' is or can be entailed, no one is driven by any degrading feeling of jealousy or any need to make *bonne mine au mauvais jeu*. It is all a matter of common sense and enlightened self-interest, and the idea of sacrifice should be resisted as a notion no more meaningful than that of 'soft-boiled boots', in the words of the novel's hero. Indeed, at the will of the author, the differences, if any, are composed in the end: Kirsanov marries Vera Pavlovna, while Lopukhov meets and marries another virtuous girl, and all four live happily together for ever after.

Chernyshevsky's own character and conduct tended to cast doubts upon his concept of reasonable hedonism, and to invalidate the ideal of matter-of-fact, unworried, common-sensical extraverts advocated by the novel. The greatest contrast, perhaps, is implied in the fact that Chernyshevsky expressed his hedonistic vision of the free life while he himself was facing with great self-abnegation the prospect of penal servitude in Siberia, and his wife went a-Maying with her amorous retinue. But, although he was not a happy man, it would be difficult to find in the whole range of Russian thought anyone whose life and convictions were more completely in harmony, or who practised what he preached. This, in part at least, enabled *What Is to Be Done?* to become a seminal book, a tract of the times, and made Chernyshevsky's fellow *raznochintsy* emulate him in their private as well as public lives. The matrimonial affairs of a number of well-known *raznochintsy* reproduce almost to the letter the pattern of Chernyshevsky's novel.[16]

Not surprisingly, the dissemination of the theory and practice of 'free love' or freedom in love, as Chernyshevsky preferred to say, provoked great indignation and moral censure, particularly in conservative circles. A rewarding target of condemnation were the first 'emancipated women', mainly students—the 'short-haired lady-nihilists' (*strizhennye nigilistki*)—who were mainly responsible for the movement's exaggerations and absurdities. They lived or tried to live in improvised mixed communities, co-operatives, and communal workshops for seamstresses, and later, with heroism but not without occasional touching and quaint irrelevance, went to the villages 'to minister to the masses'. Even outsiders fell in with the fashion. A journalist (Arkady Evald) quotes the following conversation with a young society lady sympathetically disposed towards female emancipation:

'I am reading Buckle', she told me, although I had reason to suspect that she had never read anything before in her life.

'But you don't know any history', I observed. 'What are you going to get out of him? And anyway, why read him?'

'Goodness! Everybody nowadays reads Buckle', she objected. 'There is no God, you see.'

'What has become of him?', I asked.

'There never was any. People have invented all this. There is nature, and nothing else.'

'Who told you that?'

'Everybody says so, N. and M. and P., all clever and emancipated people.'

These and the whole younger generation were mocked and caricatured by a host of minor conservative writers, such as Pisemsky—*Vzbalmuchennoe more* (The Troubled Sea), Klyushnikov—*Marevo* (Mirage), Krestovsky—*Panurgovo stado* (Panurge's Flock), and even Tolstoy, in his 'conservative' period (the comedy *A Contaminated Family*). Others, above all Turgenev (in *On the Eve* and *Fathers and Sons*), tried to depict them with greater understanding and sympathy.

The personal relations practised by the *raznochintsy*, admittedly, lent themselves to mockery, however little they may, individually, have corresponded to a type. But the imputation of immorality was quite beside the point. On the contrary, one might reproach them with too great earnestness. Their fault rather was to diminish the pleasure in love, or to take their pleasure too strenuously, although this was perhaps a more conspicuous effect of the western European movement of emancipation. Sexual licence and cynicism, as Tolstoy, a man far removed from any plebeian sympathies, insisted, flourished chiefly in court circles, among the Guards officers, the land-owning drones, and the civil servants. It was quite uncharacteristic of the radical intelligentsia, whose attitude was one of deep moral reverence which led them to reject all indecency and veniality. For them sexual behaviour was always part of a genuine human relationship. It is something of an irony that Chernyshevsky, who as a thinker scarcely ever treated of man as a solitary being, defended free love as a protest against the betrayal of human dignity, against the encroachment of society on feelings that are the exclusive concern of the individual. 'Free love', Berdyaev observed, 'is common to the Russian intelligentsia. It is part of the "Russian idea", in the same way as the rejection of capital punishment is part of it.' Chernyshevsky did not make it his business to 'rehabilitate the flesh', in the manner of Saint-Simon, George Sand, or the *fin-de-siècle* Russian aesthetes. He was merely outraged by the pretensions and hypocrisy of the social order which regulates love and turns marriage into its adjunct. That is why his detractors solemnly charged him with 'undermining the foundations of family life'.

In one sense it was perfectly true that Chernyshevsky and his fellow radicals were in avowed reaction against family life as well as against institutionalized marriage, which, in their view, promoted a limited, obtuse, and futile society. They reacted against the pious, vindictive, and covetous world of domestic tyranny, which Ostrovsky and Saltykov-Shchedrin satirized. They recoiled from 'high society' which fostered its own oppressive forms and conventions of human relations. They carried too much of the spirit of alienated, ever-migrant Russia to accept even that ideal of family life which became Tolstoy's gateway to the happiness of a state of nature and temporarily appeased his conscience. They believed that all this served to deprive woman of her individuality, by turning her into a weak, silly, expensive object of property, or swallowing her up in the small world to which she was confined. The question of the liberation of woman was, accordingly, treated almost on a par with that of the liberation of the peasants. And there was a widespread exodus of young people, and especially young girls, from their parental homes—not because of hatred in the family, but because of a love which limited and confined.[17]

The somewhat abrupt end of Chernyshevsky's brief period in Saratov, similarly, owed something to his need to move away from a sympathetic but constricting atmosphere of provincial family life. His departure was the occasion for a 'scandal'. His mother had died. 'Chernyshevsky, who loved his mother very much, was deeply moved by her death', his cousin Alexander Pypin reports.

But because he had defied the customary term of mourning, married some two weeks after the funeral and left immediately for St. Petersburg with his wife, and because, in addition, he did not sob in church, did not faint, did not throw himself howling on the coffin, the *bon-ton* society of Saratov—all kinds of lunatics of both sexes and upholders of public respectability—were quick to declare Nikolai Gavrilovich a heartless, pitiless, wanton son, who was so indifferent to his mother as to cease bewailing her and leave his father 'at such a moment'.[18]

Chernyshevsky returned to the capital in 1853. It was the beginning of the most important period in his public life. He intended at first to embark on an academic career. With this end in view he wrote his celebrated and controversial treatise on *Esteticheskie otnosheniya iskusstva k deistvitelnosti* (The Aesthetic Relations of Art to Reality), which he submitted in 1855 for the Degree of Master of Letters—a prerequisite for a university appointment. Meanwhile, he supported himself and his family (his first son, Alexander, was born in 1854) by means of irregular journalism, translations, and occasional teaching. The Degree was not confirmed at the time. But the able public defence of the thesis by the author, as well as a number of his early contributions to the 'Contemporary', established Chernyshevsky's reputation as a spokesman of radical opinion, which, of course, put an effective stop to his academic ambitions.

Speaking of the mood which prevailed at the time among the younger generation, Shelgunov, Chernyshevsky's friend and collaborator, wrote that 'the intellectual temper of the sixties was voiced for the first time in 1855, at a public disputation in the University of St. Petersburg. I mean the public defence by Chernyshevsky of his magisterial thesis. . . .' In the course of this defence, Pypin (or Herzen) reported in the *Bell*:

Chernyshevsky, in a thin but clear voice and with a slightly ironic smile, beat off vigorously the attacks of his weak-kneed opponents.

The blameless Joseph of science, professor Nikitenko, made an uncertain attempt to question the candidate on the absolute meaning
of the absolute ideal, but, alarmed, withdrew in the face of the young
man's straightforward, decisive replies. Among those present were
the ill-bred Musin-Pushkin (a Trustee of the University) and the
Minister of Popular Instruction, holy pilgrim Abraham Norov
(author of 'A Journey to the Holy Places'), poor in body and spirit,
whose acute olfactory perception scented a certain disrespect in the
disputant's attitude towards ideal art. As a consequence of this . . .,
Chernyshevsky did not receive his magisterial diploma, without
being informed of the reasons or any legal objections.

The final verdict of the Rector of the University (Pletnev) was:
'Surely, this is not the kind of aesthetics I have been teaching
you!'[19]

Chernyshevsky was now free to accept Nekrasov's invitation
to take charge of the literary and later the political section of the
'Contemporary', and, after 1859, he became editor-in-chief. His
readers immediately acclaimed him as the legitimate heir of
Belinsky and his *Ocherki gogolevskogo perioda russkoy literatury*
(Essays on the Gogolian Period in Russian Literature), 1855–6—
his first and most important contribution to literary criticism—
undoubtedly entitled him to that role.[20]

Chernyshevsky's style was a clear, plain-spoken prose,
obscured by occasional diffuseness and by the need to play
hide-and-seek with the censorship and resort to 'Aesopian'
devices in order to evade its clutches. There is no ingenuity, no
startling or far-fetched images, and no attempt to explore
recondite problems and states of mind. One would look in vain
for any touch of grace and cosmopolitan sophistication, as
practised by some of the 'fathers'. But from time to time his
manner is enlivened by outbursts of pugnacity and polemics.
It is the kind of language which appealed to the pragmatic
mood of the sixties because it fitted what seemed then to be the
main function of the writer: the illumination of man's state in
his concrete historical setting. Indeed, Chernyshevsky seldom
failed to relate his problems to social, economic, and political
activity, and, in general, he is more concerned with 'perspec-
tives' than with problems. He was fascinated by the texture
of historical situations and possessed a considerable gift for
historical analysis, while he generally produced the effect of

flatness whenever he talked philosophy or psychology. Yet he had, of course, his own values and deeply held convictions, which he never concealed and which were forthright and basically simple. The combination of these things enhanced the importance of his work in the eyes of his readers, friends and foes alike, and he became a powerful figure on the 'Contemporary'.

The 'Contemporary' occupies a special place in Russian cultural history. It is a well-known fact that nowhere were literary magazines so much guides to trends and tendencies as in nineteenth-century Russia. They were the instruments for creating ideas, ideologies, and movements as well as for recording them, and they helped to liberate Russian intellectual life from the school-room. As a rule, they were a weighty affair, nearly twice the size of any comparable English or French publication, with no convention governing the scope and nature of contributions, except that each journal was engaged in fervent *prises de position*, and hence compelled to bow and scrape or to look for any and every means of eluding the omnipresent censor. The 'Contemporary' represented one of the most exciting features of this journalistic enterprise and testified to a remarkable intellectual vitality.[21]

It began its chequered career in 1836 as Pushkin's own literary quarterly. It was taken over after Pushkin's death by his friend the poet and critic (later Rector of the University of St. Petersburg) Pyotr Pletnev, who kept up desultorily the tradition of 'literary aristocracy' which represented the Golden Age of Russian poetry. Some ten years later, when the publication of new reviews was forbidden, it was revived under the auspices of Nekrasov and Belinsky, in whose hands it became not only 'a splendidly going concern' but the most interesting and outspoken literary review in the country. Nearly all the great names of Russian literature were at one time or another associated with it.[22] It survived, rather more tamely, the most oppressive last years of Nicholas I's régime, and recovered again in 1856, when it became the platform of the radical intelligentsia and reached the height of its popularity under the editorship of Chernyshevsky. It was, as has already been noted, suspended in 1862 and finally suppressed in 1866.

Over most of this long and distinguished history there presided the elusive figure of Nikolai Nekrasov (1821–77)—the superb impresario and contact-man of Russian literature.[23] Nekrasov was himself a poet, of whom Turgenev said that 'poetry never so much as spent a night in his verse'; who was acclaimed indiscriminately by the radicals for his 'social tendency' and preoccupation with 'the sufferings of the people'; who was scouted wholesale by the conservatives and liberals for the same reasons; and who, ironically enough, came to be properly appreciated only by the 'modernists' of a later period as an innovator, responsible for what Mirsky called 'a revolution in poetic taste'.

This is not the place to discuss Nekrasov's achievement as a writer. What matters here is that through his own success as editor he became the panjandrum of Russian literature, without whom few writers would have survived the physical and moral ordeals to which conditions subjected them. He knew how to get out of almost any predicament, how and where to find and attract talent, and what the interests, sympathies, and deeper desires of the reading public were. He espoused all the right causes and, when necessary, was quick to leap to the support of the under-privileged, although his sympathy for them was mainly confined to his verse and to the sponsorship of those who were ready to commit themselves in a more direct manner. He was not the kind of man one would expect to go to the stake for his moral and political principles. Beside editorial success he acquired a reputation in society. He liked to be seen in fashionable clubs and decried snobbery while not being himself immune to it. He had large gambling gains and losses, enjoyed a régime of truffles, sturgeon, and *entrecôtes*, and drank the best vintages. With Panaev, his friend, boon companion, and fellow editor, he lived as a third party to a marriage which his presence did nothing to disturb but which was a constant source of anguish to him. His fantastic and tortuous *liaison* with Panaev's wife, a woman of astonishing beauty, intelligence, and sharpness of tongue, gave rise to some of his most moving love lyrics.[24]

Turgenev, after many years of warm and mutually advantageous friendship with Nekrasov, referred to him as 'the great enemy'. Herzen, too—a quite disinterested party, except that he accused Nekrasov of misappropriating Ogarev's money—found him extremely unattractive and called him 'a literary *ruffiano*'. 'We are unaccustomed', Herzen wrote, 'to lying in spirit and trading with talent, as prostitutes lie with their body and sell their beauty. We are unaccustomed to profiteers who lend their tears for the sufferings of the people, on interest, to manufacturers who turn compassion for the proletariat into a credit item.'[25] It must be admitted that Nekrasov's capacity for shifts and contrivances in making money was almost unlimited. Moreover, like St. Paul, he was a great believer in being all things to all men, which—to save himself and the 'Contemporary'—seems to have prompted him to write and recite in public a paean to the most ruthless of Alexander II's henchmen, Count Muraviev 'the Hangman'. It may have saved him, but it did not save the review.

And yet, despite all Nekrasov's public and private aberrations, the radicals, and Chernyshevsky in particular, remained in close and friendly collaboration with him. They admired his genuine passion for literature. They considered his sense of adaptation—not to Muraviev, but to the age in which he lived—to be a valuable public virtue, the conspicuous absence of which in the official press made it plough on from year to year, offering the same kind of ware in 1860 as in 1830. They may have been uneasy about his mixture of cynical worldliness with idealism and even sentimentality, but they also felt that his 'instinct' was right and his literary sympathies sincere. What to some appeared as a fatal inconsistency was to others the richness of a many-sided nature, or, since among the radicals this was not likely to have weighed heavily in Nekrasov's favour, a necessary attribute in a good editor. Even to be, as Nekrasov was, a successful hedonist required a certain kind of courage, since the timid are seldom hedonists. But, for all his prudence and diplomatic calculations, he gave proof also of another kind of courage, especially during the lean years of reaction under Nicholas I, when the 'Contemporary' was the only journal to retain its standards of decency. Even its distinguished companion, the 'Annals of the Fatherland', faded into complete conformity.[26] Above all, it was the stand Nekrasov took in the great division between the 'fathers' and 'sons' which showed that the opinions of the editor and the beliefs of the man were one.

The story of this division, to which reference has already been made in general terms and which became one of the greatest

literary sensations of the day, throws much light on Chernyshevsky, and on his contemporaries' estimate of him as a man
and a writer.[27] The division grew as, with the open support of
Nekrasov, Chernyshevsky's influence on the 'Contemporary' increased. The 'fathers' were represented by Turgenev, who was
ably assisted by the minor novelists and major literary critics
Alexander Druzhinin (1824-65) and Dimitry Grigorovich
(1822-99), together with Vasily Botkin, a tea merchant dab-
bling in literature and mainly known as a correspondent of
Belinsky, and a few others. The spokesman of the 'sons' was
Chernyshevsky, who was soon joined by Dobrolyubov and
Maxim Antonovich (1835-1918). A third force in the contest
was Leo Tolstoy who had returned from the war in the Crimea
in 1855 and whose *Tales of Sebastopol*, partly published in the
'Contemporary', had evoked the admiration of 'fathers' and
'sons' alike. But at the time his alignment was uncertain and he
alternately let fly at either side. It was Turgenev who declared
the paper war by starting a feverish private correspondence
after the publication of Chernyshevsky's thesis on aesthetics,
which shocked him by its apparent utilitarianism. A number of
letters to Nekrasov, Panaev, Druzhinin, and Grigorovich in
the summer of 1855 attacked the work as a 'deadly abomination'
and the 'product of wicked stupidity and blindness'. '*Je fais
amende honorable . . .*', he wrote on 10 July. 'I had the misfortune
of interceding previously for this stinking bug [i.e. Cherny-
shevsky]: accept my apologies and solemn promise henceforth
to persecute, despise and destroy him with all permissible and,
particularly, unpermissible means. I have read this disgusting
book . . . which the 'Contemporary' was not ashamed to discuss
seriously . . . *Raca! Raca! Raca!* You know there is nothing more
terrible than this Jewish curse.'[28]

The next phase in the war of words was initiated by Druzhinin, who was also a contributor to the 'Contemporary'. In a
series of articles in his own quarterly *Biblioteka dlya chteniya*
(Library for Reading), ostensibly devoted to a new edition of
Pushkin's works, he accused the 'Contemporary' (which he did
not mention by name) of 'wearing down our literature by a satirical tendency'. This he ascribed to an exaggerated imitation of
Gogol and Belinsky and to a betrayal of Pushkin's tradition,
which he claimed to be based on the principle of 'art for art's

sake'. At the time, no one in the 'Contemporary' felt inclined to
enter into open polemics with one of its own contributors; but
Chernyshevsky, in the essay on the Gogolian period, mentioned
earlier, reaffirmed the tradition of committed literature and
defended the painful training to which, before him, Gogol tried
to be true, to the exclusion of almost everything else. The essay
contained, in turn, an implied charge of betrayal against
Druzhinin. The latter replied with another sermon, repeating
at greater length and in more forthright terms his original
contention.

The outcome of this controversy was that Nekrasov found
himself faced with the prospect of losing not only Druzhinin but
many of the other pillars of his review, especially Turgenev,
Grigorovich, Ostrovsky, and even Tolstoy, all of whom now
threatened to transfer their allegiance to the 'Library for
Reading'. Druzhinin was the first to leave the 'Contemporary',
which provoked an angry letter from Tolstoy to Nekrasov.

No! [he wrote], you have committed a major blunder in allowing
our team to lose Druzhinin. With him one could hope for proper
criticism in the 'Contemporary'; but what shall we do now, with this
gentleman who smells of bugs [Chernyshevsky]? I can still hear his
thin voice, uttering disagreeable stupidities. . . . All this is Belinsky's
doing. But he spoke openly; his voice was indignant because he felt
indignation, whereas this one thinks that in order to speak well one
has to speak impudently, and therefore he is indignant. And he will
go on scowling out of his little niche, until someone licks him. . . .
Don't think I am speaking ill of Belinsky to pick a quarrel. I am
convinced that . . . as a man and writer he was remarkable and useful. But just because he had emerged from the lower social regions
he gave rise to loathsome imitators. Our criticism, and even our
literature and society at large, has been persuaded that to be outraged, bilious and spiteful is a commendable thing. To my mind,
this view is foul. They prefer Gogol to Pushkin. Belinsky's criticism
is supposed to be beyond all praise, and your verses are preferred to
all other poets. To my mind, this is preposterous. A bilious, spiteful
man is not normal.[29]

After this, relations went from bad to worse. Chernyshevsky,
too, though he bore the 'aristocratic' insults with apparent
equanimity and remained imperturbable under fire, assumed the
offensive. By 1858, and especially when Dobrolyubov joined the

editorial staff of the 'Contemporary', the controversy was fought
out with such acerbity that little coherent argument was
possible any more. Both sides over-played their hands, although Chernyshevsky showed himself on the whole the most
reasonable of the contestants: for him the only relevant question
was whether the attitudes expressed in the debate were true or
not, whereas the 'fathers' tended to shift it to one of 'tone' and
implied that their own revulsion from the 'sons' was the mark
of some superior sensibility.

It will be necessary later to consider again some of the issues
which, arrogant antics apart, divided the two sides and which
were not confined to literary matters. In any case, Nekrasov
had to choose, and he took Chernyshevsky's side. The evidence
shows that the choice was by no means easy for him, not only
because it meant breaking off relations with people (especially
Turgenev and Botkin) to whom he was genuinely attached by
ties of intimate and long-standing friendship, but also because
it did not pay: at least it did not pay to lose Turgenev and
Tolstoy, who, by the way, was himself soon to sneer at Turgenev
for his 'hypocrisy' and 'democratic haunches'. On the other
hand, Nekrasov could not sacrifice someone who stood for
those principles of social life and thought which represented his
own convictions, however ill-defined they may have been. That
this was no mere calculation on his part, no mere sponsorship
of causes he knew to have popular appeal, nor, for that matter,
a mere display of his gambler's spirit, is shown by the circumstances in which he originally engaged Chernyshevsky.[30]

The final breach between the 'old guard', headed by Turgenev, and the 'young collaborators', supported by Nekrasov,
occurred in the autumn of 1860, with Turgenev's formal refusal
(conveyed in a letter to Panaev) to have anything to do with the
review. The controversy, none the less, continued unabated
across the gulf, and its highlights were marked by a crude
skirmish into the 'Contemporary's' camp by Katkov's 'Russian
Messenger' (1861, no. 1), to which Turgenev had by then trans-
ferred his allegiance, and in which Nekrasov's review was
accused of assessing contemporary writers according to whether
they did or did not contribute to it; and, on Chernyshevsky's
side, by Antonovich's even cruder review-article about *Fathers
and Sons* ('Contemporary', 1862, no. 3), in which Turgenev was

denounced for having written a 'rancorous lampoon' against the younger generation. Subsequently, Turgenev disavowed Katkov, while Antonovich's estimate was soon reversed by the 'sons' themselves, and Pisarev, the extreme nihilist, proudly admitted the novel's hero Bazarov into their depopulated literary Pantheon.

It is evident from all these altercations that, within a short span of time, Chernyshevsky became one of the most controversial figures in Russia, not only as a writer but, as later events proved, as a public figure in general. This is something of an irony since, by temperament, he was, with all his untiring energy, a rather modest man, possessed, as has been seen, by strange delusions about his inferiority. Despite his learning and intellectual power, he never pretended to professorial authority, and he had a poor view of his abilities as a writer. There are no signs that he took his achievements very seriously, whatever dreams of 'service to mankind' he may have entertained, and however opinionated some of his utterances appear to be. His manner of life was conventional, and never more so than when he advocated radical principles. He might have been a suitable candidate for a philosopher-king in Plato's Academy. One sympathetic critic suggested that he was the kind of man who could have put all his energies into helping a state commission or a government administration.[31]

All this does not convey a very provocative figure. And yet the charges that have been levelled against Chernyshevsky by many of his contemporaries and later detractors exceed in quantity and violence the opprobrium incurred by any other Russian writer, except perhaps Dobrolyubov. Turgenev's and Tolstoy's snooty reaction owed a great deal to superciliousness and social snobbery, and in Turgenev's case also to professional jealousy, to which he was prone at times. Their distaste for Chernyshevsky's 'plebeian' qualities was equalled by his own revulsion, not against them personally, but against the whole legacy of class-conscious aristocratic assumptions and luxurious cultivated existence. Yet others, too, considered Chernyshevsky to be raw, illiterate, and underbred. He has been described as cliquish, spinsterly, Pharisaical, and intellectually immodest. The most violent attack on him came from Grigorovich who lampooned him in a short novel entitled *The School of Hospitality*

(*Shkola gostepriimstva*), whose principal character, a critic named Chernushkin ('Blacky', from *chernyi*, black—short for Chernyshevsky), is described as a moral and physical monster. He combines the qualities of a 'cynic', 'coward', 'sponger', 'timeserver', 'egotist', and 'voluptuary'. In addition, he has 'red hair', 'a long neck', and 'a squeaky voice'; he babbles interminably, uttering poisonous witticisms and pitting people against each other. Turgenev's and Tolstoy's 'bug-stinking' gives way to the euphemistic 'odour of burnt rum', which, according to connoisseurs, smells of bugs. Except for the colour of hair, thinness of voice, and length of neck, the picture is a figment of Grigorovich's imagination, although many took it to be an exact portrait of Chernyshevsky. As a matter of fact, his habits were austere to the point of asceticism. He disliked making social visits, and often forgot about his dinner, or bought himself, instead, a bunch of carrots or turnips which he consumed on his way to the editorial office of the 'Contemporary'. He smoked but did not drink. He was extremely unselfish, oddly chivalrous, and so taciturn that he scarcely spoke to any stranger. With others he talked more readily, but even then mainly with those who had won his confidence and on subjects close to his heart. As for the long neck, which to Grigorovich suggested an obscure malignance, it prompted others, Muraviev amongst them, to hint that 'il a un beau cou à pendre'.

Admittedly, Chernyshevsky's figure lent itself to ridicule. His very blamelessness was a source of annoyance, a provocation in the social and moral conditions in which he lived. There were so few saints, or at any rate so few secular saints, in nineteenth-century Russia that the impulse to ridicule one was irresistible. Chernyshevsky's very qualities betrayed him. His drastic fidelity to truth, self-dedication, and singleness of mind failed to appeal, not only to the many who upheld, from conviction or vested interest, the existing order, but also to the few whose sense of libertarian uncertainty was offended by Chernyshevsky's refusal to be diverted. The barrier dividing the single-minded great from the majestic bore is known to be sometimes flimsy. Without being a bore, Chernyshevsky may have appeared to be one.

Furthermore, a dictator lurks in every writer. Chernyshevsky's strength and influence lay in his representativeness, in his power not so much to ask questions for the first time as to make them imperative and to bring the moral and social experience of his time to bear on those questions. There is evidence that he found pleasure in the use of his influence, although there is no evidence at all that he was ever inclined to exploit it for ulterior motives or on the sly. He was cautious about declaring himself outright. Yet this was not a sign of furtiveness or insincerity, as even Herzen seemed to think when he met him in London, but of reserve and gaucherie: to quote Herzen himself, 'only banal souls achieve the sincere expression of their personality'. Nevertheless, withdrawn though he was in personal relations, Chernyshevsky was perfectly forthright with pen and paper and, indeed, became increasingly ready to take sides openly in the face of the intensified conflicts and shifts in the foundations of Russian society.

Behind the embarrassed façade, then, we are left with the impression of an intelligent, humane, and likeable person, who was, in addition, a symbol of rare integrity. This appears to be the unanimous verdict of those who knew Chernyshevsky well, and of all those who knew him not so well but had no axe to grind.[32]

What remains beyond argument is the powerful stimulus Chernyshevsky's writings gave to the younger generation. They could scarcely have served as a source of intellectual titillation. They attracted, rather, because through them Chernyshevsky succeeded in achieving a new intimacy with the younger generation, because he asked its questions and spoke to its condition. In more tranquil times such a man would perhaps have remained a scholar—a role which Chernyshevsky had chosen in the first place and which he would the more easily have accepted as he was shy of the world and found it embarrassing even to ask a shopkeeper for a pound of carrots. But he had achieved adult status at a time when nothing could be said or written in a vacuum, and when to act mattered as much as to think. Moreover, his kind of thought was, in fact, almost wholly translatable into action. The point at which his involvement became particularly close was the position of the peasants. In the end, it was they who lured him out of his study, and the 'revolutionary situation' between 1859 and 1861 succeeded in finally linking his pursuit of knowledge with a pursuit of revolution.

The extent of the latter has been the object of somewhat acrimonious debate among Soviet students of Russian political thought. Many pre-revolutionary writers, including even Plekhanov, took it almost for granted that Chernyshevsky was merely or mainly a scholar, a theoretician with a radical bias but never actively engaged in the struggles of this time: a revolutionary perhaps, but a bookish one, a revolutionary with flat feet. We have seen, however, that on more than one occasion he revealed surprising intensity of feeling, and his political aims, too, hint at a more passionate figure. He believed in the pursuit of truth and enlightenment, but he saw deeper into the nature of Russian society than any other radical, precisely because he was able to fuse a personal revolt against injustice and unhappiness with a balanced, 'scientific' view of history. This mixture of irreverence and love of truth, of violence and humanity endowed the incipient revolutionary movement with dignity, saving it from mere cynicism and occupational brutality.

Nevertheless, there is no conclusive evidence of Chernyshevsky's direct participation (i.e. as a leader or even a member) in any revolutionary organization. In fact, after the suppression of the Decembrist revolt in 1825 and the liquidation of Petrashevsky's 'conspiracy of ideas' in 1849 no such organization existed, until the fatal results of the land reform became evident. There were, admittedly, a number of scattered groups, more or less independent of each other, consisting mainly of students and a few army officers, from which there emerged eventually a Society called *Zemlya i volya* (Land and Freedom). Their activity was confined—somewhat on the lines of the French 'societies of thought'—to discussions, and the printing and dissemination of underground opposition literature. They had links with London, where, since about 1857, Herzen and in particular Ogarev tried to devise ways and means of forming them into a more coherent secret organization, of which Bakunin became later the most ardent promoter.[33] When the Society did emerge late in 1861, Chernyshevsky's part in it remained strangely aloof or 'impenetrable' (in the words of one of the Society's members), although some of its adherents—

Sleptsov, Serakovsky, Panteleev, Shelgunov, the brothers Serno-
Solov'evich, Obruchev, and others—were among his closest
friends, who regarded him as their ideological leader and the
'Contemporary' as their tribune. They are known to have been in
frequent communication with him on matters concerning their
clandestine activities. But two of the most important documents
—the memoirs of Panteleev and Sleptsov—which throw light
on this moot point confine themselves to such general statements
as 'Chernyshevsky was interested in the work of the rising
organization', or 'Chernyshevsky criticized the current projects
and gave advice'.[34]

This did not prevent some scholars from attributing to
Chernyshevsky extraordinary feats of conspiratorial intrigue
and even from implicating his wife in underground activities.[35]
The latter implication is particularly strange because, after
Chernyshevsky's own admitted caution, Olga Sokratovna seems
to have been, on the contrary, the chief cause of his circumspection, even though he himself is reported by Sleptsov to have
found an excuse for his aloofness in 'physical inability' to combine conspiratorial work with his editorship of the 'Contemporary'.[36]

Chernyshevsky's love for Olga Sokratovna never diminished,
but when the immediate object was attained he soon appreciated the wrong he had committed in marrying her, or, rather,
as he liked to believe, the wrong he had committed towards her
by exposing her to the 'inconveniences' of being married to
someone like himself. The tragedy or tragi-comedy which
resulted from this was his greatest personal misfortune, greater
in some ways than his Siberian agony, although the two were
not unconnected.

While, in Pypina's words, 'priding herself on being the wife
of Chernyshevsky', Olga Sokratovna, as has been noted, could
not help finding him profoundly uncongenial. His scholarly
figure 'beaming winsomely' through his owlish spectacles, his
modesty, the impression he gave of being uncertain of himself,
anxious only to creep back into his study, were to her both
ludicrous and irritating.

'He is always working!', she complained. 'All day long! The
moment he gets up in the morning he sits down to work, on and on,
until late at night. No time even to have his tea or to dine properly.

He snatches his glass of tea and goes off to his damned work, or even takes his plate, with the last bit of food on it, to his damned study. He is so absent-minded and unobservant that he does not even distinguish between the many young men who come to see me. He has tea and dinner with them and still does not know who they are, unless they start some learned conversation with him. What a book-worm!' 'How he bores me!', she used to say. 'One can't ask a thing: instead of answering in two words he will start a whole dissertation. Naturally, I don't listen. It's my only salvation.' 'But he himself always listens to me, and does not get bored, simply because he likes my voice. He listens, but he does not hear what I say, or forgets straight away. He couldn't possibly be interested in my pleasure trips, my turn-outs, dresses, dances and chats with young men.'[37]

However, all this only served to promote Olga Sokratovna's sense of freedom. 'Sometimes she would make her husband appear before her guests: "Let him get used to talking to people about something beside his own nonsense, which he and people like him call 'social questions'." . . . At other times, when he happened to emerge from his study, she would chase him away: "I am bored stiff with you and your '1848'. I have no time. Don't you see we are playing lotto. And you have no time either to stand about and chatter. Off with you! Put your coat on and let me see if your tie is done up!".'[38]

After Chernyshevsky's death, as an old woman, shrivelled with bitterness, misery, and resentment, Olga Sokratovna would plunge into memories of how she 'raced the Grand Duke Konstantin Nikolaevich on a trotter' and 'pierced him with a fiery look', or how 'dexterously Ivan Fyodorovich [Savitsky, an army officer] conducted his affairs: nobody suspected that he was my lover. . . . But Kanashechka [one of Olga Sokratovna's less fortunate pet-names for Chernyshevsky] knew. We used to sit in the alcove, while he scribbled at the window.'[39]

But then, even before his marriage, Chernyshevsky wrote in his Diary (14 March 1853) and later repeated to his wife: 'If she should come to love another I shall be dejected, but I shall bear no ill-feeling towards her. And what joy will be her return to me! For she will then see that, however much she may have been loved by another, no one could love her as I do.' 'He was glad', Pypina notes, 'that he had the necessary means to satisfy her "passionate inclinations".' The ample income he received as editor of the 'Contemporary' was, however, barely sufficient to meet the increasing demands of these 'inclinations'. He apologized to her, asked Nekrasov for advances (or, sometimes, she asked Nekrasov for an increase in salary) and encouraged her to spend more. He remained serene, generous, and loving. Nobody knew then what terrors of loneliness went to produce this paragon of patience, or clown of love. Of this there is perhaps only one delicate and pathetic hint in a letter to Nekrasov (5 November 1856). Speaking of Nekrasov's lyrical poetry, Chernyshevsky wrote:

I will even say that for me my personal affairs have greater significance than world-questions: it is not on account of such questions that people drown themselves, shoot themselves, or take to drink. I have lived through this and I know that the poetry of the heart has the same claim as the poetry of the mind: personally, I am more attracted by the former than by the latter. Your lyrical verse, therefore, overwhelms me. Your 'When, from the darkness where you went astray . . .', 'Long since, on the day when you spurned me . . .', 'I stood beside your grave, to-day . . .', 'O spare me, potent and unprofitable passion . . .', literally make me weep.*

---

* These are the first lines of the following poems:

> When, from the darkness where you went astray,
> My burning words recalled you to the way,
> And from the pit your fallen soul drew back;
> When, your whole being given up to pain,
> You wrung your hands, and cursed, and cursed again,
> The vice that held you on that hateful track . . .
>
> Believe me, not unmoved I heard your tale unfold.
> No! Eagerly I caught at every broken word.
> Child of ill-hap! I understood then all you told,
> Forgave all I had felt, forgot all I have heard.

> Long since, on the day when you spurned me,
>   I wandered alone by this shore;
> To the waves, in despair, I had turned me,
>   Resolved—for a moment, not more—
>   Till fear got the better of grief . . .
>
> To-day, now that you have forgotten,
>   Still alone, with lost years to deplore,
> Still alive, my soul ravaged and rotten,
>   I tread this same desolate shore.

While Olga Sokratovna's saturnalia expanded, Chernyshevsky's influence in Russia grew also. 'He became a "dangerous man",' Pypina writes. 'It was not possible to seize on anything, for he was exceptionally circumspect in his revolutionary activities, fearing as he did to endanger Olga Sokratovna's

> Again the same thought comes, now stronger,
>   As again from that cliff I look down;
> Though the waves cry their warning no longer,
>   I still feel: 'How simple to drown!'

> I stood beside your grave, to-day,
>   Friend of my years of pain;
> And in my mind your likeness lay
>   All bright and clear again.

> Before, I'd had so much to bear,
>   My mind and body slept;
> My senses numb, in dull despair
>   I came to you, and wept.

> Your laughter and high spirits failed
>   To chase my gloom away;
> My sick and irritable temper quailed
>   And fretted at your play.

> Within your unencumbered heart,
>   Nought, I felt, chimed with mine,
> Where grief, as I still fumed apart,
>   Engraved a deeper line.

> O spare me, potent and unprofitable passion—
>   Now common sense returns with dawn—
> The scornful glances of that queen of fashion
>   Round whom performing lions fawn:

> Their gait is confident, their tone assured,
>   Their terms are apt, their views correct.
> I enter stumblingly, confused and awed,
>   And dare not hold my head erect.

> Imaginary fetters clog my feet;
>   My head feels like a lump of lead:
> My hands are neither eloquent nor neat;
>   My words upon my lips drop dead.

> If I dare smile, my smile's a mirthless grin,
>   A spasm passing for a smile.
> I joke: they ask me where the point comes in.
>   I blush; and my hard fate revile.

> In disconcerted silence I retreat
>   And gaze despondently about,
> Fixed like a statue in my corner seat,
>   And try to last the evening out.

well-being. Yet he foresaw difficulties. There was no point in speaking of his apprehensions in general, least of all to his wife.'[40] Subsequent events showed that Olga Sokratovna, who flared up at the slightest mention of possible 'complications', was not unduly moved by anxiety for her husband.

Meanwhile, the reversal in Government policy gathered momentum. The peasant risings strengthened the forces of reaction. The risings were followed, in the autumn of 1861, by student disturbances and student arrests in the two capitals and in Kiev and Kazan, mainly in connexion with the new restrictive measures concerning the admission of students and the prohibition of all extra-academic activities.[41] A novel feature in the changing circumstances was the appearance at this time of a number of anti-Government underground proclamations which originated in student and partly in military circles. The first of these, a 'gazette' entitled *Velikorus* (The Great-Russian), was distributed fairly widely in the capital.[42] It was succeeded in the spring of 1862 by another one, *Molodaya Rossiya* (Young Russia), the tone and contents of which were considerably more vehement and subversive, reflecting the desperate revolutionary mood of the peasants shortly after the emancipation. As one contemporary put it, 'it crashed like thunder over the capital'. It originated in Moscow, in a revolutionary student 'cell' of 'Land and Freedom' headed by Zaichnevsky, the son of an officer, and Argiropulo, a Graeco-Russian nobleman.[43]

The threats of 'Young Russia' caused considerable nervousness in Government circles and among the liberals. The proclamation conjured up the phantom of a strong political organization, which, in fact, did not exist. Herzen, who was not uncritical of the manifesto, wrote that 'the Ministers of progress and the directors of liberalism, the police of human-kindness and the red-tapists of emancipation had all vanished like dust, from fright at the words spoken by "Young Russia", . . . The fear inspired by a small group of energetic youths was so great that, a year after, Katkov congratulated the Government and all Russia on having escaped a terrible revolution. The persecutions by the Government, therefore, have their natural explanation: *ante tubam trepidat*.'[44]

Nevertheless, the fear seemed genuine and widespread, and it was aggravated by a series of fires which broke out in the middle

of May in the capital and in the provinces. The conflagration
in St. Petersburg assumed enormous proportions, lasting for
more than two weeks and completely destroying large parts of
the city. The origin of the fires remains a mystery to this day.
They may even have been an outright provocation on the part
of the police and the Ministry of the Interior, with the aim of
'frightening the Emperor above and the weak souls below'.
Such at least was the allegation made by Herzen's *Bell*. In any
case, the Government seized on the opportunity and tried to
implicate the 'revolutionary party', by linking the disaster with
the incendiary proclamations. A systematic press campaign
against the students ensued.[45] Two commissions were instituted
by the Senate (the supreme judicial organ dealing with,
amongst other things, political crimes) to investigate the origin of
the fires and of the proclamations. As regards the fires, no
evidence whatsoever could be found incriminating the students,
and the commission concerned with the matter receded into
mystifying silence. But the existence of student circles engaged
in clandestine revolutionary propaganda was an undisputed
fact, and the commission succeeded in preparing a number of
large-scale administrative actions against the students or groups
of students, of which the so-called 'Trial of the 32' was the most
notorious.[46]

The greatest amount of energy and ingenuity was expended
on the case against Chernyshevsky, and early in 1862 a secret
report of the Chief of Police (Dolgoruky) to Alexander spoke of
Chernyshevsky's responsibility for the underground literature
and for 'hostile feelings towards the Government'. The police
were anxious to strike at the right moment so as to forestall
possible disturbances as a result of Chernyshevsky's untimely
arrest. 'The slightest mistake . . . in Government plans of such
importance', Dolgoruky wrote, 'can lead to a premature out-
break, the consequences of which are unpredictable.'[47] From
then onwards Chernyshevsky was continually shadowed (this
was known as 'the tail') by secret agents ('archangels') and by
informers ('angels'), one of whom turned out to be the Cherny-
shevskys' housemaid, and all his movements, the people who
came to see him and whom he went to see were weekly and
sometimes daily reported to the Third Section. Anonymous
denunciations spoke of him as 'the ringleader of the young', and

the official press joined in spreading inspired rumours about his 'treasonable deeds'. 'Unless he is eliminated', one report suggested, 'we shall not escape revolution.' Chernyshevsky himself received threatening anonymous letters: '. . . your hands are drenched in blood . . .', a correspondent wrote. 'We do not wish to see an Anton Petrov on the throne, and if it should really come to a bloody rising, we will find you out, you and Iskander [Herzen], or some other member of your race, and we'll leave you no time to secure a body-guard.'[48] Chernyshevsky concealed these letters from Olga Sokratovna, who reacted to the badgering with more and more frequent fits of hysteria, accompanied by complaints about her husband's heartlessness in having 'done such a thing to her', and by impassioned reminders that she 'did not love him now, neither [had she] ever loved him before'. Eventually, he found a pretext for dispatching his family to Saratov, while he himself remained in the capital 'to await the inevitable'.

Meanwhile, the Minister of the Interior wrote impatient letters to the Third Section requesting an early completion of Chernyshevsky's dossier: since no evidence could be found for attributing the proclamations to Chernyshevsky, 'would it not suffice', he asked, to proceed with the arrest 'on the basis of the generally known fact that communications are being maintained with London, and that links existed with persons already under arrest?' Indeed, very soon, with the help of a frequent visitor to Herzen's London home who turned out to be a secret agent, it was possible to arrest a person at the Russian frontier carrying a letter from Herzen and Ogarev to Nikolai Serno-Solov'evich. In it the London émigrés suggested that they would be 'prepared to publish with Chernyshevsky the [suspended] 'Contemporary' here or in Geneva'. The mention of Chernyshevsky sealed his doom. He was arrested and imprisoned in the Alexis ravelin of the Peter and Paul Fortress on 7 July 1862.[49]

For two years Chernyshevsky awaited his secret trial. Some members of the investigating commission and other influential persons, notably Suvorov, Governor General of St. Petersburg, who showed a vague sympathy for the prisoner, believed that Chernyshevsky's case was ill-prepared and the evidence too flimsy to make it convincing in the eyes of those to whom his condemnation was to serve as a lesson. The disagreements resulted in a serious clash between Suvorov and the Third Section which was eventually resolved in favour of the latter by the direct intervention of the Emperor. Chernyshevsky made one deposition after another proving his innocence and, unlike some other Russian revolutionaries in a similar position, refused to 'repent' of his views.

You remember what I told you when you went away [to Saratov] about the rumours of my impending arrest [he wrote to his wife from prison]: 'I don't think they will arrest me; but if they do, you should know in advance that nothing will come of it, except that the Government will be compromised by an unconsidered arrest, for which they will have to apologize. I am not implicated in anything: more, it is impossible to implicate me in anything.' . . . Having arrested me, they now begin to think 'what charge shall we level against him?' This sort of thing happens often with us: something is done and afterwards people begin to think up something. . . . They have been thinking for four months . . ., and for yet another month . . . but nothing happens . . .

Chernyshevsky could hardly have been so naïve as to think that 'they' were going to apologize for wrongly arresting him. The words were evidently meant to reassure his wife, while the Assistant Chief of Police duly noted on a copy of the intercepted letter: 'He is wrong, no one will have to apologize!'[50]

Whatever hopes Chernyshevsky may have harboured for a favourable outcome, he was deeply depressed, particularly because for many months he was not allowed any visits from his family, including his wife. As a protest, he began a ten-day hunger strike. When told that unless he ate he would not see his wife at all, he replied every time: 'after the meeting, but now you can take the food away.' Nothing but an unyielding, drastic quality of will and a miraculous power of application can explain that in these conditions Chernyshevsky was able to go on writing and even produced a full-length novel (*What Is to Be Done?*). It is similarly a miracle (actually, it turned out to be no more than a blunder or oversight on the part of the investigating commission, and it was soon rectified) that the novel, written as it was by someone held in solitary confinement and indicted of major political crimes, found its way out of the Fortress into the pages of the 'Contemporary', which by then (1863) had been allowed temporarily to resume publication.[51]

All this largely by-passed Olga Sokratovna. The uncertainty became a source of extreme irritation to her. She wanted to know where she stood. 'She got bored and amused herself; she amused herself and got bored again.' Life with the Pypins, to whom she had moved on her return from Saratov, was a burden to her, although they tried to look after her and provide for her as best they could: their life was completely absorbed in hopes, expectations, disappointments, and unending conversations about Chernyshevsky's case. When at last she was allowed to visit her husband she complained to him, as she had done before and was to do again later in her letters to Siberia, of his 'tiresome relations', thereby increasing his anxiety on her behalf. She longed to get away from the depressing atmosphere. 'She raced all over Russia', 'boated up and down the Volga with her *entourage*', and nearly missed the day on which her husband was taken to penal servitude in Siberia.

The verdict, confirmed by the State Council, came on 5 May 1864. Chernyshevsky was condemned to fourteen (later reduced to seven) years forced labour and perpetual deportation to Siberia, with permanent loss of all rights. This punishment was in no way based on the facts at the disposal of the Senate. Hard as it tried, the Senate commission could not find even circumstantial evidence of Chernyshevsky's guilt. Apart from being branded as 'a particularly dangerous agitator', whose writings —previously passed by the censorship—were 'contaminated with extreme materialist and socialist ideas', he was convicted on three counts: communicating with Herzen (this charge, central to the whole case at the beginning, receded later into the background), composing an unpublished appeal to the peasants, and harbouring 'an evil intent to subvert the existing order'.[52] The crimes, or rather the only tangible crime, namely, the appeal to the peasants, remained unproven, despite the fact that in the last stage of the trial the Senate used a false witness and faked evidence. The proceedings turned, in fact, into a cruel farce, and they stand as one of the greatest judicial crimes in Russian pre-revolutionary legal history.

Asked later if the case against Chernyshevsky could be regarded as established, one senator replied that 'no legal proofs have been found', but that 'the moral case against him was complete'.[53] The heart of the matter lay, indeed, not in legal proofs. The Government had come to realize the extent of Chernyshevsky's influence on the younger generation; it knew what his views were, and it had taken fright. It was essential to smother him for, undoubtedly, he represented a real danger to the existing order.

A special ceremony, devised for political prisoners and known as 'civil execution' (*grazhdanskaya kazn'*), accompanied the announcement of the sentence on 19 May. A number of eye-witnesses left records of what took place in the early morning of that day. Chernyshevsky was brought into a public square accompanied by two executioners and put on a scaffold.

He had changed a great deal. His pale face was swollen and bore marks of scurvy.

After the sentence had been read out he was forced to kneel, a sword was broken over his head and he was then set in a pillory by a chain.

While he was being freed from the iron rings . . . someone in the assembled crowd shouted 'Farewell! Farewell!'

'Who said "farewell"?'

The crowd stood silent. Then a bunch of flowers landed at Chernyshevsky's feet. Another one.

'Who threw the flowers?'

Again silence. The police began to question some people in the crowd.

'It's you', a policeman turned to a young woman.

'Yes, it's me. He is a good friend of mine. . . .'

The girl is arrested. Other arrests follow. Chernyshevsky is driven away. That is the end of it. Quietly the crowd dispersed, drenched and cursing the rain. A feeling of weariness, of moral sickness seemed to fill everyone. But some were indignant. . . .[54]

'Chernyshevsky is condemned . . .', Herzen wrote on receiving the news: 'May this monstrous crime spell the damnation of the Government, of society, of the foul, corrupt press which courted the outrage. . . . Congratulations to all the Katkovs! You have gained your victory over this adversary. Why, now you can draw a deep breath! Chernyshevsky was put in the pillory for a quarter of an hour, but what about you, what about Russia which is chained to a pillory for so many years? Curses on you, curses on you, and, if possible, revenge!'[55]

The station-master of a small Siberian village near Irkutsk gave the following account of Chernyshevsky's deportation:

They drove him by post-cart, his feet shackled in chains, with two gendarmes, who looked like being from Peter [St. Petersburg]. It was summer then. [The prisoner] seemed like a little child to me, quiet and courteous—the kind of fellow who wouldn't hurt a fly. . . . Couldn't make out why a fellow like that should be sent to forced labour. The gendarmes themselves told me: 'While we drove, day and night, he sat between us . . . and kept silent most of the time. Still, being together for so long, we got to know him a bit and managed to find out a thing or two . . . I am from Russia, but this my mate is from your parts, a Siberian. His village and his people are only a few *versts* away from here. So, when we approached your place my mate felt homesick, . . . but we couldn't turn in: "secret charge", "strict instructions", and all that. "Maybe on the way back", he said. Chernyshevsky listened all the time to what we were talking about and suddenly says: "Friends, do let me rest for a day or so! I am tired and aching after all this driving. You can go if you wish to your village. Leave me at the station, in the waiting room . . . I won't go anywhere: you can trust me, I won't leave the room." It was very tempting. . . . My mate longed to see his people.' They believed him and went away, . . . leaving [Chernyshevsky] in my charge. I put him in that room over there, at the side, away from other travellers. The gendarmes took a horse from the stables and left for their village. And he sat here, like a child, mostly on the couch, . . . looking rather shrivelled, sun-burnt, with glasses, and all the time sort of thinking to himself . . . I tried to draw him out as best I could: I was rather curious . . . 'Would you like a glass of tea?', I asked, and he replied: 'No, thank you. But I would like some milk, if you can spare any. I'm tired, very tired, I must rest now.' Still, I kept him under observation, if you know what I mean. You never know. After all, I was in charge. But during all those hours he never left the room, except a few times for a wash. And before leaving, always asked for permission, and I showed him the place. Once I asked him, as though by the way: 'What would be your station?' 'What do you mean?' he replied. 'I mean what's your trade at home, in Russia?' He looked at me, smiled, thought for a while, and then said: 'In the scribbling line, that's where I used to work, in the scribbling line, sort of clerical work.' And went on smiling. . . . A remarkable man he was, quite remarkable! Just like a little child—and yet on the way to penal servitude! . . . He lay there for a few hours on the couch, and then he would get up and walk around the room, and then lie down again. I could see and hear everything from my part of the station-cottage. There were no new travellers all this time, when he was, so to speak, in freedom, and no post-chaise. The gendarmes returned from their village in high spirits, . . . harnessed the horses, stamped the papers, and then they were off. In three weeks' time they stopped again on their way back, having safely delivered the convict. They said of him: 'Such a fellow could be safely dispatched to forced labour on his own, without any guards. Just put him in a cart and tell him: "drive to penal servitude!" . . . Our orders were to escort a criminal, but we were escorting a saint.'[56]

Nearly a quarter of a century, that is, about half his life, Chernyshevsky spent in penal servitude and deportation: seven years at the Kadai mines in the penal settlement of the Narchinsk mountain district and at the silver-melting furnaces of Alexandrovsk; twelve years in Vilyuisk jail, which was virtually a continuation of penal servitude but where he was allowed to walk 500 steps beyond the prison walls; and nearly six years in Astrakhan, his last place of deportation. He was moved to European Russia as a result of secret negotiations between the populist terrorists and the Government. The revolutionaries promised to refrain from terroristic acts during the coronation of Alexander III in return for Chernyshevsky's repatriation. Four months before his death Chernyshevsky was granted permission to settle in his native Saratov.

Strangely enough, the Siberian part of his life (especially the seven years in Kadai and Alexandrovsk) is fairly well documented, owing not so much to his own correspondence as to a number of reminiscences left by political fellow-prisoners, who had seen him or heard of him in the course of their wanderings through the Siberian penal districts.[57] None of these could be published in Russia before the revolution of 1905 because until then all references to Chernyshevsky in print were forbidden and all his writings were withdrawn from public libraries. This served to contribute to his being treated, at any rate by the radical intelligentsia, as a legend, almost at times as a myth, a remote dedicated figure half-glimpsed by the returning convicts in the places of his deportation. The only exception to this imposed silence was Dostoevsky, who could afford or had the courage to give open expression to his 'respect for an opponent' and 'deep sympathy in Chernyshevsky's misfortune'.[58]

The evidence about Chernyshevsky's experience among the

PLATE 2

a. Chernyshevsky, aged 6o

b. Vilyuisk prison where Chernyshevsky spent 12 years

criminals and 'politicals' in Siberia has something of the night-mare humanity of so many specimens of Russian prison litera-ture. He lived in a world in which Dostoevskian extremes of degradation and self-degradation are inevitable, and where those potentially most virtuous are the most extreme. It is almost unbelievable how in these terrible conditions Cherny-shevsky managed to be so noble, especially as physically he soon became a very sick man indeed, suffering from scurvy, stomach ulcers, acute rheumatism and, later, malaria. His human dignity never collapsed, not even when prisoners, snarling like dogs, would fight each other for a cabbage leaf and were treated as objects with no personality or opinion. He remained as un-selfish, as kind, as courageous and upright as ever, or more than ever. It seems as if a new serenity had come into his life, in which even the ideological acerbities of his active years appear in a new light. But he never wavered in his convictions or repented. Apart from an unsuccessful attempt by some revolutionaries to arrange his escape—to which he did not agree and which served to aggravate his position—he was approached by the authorities with a view to inducing him 'to beg for the imperial mercy'. The measure was aimed at destroying 'the myth of Chernyshevsky'. 'I thank you,' Chernyshevsky told the special emissary who conveyed the message to him in person, 'but, you see: what exactly am I supposed to petition for? That is the heart of the matter. It seems to me that I have been deported because my head and that of the *chef de gendarmes* Shuvalov are shaped in different ways. Is this something about which one could ask for mercy? I am grateful for your efforts, but I positively refuse to make the petition.'[59] A number of petitions on his behalf by his family, on the other hand, remained ineffective and only caused him bitter disappointment.

He lived for the most part in solitary confinement, and when-ever possible preferred to live in a cell of his own. The only request of a private nature made by Chernyshevsky to the prison authorities was to be allowed not to wash the floor of his cell: he had a phobia about damp floors, mainly on account of his rheumatism, which, he believed, would finally immobilize him if his floor was washed regularly. His cell—in Vilyuisk—was a bare room with a table, a chair, a bunk, and a fair quantity of books, acquired more or less by chance; later Pypin was allowed to send him books from Russia. When not digging ditches, he worked in his cell, carving small articles with a pen-knife or writing. At times he worked with an almost rigid frenzy, writing and then burning what he wrote, as if something was burning at the back of his mind. 'These works were not the result of my will', he wrote at the beginning of his imprison-ment in an autobiographical passage of a short story called 'Alferev'. 'I had no choice in the matter. Nature, which from time to time sends down a thunderbolt, produced them through me. They are not books but phenomena of life and nature.' A few of Chernyshevsky's Siberian writings have been preserved, although manuscripts were apt to be confiscated or destroyed, and most of them are fictional matter—unfinished novels, stories, allegorical plays, fantastic adventures. The flow of ideas seemed irrepressible in him and, from time to time, he regaled his fellow prisoners with them and, in Vilyuisk, even occasional people from outside, keeping his listeners as spellbound as his pupils in the Saratov school, by his versatile knowledge and narrative gift.

There were, however, periods of deep spiritual anguish. His loneliness was frightful. He invariably concealed his feelings, but people sometimes heard him sob behind the walls of his cell. 'It happened that on some nights . . . he would talk or sing to himself, or laugh, or sob. It was a strange sobbing, loud and heart-rending. He wept especially after receiving letters from his family. It was said that he was very fond of his wife. . . . After such nights he felt so distressed . . . that he did not speak to anyone for a long time.'[60] The letters from Russia, arriving at very infrequent intervals—about three or four times a year— were an enormous event for him. His own strictly rationed letters to Russia, though graceless and sometimes trivial, and written with a view to the censor, have a peculiar unobtrusive power which nothing, or nothing short of a recapitulation of his moral history, can explain. They are chastely objective and free from self-pity. There is no trace of morbidity in them, no unhappiness that has turned sour. 'As for myself', he wrote to his wife (12 January 1871), 'I am not sure if I would agree to have this ordeal, which has brought so much distress and deprivation to you, struck out from my fate. I am deeply sorry for your sake that it should be so. But I am content for my sake

And in thinking of others—of those tens of millions of paupers—
I am glad that without will or merit on my part my voice should
have acquired more power and authority than before and should
have enabled me to plead their cause in this way.' In reading
Chernyshevsky's letters to his wife one derives a new appreciation of his lofty, quixotic soul.

Olga Sokratovna did not emulate the Decembrists' wives
who followed their husbands into penal servitude, although she
did go to the considerable trouble of travelling once to Siberia
to see her husband for a few days. She remained in Russia not,
as she liked to believe, because of the education of her children,
who, in any case, were brought up by the Pypins and lived
with them; nor because, after the Karakozov affair and the
absortive plans to arrange Chernyshevsky's flight, it would, admittedly, have been difficult to obtain the permission of the
authorities to reside near her husband. She was otherwise
engaged, 'agreeing' with Chernyshevsky in her letters to him
that Siberia could not offer 'sufficiently comfortable living
conditions'. Chernyshevsky, meanwhile, overwhelmed her with
epistolary solicitude for her health (which was robust and
enabled her to survive her husband by nearly thirty years); for
her comforts (which her 'position required'); and her amuse-
ments (with which she solaced herself 'in [her] great misfortune'). He insisted that she take fuller advantage of her freedom,
abandon him altogether, marry another. It is *she* who suffered
because of him: *he* failed to protect her against the vicissitudes
of life, and *he* made her undergo privations.[61]

Although he could not help seeing his love leading nowhere
except to obliteration in the sands of time, Chernyshevsky was
in a way happy in his unhappy, selfless love, which claimed
nothing and forgave everything. 'I leave it to you to judge',
he wrote to Olga Sokratovna on 10 April 1883, 'if there is
among the women you know now, or have known in the past,
a woman gentler, better, more intelligent than you. But remember one thing: I love you, only you, and not one of the
women I have ever seen could have been loved by me, even if
I had never known you at all.' 'His feeling for Olga Sokratovna', Pypina writes, 'remained as alive then as it was at first,
but he was worn out by his love.' In the end, he may have
realized that the essence had gone out of it and that the dream

had vanished. 'Do you think that my Siberian deportation was a misfortune?' Chernyshevsky is reported to have said to a relative, referring obliquely to his conjugal life after he had rejoined his wife, 'it is only there that I was happy.'[62] He never knew when he was himself being comic, nor what is more, when he was being tragic; perhaps it was his own tragedy that had destroyed the tragic sense in him.

Chernyshevsky's deportation in European Russia in the last six years of his life was a comparatively mild affair. He was allowed to live in a private house with his wife and family. But instructions from St. Petersburg laid down that

in view of the special importance of Chernyshevsky, of his popu-larity among evil-doers who have made several attempts to liberate him, as also in view of the likely appearance in Astrakhan . . . of ill-intentioned persons for whom Chernyshevsky might serve as a means towards the realization of criminal aims—[it is necessary] to subject him not only to general surveillance, but also to make arrangements with the local police authorities for the most vigilant secret observation of all communications and, generally, of his way of life. . . .[63]

The instructions were carried out to the letter and, in a sense, Chernyshevsky found himself no less of an outcast in Astrakhan than in the penal settlements of Siberia. He was shadowed and censored by the police, people feared to come into contact with him, and they were officially discouraged from doing so. 'Now, my dear friend, if you were to go and convey to the appropriate persons what has been said here to-night', he observed jokingly to one of his rare visitors (Khovansky), 'it will be sheer patrio-tism . . . ha, ha . . . a truly patriotic deed!' Yet then as before, he was least of all prone to parade as a man of sorrows or a martyr, although once or twice he was heard to remark in desperation: 'My God, when will they [the police] at last leave me alone?' He preferred to shelter behind a rough and slighting gesture of unconcern. He lived now in very straitened material circumstances which were a constant source of grumbling by his wife, who by this time had turned into a cantankerous, neurotic termagant. He existed on the proceeds of translating, anonymously, Georg Weber's voluminous *Universal History*. Apart from this he wrote little.

Some witnesses report that Chernyshevsky had lost all

interest in public affairs, that he had become odd or even un-
settled in his mind. In fact, though a complete invalid in body,
his intellectual capacities were unimpaired and the spirit remained irrepressible in him. But Korolenko was probably right
in observing that 'Chernyshevsky returned to us not only from
the depth of Siberia, but also from the depth of the sixties. . . .
The trouble was not that he had "changed": the fact is that, on
the contrary, he remained the same, . . . whilst we had lived
through the historical experience of a whole age.'[64]

There is no doubt that the Siberian agony had narrowed
him, but it did not distort anything. In the last resort, his
tragic fate goes beyond the personal. It helped him to live on
as a moral and social influence superior to the sectarian attitudes which he may have assumed in his lifetime, and it
established his status as the comfortless saint of Russian
radicalism.

He died on 17 October 1889 from an attack of malaria.

2. *In Defence of Humanism*

It has become a largely unquestioned commonplace that
Russian thought was linked with social and political attitudes
to an extent unknown almost anywhere in contemporary
Europe. The idea of philosophy as a neutral technical enterprise, as mere methodology, is naturally alien to the Russian
intellectual scene. Unless this is fully realized, Chernyshevsky's
philosophical ideas might strike one today as a desert full of dry
bones into which no prophet could breathe new life. Seen in the
context of events, on the contrary, they express problems and
perplexities which are still our own.

There was about Chernyshevsky, as a thinker even more than
as a character, a certain grand and sturdy simplicity, an intellectual certainty, a clear conviction of what is good and bad,
right and wrong, real and imaginary.[65] True, he never pretended that he was unperturbed in his convictions, or that he
had an ice-cold intellect. He said that 'only the unimportant
things in life can be done in cold blood, dispassionately, judi-
ciously, rationally'. But an idea was to him not something
which he had to question, or which he had to seek to recon-
stitute: it was something by which he lived. His pre-eminent

gift was truthfulness. He positively relished speaking the truth, especially when it was unpleasant. He also had a tendency to think against, instead of simply thinking, and so indulge in contentiousness. This had the effect of both blunting and sharpening his perception. In the first case, it offered him little room for doubt and hence spared him the refinements and subtleties of the intellect; in the second case, it produced a sense of 'engagement', which enabled Chernyshevsky to see problems in relation to the contemporary conflicts of values, ideas and personalities. It may be said that his main interest lay not in ideas as such, i.e. in their relative validity, or in what canons of criticism may be validly applied to them, but in the interdependence and status of ideas. Next to his scientific preoccupations, he was concerned with the conditions which made a thinker hold the views he holds and the way in which his thought reflects his vision of the world.

Even in his early contributions to the 'Contemporary' (e.g. in his excellent essay on Lessing's life and work written in 1856) Chernyshevsky urged his readers to accept not only political institutions but philosophical schools as 'relative', rooted in peculiar historical contexts and in the social and economic conditions of their time.[66] Like Marx, but quite independently of him, he attributed to every philosopher a bias which belied the philosopher's claim to pursue 'objective' truth. Later, in a work dealing specifically and at length with philosophy (*Antropologichesky printsip v filosofii*—The Anthropological Principle in Philosophy, 1860), he wrote that 'all philosophical doctrines have been at all times conceived under a strong influence of the situation in society to which the philosopher belonged, and every philosopher represents one of the political parties struggling for social supremacy. . . . We shall not mention those thinkers who were avowedly concerned with the political side of life. Their involvement in political parties is self-evident.'[67] Hobbesian doctrines are shown to be appropriate to political absolutism, Locke embodied the prejudices of Whig mercantilism, Milton, of Protestant republicanism, and Montesquieu, of liberalism *à l'anglaise*, while Bentham's individualism hustled England into the full acceptance of the gospel of laissez-faire. The philosophy which suffered most from Chernyshevsky's deflationary treatment was idealism. Schelling, in his view, represented 'a party scared by revolution, seeking repose in medieval institutions and hoping for the restoration of the feudal State, destroyed in Germany by Napoleon I and the Prussian nationalists'. Hegel is described as a spokesman of 'moderate liberalism, extremely conservative in its conclusions, but admitting of revolutionary principles as a weapon against extreme reaction and aiming at the prevention of the growth of the revolutionary spirit which threatened an already crumbling antiquity'.[68]

Chernyshevsky did not consider how far the principle of social causation is to be carried, whether it should be applied to the technical problems of philosophy and to the criteria of scientific truth, or how to deal with the difficulty of infinite regression, since the belief that beliefs are socially conditioned must in itself be socially conditioned. But he was not, in the first place, concerned to show whether it is a good or a bad thing for man to be, intellectually and materially, a function of something else: rather he wished to identify man as he actually is in relation to his environment as well as to himself, to the changes in society as well as to 'objective' truth. Moreover, he was by no means consistent in his historicism. Side by side with statements that are strongly reminiscent of Marx's treatment of 'ideology' as 'super-structure', i.e. as the adoption of intellectual attitudes which embody and sanctify the interests of particular sections of a society, there are others which suggest that he believed in innate ideas, in the perennial conflict between good and evil, virtue and vice, the forces of change and immobility. The essay 'On the Causes of the Fall of Rome' (*O prichinakh padeniya Rima*) (1861), for example, illustrates largely the eighteenth-century doctrine that 'c'est l'opinion qui gouverne le monde'.[69] If challenged, Chernyshevsky would probably have been content with the common-sense view that what men do is governed by what they think, though what they think is partly or mainly governed by the conditions in which they live. On the whole, Chernyshevsky is more interesting and convincing when he talks about ideas as governed by social and historical circumstances than when he discusses them, as at times he does, in isolation and on their own merit.

It is the idealist Hegel, the dominant figure in nineteenth-century Russian intellectual history, who is largely responsible for introducing change as the essential category of philosophical and social thinking. And it is Hegel who taught Chernyshevsky that only to the extent that man understands the historical situation in which he is placed, both intellectually and materially, can he assert his freedom in that situation. As early as 1849 Chernyshevsky noted in his Diary that he was 'almost completely an adherent of Hegel', although he added that he might have 'to blush for this later on'.[70] Admittedly, at the time, he had to deal mainly with a Russified Hegel—Hegel as expounded and interpreted by such 'left' Hegelians as Bakunin and Herzen, who had an enormous influence on Chernyshevsky's early intellectual development. But even his somewhat later work on the Gogolian period in Russian literature contains an enthusiastic tribute to Hegel.[71] He was particularly impressed by what he took to be the revolutionary meaning of Hegel's Reason, which negates existing reality in the name of a more rational (and therefore more real) reality which it brings into being. Whenever Chernyshevsky shows a tendency to rationalism, this must be ascribed not so much to any influence on him of the eighteenth-century French *philosophes* (as some, notably Masaryk and Chizhevsky, have done) as to Hegel; for, with all his inconsistencies, he was deliberately working away from the idea of abstract, static divine Reason, or of abstract, static natural Reason, towards that of human reason which works in ever-changing historical circumstances.

And yet, Chernyshevsky soon came to vie with the earlier Russian critics of Hegel in saddling him with responsibility for the greatest imaginable, actual and potential crimes. Above all, Hegel now appeared to him as the great retarder of atheism, materialism, and revolution in virtue of the grandiose attempt he made to persuade one of the divinity of existence. 'He is', Chernyshevsky wrote in his Diary, 'a slave of the present state of affairs, of the established order, even to the point of hesitating to repudiate capital punishment, and so on. He draws only timid conclusions. . . . After all, did not Fichte arrive at a deification of the existing order? The characteristic feature of his (that is, Hegel's) philosophy is to keep away from radical transformations, to be *die zarte Schonung des Bestehenden*.'[72] In addition, Chernyshevsky increasingly found Hegel an incomprehensible, cloudy, and verbose writer who intoxicated and obfuscated the susceptible mind with a vast outpouring of abstractions.[73]

With Chernyshevsky's exceedingly irreverent attitude to recognized authorities of every kind, no philosopher seems to have kept a hold on him for any length of time. The one exception was Feuerbach, who was his first and enduring philosophical love. As before with Belinsky and Herzen, Feuerbach's celebrated *Das Wesen des Christentums* (forbidden in Russia) had the effect of an intellectual illumination on Chernyshevsky. 'I like his nobility, veracity, frankness and trenchancy', he noted in his Diary (25 February 1849) on reading the book for the first time. Much later, in 1877, he wrote to his sons from Siberia: 'If you wish to know what my views on the nature of man are, you can find them in the only thinker of our time who, I think, had a true understanding of things. This is Ludwig Feuerbach. I have not re-read him in the last fifteen years. Even before that I had little time to do so. But when I was young I knew whole pages of his book by heart. And as far as I can judge from my dim memory of him, I remain his faithful follower.'[74] At least two works by Chernyshevsky—his thesis on aesthetics and 'The Anthropological Principle in Philosophy' —were explicitly designed as essays in 'applied Feuerbach'. Feuerbach's influence on Chernyshevsky, nevertheless, has been disputed by some historians of Russian thought.[75]

There is little intrinsic interest in hunting for influences, since it is not the raw source that matters, but what is made of it. One can borrow what others say, but not the experience, the history, and the force which make one say it. It may be useful, however, to mention here that in three respects at least the undeservedly forgotten German thinker did play an important part in Chernyshevsky's intellectual development. Chernyshevsky became acquainted with him at a time when he, Chernyshevsky, was reconsidering his whole attitude to his religious past. Feuerbach seems to have given point to his growing conviction that to attain maturity he would have to face the future without any such 'irrational support' as is provided by religion. In the second place, Chernyshevsky readily yielded to Feuerbach's principal claim that in 'wishful thinking' is to be found the clue to all man's 'ideal' aspirations, and that man will recover his identity by ceasing to nourish himself on a dream. Finally, he felt more and more inclined to Feuerbach's view that 'philosophy had out-lived its time' and that 'the essence of philosophy consists in denying that it has any'. As a consequence, he took increasingly less interest in philosophical questions.[76]

Although modest as a man and ready to revise his views when confronted with incontrovertible evidence, Chernyshevsky leaves the impression of a rather assertive thinker, inclined to ignore or to underestimate theories and values which were outside his range. He would push aside thinkers who did not fit his pattern and treat with exaggerated importance those who happened to be going in the right direction. He would swear by Leucippus while scoffing at Kant, Helmholtz, and Lobachevsky. He was a great *simplificateur*, who, from unwillingness or lack of opportunity, at times failed to examine thoroughly the many scientific matters on which he entertained strong opinions, and who was misled as well as fascinated by the fact that classifications and generalizations are a necessary part of scientific thought. Chernyshevsky's unfaltering confidence is, indeed, better understood when it is realized that he lived, as we do, in a scientific age; that then, as today, nothing was so comforting as to be thought scientific; and that he was impressed, as perhaps we are not, by the beneficent results of all scientific activity.

The natural sciences [Mikhailovsky wrote] have from the very beginning of our revival, immediately after the Crimean war, drawn the attention [of the intelligentsia]. A great number of scientific books were translated and there appeared many popular articles on various scientific subjects. This is only partly to be explained by the fact that in pre-Reform times natural science enjoyed the curious status of a half-forbidden, and in a sense wholly forbidden, fruit. For this was largely true of every pursuit of knowledge in Russia. But even apart from the inevitable reaction, the awakened search for enlightenment was bound to be centred on the natural sciences. They provided genuine knowledge, because their evidence was based not on mere speculation but on observation . . . and experiment, leaving little room for equivocation. We stood in need of something unambiguous in order to cope with the mass of problems which showered down on us. Not surprisingly, sometimes we expected science to do what is not on its agenda.[77]

When the products of this scientific activity percolated down to the level of the ordinary mind they became translated—sometimes precipitately and often by men who were not themselves scientists—into a new world-view, reflecting both the rate and direction of scientific growth and the moral changes in Russian society which had affected that growth, or were affected by it. The moral enrichment which the new scientific culture gave to Russia was, indeed, very great. Whether professional scientists or not, most of its representatives were high-minded men, almost totally immune from indifference, self-indulgence, and moral vacuity.

For all the immense technical achievements of our age, they do not change our attitude to life, even when they promise to destroy an infinitely great number of people in infinitely little time: we have become accustomed to learn of a new scientific advance each week. But in the nineteenth, just as in the seventeenth, century science effected a revolution in the mental and moral climate. For Chernyshevsky, too, scientific activity was more than individual discoveries or items of accepted knowledge: it meant a manner of thinking, a perpetual reconstruction, in whole or in part, of one's experience of the world.

This explains, to some extent, the importance Chernyshevsky attached to the 'dialectical method', which also owed something to his Hegelian antecedents. Despite the assertive character of his thought and a preference for uniform explanations, it would be wrong to say, as some have done, that he suffered from a compulsive need for dogmatic finality. There was for him 'a perpetual change of forms, a perpetual rejection of all forms' springing from changes in man's condition. The dialectical method ensured that one was

not being lulled by any positive conclusion: it compelled a thinker to look for qualities and forces in a given object of thought which contradict anything that might have been gathered from it at first sight. In this way, a thinker was obliged to survey an object from all sides and truth appeared to him only at the end of a variety of conflicting notions. Instead of previously held one-sided views . . . he was enabled to perform a complete . . . inquiry and form a vital conception of objects as they really are.[78]

Seeing scientific activity in the context of human activity at large, Chernyshevsky sought from science guidance in human affairs. He never failed to realize the interdependence of science and the problems of human relations. He called for a wider vision among scientists and against rigid specialization. He considered scientific knowledge to be not only a means of finding the truth but also a way of gaining mastery over man's environment, not only a description but a therapy—in fact, a weapon for the establishment of a new society and civilization.[79] Hence the longing for the field to be wide open; hence the confident tone, the certainty that 'history' is on man's side; hence the brashness, the challenging and revolutionary temper. With Chernyshevsky's concentration on the sheer mechanics of living, on how men eat, work, build, and destroy, this intellectual attitude seems harsh and bare, but it is bracing in its directness.

. . . . .

Chernyshevsky was a materialist (although, curiously enough, he nowhere describes himself as such), that is, he believed that reality possesses one fundamental quality which is material, or that it is the sole perception of quantitative, measurable characteristics, such as extension, weight, motion, &c., which reveal to us reality. 'That which is is called matter', he stated. But what matter really is was never conclusively defined by Chernyshevsky (if, indeed, it is definable), for in this respect he is, as a rule, content with description, with oblique analogy, and we often find ourselves thrown back upon the short catechism: What is matter?—Never mind. What is mind?—'Tis no matter. At times, he uses arguments based on the atomistic theory upheld by many natural philosophers from the time of Democritus, according to which matter is composed of small indivisible particles. He assumed that any event which did not seem to flow from its antecedents was sure to do so if one broke it down into smaller and smaller pieces either of fact or of matter.[80] As is well known, the atomistic theory, although now largely abandoned, provided a stimulus for the study of physics and chemistry (based as these were believed to be on measurements); and Chernyshevsky, who always wished to be scientific, offers many proofs in favour of materialism which are derived from the armoury of the physical and chemical sciences.[81]

Elsewhere Chernyshevsky endows matter with vital and psychic qualities, so that it becomes, in many of its functions, energy, force, motion and mind. This resembled the early Greek, hylozoistic idea of nature as an organism, restated in fifteenth- and sixteenth-century philosophies, and later replaced by the idea of nature as a machine. 'Movement is reality', Chernyshevsky writes, 'because movement is life, and reality and life are one and the same thing.' The dehumanized, immutable matter of the atomists and eighteenth-century French materialists is forgotten, and matter is conceived in close relation to man's action upon his material environment, in the manner of Marxism. 'The chief element in life is work . . . and the truest sign of life is action.'[82]

At the same time, following Spinoza and often using Spinoza's language, Chernyshevsky stressed the unitary character of his outlook, inasmuch as he held that matter, or nature, is the only ultimate reality, containing all things, living as well as lifeless, conscious as well as unconscious. Every object or event is dependent on innumerable others, which ramify in all directions, and are each of them similarly dependent on others. The so-called mind is described by Chernyshevsky as a number of extremely complex reactions in the central nervous system. Thus he establishes a baffling identity between 'the process which occurred in the nervous system of Newton when he discovered the law of gravity and the process which takes place in the nervous system of a hen picking grains of oat in a heap of rubbish and dust'. And there is a lengthy explanatory passage which shows such an excessive preoccupation with animal behaviour as seemingly to turn Chernyshevsky into an animist and to revive the Greek notion of psychic and intellectual kinship between beans, cats, and human beings: animals, though inferior to men in their possession of a smaller amount of 'grey matter', find themselves endowed not only with 'memory, imagination and thought' but also with 'lofty, disinterested and ideal sentiments'. We are also told that all things, whether physical or spiritual, require the same method of inquiry, namely, the method of strict determinism used in natural science.[83] In applying the notion of the necessary interrelation of all things and all creatures to morality, Chernyshevsky concludes, somewhat unexpectedly, that 'the same law [of interrelation] reigns in moral life, and the moral law [sic] governs the life of man'.[84] In this as in some other respects, the legacy of Chernyshevsky's thought was diverse and contradictory enough to ensure dissension among his interpreters.

Although his philosophy is monistic as regards the one ultimate fabric of reality, it often appears pluralistic in regard to the material and mental attributes with which he credited it. 'While possessing a single nature,' he wrote, 'we recognize in man two different series of phenomena: those which possess a so-called material character (man eats, walks), and those which possess a so-called moral character (man thinks, feels, wills).'[85] He resisted the statements of certain contemporary German materialists (Vogt, Moleschott) to the effect that mental acts consist of matter and that the brain secretes thought in the same way in which the gall-bladder secretes gall. 'Thought has no material form', he said.[86] But Chernyshevsky's predominant view of matter as infinite in extent and permeated by movement, yet devoid of ultimate qualitative differences and moved by uniform quantitative forces, led him to seek to express too many things in mechanistic terms. He drew large cheques on non-existent scientific assets in favour of his materialistic interpretations, and dismissed awkward facts by the use of such vague terms of abuse as 'metaphysical', 'fantastic', or 'illusionist', much as indignant schoolgirls use the epithets 'frightful' and 'beastly'.

Sometimes, it is true, he seems aware that no kind of physical or chemical process in the nerve system is remotely like suffering and rejoicing, or composing music and painting pictures. He even admits that, strictly speaking, there does not exist a science without unverified if not unverifiable hypotheses; that science may turn anything into a problem, even if it has not yet shown the courage to admit that the nature of truth itself is problematic.[87] Similarly, he admits that physical explanations use similes and analogies which, while enabling us to make inferences and generalizations about things of which we have no direct experience, also serve to underline the fact that there are no instruments, or there are not yet any instruments, to measure thought and feeling. He even said that physical and mental acts denote 'wholly different qualities, and there is no concept to which one could reduce them, except the general concept of quality'. Plekhanov, who was a great admirer of

Chernyshevsky and to whom we owe one of the best monographs on him, is particularly insistent on this point.

Yurkevich [he writes about one of Chernyshevsky's philosophical opponents] has fathered upon Chernyshevsky the idea that there is no difference at all between material and mental phenomena, and asks with triumph, how it is that sensations arise from the twitches of nerves? This is a piece of hoary nonsense with which materialists have been pestered for ages, and from which one can only infer that those who claim to criticize materialism are ignorant of its first elements. Nowhere in his essay ['The Anthropological Principle in Philosophy'] does Chernyshevsky contend that there is no difference between so-called physical phenomena . . . and mental phenomena . . .: on the contrary, he positively acknowledges the existence of such a difference, yet he thinks that this gives no justification for ascribing mental phenomena to some special non-material agency.[88]

Nevertheless, Plekhanov, who as a dialectical materialist clearly distinguished between the way in which human minds behave and the way in which material objects behave, tended to read into Chernyshevsky a more radical and consistent distinction between physical and mental acts than seems to be justified by the evidence. For, whether or not Chernyshevsky may have flirted with two or more different theories, the essay in question contains passages where life is unmistakably reduced to 'a complex chemical process'. Mental phenomena are seen as the result of a greater number and a more intricate arrangement of quantitative, physical elements, different in degree and in the stage of development, but not in kind, from material phenomena.[89] This prompted Steklov, the Marxist author of another important work on Chernyshevsky, to say that 'he carries materialism to excessive logical conclusions'.[90] Towards the end of Chernyshevsky's life, however, his mechanistic views became less pronounced, and his commentaries on Weber's *Universal History*, which he was translating after his return from Siberia, are largely an explanation of the idea that 'the development of the mind' is the governing factor in life.

· · · · ·

It was essential for Chernyshevsky's materialism to deny the reality of 'ideas' and 'sensations' as conceived by idealist and empiricist epistemologies respectively. Accordingly, Chernyshevsky's theory of knowledge is 'realistic', to be more precise, 'naïvely realistic'. The existence of objects, in his view, is independent of their perception and they are apprehended directly as they are. He thought of the mind as a kind of camera taking snaps of reality. A camera must take objects independently existing, otherwise it would not be a camera but a machine for the production of uninformative patterns. Assuming the validity of this photographic analogy, Chernyshevsky (who preferred to speak in terms of reflection in mirrors rather than of photography) does not explain how a camera can take scenes which do not satisfy certain conditions of photography, or how a picture of 'reality' can be recorded unless it is photogenic. The very problem of the 'correlative' nature of human knowledge appeared to Chernyshevsky to be a piece of 'naturalistic nonsense'.

Most naturalists who attempt to construct comprehensive theories about the laws that govern human understanding [he wrote] repeat Kant's metaphysical theory about the subjective nature of our knowledge. They say, as Kant said, that the forms of our perception do not resemble the forms of really existing objects; that, therefore, objects, their real qualities and inter-relations, are unknowable. When naturalists will cease talking such or similar metaphysical nonsense they will be able . . . to elaborate a more precise and adequate system of knowledge based on natural science.[91]

By 'naturalists' Chernyshevsky meant a great variety of thinkers, including agnostics, neo-Humians, and neo-Kantians as well as traditional idealists and empiricists, for whom cognition provides patterns of sense data for interior interpretations, but does not make us aware of real things, or 'things in themselves' (*Dinge an sich*). He himself tried on several occasions to formulate his epistemological views. The following attempt, taken from the essay entitled 'The Character of Human Knowledge' (*Kharakter chelovecheskogo znaniya*), aimed at idealists and empiricists alike, is as typical and simple as any other:

Do we know of ourselves that we are human beings [Chernyshevsky asks]? If we do, our knowledge of the existence of the human organism must needs be an immediate knowledge, knowledge . . . without the admixture of any kind of cogitation. And if we have knowledge of our organism, we also have knowledge of the clothes we wear, the food we eat, the water we drink, &c. In short, as human beings we have knowledge of an infinite variety of objects—

a direct, immediate knowledge of objects in themselves: it is given to us by real life.

If this could still be construed into a recognition of self-awareness as the basis of our knowledge of external reality, the following quotation is unequivocal:

> We know objects. We know them exactly as they are in reality. Let us take the example of the sense of vision—a subject widely discussed by naturalists. They contend that knowledge gained by this means is untrustworthy or does not correspond entirely to the real qualities of objects. We see something, for example, a tree. Another observer sees the same tree. Look into his eyes! His pupils reflect exactly the same tree as seen by us. Two identical pictures: the first is seen by us directly, the second in the mirror of the other's eye. The second picture is an exact copy of the first one. What follows? The eye neither adds nor takes away anything whatever. . . . There is no difference between the two pictures. But does not 'the interior sensation', or 'the central tissues of the visionary organ', or 'the soul', or 'the activity of our consciousness' alter something in the picture? We know it does not. . . . The original and the copy are the same: our sensation is identical with the copy. Our knowledge of our sensation is one with our knowledge of the object. . . . We see objects as they really exist.[92]

All this does not appear to take us very far in understanding how knowledge is at all possible, as distinct from how one can get hold of some particular piece of information. It seems crude in matter and manner. But then Chernyshevsky was deliberately using his 'naïve realism' as a weapon for eliminating complexities which he tended to regard as narrow and obstructive pedantry. His account of human knowledge was an attempt to look reality straight in the face, instead of trying to explain it away with a myth, a word, and impression, or a preconceived idea. He wished, as he himself said, that a thinker should remain under the 'perpetual discipline of fact and reality'.

If Chernyshevsky's epistemological realism matched his materialism, this in turn goes some way towards explaining his utilitarian morality. Following Bentham and the Philosophical Radicals, Chernyshevsky had no use for *a priori* judgements about man's moral behaviour. His test of right and wrong was utility or pleasure or desirability. He argued, with Helvétius, Bentham, the Mills, and the other utilitarians, that just as the only things visible (and therefore real) are things seen, and the only things audible are things heard, so the only things desirable (and therefore good) are things desired. 'On examining closely the motives which guide man's behaviour,' Chernyshevsky wrote, 'we find that all actions, good and bad, noble and ignoble, heroic and cowardly, spring . . . from one source: man behaves in the way which pleases him most. He is influenced by considerations of expediency, prompting him to renounce the less advantageous and desirable for the sake of the more advantageous and desirable.' 'The aim of man's striving consists in finding pleasure.'[93] In confirmation, Chernyshevsky quotes the example of a wife mourning her husband, and explains that her grief is due to self-pity. Even heroic actions are self-regarding. Lucrecia stabbed herself because this was 'less unpleasant than living in a state of humiliation'. 'On closer scrutiny we shall discover that an action or sentiment which appears to us disinterested has, none the less, its origin in the consideration of personal advantage, personal pleasure, personal welfare, i.e., in the sentiment known as egoism.'[94]

Thus, following Bentham, Chernyshevsky denied that human behaviour can be intrinsically good or evil, and judged it by its ascertainable effects, or as an outgrowth of human 'inclination' or 'self-realization'. The preference for 'inclination' and 'self-realization' owed perhaps not so much to Bentham as to Rousseau, for whom Chernyshevsky had a great if critical regard.[95] Since a moral system created from ordinary human experience cannot be viable for anything more than a given time and place, Chernyshevsky maintained, with perfect consistency and more explicitly than Bentham, that all morality is historically and individually conditioned. He rejected natural law in both its theological and metaphysical forms as a sanction of moral standards. This was sustained by Chernyshevsky's identification of the order of the human world with that of the material universe. There was no transcendent purpose in the universe, but there was human purpose which can be known from a scientific analysis of the material conditions of human life and human society. It will be seen later, in connexion with Chernyshevsky's discussion of Darwinism, that he was not unaware of the limitations of naturalistic categories when applied to the study of human society. Still, 'moral events', he wrote, originate in other moral events and in external circumstances according to the law of causality: hence it is erroneous to conceive the idea of a phenomenon which is not derived from antecedent phenomena and from external circumstances. Modern psychology does not . . . admit such a proposition as this: 'man has committed a bad action in a given case because he willed to act in this way, whereas in another case he has committed a good action because he intended to do so'. It holds that a bad or a good action is necessarily due to some moral or material factors, or a mixture of these, whilst the 'willing' here denotes merely the subjective impression of our consciousness which accompanies the inception of thoughts and actions from antecedent thoughts or actions or external facts.[96]

This kind of language, derived in part from eighteenth-century idiom, left no room for the irreducible and irrational in human behaviour, for all those facts where we deal not with things and objects, but with willing and choosing human beings and their relationships. The problem of freedom was Chernyshevsky's greatest stumbling-block, and he would have swept it away into unreality had he not let it reappear by the backstairs in his idea of man as the creator as well as the creature of his environment. The preference for seeing freedom as essentially a force which, in a given situation, controls or modifies or compels the world to behave in a certain way, rather than as an assumption by man, or an imposition on man, of moral responsibility for the consequences of his actions, was largely due to Chernyshevsky's instinctive aversion (which he shared with Herzen) for what might be called 'forensic morality'. The idea of free will and responsibility should not be confined to those aspects of behaviour which were amenable to reward and punishment, for then it could equally well be applied to rats in mazes. Chernyshevsky's dominant reaction was to treat nothing as irrational or fortuitous that could conceivably lie within man's control. He had nothing but contempt for those who make use of a pretended insight into human behaviour to obscure the social truth and who are prompted, as, for instance, Kavelin and Samarin were prompted, to agree with Muraviev, who justified hanging people with the argument that it served to demonstrate the moral freedom and accountability of the hanged victims for the consequences of their actions.

Still, it is impossible for necessity to emancipate itself; nor can natural science alone prove that, for instance, it is bad to enjoy the infliction of cruelty. As it happens, with all the rigidity which causal and utilitarian categories imposed on his ethical reflection, Chernyshevsky began with the bias of a man endowed with an acute moral conscience and sense of moral discrimination. His attempt to elaborate a view of what is likely to produce the greatest good was, in fact, to a large extent a rationalization of his innate moral bias. This was strong enough to move him to impress on his sons in letters from Siberia that 'honour and conscience are the foremost standard for judging historical facts at all times and in all nations'. It also had a self-defeating effect on his utilitarianism for 'pleasure' is a theoretically useless category if one has to qualify it, as Bentham, Chernyshevsky, and some other utilitarians often did, by explicitly or implicitly distinguishing between good pleasure and bad pleasure. For Bentham a rational assessment of self-gratification and expediency was to result in universal contentment. 'To possess social virtue', he wrote, 'means to sacrifice one's own pleasure, in order that by means of serving the interests of others we may attain a greater degree of pleasure.'[97] 'Pleasure' here meant, no doubt, nothing more or less than that moral good consists in the tendency of an object or an action to conduce to happiness as an end, or, in brief, that, as another utilitarian said, 'if goodness is not this then heaven knows what it is'. But Bentham's incurable optimism inclined him to the view that the steady pursuit of one's own aggrandizement is a guarantee for the happiness of others. 'Reproducing in a . . . spiritless fashion what Helvétius had said before him more brilliantly', Marx observed unkindly, 'this pedantic arch-philistine' assumed 'a modern petty *bourgeois*, and a modern English petty *bourgeois* at that, to be the normal man. Whatever seems useful to this queer sort of normal man and to his world is regarded as useful in and by itself.'[98]

Chernyshevsky had no such optimistic estimate of human conduct, and, as will be seen later, he did not share the belief in the natural harmony of interests. What he did was to invert Bentham's hedonistic calculus: he declared that it is the failure to pursue the common good as one's own which brings ruin to oneself. In other words, he qualified every expression of his belief that the goodness of man would lead him to follow his best interests by a statement, not unfamiliar among revolutionary apologetics, of the disaster in store if he failed to do so. '"They perished like the Avars"', says Chernyshevsky, referring here to groups of men rather than to individuals: 'these words from an ancient Russian Chronicle are spoken by history over each people and each estate that has fallen into the fatal error of opposing its own advantage to the human interests at large.' 'The Spaniards devastated Europe at the time of Charles V and Philip II and themselves came to grief. The French devastated Europe at the time of Napoleon I and were themselves destroyed in 1814/1815.'[99]

Clearly then, Chernyshevsky was no mere Benthamite. At any rate, his utilitarianism did not entitle him to a place among the comfortable individualists who pretend that their natural impulse to promote their own interests serves the needs of others. Altogether, one cannot help thinking that the life of the hunted radical in the Siberian wastes is a sad comment on his utilitarian speculation. But, in addition, Chernyshevsky paid lofty tributes to entirely disinterested actions, and this drove him into inconsistencies.[100]

In the last resort, it was impossible to be a thorough-going utilitarian in nineteenth-century Russia. As a matter of fact, although a branch of nineteenth-century positivism, utilitarian doctrines did not seem to fit into the pattern of European nineteenth-century thought as a whole, which expressed itself more characteristically in Hegel and Marx, in Nietzsche and Dostoevsky than in Bentham, Malthus, and the Mills; and even John Stuart Mill found himself using arguments which helped to destroy Bentham and utilitarianism. But in so far as the utilitarian analysis was made in terms of individual rather than social behaviour, Chernyshevsky had learnt from it. His readiness to do so was due partly to his own inability to make reason supple and subtle enough to include the incalculable; partly to his refusal to disguise realities. He owned to a rooted dislike of 'the lovers of fine ideas and the advocates of sublime aspirations', and he took a Rochefoucauldian pleasure in showing how even the most generous impulses can be traced back to the basic animal necessity of defending one's material interests.

．　　．　　．　　．　　．

A history of ideas must do more than tell us what past thinkers thought, or even whether they were right or wrong in thinking as they did. It must explain how they came to hold their views. It is important, therefore, to look for the governing factor in Chernyshevsky's philosophical doctrines, for his *idée maîtresse*, for what Balzac called the 'dominant passion'. Such a procedure seems particularly suitable in the case of Chernyshevsky, for much of the 'outside' in his outlook is rough and springs from misconceptions, while the 'inside' contains a profound moral and intellectual experience, into which it is necessary to enter.

Ever since man emerged from the primitive state, the physical and spiritual sides of his being have been in conflict. This has been the price and condition of his self-consciousness, and, as often as not, the victories of the spirit, because they have been one-sided or illusory, have been followed by defeats as the alienated body reasserted its rights. The same pattern of conflict is seen in the ancient feud between idealism and materialism, in which religion and natural science have in more modern times assumed leading roles, even though their opposition seems to stir only faint echoes today. There was nothing original in Chernyshevsky's attitude to this controversy. Indeed, a comparison with the materialistic (or 'anthropological') ideas of Feuerbach, or Herzen, or even Belinsky will show his materialism as commonplace and lacking that keen insight which enabled Herzen to see 'matter' and 'spirit' at, as it were, their full stretch. And yet, Chernyshevsky's concentration on material reality never took him beyond the pale of human values, as was largely the case with the 'vulgar' or 'metaphysical' materialists of the eighteenth century. His materialism could dispense with the idea of matter as an object, or a special substance, which is as much an ideal construction—a 'skeleton in the cupboard'— as the 'spirit' or the 'transcendental ego' of the idealist school, and which prompted the French materialist Holbach to close his famous work *Du système de la Nature* with what is nothing more or less than a prayer to matter. In Chernyshevsky's time eighteenth-century materialism was to all intents and purposes already dead, alike in Russia and in western Europe, and Hegel had prevented it from striking any deep roots in Russia even before then; although its spirit, acquiring a new surcharge of knowledge (especially biological knowledge) and reforming ardour, may have lived on in many Russian and non-Russian radicals.

Before deciding to reject or to accept Chernyshevsky's position, then, it is essential to take into account the starting-point of his materialistic speculations. This will show that, in the last analysis, metaphysical materialism and idealism alike falsified, in his view, the relation between man and the world. It may be said that the notions of spirit and matter, of subject and object, fail to convey anything important about human existence, except, perhaps, in so far as they are rationalizations of certain deplorable possibilities of human arrogance and human impotence. A man so completely self-centred as to behave like a sovereign ego is insane; a man so oppressed by circumstances as to react like matter is dead. Chernyshevsky insisted that unless we begin by focusing attention on the living organism and its functions, we shall continue to regard experience as divided into spheres—the material and the spiritual—between which there will remain an unbridgeable gulf. 'Life' and 'consciousness' are not merely connected: they are identical. The underlying idea is not of an allegedly all-material or all-spiritual universe but of man who is both spirit and matter. The point is simple enough, indeed so simple as to make it almost superfluous to say it. Chernyshevsky made the point by the very title he chose for his most avowedly materialistic work —'The Anthropological Principle in Philosophy'. He made more of it by insisting again and again that man cannot be 'divided into compartments' and 'truncated by means of surgical operations'; that 'the obsolete pursuit of confining human life solely to the head or to the stomach is absurd and obnoxious'; that the mind-body dichotomy is inapplicable to man.[101]

Admittedly, having rejected the dichotomy, Chernyshevsky often goes on to maintain with the fervour of a proselyte that only one of the alleged opposites exists. But the heart of the matter is in man himself, and nothing could deflect Chernyshevsky from that conviction. The process of life is unitary, embodying mental and spiritual as well as physical and material qualities, but the focus of the process is man. Spirit is not matter, Chernyshevsky admitted, but we can never conceive of the spirit of anyone whom we love detached from the look and smile through which we recognize it.

What is a human face: eyes, voice, gesture [Chernyshevsky asks with Belinsky]? It is all body, external appearance, that is, something transient, fortuitous, of no account: it is neither feeling, nor mind, nor will. Yet through it alone we glimpse feeling and mind and will. Mind without body, without countenance; mind which does not act on the blood and does not absorb its action into itself is a figment, a deathly abstraction. Mind is man in the body, or rather man through the body—in short, a person.[102]

Wherever Chernyshevsky and Belinsky or, for that matter, Herzen differed, they were at one in using their materialist interpretation as a way to express their vision of man as a whole, from within as well as from without, and as the centre of life rather than an object or instrument or symbol of supra-human forces. Their common attack on the metaphysical cult was nothing if not a search for the human meaning of existence, although Herzen had the perspicacity, lacking in Chernyshevsky, to admit that people will strangely persist in asking metaphysical questions, even if they cannot answer them.

Chernyshevsky's writings abound in declarations of impassioned humanism. 'However much one may be attracted by natural science', he wrote, 'the most important and fundamental science is and will remain the science of man'; 'in the whole sensible world man is the supreme being. . . . Man and human life are man's most intimate and dearest reality'; without man there is neither nature, nor life, nor 'reality'—all these are merely 'allusions and prefigurations of the revelation of man'; 'only he who seeks to be completely human is good'; 'man must look at everything through human eyes', &c.[103] A perceptive critic of Chernyshevsky, Kotlyarevsky, called attention to the fact that Chernyshevsky responded eagerly to Feuerbach precisely because the latter's *Essence of Christianity* was received in Russia as a kind of canonical book of the 'religion of humanity'.[104] But Chernyshevsky rightly suspected that in raising man to the status of a deity Feuerbach had lost sight of real man, known in the here and now; that he had substituted an abstract idea of man, or the genus man, or humanity in general for the concrete human person who, as often as not, fell victim to the claims of the abstraction mankind.

It is particularly important to take account of Chernyshevsky's treatment of the traditional problem of the relation between 'the universal' and 'the particular', although scarcely any student of his thought has considered it in this connexion. Criticizing in his treatise on art some of the familiar propositions of idealist aesthetics, notably the idea that excellence in art consists in its 'universalizing virtue', Chernyshevsky says: 'It is impossible to agree with this view, for it is based on a false opposition between the universal significance of a being and its actual reality, on the presupposition that "by assuming individual character the universal loses its universality".'[105] For Chernyshevsky the particular and individual are primary qualities. The universal does not lie in an ideal transcendental sphere which exists above man, in its own right, or which stands to him in the relation of a whole to a part. On the contrary, it owes its origin to the particular; it exists solely in singular beings, *in rebus*, not as an objective reality with an independent life of its own. It is by 'incorporation' in the singular, in the total experience of a human being that the universal becomes real. As a rule, we notice in men those things which they have in common, that by which they conform to type; but it is the dissimilar, the peculiar in them which is important and significant. 'Do real events have a universal aspect?' Chernyshevsky asks. His answer is in the affirmative, but he concludes that 'the original has universal meaning in its very individuality'.[106] Hence his predominant interest—even when he was talking about philosophy—in the flux of human life, before it has been forced into the abstract categories of speculative thought: 'there is no abstract truth', he says, 'but only concrete truth' and 'a definite judgement can be made only about a definite, particular thing'.

Chernyshevsky's business was man as he is known, face to face with other men—a seeing, feeling, willing, acting being, weighed down by flesh and blood and enduring his common, or rather uncommon, human plight. Far from preventing Chernyshevsky from recognizing men in their unique, personal character, his materialism helped him to see the inevitability with which they disclose their individuality, even when they concentrate on reaching an altogether worldly, material object. On the contrary, it was in the search for salvation in

other-worldly regions, whether in life after death or in intro-
verted beatitude here and now at the expense of the endurance of
the human world, that Chernyshevsky saw a betrayal of man. And
it was the search for teleological explanations, turning man into
a means to the accomplishment of all-embracing transcendental
aims, which, in his view, served to cast out the human element
in life. The erasing of the line drawn between the existing
world and that in which deity or absolute excellence existed,
therefore, implied for him a liberation of humanity. Materialism,
restrictive though it was, proved justified in the end: it was a
necessary step which enabled Chernyshevsky to build up his
case for man.

In this context, even Chernyshevsky's 'naïve realism' will
appear in a new light. His resistence to epistemological idealism
was prompted by a desire 'to see things as they are'; but it also
came from his unwillingness to see knowledge as exclusively
discursive, and man as a purely cognitive being, standing outside the world, with a set of self-regarding intellectual states, or
waiting for Aeolian visitations. Knowledge to Chernyshevsky had
for its principle a real, conative and social being, who attains
knowledge not in the abstract, by passive illumination, but by
identifying himself with the world which he is trying to survey.

Reality [he writes] embraces both dead nature and human life,
the present and the past (inasmuch as it embodies human action)
as well as the future (inasmuch as it is projected by the present). . . .
Thought is not opposed to reality, because it is born of reality and
seeks realization. . . . What is opposed to reality are idle dreams born
of inaction—the pastime of those who sit tight, aloof and with
screwed-up eyes. In the same way 'practice' embraces man's
intellectual and moral as well as his material activity.[107]

Man does not stand outside the world: he goes to make it, even
while striving to know it. 'To see things as they are' is not, after
all, sufficient to define the philosopher's task. It is only a part
of the process of acting with reference to them; and it reflects
the 'relative' character of reality which consists in the constant
interaction of subject and object, of man and his environment.
Chernyshevsky recognizes that, oddly enough, no philosopher in
fact confines himself to the disinterested pursuit of timeless truth.[108]
We see philosophers trying to impose their vision on the world;
we see them writing books and gaining power, or seeking it.

Admittedly, despite his Hegelian training, Chernyshevsky belonged to a world in which the cult of mechanistic explanations was still alive. He considered science to be largely a mechanism, even if he wished it to be a mechanism that would help to modify and control the world, rather than an activity in the post-Einsteinian sense, surrounded by an area of uncertainty and unpredictability and working with ill-defined quantities because it is built from them. He could not imagine matter becoming energy, as physicists have now proved all too devastatingly to be the case, although he came near to this notion by endowing matter with the qualities of force and motion. But his idea of facts and objects as a 'presentation of human activity'; his attempt to put man's creative mind at the centre of knowledge, as part of the structure of the world which is to be known; and his insistence on 'practice' as 'the crucial test of every philosophy' all have an unexpectedly modern ring about them.[109] Not surprisingly, traditional academic philosophers in Russia dismissed him as too pragmatic. Like Marx, he wished to substitute the philosophical task of changing the world for that of interpreting it. Reading some of Chernyshevsky's remarks about the function of mind in human life, or about reality being what man makes of it, one might even conclude—rashly no doubt—that the Berkeleian or Kantian wheel has come full circle. But it is beyond question that knowledge for Chernyshevsky at once embodies and justifies man's creative effort, and that man the maker, the 'practitioner' takes precedence for him over the thinker and observer. It will be seen later that Chernyshevsky also approached Marx in his idea of labour as the fullest expression of man's humanity.

It has been said that whatever importance Chernyshevsky may have attributed to man in his social doctrine, his views on morality show him up as a pronounced anti-humanist and anti-individualist, and that his notion of the good as synonymous with the useful militates against the value and dignity of man no less than the notion of the good as synonymous with the necessary or inevitable, later adopted by some Russian Marxists.[110] This is not the place to compare Chernyshevsky's utilitarianism with the 'necessitarianism' of the Russian Marxists. There are reasons to believe, however, that the utilitarian morality of

Chernyshevsky carried in itself the articulation of his essential belief in man and in the human person.

It was inevitable perhaps that the very word 'utilitarian' should accumulate a semantic load of disapproval, because all criteria of rightness which make it a mere function of expediency, of private or collective advantage, call in question the existence of truth. Whilst little evidence can be adduced for the usefulness of truth, history abounds with instances of the enormous advantages falsehood can bring. The leaders of human societies have always set a high value on the socially useful lie and have consistently employed elaborate religious, national, and political mythologies in pursuing it, and even claiming scientific value for it. Similarly, common interest or agreement among men has proved to be of doubtful value as a criterion of goodness. Actually, the converse statement that morality is a function of disagreement, dissent rather than consent, may define more clearly genuine morality. Few things show this more than Chernyshevsky's own drama of dissent and martyrdom.

Nevertheless, there was an important truth in the utilitarian idea of goodness, precisely because it gave expression to moral value as a function of human existence, as something which served a foremost human purpose. By taking as its object the happiness of man, by insisting on the maximum development and co-ordination of each man's individual powers, it became an instrument of practical humanism. In deriving his ethical notions from human experience, from human 'inclination', rather than from any abstract principle of man's destiny, the utilitarian gained an understanding of the real human situation. It is this that made Chernyshevsky discredit marriage as an institution, a socialized relationship between individual human beings. No social institution ever has been or will be built on an idiosyncrasy. Yet, as has been seen, the idiosyncratic basis of marriage was precisely what Chernyshevsky was advocating, as against marriage based on a body of built-up law and custom, or on the relations of property and domination, and acquiring gravity in the face of all personal sentiment.

The classical objection to morality based on human experience is that no moral theory is genuine unless the ethical imperative is seen as something which imposes itself on us, i.e. that there is a fundamental distinction between what men do and what they ought to do, and not as a mere outgrowth of human inclinations. But a pragmatist may reject as vain fabrications of the mind any ideal world or rule of life precisely because he believes moral value to reside in the ability to choose without any general guiding principle, without extraneous, objective standards by which to decide what is good or bad.

These, however, were not questions with which Chernyshevsky concerned himself, except perhaps in so far as he helped in the undoing of Absolutes and shining moral credos, which appeared to him as masks for other views and other conduct. His, as Bentham's, effort to add up pleasures in a hedonistic calculus was pedantic or inhuman. It may be said that the world's great values arise not out of pleasure but out of affliction. Still, though one might regret the ending of such values, one would welcome their end if it heralded the end of misery. And Chernyshevsky's utilitarianism showed that, though to seek one's own well-being may be trivial and inhuman, to seek to reduce the misery of others is both important and eminently human.

. . . . .

Nothing is likely to provide a greater understanding of the driving force of Chernyshevsky's speculations than his celebrated controversy with Yurkevich. Pamfil Yurkevich (1827–74) was a professor of philosophy at the Kiev Theological Academy. After his indictment of Chernyshevsky he was promoted in 1861 to the chair of philosophy at the University of Moscow. As a private individual Yurkevich was unimpeachable, and as a technical philospher, though grave, sententious, and often dull, he was more competent and skilful than his opponent. His philosophy was eclectic—a mixture of Platonic metaphysics with Kantian ethics and Berkeleian epistemology. He believed that all objects are mental in character or, at any rate, that their existence depends on an apprehending or knowing subject; and he tended to regard this subject not as a finite human mind but as the Absolute, or absolute goodness, which 'turns ideas into reality'.[111] In 1860 Yurkevich published two articles on materialism in the 'Transactions of the Kiev Theological Academy' (*Trudy Kievskoy dukhovnoy akademii*, No. 4), one of which—'An Essay on the Human Spirit' (*Iz nauki o chelovecheskom dukhe*)—was specifically aimed at Chernyshevsky's 'The Anthropological Principle'. The 'Transactions', however, offered little opportunity of reaching the wider public and Yurkevich was invited by Katkov to avail himself of the 'Russian Messenger'. The article in question duly appeared in Katkov's paper in a slightly abridged form, but provided with extensive and incisive commentaries by Katkov himself.

Although lucidly written, reasonable in tone—the acrimony was supplied by Katkov—and containing lines of argument admirably pursued, it proved, nevertheless, one of those statements which are more effective in confirming the prejudices of the convinced than in persuading the doubters. It was a piece of dissociated cerebration, a spider's web of obsolete ingenuity. To Katkov Yurkevich was a godsend and he put the professor to his own uses by publicizing him as a great Russian tom-cat playing with a horrid little mouse before strangling it. Yurkevich, a well-meaning and good-natured man, left the strangling to others. To change the metaphor, he just charged on—painstakingly if not very stirringly—into an empty countryside, while the real battle was being fought out elsewhere. What he saw was Chernyshevsky's 'materialism', in dominant close-up, with everything else out of focus and oblivious of the fact that Chernyshevsky could not be judged by mere technical arguments.[112]

Indeed, no intellectual change can occur when one system of thought gets, or claims to get, the better of another: it appears only when the underlying conviction yields to criticism, and the mind receives an impulse to new insights. Yurkevich was manifestly incapable of such criticism. Instead of trying to understand his opponent's position by seeing what led or might have led him to adopt it, he was looking for technical objections, based mainly on deductive reasoning, which might prove or disprove it. He came down from 'upper reality', from 'the higher forms of being', where, in his view, man's 'natural home' lies, to show the category mistakes committed by the materialists. He wished to induce a new appreciation of idealism which inspires 'all minds and hearts inclined towards goodness and beauty' with the noblest sentiments, and to preach 'peace with one's fellow-men as a condition of Christian social living'. Admittedly, he insisted on the need to take into account 'the empirical approach', to accommodate philosophy and religion to changes in the development of human opinion. He was even prepared to veer with the winds that blow from scientific laboratories, while fighting shy of any field in the new scientific experience where knowledge could possibly be perilous. Chernyshevsky, haunted as he was by a sense of historical urgency, could not help being struck and shocked by the sheer distance at which Yurkevich's anti-materialist credo stood from reality, both factual and human. The credo was made real only to the extent to which it was harnessed to Russian actualities and moved towards the standard end of vindicating divine providence in them. These issued, in fact, in a special kind of materialism and utilitarianism, in a profession of faith, which, for all its avowed spirituality and godliness, depended on material guarantees and advantages, or even became conterminous with the material conditions in which it grew and seemed like perishing. No real discussion could possibly take place between the two opponents. They were divided from each other not so much by the barriers of different philosophical assumptions, however real these may have been, nor by the occasional deftness of Yurkevich's metaphysical argumentation and Chernyshevsky's tone-deafness to metaphysical problems, as by totally different conceptions of what is and what is not important.

It is true that a thinker can be out of touch with reality and still stimulate, as Konstantin Leontiev proved. But in that case he must be genuinely controversial, and controversy, that is to say controversy about the basic experiences of human life and society, was something which people in Yurkevich's position avoided like a plague. Unlike Chernyshevsky, Yurkevich had neither pondered nor felt the human situation, nor did he speak the intellectual language of moral and historical experience. He remained fixed in the posture of a theological professor uttering timeless truths, but cushioned by bishops, Putyatins and Katkovs from shock, displacement and want in the real world around. Indeed, his metaphysical truths appeared like a machinery of acquiescence whose by-product was Bezdna, the Alexis ravelin, and Siberian penal servitude for the materialists.

No wonder that Yurkevich's dialectics served only to provoke exasperation in Chernyshevsky. And this was enhanced by a simultaneous campaign against him and his group of collaborators on the part of the conservative and liberal press, with the 'Russian Messenger' in the vanguard: they were branded as 'the monsters of negation' who 'must be destroyed before they succeed in undermining the foundations'. Accordingly, Chernyshevsky's reply to Yurkevich ('Polemical Beauties' — *Polemicheskie krasoty* in the 'Contemporary', 1861, nos. 6 and 7) turned into one of the most ill-tempered utterances he ever made throughout his journalistic career. Perhaps he would not have been *raznochinets* if he did not lose his head, grow irritable and dogmatic in turns, forget his subject in his concern to rebut a socially compromised and therefore untenable position, and rush in with views and even abuse. He cut short a quotation from Yurkevich's article on the explicitly stated ground that he had neither the time nor the space to go on, and he declared that his opponent's views were utterly uninteresting to him and that it bored him to argue with 'stiff-necks' (*rutinyory*).

I was myself a seminarist [he wrote in a slightly milder passage]. I know from experience the conditions in which people like Yurkevich have been brought up. I have seen people holding his position. It is distressing to laugh at him: it means laughing at the inability to obtain decent books, at the extreme frustrations which attend one's intellectual development, at conditions of unimaginable oppression in every respect. I do not know how old Mr. Yurkevich is: if he is old it is too late to come to his assistance. But if he is still young I will with pleasure supply him with books from my inextensive library.

And when Chernýshevsky was accused by the 'Annals of the Fatherland' of side-tracking the issue he offered his critic the loan of his seminary cribs which, he claimed, repeated word for word Yurkevich's arguments. 'These people adopt a tactic', Chernyshevsky concluded obscurely, 'of whose spuriousness they must know themselves.'[113] Since he did not enjoy Yurkevich's protected status, Chernyshevsky had to veil his counter-attack in the customary fashion, but it was sufficiently outspoken to have become an important contributory factor in his own elimination and in the suppression of the 'Contemporary'.[114]

Hardly anybody heeded Chernyshevsky's concealed warning that his opponents were dealing not merely with speculative abstractions but with other, more urgent issues. There were, however, two memorable exceptions: Dostoevsky (before he began making up to Katkov and Pobedonostsev) and Bukharev (before he was rendered harmless by the ecclesiastical authorities). 'Who else but you would think, especially at such a time as ours,' Dostoevsky addressed himself in his own paper 'Time' to Chernyshevsky's detractors, 'of jeering and taunting such people from the recesses of your studies, where you sit in Olympian quiet? Blessed is he who, even in the unadorned, can recognize its historic, serious side! Are you not yourselves guilty of the phrase-mongering of which you accuse your opponent? But your capacity for rant does not conceal your real aim. You merely pretend to worry about science. Nothing distresses you. You merely want to show up all progressives as dishonest people. . . . No serious person, capable of sympathy and discernment . . . could have adopted such a supercilious attitude. You have only succeeded in displaying the depth of your cynicism' and 'your love of stability and repose', which 'serve current material interests, often to the detriment of the majority of your fellow men. . . .' 'Why should someone who is mistaken be branded as a scoundrel? There are times when . . . upheavals and a sense of urgency testify to the abundance . . . of life. . . . These outcasts at least try to do something; they delve in order to find a way out; they err and thereby save others . . . , but you can only grin in a melodramatic posture of unconcern.'[115]

Dostoevsky realized that in Chernyshevsky's materialistic discourse, behind the owlish spectacles of this 'bug-stinking gentleman', the decisive moral and intellectual battle of Russia was being fought out. Yurkevich, on the other hand, was merely known to exist.

Dostoevsky got away with his defence of Chernyshevsky. Alexander Bukharev's lot led him along no easy path. He did not take a direct part in the controversy, but his already quoted book *On Orthodoxy in Relation to the Contemporary World* appeared while it was still raging, and he was the only ecclesiastical writer who declared openly, but with characteristic amiability, that to taunt an unbeliever such as Chernyshevsky with the shallowness of his thought is no solution of the problems he had raised. These, he said, arise from the increasing and gnawing sense of unreality and insincerity that accompany the religious ideals and aims of man. A Christian's faith ought to enable him to admit the possibility of it being thrown back at him; he ought to speak with relevance not so much through

his possession of an unassailable truth as through his closeness
to the sufferings, the perplexity, and the hope of his time, in
which and with which, Bukharev believed, the spirit of Christ
was working.[116]

A prominent ecclesiastical journalist, Askochensky, whose
denunciations of Bukharev exceeded even Katkov's diatribes
against Chernyshevsky, was horrified at the suggestion that
as he (Askochensky) wrote, 'spiritual and secular literature
could pursue the same aim of truth and goodness; that, for
instance, the "Contemporary" with its whistle [a reference to the
satirical supplement of the review called "The Whistle"] or the
"Russian Word" with its husky scream . . . share the aims of
"Christian Reading", "Spiritual Conversation", "Reading Useful
for the Soul", and similar pious journals that have not succumbed
to sinful modernity'.[117] But Askochensky was mistaken. Bukharev
never supported such lofty claims for the latter publications.
The whole burden of his argument was that, in an age of cant,
make-believe and expediency, both in religion and politics,
a persecuted radical whose beliefs are lop-sided is more interesting from the point of view of 'truth and goodness' than a comfortable professor whose beliefs are beyond question.

It remains to say a few words about Chernyshevsky's personal
attitude to religion. Attempts have been made to present much
of his work as a secularized version of traditional religious
attitudes, as an embodiment, or an inversion, of the beliefs of
his fathers.[118] In doing so some commentators tend to build
too much on too little and to indulge in flights of fancy. None
the less, it is true that Christianity played a large if not very
deep part in Chernyshevsky's early life, and it remained to some
extent an element in his consciousness, and to a larger extent
in his conduct. His way of life had the self-dedication and
singleness of mind and purpose normally reserved for religion;
and he employed the tenacity imparted by his religious education to rid himself of the restraints which this education had
laid upon the mind. Religious attitudes can be detected in his
Diary references to the radicals who, while professing an optimistic philosophy, are committed to a world which they see as
a malevolent, lying and loveless place, and who are guilty of
'the really terrible thing': to want it to be good. Traces of the
same are to be found in the novel *What Is to Be Done?*, in which

one character, Rakhmetov, renounces the flesh and sleeps on nails in order to prepare himself for suffering in the cause of revolution; and which contains even the character of an enlightened priest (Mertsalov), who dedicates himself to the work of the 'communal association'. At any rate, the claim supported in some quarters that Chernyshevsky was an atheist and a materialist in his teens if not in his cradle does not bear scrutiny.[119]

The evidence suggests that at the age of twenty-two Chernyshevsky was still wavering. 'What if we are to expect a new religion?', he wrote in his Diary in 1848. 'I am disturbed and shaken in heart and mind by the idea: I would have liked to keep the past alive . . . I would feel greatly grieved at parting with Jesus Christ, who is so righteous and so dear for his goodness and love of men.' In a 'confession' dated 2 August of the same year he noted: 'Theology and Christianity: cannot say anything definite; at bottom, am probably still holding on to the old—more from habit. But somehow or other this does not seem to go together with my other views and notions and is, therefore, seldom remembered and has little effect on life and on the mind.' He ends the confession with the words 'Thy will be done, O Lord!' as if submitting his unbelief to God. Later still (29 February 1849), he noted again: 'Religion: I know nothing. I believe in God and pray to him on important occasions—from habit, that is, in virtue of ingrained notions. But is this real conviction?' There followed moments of even greater indecision and vacillation (20 January 1850). Towards the end of that year he wrote that he had reached 'such scepticism as to surrender almost completely to the teaching of Feuerbach'. But Chernyshevsky was not a man of sudden revelations, and the religious crisis meant no serious spiritual disorientation for him. There were no agonies and no 'dark nights': only uneasiness at the necessity of tearing himself away from at once loved and hated roots. 'There are moments in life', he said, 'when one envies people of deep religious faith: for me such a moment was my mother's death. I knew that everything between us was finished. I did not expect any meeting in the other world. There would be no more explanations. Yet so much has remained unsaid, and one was left with the void of separation.'[120]

At the end of this road, however, there was a sense of release on losing a burden which he was no longer capable of enjoying and which, above all, had ceased to fit his convictions and the real world around him. Having abandoned religion, he was no longer haunted by the ghost of the dead faith. But he retained throughout his life a respect for genuine religious conviction, as is shown not only in his attitude towards his father (who died about a year before Chernyshevsky's imprisonment) or towards another priest (Ioann Popov), whom he used to meet during his term in Vilyuisk jail, but also in the tone of some of his articles dealing with religious matters.[121] His unbelief differed from the moral protestations of Belinsky, from the Promethean anti-theism of Bakunin, and the iconoclastic irony of Herzen: it was unequivocal, yet unobtrusive, austere, and matter-of-fact.

3. 'Marxist' or 'Jacobin'?

Idealism, at any rate the kind of Platonic idealism with which Chernyshevsky was confronted in the person of Yurke-vich, can be attacked in two ways. There is a philosopher's attack on the cult of *a priori* concepts and general ideas or truths; on supra-sensible, immutable forms elevated to the status of sole or dominant objects of knowledge. And there is a sociologist's attack on a discipline whose virtue is seen in timeless abstraction from mundane activity; on a scale of values according to which any science concerned with the production of material goods is regarded as trivial. The connexion of these two aspects of idealism appeared for the first time in Plato. The Platonic soul pursues superior aims, while the body is subjected to base material interests. Plato's aristocratic idea of society consisting of the governors, initiates who cultivate the intellectual way of life, and the governed, ordinary men working for their living and cultivating inferior pleasure, followed from his dualistic conception of truth as lying beyond, in a world of eternal ideas to be discovered by contemplation, and of man detached from physical desires and involvement in the terrestrial world. This, in turn, gave rise to difficulties in regard to history. Aiming as the Platonic idealist does at the ideal of an unchanging and eternal object of knowledge, he is made insensitive to history, with its fleeting actualities and catastrophic changes.

On the whole, Chernyshevsky was more disturbed by the social and historical than by the philosophical implications of idealism. His whole case for essentially indivisible human nature depended on the idea of man inextricably involved in history, which could not be reconciled with any distinction between so-called higher and lower pursuits, interests, and responsibilities. He repudiated idealism because it treated, or tended to treat, history as something which ultimately ought not to be possible, or as something towards which one could remain in the attitude of an uncommitted onlooker; and because it treated, or tended to treat, all social activity as morally inferior. If permitted to flourish freely, it would subvert the static order, for the new was the enemy of the good and the practical the opposite of the true. It is no accident that the Greeks justified slavery on the grounds that without it free citizens would have been enslaved by the necessities of life. Others may have had the same excuse for child labour.

Admittedly, Chernyshevsky himself displayed on occasion a tendency to think of history in idealistic terms. As has been noted already, he was disposed to look for the key to the history of human deeds in the development of human ideas, whose custodians are the intelligentsia; and he toyed with the notion that the solution of human problems lay in the spread of education.[122] This belief, founded on the conviction that man is a rational being, so that once enlightened education has become universal and scientific techniques widely accepted truth would come into its own, lies on the long and familiar curve running from the renaissance through the Encyclopedists to the Utilitarians. Chernyshevsky's foremost question in this connexion, however, was not who are the standard-bearers of truth, but where is the standard? He looked for this in concrete historical situations, in the peculiar conditions of time and place. 'Without the history of an object', he stated, 'there can be no theory of an object.' No one could be less prone to evasion of real situations, however rationally convincing, than Chernyshevsky. Among the Russian thinkers of the nineteenth century he stands out for his extraordinary sense of historical momentum. The right view of history and of society for him was the one which enables one to understand and cope with reality in its existing form. It must be about what is contingent, and it must be scientific.

Wide as are the varieties of so-called scientific history, they all have this in common: they included man in nature, and everything of which account should be taken was seen as lying within the existing world, in things susceptible of demonstration. One of the chief complaints by Chernyshevsky's idealist detractors was, indeed, that he was excessively involved in scientific applications which led him to see history in causal terms, obedient to the laws of nature. Yet, whatever the simplifications entailed in the assimilation of historical method to the methods of natural science, it offered thinkers of Chernyshevsky's persuasion a means for recognizing and understanding historical origins and processes. Chernyshevsky criticized Greek historiography for its failure to admit the changeable as worthy of serious consideration: it was thus unfit to show the origin of anything and to account for the interrelation of material and spiritual facts in history.[123] But even the contemporary historians (Guizot, Thierry, Niebuhr, Schlosser, Macaulay, or Karamzin and Polevoy in Russia) failed to satisfy him. They all fell short of a comprehensive view of these relations: 'their deficiencies do not consist so much in particular errors as in the inadequacy of historical approach, in a one-sided, incomplete view of the life of mankind. The life of the human race like that of individual men, is constituted by the interpenetration of a great variety of factors. Of all these only a few have until now been considered in the account of mankind's history.'[124]

In his critical examination of the traditional schools of writing history, Chernyshevsky takes particular exception to their 'undue confinement to political history', to an excessive concern with kings and battles, with isolated individuals, incidents, and institutions, without ever seeking to answer or even to ask the questions dealing with society as a whole. Even when he spoke of ideas as the ruling factor in life, he regarded these as an outcome of men's actions and as such virtually identical with social relations between men. The basic data and the proper subject of history for him were not the abstraction 'state' or 'nation', but the social and moral activity of men in community. In fact, he all but substituted sociology for history.

For the first time in the history of Russian political thought 'mass civilization' became a real historical problem. A deliberate attempt was made by Chernyshevsky to incorporate the innate interests and tendencies of 'the masses', or 'the simple people' (*prostolyudiny*) as he called them, into the historical outlook as something in no way inferior to political and cultural pursuits. Chernyshevsky was completely free from contempt or fear; his attitude to 'the people' was neither adulatory nor apologetic, unlike that of most intellectuals. He believed that no values could be maintained or promoted except through solidarity with the many, even if the values might be debased thereby. He consciously sought a revolution that would break down all the barriers of communication and convert the experiences and forms of self-expression of limited groups into a common human experience and shared forms of self-expression. This ensured a wide human range, but gave Chernyshevsky little opportunity to reflect on the complexity of human life and human relations. The habit of thinking 'democratically' places him in the main stream of Russian historical thought, which even at its opposite poles, such as early Slavophilism and Westernism, had a distinct 'popular', 'democratic' character, although it had not as yet concerned itself with a situation in which the masses were asserting themselves not as intruders but, in Chernyshevsky's own words, as 'the subjects of history'.

As regards Russia's position in history, Chernyshevsky differed from most of his radical predecessors, as well as from the Slavophils, in that his views were, at first, exceedingly gloomy.

What have the Russians given to science [he wrote in Chaadaevian vein]? Alas, nothing. What has science contributed to Russian life? Again nothing. . . . Is our mission merely to possess an army of a million and a half and the power, like the Huns or the Mongols, to conquer Europe if we so desire? Should we not pity the existence of such peoples? They have lived as if they had not lived. They passed like a storm, destroying, burning, imprisoning, plundering everything—and that is all. Is this our mission: to be all-powerful in military and political terms, and nothing as regards any other, superior aspect of national life? It would be better not to have been born than to have been born a Hun, Attila, Genghis Khan, Tamburlaine, or one of their warriors and subjects.[125]

But this dismal outlook soon gave way to the somewhat milder notion that to be a Russian was to have inherited most things of cultural value from western Europe or from the world at large ('they are men, and we children', he said); that Russia was the great assimilator, weaving all strands into a complex web and making a virtue out of necessity. The more he allied himself with 'the people', however, the more he came to believe in their latent 'creative possibilities', their power to bring to realization a more humane and just society, in spite or because of their historical retardation, and the less disparaging his estimate of Russia became. 'History, like a grandmother, is very fond of her grandchildren', he said. '*Tarde venientibus dat non ossa sed medullam ossium*: and when western Europe tried to get at the marrow it cut its hands badly on the broken bones. . . . The last shall be the first.'[126]

At a later stage Chernyshevsky approached Herzen's and Belinsky's final views on the matter. He even quoted with approval the latter's somewhat unexpected messianic notion that 'Russia is called to proclaim to the world its message and idea, although what this message and idea will be is still undecided. Posterity will recognize them without the effort of premeditation, because it is through it that the message and idea will be uttered.' And later still, he expressed his bewilderment at the 'fantastic certainty with which people believe that western Europe is a paradise on earth, whereas, in fact, it is nothing of the sort'.[127]

But the problem of Russia's relations with western Europe had never had for Chernyshevsky—except, perhaps, when he was a very young man—that obsessional acuteness, ranging from ardent love all the way to horrified repudiation, which was typical of many Slavophils and Westerners. He believed, with the Westerners that influences from outside were to be welcomed, and that they could only serve to promote social and cultural development and to widen as well as sharpen the sense of one's identity. As for the Slavophils (to be more precise, the early Slavophils), he respected their search for the true sources of national life and forgave them a great deal for having extolled the Russian peasant commune, but thought that there was something undignified in their emphatic, nervous claims to national originality; that, by falling over themselves

in protestations about the superiority of Russia *vis-à-vis* western
Europe, they were merely providing evidence of inferiority and
a sense of frustration.

A preoccupation with originality [he wrote] destroys originality
itself, and true independence is given only to those who do not stop
to think of the possibility of not being independent. Only the feeble
talk of their strength of character. And only the man who is afraid
of being easily discomfited is afraid of exposing himself to the influence of others. Current preoccupation with originality is a preoccupation with form. A man who has any real content will not
worry unduly about originality. Preoccupation with form leads to
baseless fabrications and emptiness.[128]

Russia never turned in Chernyshevsky's mind into a metaphysical concept, or an unrealizable dream. He believed in
Russia and lived for her entry into an area of freedom and
happiness, but he also knew, together with her best and most
truly loyal citizens, her most sensitive poets and writers, that
the reality of Russia, at any given moment, had always mocked
this belief. 'Wretched nation, wretched nation', he (Volgin)
exclaimed, 'nation of slaves from top to bottom!'[129]

Chernyshevsky's attitude to Russia was expressive of his
general view of history, which cannot be fairly described as
either fanciful and idealistic or as compulsively bounded by
predictable facts. He has, none the less, been made responsible
for precisely such tendencies and, in particular, made to answer
for historical utopianism by some, and for a rigid 'scientific'
determinism by others. An animated controversy took place
around this question at the beginning of this century between
the Russian Marxists (especially Plekhanov) and the late populists (especially Ivanov-Razumnik). It is important to examine,
in the first place, the grounds on which it might be said that
Chernyshevsky upheld utopian views and, in the second, how
far his idea of history was scientific or determinist.

.   .   .   .   .   .

Roughly speaking, Chernyshevsky was a utopian to the
extent to which he maintained that an historical structure
without reason or idea or ideal leads inevitably to ossification,
or turns, as he put it, into 'a machine with no opinions'. In
view of what is known of his moral beliefs, he was in no danger
of seeking at all costs some virtue or ideal that would bridge

the gulf between what is and what ought to be by suppressing or mutilating existing human needs and desires. But, at the same time, he belonged to the generation of 'sons', far removed from the kind of reaction against utopianism which is symptomatic of a tired and disillusioned age that has settled into middle-aged conformity, and can be indulgent to childhood but is severe to adolescence. It was easy to be non-utopian in nineteenth-century Russia, to concern oneself with order—or disorder, to believe that everything that has not happened must be utopian. Those who fear anything that might challenge settled conditions, those who are under the domination of the ready-made, are never utopian. They may tolerate any belief, so long as it is not too ardently held. History for them is history with passion left out, and technique and efficiency put in. They will greet every rejection of the present for the future with frantic warnings that such rejection is always for the worse, and greet every challenge to the old world with forebodings of doom and decay.

To Chernyshevsky's mind such anti-utopianism betrayed a survival from a leisurely age of privilege which fitted ill into the exacting framework of his day. In addition, he was tormented by a sleepless conscience roused whenever and wherever injustice was committed. But he derived no comfort from contemplating injustice: he preferred the effort to diminish it. Few things for Chernyshevsky were more inimical to man than resignation in the face of things as they are: such resignation, in his view, could only lead to moral bargains, to 'small deeds' and to ennui. The remedy against stagnation and mediocrity lay in a radical transformation of life. It was a 'utopian' remedy, because it threw suspicion on the solid appearance of the existing order; because it admitted the fundamental fact of change in nature and history and, therefore, expressed an urge for the future, for perfection, against a closed, mean and inhibited world. But in Chernyshevsky's case, it was not mere escape or compensation, a desire to be somewhere else and for things to be otherwise; it was more than dissatisfaction of the kind that keeps romantics eternally angry as well as eternally young. Behind the dissatisfaction there lay the need for the creation of a new reality.

Utopias are often symbols of lost opportunity, of suppressed instincts, and imagined memories of a society's pre-civilized days. A utopian could be a conservative in search of a lost paradise, intent on regaining old, lost territory, or on preventing its loss. The Slavophils were typical utopians in this sense. For Chernyshevsky utopia was not a dream born of a sense of loss and confusion, or even a way of rationalizing life according to some primordial plan, but an expression of conscious, self-directing activity, a project, a design for the future, as well as an assertion of his time's deficiency. The difference between these forms of utopianism resembles the difference between a missionary converting pagans and a pioneer discovering a new world. Chernyshevsky did not wish to convert and to persuade: this way had led nowhere, and the mood it begot did not survive the experience of betrayal which had impressed itself so grimly on the radical intelligentsia. Nor did he indulge in lyrical effusions about some hypothetical Golden Age: his business was, on the contrary, deliberately to tear off the romantic mask from past and present reality. He remained throughout completely realistic, responding to the demands of current events, abreast as well as ahead of time. 'I have always laughed at every kind of enthusiasm', Chernyshevsky wrote from Siberia, 'except when I thought a serious rebuke was more called for than laughter. Enthusiasts are silly; they are silly little boys grotesquely contained in an adult body. Most of them are good people, and we must be lenient with them. But they are children, small children who beguile this century in a way unworthy of grown-up men.'[130] There was, indeed, a strong practical strain in him and a sense of tactical timing. He showed a rare ability to learn what the world ought to be by examining what it is and how it became what it is. He never tried to reconstruct history on an *a priori* basis. He thought of it as a continuous process by which man adapts himself to his environment.

But it is also undeniable that Chernyshevsky passionately believed in the need for and the efficacy of man's decision and action (or what he calls 'guidance by the conscious resolve of man') which sets the new world in motion. Hence the mixture, sometimes plausible but often incongruous, of fantasy and realism in his novel *What Is to Be Done?*; hence the hortatory as well as factual, the ethical as well as scientific manner of his social thinking; hence the contrast between the revolutionary will and the caution with which he conducted his literary and revolutionary life; hence the oscillation between idealism and materialism in his historical interpretations.

There is a great deal of 'dialectics' in these interpretations (especially in Chernyshevsky's attempt to define the place of communal ownership in social development). But it is important to stress that it is neither a purely idealistic nor a purely materialistic dialectic: it becomes significant as an expression of the mutual relations and conflicts between persons and things, ideas and facts. And it is this twofold aspect of Chernyshevsky's view of history, as well as the peculiar nature of his utopianism, which suggests the comparison with Marx and the Jacobins. Did Chernyshevsky speak as a Marxist, or as some Marxists, in terms of scientific determinism, in which human action has to wait for the forces of evolution to perform their inevitable function; or did he reflect the mood of the Jacobins, depending on man's active intervention in the course of events, or even on revolutionary violence? The evidence shows (notably in the essay on Lessing quoted earlier on) that he spoke with both voices—a logical contradiction, if such it is, which has been attributed to Marx himself and, even oftener, to Lenin. Both Marx and Lenin spoke of 'iron laws' governing social development, and yet they believed in the decisive historical role of the revolutionary will, for which, strictly speaking, there are no fixed, immutable natural laws, subordinating man to an environment that he cannot control.[131]

This seems to put a peculiar interpretation on the materialism of Chernyshevsky, as well as, for that matter, on that of Marx and Lenin. For materialism in the common sense of the term is a basically conservative, reactionary doctrine, highly unfavourable to revolution. One of the most apparent forms of slavery is slavery to material necessity. 'Matter' (unless it is made to undergo a self-denying transformation) denotes inertia, dependence, resignation, whilst 'spirit' is revolutionary and asserts man's freedom in regard to his material environment. This accounts for the fact that the typical *bourgeois* is born materialist: his belief in the spirit is for the most part traditional hypocrisy, and he appeals to faith and religion to safeguard his position in the material world. Marx aimed at man's liberation from material and economic necessity, not at subjection to it, even though he sought such liberation within the world of material and economic relations. So did Chernyshevsky: economic dependence was for him one of the worst forms of servitude. The assumption that the mainspring of human endeavour is to acquire more and more wealth appeared to him as a piece of *bourgeois* materialism insulting to man. He reproached Chicherin with complacent historical necessitarianism, and attacked the apologists of liberal economics for their 'worship of the golden calf'. 'We must not', he said, 'yield to quietism, according to which all things occur by the force of nature and history: we must fight our way and change the shape of things.' And, on being asked what he thought of 'economic materialism', he replied: 'it may provide the material for stating the problem [of life in society], but not the solution'.[132]

Man's thoughts and actions, then, are conditioned by his social situation, but Chernyshevsky, no less than Marx, expected man to bring about what otherwise appeared as inevitable; and the interrelation between these terms constituted part of the celebrated dialectic of history.

I have already mentioned Hegel's influence on Chernyshevsky. We gather from one of his notebooks that he was particularly impressed by the Hegelian idea of history as 'an eternal struggle, and eternal movement forwards, which in essence represents a gain and which in form brings back the end to the beginning'. He was similarly attracted to Heraclitus, 'the dialectician at the mythological stage'. History does not lend itself to fixation: everything is in flux, consumed by the flames of ubiquitous 'chance'.

Whoever has learned to apply this [the continuous rejection of existing forms] to every manifestation of life will boldly hail the forces of chance which alarm the faint-hearted. He will echo the poet [Goethe] who said:

> Ich hab' mein Sach' auf nichts gestellt
> und mir gehört die ganze Welt' . . .[133]

It is almost strange to read such and similar statements alongside so many of Chernyshevsky's uniform and savourless reflections: they show that he was not insensitive to the multiple factors of history, the devious paths, the disruptive agencies, the paradoxical conjunctions and turns of events.

. . . . . .

Evolution, whereby all existing things had come to be what they are, was the master-key of nineteenth-century thought, and, like many of his contemporaries, Chernyshevsky relied on it for his understanding of the world. Though by no means a new idea, it was, he observes, not until the works of Lyell in geology and Darwin in biology that the actual means by which development had taken place were shown. But the doctrine of evolution affected many other branches of knowledge and converted them into a science. Chernyshevsky, too, approached all the phenomena of nature and of human nature by trying to discover the way in which they had acquired their existing qualities.[134] It has been shown already that he assumed that, in principle at any rate, one could discover 'laws' in every sphere of investigation, because unvarying law, i.e. a sequence of cause and effect, marked all the processes in which evolution could be traced.

Yet, significantly enough, he failed to apply this with any consistency to human history and society, and his belief in a process of gradual unfolding or natural development is shaken by the admission of a succession of catastrophic, if not, of course, unrelated, events in history and society. In particular, he refused to accept 'the vulgar (poshlaya) idea' that all evolutionary changes are bound to be for the better, and that a gradual and general improvement in human existence is in the very nature of things. 'I have always laughed at progressives of all kinds', he wrote to his sons from Siberia. But the most important evidence to this effect is to be found in the already quoted essay on the "Fall of Rome". It presents a picture of western European history as a sequence of hazards and catastrophes, as a development proceeding by leaps and bounds and interrupted by unforeseen circumstances. Far from regarding such catastrophes as accidental and, therefore, irrelevant, he deliberately emphasized them as of decisive significance for a proper understanding of the course of history. In history, he said, 'no peaceful, gradual development is possible'.[135] There was progress, but very much a progress against the grain, in spite, rather than because, of the supposed uniformities of the historical order. Chernyshevsky does not go so far as to say with Herzen that the idea of progress has gone to join the lost illusions of mankind, that it was a secular illusion which had arisen in place of religious teleologies. But he was no evolutionary optimist, and one of his main charges against nineteenth-century history-writing, and against Guizot in particular, is that it indulged in unwarranted optimism, which made it view everything in history as conducive to gradual improvement; whereas most things in history served to belie such bright expectations. He even anticipated the *ultima ratio* of Marx, the logic of catastrophe, according to which things will have to get far worse before people will be persuaded to make them better.[136] He confessed that he felt little inclination 'to delight in the alleged successes of humanity'. In the end, progress, that is human progress as distinct from mere technical and scientific advance, appears not as a law, not even as a fact, but as a pressing demand, an urgent need.

Chernyshevsky's critique of historical optimism is further elaborated in one of his last articles, 'The Origin of the Theory of the Beneficent Effects of the Struggle for Life' (*Proiskhozhdenie teorii blagotvornosti bor'by za zhizn'*), published anonymously in 1888 and specifically concerned with Darwinian and Malthusian doctrines. The article confirms that, though a believer in science, Chernyshevsky was not entirely misled by his own attempted reduction of the science of man to the rank of the natural sciences. Even earlier on he had expressed the view that, unlike the scientist, the historian cannot confine himself to saying what the facts are: he passes judgement on them. He does not enter a world of animal nature, but one which mankind has previously conquered by action, discovery, sacrifice; his facts are man's experiences. Historical events, therefore, require interpretation before they satisfy the conditions of comprehensive facts, and the historian's task is to supply the interpretation, 'to describe . . ., to explain and to judge'.[137] He is recorder, arbiter, and partisan. Now Chernyshevsky wrote that

the rules of genuine inquiry prohibit the construction of theories for the relatively precise facts of natural science, such as botany and zoology, by analogy with the social sciences. . . . In the life of plants and animals there are some factors which have given rise . . . to

fantastic attempts to draw parallels between the internecine strife
in one species, or the attacks of predatory on herbivorous animals,
or the suppression of some plants by others, on the one hand, and
the activities of economic competition in human society, on the
other. But such parallels, even if they were made with full knowledge
of economic theory, can be no more than rhetorical embellish-
ments. . . .

It does not matter to us [he says elsewhere] if a few small trilobites
or fossilized ammonites disappear and give way to other zoological
forms. But supposing the African Negroes fight each other: is that a
good or a bad thing? According to Malthus and Darwin it should
be welcomed. And, no doubt, if we, white people, eliminate all the
Negroes this will be even better. It might indeed be better but for
one thing: once we begin to slaughter all the Negroes, we shall
become, on account of these very precious deeds, barbarians ourselves, wild beasts and savages. . . .[138]

In *The Origin of Species*—the only work by Darwin that
seems to have been known to Chernyshevsky—Darwin hardly
concerns himself with the social and ethical significance of
his theories. But Chernyshevsky correctly detected the ideological implications of natural selection as a 'struggle for existence' and the 'survival of the fittest'. It commended itself to
many followers of Darwin because it suited the book of Victorian *laissez-faire* capitalism with its tooth-and-claw ethics.
It was quite incapable of explaining the peculiarly human
phenomenon of 'pre-Darwinian' conscience which subordinates
the principle of competition. It could not inspire solidarity
with those who, on Darwinian premisses, stand in need of
extinction, or expend human energy on rescuing the 'unfit'.
Similarly, Chernyshevsky attacked Malthus's gloomy theory of
population which, extended to the world of animals and plants,
provided the stimulus for Darwin's idea of evolution. It also
gained favour because it was an expression of the competitive
order in which wage-earners were expected to earn always the
smallest amount that would keep them and their families alive
but prevent them from multiplying. 'Poverty and suffering',
wrote Malthus, 'have their origin in natural law which cannot
be shaken by any human institution.' Chernyshevsky rejected
any such inevitability and asserted, on the contrary, that 'these
things [poverty and suffering] result not from natural law but

from existing human relations. . .'.[139] The whole concept of
a struggle for existence, in which the fittest would survive
if natural forces were allowed to take their course, appeared
to Chernyshevsky as a piece of ruthless complacency when
adapted—as one of Chernyshevsky's pre-eminent *bêtes noires*,
Herbert Spencer, adapted it on a systematic scale—to social
relations.

While rejecting the application of natural laws to life in
society, whose struggles, if left to itself, would result in the
inevitable and deserved victory of the animals that most resemble the successful haves over those that most resemble the
unsuccessful have-nots, Chernyshevsky was far from denying
the existence of social conflict. On the contrary, he was one of
the most important progenitors (although Saint-Simon preceded him in this by some forty years) of a philosophy of history
based on the conflict of opposites in society. In this, too, he can
be regarded as a spiritual forerunner of Marx. Unlike Hegel,
Chernyshevsky envisaged conflict specifically in terms of class
conflict—not as a metaphysical or a biological necessity, but as
an economic fact—and thus, more directly, anticipated the
Marxist scheme. His conception of class remained ill-defined
and fluid, as indeed was Marx's in some measure. But, broadly
speaking, he thought of society as divided between property-
owning and property-less classes or, with reference to Russia,
between the landowners and the peasants, and of this division
as one of the main motive forces of the historical process.[140]
Before discussing Chernyshevsky's treatment of economic questions, however, it is necessary to say more of his revolutionary
ideas.

.   .   .   .   .

The year 1850 appears to have been a decisive moment in the
development of Chernyshevsky's revolutionary conviction, for
on 15 May of that year—his last at the university—he made
the following entry in his Diary: 'Now I feel no more like
someone holding certain vaguely socialist views . . ., imbued
with hostility towards stagnation and oppression: I am conscious of being a personal adversary, placed in a new situation;
I feel like a conspirator, a soldier face to face with his enemy . . .;
I feel within that I am capable of perhaps the most desperate,
the boldest and maddest actions.' He wished to challenge the

whole concept of the game, rather than the incidental way the cards had been played. There is evidence that at this stage he already had designs for some definite subversive action. He thought of 'a secret printing-press' with a view to 'issuing a manifesto that would proclaim freedom for the peasants'. The manifesto was to be sent out ostensibly on behalf of the Holy Synod, with instructions for immediate implementation.

Such a measure will instantly result in terrible disturbances, which will be suppressed and, for a time, bring unhappiness to many. But it will also unfetter and incite the people to such an extent that nobody will be able to restrain them for many years to come. It will give support to widespread risings. The prospect filled me with great resolve and no regret at all if this cause should result in my own destruction. . . .

Still, he hesitated and eventually rejected the plan on the characteristic grounds that 'a lie must always prove harmful in the end. It would be better, therefore, just to summon to a rising . . . without any subterfuge, to describe the position in seditious language, and to say that they alone [the peasants] can free themselves, and that they can do it only by force. . . .'[141] This plan did not materialize until much later, when Chernyshevsky wrote his fatal proclamation 'To the Landowners' Peasants', if indeed he was its author.

Living in a society in which conscience was daily harrowed by the fate of millions of dispossessed, and where everything seemed to be a means to enslave the peasants, he thought of himself from the very start as a spokesman of the peasants, and of revolution as primarily a revolt by the peasants. 'The only thing that was lacking', he wrote, curiously echoing the frightened Pogodin, 'was co-operation between the various local risings.' But they charged the air intermittently with menace. Chernyshevsky almost longed for revolution to swoop like some black cloud over the whole of Russia, carrying everything in its wake. Again and again we read in Chernyshevsky's Diary of the impending upheaval. 'This is my view of Russia:' he stated in 1850, 'irresistible expectation of the revolution to come and a longing for it.' And two years later:

. . . We shall soon have a revolution, and if it happens, I'll certainly take part in it. . . . It will happen without fail. . . . Only a spark is needed to start a conflagration. . . . But when will it be lit? Perhaps in ten years' time, but possibly sooner. And when it strikes . . . I shall not be able to restrain myself. I am sure to be in it. Neither filth, nor drunken peasants with cudgels, not even slaughter will frighten me. . . . I do not yield to Iskander [Herzen] in fierceness of outlook.

Still later, in a reference to Razin and Pugachev, Chernyshevsky reminded the readers of the 'Contemporary' that

from the beginning of the seventeenth century almost all the dramatic episodes in the history of the Russian people owe their origin to the energy of the peasant population. . . . These are difficult times, reader! . . . Difficult times, in which we witness all around us the fulfilment of the mighty words uttered by the spirit of the age: 'arise from your sleep!'[142]

Earlier on, Chernyshevsky toyed with the idea of tyrannicide, apparently believing for a time that the removal of an individual would somehow usher in the reign of justice.[143] It was the first indication of that mood which later dominated the conduct of the populist terrorists, who believed that individuals still bestrode events and miracles still happened; or that political organization tends to depersonalize, while terrorism restores individuality. But Chernyshevsky soon realized that the enemy was a faceless enemy, that the collective forces had sunk so deeply into society that only the destruction of the whole system could effect change.

I attacked Herzen [he told Stakhevich, a fellow prisoner in Alexandrovsk, about his disagreements with Herzen] for the denunciatory character of the *Bell* [i.e. for merely speaking of administrative abuses]. I told him that if our government had been a little more sensible it would have thanked him for his denunciations: they assisted it in the task of keeping its agents in slightly more decent shape, while at the same time leaving the political order intact. But the crux of the matter is in the order, not in its agents. . . . *Cæterum censeo Carthaginem delendam esse.* . . . He should have repeated tirelessly his *cæterum censeo*.[144]

Although the criticism is scarcely justified—Herzen himself used exactly the same arguments against the liberals—it conveys Chernyshevsky's attitude at the time in question.

This coincided with a perceptible change in revolutionary mood. He wanted to use it constructively and even with restraint. He became less communicative, but no less determined for all that. 'For a long time, for a very long time perhaps, it [revolution] could lead to no good.' 'It is terrible to think', he wrote in a reference to revolutionary currents in western Europe, 'how much suffering and loss it [revolution] has already cost and how much more it will cost in the future.' Nevertheless, the errors and crimes of revolution were no argument against revolution itself, and most certainly not against the judgement of revolution. 'Anyone not blinded by idealization and capable of judging the future from the past', Chernyshevsky wrote, 'will not be alarmed . . . in spite of all the evils that accompany revolutions. He knows that one cannot expect anything else from men and that peaceful development is impossible. . . . Not a single step forward in history has occurred without convulsions.'[145]

This sentiment pervades all Chernyshevsky's subsequent revolutionary ideas, although he could express them in public only indirectly, for the most part by reference to events outside Russia, in France, Austria, Hungary, and particularly in Italy.[146]

He who fights for the cause (*delo*—the accepted synonym for 'revolution') [he said] must know what it leads to. If he does not wish to have anything to do with its implications he had better abandon the cause altogether. Political upheavals have never happened without incidents of outlawry. . . . Upheavals excite popular feelings, and excited feelings disregard forms. If we do not know this, we shall never be able to understand the nature of the forces which move history, neither shall we know the human heart.

'The pathway of history does not resemble the pavements of the Nevsky Prospect: it cuts now across dusty, dirty fields, now across swamps, now across wilds.'[147]

Chernyshevsky was by no means insensitive to the moral problem which revolutions raise. Indeed, the whole 'other world' of the *raznochintsy*—the high-minded, uncorrupt radicals desperately trying to throw off old chains and loath to forge heavier ones—could hardly have been immune to it. 'The people are ignorant,' Chernyshevsky wrote apropos of the popular revolutionary threat in his 'Open Letters' (*Pis'ma bez adresa*), 'dominated by primitive prejudices and by blind hatred for anything different from their own barbaric habits; they do not distinguish between the members of a class who wear different clothes from their own. They will act against them all without distinction and will spare neither our science, nor our poetry, not our arts; they will destroy our civilization.' But Chernyshevsky also saw that not only are revolutions never accompanied by distinctions but our moralizings about them often involve self-deception. He found himself in a social and political situation—especially after 1858, when he began to see and to predict the illusory nature of Alexander II's liberal promises—a situation which must lead to a conflict if one had a conviction of the rightness of one's chosen position. He could not accept the moral issue as presented, for example, by Kavelin, who considered anything better—morally and politic-ally—than 'the irregular and the anomalous' which endangers the existing order. In Chernyshevsky's view this attitude ensured only greater moral and social disaster. In the end, it was not even a question of killing the existing order: the latter per-versely insisted on committing suicide by its very terror of what might be its fate should it be called in question and its repressive control be relaxed. To recognize this and to act ac-cordingly was for Chernyshevsky not a way of evading the moral issue, but of dispelling the moral fog and moral pretexts whereby its real significance was concealed.

It has been argued that the just-mentioned 'Open Letters' marked Chernyshevsky's considered step away from revolution. This view is based on a misapprehension, which a closer study of the 'Letters' themselves and of Chernyshevsky's subsequent writings will easily dispel. The 'Letters', whose real addressee was none other than Alexander II, were written at the beginning of 1862 for the 'Contemporary' and were seized by the censorship. They must be read in the light of Chernyshevsky's belief, which he held until 1861, that the peasant Reform would precipitate an immediate popular revolution. This belief did not survive the successful and melancholy suppression of the widespread pea-sant risings which the reform provoked. He realized that, on the one hand, these heroic but hopeless revolts were little more than acts of despair mixed with millenary expectations, explosions without any clearly defined objective in which the people, re-moved from the modern concepts and agencies of power, were merely swarming to die under the fire of punitive expeditions and waiting to be killed. On the other hand, he saw that there were no leaders and no group or groups of men among the radicals with any viable revolutionary strategy; and that the peasants for their part were not even aware of the possibility of such leadership, except to the extent of knowing that, as a peasant said to Chernyshevsky, 'whoever is on the side of the people goes to Siberia'. In the face of all this Chernyshevsky made a last effort to test the applicability of the reformist attitude, against a background which, in his view, continued to point towards crisis and catastrophe. He explained to the Tsar in a restrained and dignified tone the disastrous consequences of his reforming activity. He drew his attention to the known impracticabilities and calamities which the new measures entailed, and to the justified grievances of some landowners and most peasants alike.[148] So far, however, he did not say more than did the liberal gentry of Unkovsky's persuasion who were at this very time pressing for constitutional changes. In fact, he even showed readiness to side with them inasmuch as they sought political freedom for all, thereby ensuring the possibility of a wider appeal of the very revolution which Chernyshevsky was advocating, and challenging a régime that, in the words of the 'Letters', 'acted always like a machine with no opinions'. But the burden of his address lay not in mere dissatisfaction with the reforms of Alexander. He told him that these may have changed the appearance of the relations between serfs and serf-owners, but that they had left the reality intact. And even more, he suggested in the customary Aesopian manner, that, although violence was regrettable, revolution was the only way out of the predicament: 'no amount of trouble taken by anyone else can produce the results which are given by action for oneself. . . . All the persons and social classes estranged from the people are scared at the prospect of this expected outcome.'[149]

Describing the mood which governed Chernyshevsky at the time, Rusanov, a contemporary member of 'Land and Freedom', wrote that

in those days Chernyshevsky and his associates in the democratic camp were faced with a dilemma: either to surrender to reaction without a fight . . . or to persist in the movement forward. . . . Nikolai Gavrilovich was too far-sighted not to realize that in Russia

in the sixties the democratic elements were weak and ill-prepared
for a decisive conflict with the old order. . . . Nevertheless, having
considered the possibility of such a conflict, and having recognized
that there was no other solution and even some chance of success,
he opted for active intervention in the course of events. This decision was taken . . . not without the most careful weighing of all the
pros and contras. But having once taken up his position, he never
abandoned it. . . . Circumspect as he was, where circumspection was
indicated . . ., he took unhesitatingly such steps as were demanded
by the historic confrontation between old and new Russia.[150]

That this was, in fact, Chernyshevsky's attitude is shown in
a veiled form in *What Is to be Done?* (particularly in the last
chapter) and, more conclusively, in his autobiographical novel
'Prologue' (i.e. Prologue to revolution). This novel, written in
1868 in Alexandrovsk, though unimportant as literature, gives
a suggestive picture of events and trends in Russia in the
sixties, including an account of a peasant rising. Its hero,
Volgin—Chernyshevsky's *alter ego*—is a professional revolutionary. Volgin admits the two extremes and dislikes all that is
in the middle. He understands, although he militates against,
the unbending reactionary, but he cannot stomach the liberal—
the man with principles who does not live up to them, the reformer who stops half-way, the fellow-traveller who wants the
fruits of radicalism without its terror. The novel disposes completely of the idea that Chernyshevsky had ever abdicated 'the
cause', or had ever been tempted to fall into the trap of simple
gradualism, even if, as Alexander Sern-Solov'evich reports, he
used to 'rejoice like a child in every sign of life in Russia, and
in every event that brought to light conscience and energy'.[151]
It is not by accident that he expressed on more than one
occasion a sympathy for Blanqui, the revolutionary agitator and
activist who carried on the insurrectionist tradition of the
Jacobins and regarded any mere reliance on historical inevitability as treason to revolution. Chernyshevsky's declaration to
Herzen to the effect that 'only the peasants' axes can save us'
was, in the end, as relevant after as it was before 1860.[152]

Being a fundamentally sane and temperate man, however,
noisy exhibitionism and indiscriminate preference for violence
were untypical of him. Rebellious feelings were the outcome
not so much of his psychological make-up as of political

conviction. He did not delight in destruction, as do, in his own words, 'those strait-laced revolutionaries who are unable and unwilling to take into account the circumstances of time and place'. Some are iconoclastic not because they are 'debunkers' by inclination, as Bakunin was, or because, like Herzen, they are not impressed and must clear away accretions of prejudice and bigotry, or simply because they wish to cover up obsessive class-consciousness, but because they are placed in an explosive situation ·and no other course is available to them. Chernyshevsky belonged to this latter type of revolutionary, and, in this respect, he approached a 'Marxist' rather than a 'Jacobin'. He was no alarmist when he talked of distress, no wild-eyed visionary when he anticipated vengeance, danger, and the clash of wills and interests. Faced with the impasse of Russian society in the sixties, he could not help seeing the spectre or the vision of revolution. Behind the fierce revolutionary sentiment lay the most empirical recognition of Russian facts described in the first part of this study.

It is both strange and significant that Chernyshevsky, who for many years had used the pages of the 'Contemporary' as a forum for discussing a great variety of problems connected with the preparation of the land Reform, met the Emancipation Act of 1861 with almost complete silence. It is true that once the Act was published a strict embargo was put on any critical discussion of it. But Chernyshevsky did not speak, because he had nothing to say: for him, as for the peasants, the Emancipation statutes were not worth the paper they were written on. 'The reader, no doubt, expects me', he noted in the 'Contemporary' of March 1861, 'to converse with him on the matter about which all the journals, newspapers and broadsheets are shouting today . . ., that is, about the freedom granted to the peasants. You are wrong, reader, in your expectations. I am distressed that you should think so ill of me.' The same issue contained a Russian version of Longfellow's *Poem on Slavery* and an article on the American Negroes in which the author asked what would happen 'if the enslaved Samson should rise?'

The original announcement of the Tsar's intention, admittedly, raised Chernyshevsky's hopes—hopes, though scarcely expectations. In the February issue of the 'Contemporary' of 1858, in an article entitled 'On the New Conditions of Village Life' (*O novykh usloviyakh selskogo byta*), he even wrote brightly that 'the blessedness which is promised to the peacemakers and the humble will crown Alexander with joy that has never yet crowned any of the rulers of Europe—the joy of having alone begun and completed the liberation of his subjects'.[153] He had vague hopes that the Reform would meet some of the essential needs of the people, 'provided the peasants obtain land without redemption payments'. His articles in the 'Contemporary' during 1858 and 1859, which represent one of the most important contributions to the discussion of contemporary economic problems in Russia, are accompanied by a persistent plea for the abolition, or at least the reduction, of the proposed redemption norms. But very soon he arrived at the conclusion that the Reform would turn into a 'deal (*sdelka*) between the monarchy and the serf-owners'. The 'deal', in his view, would serve to enslave and impoverish the peasantry; and he explained this by the contradiction 'between the essence of the task undertaken and the quality of those who undertook to carry it out'. 'To take a thing from a man', he wrote of the whole redemption scheme, 'or let him keep it and take money for it instead is one and the same thing.'[154]

Inasmuch as Chernyshevsky confined himself to a mere demand that the peasants should be exempt from payments for the land which they had been farming for themselves, he may be said to have assumed that the landlords would legitimately continue to own their estates, even if he did not, of course, envisage the continuation of the obligatory work by the peasants on the estates. In effect, however, he was convinced—after the peasant Reform—that all the land should belong to the people who work on it, even if such a possibility may have appeared to him as unlikely at the time. The matter was clearly set out by Chernyshevsky in his essay 'On Landownership' (*O pozemelnoy sobstvennosti*), in the formula 'state property in the possession of the commune' (*gosudarstvennaya sobstvennost' v obshchinnom vladenii*), which meant the nationalization of the land and the elimination of private property. Later, in 'Prologue', he asked: 'should they [the estates] belong to the landowner or should they too be given to the peasants?' To this Volgin (that is, Chernyshevsky himself) replied: 'The land-owners have not the right to a mite of redemption; whether they are or are not entitled to an inch of Russian land must be decided by the will of the people.'

This proposition was based not only on a factual assessment of the productive forces in the country, but also on a close analysis of the principles of 'political economy', which he defined in his commentaries to a translation of Mill's *Principles of Political Economy* as 'the science of men's material welfare depending on the objects and situations of labour'. According to this, ownership was concomitant with labour, and economic inequality and socially wasteful enterprises were to be elimi-nated. It was a view which, as we have seen, was shared instinctively by the Russian peasants. With characteristic austerity, Chernyshevsky considered work to be desirable and admirable, and idleness a curse. A Platonic 'cave' suggesting the shadowy, delusive nature of the material world of action was to him an unquestionable blasphemy against man; and the privilege of not doing anything in particular—the traditional delight and congenial paradise of the Russian gentry—was his idea of hell. 'The principal element of life', he said, 'is labour; and action is the truest token of reality.'

In more concrete economic terms, Chernyshevsky considered the value of a product to be proportional to the labour ex-pended on it. In treating labour as the source of value, he continued an established tradition of economic theory which owed its origin to the Physiocrats, had passed through Adam Smith, Ricardo, and Mill to Marx, and has come in for a great deal of criticism by more recent western European economists. For a time, the belief that man has a natural right to property created by his labour, and that wealth is the product of per-sonal effort and enterprise, served admirably the turn of the emergent *bourgeoisie*. In its formative, middle-class period, in the England of the great Reform Bill and the France of the July Monarchy, this belief stimulated the working of a free market which continually enlarges the *produit net* and uses the iron law of wages for the purpose. Labour, or rather the labour of others, was turned into a commodity freely bought and sold on the market by the employer. It enabled him as a matter of course to annex as his profit the difference ('surplus value')

between the amount produced by a given quantity of labour at
the margin and the wages of that labour, or, in Marxian terms,
all receipts from the sale of commodities that did not pass to
the labourer in the form of wages. This led the way to economic exploitation and ushered in a class antagonism between
the receivers of surplus value and the producers of it. Thus the
labour theory of value became a fatal chink in the armour of the
successful middle class, for it provided both pre-Marxist and
Marxist socialism with a case against the capitalists themselves
who deprived men of the fruits of their labour. Some liberal
economists—for example, John Stuart Mill—were conscious of
this development. In Chernyshevsky's view, however, Mill,
though responsible for a revolution of social conscience in
Victorian England, missed his mark by continually having it
both ways.[155]

The most important part of Chernyshevsky's economic
doctrine is probably his critique of liberal economics and, in
particular, of the whole system of hired labour. In his essay
'Capital and Labour' and in his commentaries on Mill he argued
that the labourer had a right to receive in exchange for his
labour the full value which he had contributed, i.e. the whole
value of the product. Anything short of this meant that his
labour was being exploited in the interests of those who did not
contribute to the value. Labour, in Chernyshevsky's view,
should not be treated as a commodity, for labour was inseparable from man and the selling of labour was tantamount to
selling man. 'Labour', said Marx, 'is the metabolism between
man and nature.' Chernyshevsky held, independently, that
man's humanity expresses itself most fully in labour: man can
defend himself against enslavement only by building up a world
of his works which extends his powers through space, which is
certain and controllable. But 'capital', too, Chernyshevsky refused to treat as a sum of alienable, marketable value, such as
money, commodities, factories, yielding income rights to their
owner at the expense of the producer: it was 'the embodiment of
labour, serving as a means for human existence', 'the creation
and the property of all who contribute to its making'.

The laws of those countries which have repudiated slavery,
[Chernyshevsky wrote] prohibit man to sell himself. No one will
hold that this restrains human freedom. On the contrary, it only

serves to protect it from the disastrous effects of men's presumption. But in what does the buying of labour differ from the buying of man which the laws of these countries prohibit? In only two respects: first, in the length of time for which the purchase is made; secondly, in the extent of power which the buyer exercises over the seller. Yet it is clear that both differences are differences of mere quantity, not of quality, of degree, not of essential character.[156]

A man who is driven to sell his labour is driven to sell his humanity: he is the proletarian, the alienated human being *par excellence*.

As is known, Marx also described the capitalist wage system as a system of slavery which turns man into an impoverished 'thing', an article of commerce. Indeed, their analysis of capitalism was in this respect almost identical. Marx, however, particularly in his controversy with Lasalle, defined the proletarian not as a mere individual engaged in the production of a specific commodity but as a contributor to a social process of production, in which he is exploited not only by individuals but by a class, and not as an individual labourer but as a member of the working class as a whole. Unlike Chernyshevsky whom he criticized for 'misconceiving the capitalist mode of production', even while approving his strictures of *bourgeois* economics, Marx was thinking in terms of large-scale industrial civilization, in which the principle of man's right to the produce of his own labour had to be complemented by the methods of organizing production and distribution in favour of the community as a whole. Chernyshevsky was fully aware of the industrial boom in Russia in the sixties, of the spread of capitalist enterprise, business property, and capital accumulation. But he saw in 'the technical side of economic progress a tendency to lower the well-being of the working class'.[157] Faced with the actual manifestations of the capitalism of his day, he considered contemporary social conditions in Russia to be largely the result of a process that enabled rich men to corner all the land, thus pushing the surplus rural population into cities and creating an urban as well as a rural proletariat. As capital accumulated and industry spread men decayed. Whatever they did, morally and amorally, their well-being and health and productivity decreased, bringing cumulative impoverishment, spiritual as well as material, to the masses.

Arguing from the particular to the general, i.e. from the prevailing state of affairs, Chernyshevsky concluded that 'unlimited competition must result . . . in the growing concentration of wealth in the hands of the few, while the position of the
poor becomes increasingly more difficult'.[158] As has been noted
in another connexion, he believed in what Marx called the
'immiseration' (*Verelendung*) of the proletariat as capitalism
develops and the owners of capital are enabled to appropriate
the benefits of increasing productivity. There was indeed nothing
in the contemporary capitalism that could have invalidated
this belief, and if the trend towards misery has stopped at all,
it does not appear to have been due to any inherent qualities
of capitalism and of capitalist growth.

From this Chernyshevsky drew two important conclusions.
First, he asserted the primacy of distribution over production,
i.e. that expansion in national wealth and capital production
should give way to the supply of available goods to the producer. The idea was later naturalized among the majority of
populist economists and won them the reputation of incurable
romantics and utopians in the eyes of the liberals and Marxists
alike. It was formulated by Chernyshevsky in opposition to the
Russian liberal economists who preached the virtues of thrift,
abstinence, postponed consumption and present hardships,
which, in fact, meant plenty for some while others starved.
They believed that the nation's well-being could best be
achieved by extending production and removing every restriction on the accumulation of capital: like the leaders of the
Anti-Corn-Law League in England, they saw in Manchester
the entrance to heaven. For Chernyshevsky, it was the entrance
to hell: 'sooty Manchester . . . built upon the infinite abysses'
(Carlyle). He did not, however, simplify the issue unduly. He
saw what Ivanov-Razumnik calls the 'tragedy' inherent in
economic development. 'Man needs for his well-being', Chernyshevsky wrote in the commentary to chapter viii of Mill's
Political Economy, 'the spread of production, and this requires
division of labour [characteristic of capitalist society]. . . . We
thus have two propositions, leading to the following conclusion:
the factor [increased production] which is indispensable for the
well-being of society proves disastrous in its effects on the
masses.' Or, to put it still more paradoxically: the greatest

unhappiness of the greatest number provides the capital for the greatest happiness of the greatest number.

The liberals defended freedom not so much because men as such had value as because it was necessary to society's material growth and efficient working that they should be unmolested in the competitive exercise of their economic liberty.[159] They postulated a kind of absolute competitive society, in which there are no vested interests, no pressure groups, no frictions, and in which considerations of real welfare are left out of account, except for the assumption that an undefinable maximum of total wealth means maximum total welfare. The idea finds its advocates even today, with the additional paradoxical complaint that there are not enough people out of work, which means that people do not work enough, which means inability to compete with foreign producers, which means general poverty and unemployment. Chernyshevsky, on the contrary, regarded 'national wealth' as a misleading abstraction, standing in direct proportion to a man's distance from the material objects from which wealth is ultimately derived, and therefore inhuman in its effects. The thought uppermost in his mind was the net individual, not the net social result. 'The aim of production for those who work is to consume the values produced, but for the capitalist it is to sell them to others for a gain through exchange. For those who work, the real needs of consumption serve as a criterion for production, . . . whereas for the capitalist the criterion is the scale of market value', which Chernyshevsky considered an artificial value that has no bearing on the consumer's real needs.[160] 'To the democrat', runs his famous dictum, 'our Siberia, where the ordinary people enjoy well-being, is superior to England, where the majority of the people suffer extreme want.'

The other conclusion drawn by Chernyshevsky from his version of the *Verelendungstheorie* was that in certain circumstances it is possible and desirable to skip the stages of industrial development, or at any rate 'to reduce its length and deprive it of all tangible effect', and to advance directly to a free and full-blooded socialist society based, in Russia, on the liberated peasant class.[161] This, Chernyshevsky believed, could be achieved by reviving the peasant commune, the essential collective institution of the people. Unlike the Slavophils, he did not view the commune as a uniquely Russian phenomenon, a kind of invariable, solid, metaphysical entity, obeying the rules of the *Volksgeist*. He took it for what it was: a form of social organization characteristic of primitive societies and preserved in Russia after its virtual extinction in western Europe, as a consequence of Russia's arrested social and economic development. Still, for him, as for Herzen before him and for the populists after him, the commune was at the centre of his hopes for the future—an opportunity for avoiding the errors of more advanced societies, a means whereby Russia could be spared 'the ulcer of proletarianism'. The hopes were sustained by the conviction that there are no inexorable 'necessities' in economic development, just as there are no historical necessities that hold man in irresistible bondage to his environment, or deprive him of the power to affect the forces of circumstance. Thus, the misfortune of Russia's backwardness could be, by conscious effort, turned into a blessing. The current theory of evolution made the most progressive country still more progressive. In the case of Russia the theory failed. Russia would revolutionize human society *because* it was the most backward country in the world of progressive liberalism. The backwardness would be a positive help towards the establishment of a new order: it would forestall and quicken it. More specifically, this could be achieved, according to Chernyshevsky, by raising primitive communalism to a 'higher plane', by taking advantage of the experience of western Europe (and, indeed, overtaking her), by mechanizing agriculture and, eventually, by passing from communal land-tenure to communal cultivation. The Slavophils advocated the peasant commune as a safeguard against corrosive western influences and as a support of paternalism and individual land-ownership by the gentry; the Government upheld it in order to ensure the payment of taxes by the peasants; for Chernyshevsky it was the basis of all productive processes in an advanced socialist society.[162]

In a number of articles published in the 'Contemporary' during 1857 and 1858 Chernyshevsky attacked the liberal economists, who stood up for individual ownership as alone conducive to social development, and he adduced arguments and an impressive array of more or less convincing historical and sociological evidence in favour of the 'spiral' (or 'dialectical') idea of social progress. This served to prove that communal land tenure had been reinstated even after society had grown more complex and individualized, because it showed itself stronger and more liable to promote the interests of the landholders.[163] Though admitting that some would and did always desire separate individual property in land—the 'strong and sober' on whom, later, Stolypin proposed to build—the majority, in his view, dreaded the rise of new masters and the end of the old egalitarian order, and of the opportunities of livelihood which the communal system ensured. It is important to stress, however, that Chernyshevsky's belief in the commune never stood in the way of his rational assessment of the peculiar complexities and 'contradictions' which men cannot escape when they try to live and work together in highly developed industrial societies. Yet it is equally important to recognize that no one has challenged the optimistic claims made on behalf of capitalist expansion in Russia more effectively than Chernyshevsky: contrary to the belief and the hopes of the contemporary liberal economists, these claims proved untrue as a description of fact and disastrous and inhuman as a guide to action.[164]

Chernyshevsky's knowledge of economics, and of liberal economic theory and practice in particular, was very impressive indeed. He understood perfectly well the historical context in which liberal political economy successfully questioned the old, feudal, authoritarian order and substituted for it the idea of a natural order, which, it was held, would 'go by itself' and could operate only when man was left unfettered by divine rights, codes and sanctions. The individual must pursue his self-interest, and in so doing, he was promoting the common good. Thus the Physiocrats coined the slogan *laissez faire, laissez aller*, in opposition to all claims to regulate economic affairs, while the English economists, following Adam Smith, set forth that imposing symmetry of economic harmonies which would come about if it were not frustrated by unnatural intervention from above. And both were formulated as a direct apologetic of individualistic capitalism.[165]

Chernyshevsky acknowledged the relative importance of the problems raised by these doctrines. Indeed, he went beyond such acknowledgement. The whole concept of progress as a result of change in environment; the deliberate substitution of economics and sociology for divine right and prerogatives, which seemed to render all efforts to improve human society futile; the notion of human individuals as separate entities obeying the same law even while pursuing their own aims; moral utilitarianism: these and other ideas that grew up in partnership with liberalism in the days of middle-class supremacy characterize some of Chernyshevsky's own views.

And yet intellectually as well as temperamentally he was deeply opposed to liberalism. To his mind, it had faltered and failed before the social and human question. He looked at it as ultimately serving to perpetuate the injustice of existing social relations, as a form of cruel complacency, precisely because it sprang from the belief that life grows inevitably better and more prosperous as history progresses; that all human problems can be solved with the gradual extension of liberal economic and political practice. Believing in the liberal future, the liberal could afford to flout the illiberal present. Moreover, as in the case of the labour theory of value, he found himself fighting against the further application of the very principles which sustained him. While equality and progress served the purpose of the middle classes, Chernyshevsky contended, they adhered to them; when the masses began to threaten property and privilege, the dangers of such application became obvious and all demands for revolutionary change began to be described as anarchism or nihilism or oppression, whether it was in fact so or not. Such was, indeed, the attitude of the Russian liberals —of Korsh, Kapnist, Chicherin, Vernadsky, and even Kavelin —all of whom upheld the existing order in the hope of adapting it to the needs and prospects of capitalist development in post-Reform Russia.

None of these liberals could have been described as cruel or cynical: on the contrary, they were patient, sensible, and sober. It was 'history' which had grown cynical and brutalized. Once the Reforms had shown their real face and a split revealed itself in the attitudes towards them, liberal patience became for Chernyshevsky a moral and political luxury that one could not afford. 'There was a time', Chicherin observed, 'when Russia pursued a healthy and greatly promising course: it happened in the first years of Alexander II's reign. But then there started this revolutionary ferment; everything became confused, and so it goes on up to the present day. It is all Chernyshevsky's fault: it is he who infused the revolutionary poison into our life.'[166] To suggest that Chernyshevsky's anti-liberalism was mere impatience and 'revolutionary itch', however, was to misunderstand his mood and the whole situation. He was driven to extremes not because he was irresponsible but, on the contrary, because he recognized the plight of millions of peasants, of whom the liberals were prepared to wash their hands, in virtue of their very belief that no insoluble problems or insuperable barriers could arise to bar the steady march of Russia towards a fuller and better life. To express sympathy, as many liberals did, with Muraviev or Apraksin and their victims at the same time, with the executioner and executed, was not mere evasion. It was something blunter and cruder: it was, for Chernyshevsky, a way of keeping in countenance a system by which the liberals themselves were ultimately the beneficiaries; it concerned the fight of one social group resisting the effort of another group to take away whatever it wanted to hold.

Chernyshevsky's conviction that conflicts could no longer be resolved by compromise shows that, despite his belief in the reasonableness of man, he had already ceased living on the capital of the Enlightenment, that his problems were no longer of the kind which lend themselves to solution through a process of rational discussion. That is why he came eventually to regard the committees and commissions, which dealt with the peasant question and to which the liberals gave their faith, as irrelevant, as abstracted from political and economic reality. While sharing the liberal belief in reason, happiness, and improvement, he did not live in the settled world of western European liberals, in which wisdom and truth appeared to be ever expanding. He anticipated what became the dominant idea in our time—too unorthodox and too vulgar to be taken seriously by nineteenth-century enlightened opinion—that helplessness, desire for power and the pursuit of their own interests weld men together into the collective group, that power can be pursued for its own sake, and that private and public interests recurrently collide.[167]

It is not surprising, therefore, that he should have viewed the social and political set-up of his day as a dictatorship of one class over another.

Participation in the exercise of political power [he wrote], or influence in social affairs depends not on whether certain people or certain classes have obtained the formal right to share in the formal acts of government: it depends on whether such people and such classes are so situated in the life of society as to be able to have real significance in it. . . . The point is not to provide formal conditions for exercising one's influence on political life, but to have the power to exercise such influence.

And, speaking of political freedom in this connexion, he said:

Freedom is a very pleasant thing. But liberalism understands freedom in too narrow and formal a way: it is conceived in terms of abstract rights, as a paper dispensation, as absence of legal restriction. Liberals will not understand that juridical freedom has value for man only when he possesses the material power to take advantage of it. Neither you, reader, nor I are debarred from eating off a golden dinner-set. Unfortunately, neither you nor I are likely to have the means of assuring such a refined prospect. I must frankly say, therefore, that I do not in the least cherish my right to possess a golden dinner-set and am ready to sell this golden right for one silver rouble, or even for less. The same could be said of all the rights for the people about which our liberals fuss.[168]

As far as the antagonism between the political ideals of liberal democracy and the economic ideals of socialism is concerned, Chernyshevsky did not, of course, say anything that was new. Babeuf lost his head for being the first to maintain that economic equality was the natural and necessary corollary of political equality. Louis Blanc made fun of 'formal freedom' by recalling the story of a rich *bourgeois* who was taking a stroll in Paris and saw a cab standing at the corner of the street. 'Are you free, driver?', he called out. And when the driver replied that he was, the gentleman retorted, 'Long live freedom!' and went on his way. Marx inherited and popularized the thesis of the inadequacy of political democracy. But he at least maintained that the realization of *bourgeois* democracy as well as of capitalism, was a stage—and a stage that could not be skipped—towards the realization of socialism, so that the two ideals, while in some respects antagonistic, were necessary in their own time and place. Chernyshevsky was rather more extreme in his conviction that political democracy was a sham and a delusion. 'A poor man's freedom', he concluded, 'is a form of slavery.'

This is not to say that Chernyshevsky disbelieved in political freedom as such. On the contrary, he stated explicitly that 'there is no happiness without freedom'. According to Stakhevich, he even displayed great vehemence in standing up for civil liberty. 'You gentlemen declare', he is reported to have told his fellow prisoners in Alexandrovsk, 'that political freedom cannot feed the hungry. True indeed. But can the air feed the hungry? Of course not. And yet man might survive for a few days without food, but he will not live ten minutes without air. As the air is necessary for the life of the human individual, so is political freedom necessary for his normal social life.'[169] Nevertheless, Chernyshevsky was genuinely troubled by the actual incompatibility between the two ideals and could not take their marriage for granted. He did not ask, in the manner of Dostoevsky, What is to be done if men with their eyes wide open, conscious of their freedom, none the less choose a conformist, manipulated society, that is to say, What if the Grand Inquisitor was right? But at least he saw through the clever conjuring trick of the harmony of interests and rejected all reconciliation, inasmuch as it meant compromise that ignores or dismisses, as the Russian liberals persistently ignored or dismissed, the existing conflicts. He believed fervently in the right of men to be regarded as an end, never as a means. But this meant for him a new world of human relations, a total social revolution, without which he could not see any prospect of real democracy.[170] That is why he proved so stimulating to his fellow radicals and infuriated so extremely the conservatives and liberals. 'I have never seen such a *brouillon*,' Kavelin complained to Herzen, 'a man so lacking in tact and so full of presumption.'

Chernyshevsky's writings bear few if any signs of lustre, but he is pithy when, in turn, he is dealing with current liberal attitudes. He had a remarkable gift—superior to that of the contemporary detractor of liberalism, Lasalle—for stripping away the top layer, the façade of liberality, and finding the second line of defence—the *penkosnimatel'* (the 'skimmer of cream'), the toothless time-server, the broken-down gentleman, the master of sitting on the fence, the *bien-pensant*, the apostle of

'make-haste-slowly', and, in the end, the iron-fisted bully, phoney
perhaps, but alarming in his hollowness. The facts thus stripped
of the web of verbiage formed an ugly pattern, far more suggestive and dangerous than pretentious folly. Nowhere has
Chernyshevsky shown more devastatingly the heartlessness and
lack of imagination disguised in remote platitudes and soft
banalities falling from liberal lips than in his novel 'Prologue'
which contains a subtle satire on Kavelin, in the person of
Ryazantsev. But Turgenev, too, became for him a symbol of
liberal tameness. He admired him as an artist, but he could not
bear, or perhaps he misunderstood, Turgenev's inability to
take up a position without hedging his bets, the ineffectual
appraisal in face of every problem, the languor at the source,
the want of creative energy both in himself and in his male
characters, the series of charming rendezvous in the lap of nature leading nowhere and reappearing with chafing punctuality
in so many of his stories.[171] 'The habitual failing of our liberal
classes', Chernyshevsky wrote, 'does not consist in mistaken
ideas but in the lack of any idea; not in mistaken feelings but
in the impotence of intellectual and moral sensibility, of social
interest.' Elsewhere he referred to them as 'the weather-cocks,
turning this way and that as the wind blows. They are the
people of whom the Scriptures say that they must be broken
with a rod of iron.'[172]

When it came to specific political problems, Chernyshevsky
liked, or was compelled, to choose his texts from contemporary
western European, especially Italian, history. Against the background of events in 1860, when Sicily turned into a true radical
paradise, he described the idealism of the radicals and the incomparable lack of principle of Cavour—the man who succeeded in
discrediting Garibaldi, who killed the radicalism of the radicals
by baiting the hook of liberal promises, and settled down on
the misery of the people.[173] Earlier, speaking of the 'moderate
republican' Cavaignac and the crushing of French workers by
him in the June Days of 1848, Chernyshevsky depicted liberalism
as a basically anti-popular, reactionary force: 'the workers of
Paris paid for their alliance with the moderate republicans by
starving, by dying in thousands in the struggle, and by being sent in
thousands to prison; while the moderates forfeited the cherished
loyalty of all classes and aroused them against themselves.'[174]

Indeed, Chernyshevsky's despair of liberalism drove him to the point of what some thought to be playing into the hands of reaction. Thus, he came out publicly against the political exile Carlo Poerio, who spent ten years in prison for his part in the Italian movement of liberation. Chernyshevsky's derisive verdict was that it served Poerio right, for surrendering to 'liberal illusions' and trusting in the pledges of absolute monarchs. This provoked a paroxysm of indignation in Russian liberal circles and offended even Herzen. Chernyshevsky ignored the reaction of the first, but to Herzen, with whom relations had fallen to a low ebb at the time, he said: 'our derision is a cry of anguish'. As Venturi aptly observes, Chernyshevsky was prepared to pay for the right to pursue his radical vision with twenty years' Siberian deportation. 'Soltanto a questo prezzo poteva differenziare la propria voce da quella dei liberali russi, e Černyševskij non esitò a pagarlo.'[175]

Attacks on liberals, on mere 'reforms', on passive acceptance of explicable evils, on entrenched privilege and social compulsion did not prevent Chernyshevsky from seeking to answer the positive question, What is to be done? Some of the answers are naïve in the extreme, showing his occasional tendency to mismatched, bizarre combinations. His belief in scientific procedure side by side with visions of a free and happy world, where self-dedicated women sow, study medicine, and have lovers whose number is not limited otherwise than by the liberality of providence, where workers inhabit palaces built of metal and glass, sit on aluminium furniture and eat off steam-heated tables, is a case in point. But even these imaginative splendours and 'crystal palaces', which, as Dostoevsky perversely believed, would make man at best soporific, at worst slavish in order to be happy, had a core of truth and plausibility in them, despite what appeared to be their airless utopianism. For Chernyshevsky, the first men to read the riddle of what would make society worth its members' loyalty, inspire them to work and sacrifice for it, believe in its future and help make that future come to pass, would prove the masters of a new world.

His practical—or unpractical—answer, worked out with considerable detail in the essay 'Capital and Labour', in the commentaries on Mill, and especially in *What Is to Be Done?*, was 'co-operation'. The model or prototype was the Russian village commune. Chernyshevsky saw Russia covered with productive communities or associations (*tovarishchestva*), comprising 1,500–2,000 members, in which collectivization was to be carried to the point where private ownership of the land and of the means of production would cease to exist, and where there would not be any such things as monopolies, differential powers and privileges. The communities would have nothing to quarrel about and would be for the most part self-sufficient, combining agriculture with industry and exchanging their surpluses one with another. Chernyshevsky proved to his satisfaction that their living standards would continually grow. But this would result in an increased variety of intellectual enterprise rather than in 'the absurdity of creating demand for goods instead of goods to supply demand', in a needless multiplication of material wants, which he tended to regard as the trappings of the self-seeking, philistine property owner, weighing like chains on a slave.

Contrary to Dostoevsky's suspicions, the general trend in this scheme was to make a society in which the individual could express himself in free collaboration with his fellow men and engage in as great a variety of unspecialized pursuits as possible, without becoming a mere unit in a machine too vast for him to control, or even to influence. Internal State action was, therefore, to be confined in the main to subsidies or repayable, interest-bearing loans. Chernyshevsky had few prescriptions for the political ordering of future society since, fundamentally, he believed with Saint-Simon that 'the government of men' must give way to 'the administration of things'—a technical process which might be necessary even in the epoch of freedom. As for external State action—foreign relations, diplomacy, alliances, spheres of interest, &c.—he thought that, in the existing social and political conditions, they were in any case or in the main a racket of and for the privileged. He had little liking for the State: 'the most terrible thing', he is reported to have said, 'is the shapeless monster, the omnivorous Leviathan.'[176] In an essay entitled 'Economic Activity and Legislation' (*Ekonomicheskaya deyatelnost' i zakonodatelstvo*), published in the 'Contemporary' in 1859, he wrote that 'some ascribe to the State an aim which transcends the needs of individuals, i.e. a realization of the abstract ideas of justice, truth, and so on,

Undoubtedly, it is easy to deduce from this principle wider prerogatives on behalf of the State than from the other theory, which has only the good of individuals in view. Generally speaking, we uphold the latter theory and do not accept anything higher in this world than the human person.'

These statements, however, must be qualified by the fact that the changing economic conditions in the sixties impressed Chernyshevsky with the need of State intervention in economic affairs which, in any case, already played an important part in the Russian economy. The question was how to shape and direct such intervention in the interests of the people. 'The essence of socialism', he said, 'applies, strictly speaking, to economic life.'[177] As has been shown, he denied that the conditions postulated by the Manchester School of Economics, gaining increasing favour as it was with the Russian liberal economists, were part of the natural order which, in the absence of or with reduced intervention, would maintain itself. In fact, he held that far from being an essential spur to progress, private interests obstruct it, and that in the circumstances the function of the State should be to provide a rational framework for collective institutions within which social life could develop justly and freely. Federated working co-operatives or associations were to be such institutions.

Plans for various kinds of co-operative enterprise had found advocates before Chernyshevsky, and he learned from all of them.[178] One of the first practical experiments to arouse widespread attention were Robert Owen's spinning factory in New Lanark, and his later communal settlements in America and England. The pathetic misfortunes which these communities had met with did not shake Chernyshevsky's, nor had they shaken Owen's, faith in the fundamental soundness of working associations. The other social thinker who made a strong appeal to Chernyshevsky and who insisted on the importance of 'community making' was Louis Blanc. His book *Organisation du travail*, in which he elaborates a programme for the construction of socialism by means of communal workshops and widespread measures of nationalization, served as a pattern for Chernyshevsky's plan of industrial co-operatives set out in 'Capital and Labour'. 'My theoretical sympathies', Chernyshevsky wrote in 1849, 'are with L. Blanc, for he was my first teacher.' Even greater similarities might be found in this respect between Chernyshevsky and Lasalle, although Chernyshevsky appears to have read Lasalle only in Siberia. Lasalle also believed in economic emancipation by means of co-operative enterprise, but, unlike Blanc and like Chernyshevsky, he held it impossible to achieve this without the help of the State and as long as private property in land and capital remained intact. 'He [Chernyshevsky] is a Lasalle in his own manner, in the Russian manner,' Shaganov remarked,'—or even better than him, for he does not suffer from Lasalle's muddleheadedness.'[179] What kind of muddle Shaganov had in mind is uncertain. But, whatever practical significance in the economic sphere Chernyshevsky may have attributed to State action, he was far removed from the entire Lasallian conception of the State as a political expression of *Volkstum*. The nationalistic gullibility imputed by Chernyshevsky to Mazzini could have been laid, as Marx has done, with equal justice to the charge of Lasalle, who linked his notion of the State with that of the national unity of Germany, and with Prussian hegemony in particular.[180]

But the man who must be counted as the main influence on Chernyshevsky in this connexion was Fourier. Fourier belongs to the category of people known as forerunners: he was a forerunner of Marxism, of the emancipation of woman, of child psychology, of town planning and industrial co-partnership, of collective farming and the co-operative movement. Chernyshevsky's admiration for him has received special expression in *What Is to Be Done?* It was due, however, not so much to the many absurdities which Fourier prescribed as a guide to his inventions, or even to his ideal society organized in 'phalansteries', as to what Chernyshevsky considered to be 'the wide philosophical range which marks his solution of some of the essential social and moral tasks'.[181] This claim, like a similar claim made by Chernyshevsky on behalf of Saint-Simon, is scarcely justified, but in one respect it was genuine and, in the context of Chernyshevsky's private life, significant, for Fourier was to him what, two generations later, Ibsen became for some: the prophet of the moral liberation of woman and, indeed, of the liberation of society through the liberation of women.

Fourier's influence was indigenous to Russia. He had won

some following in the forties, and his Russian disciples, of whom the most important was Mikhail Butashevich-Petrashevsky (1821–66), conducted an active Fourierist propaganda, until the suppression of the Petrashevskists in 1849—the year which also marked the virtual end of the great period of utopian socialism in western Europe. The 'Petrashevsky circle' was a fairly important factor in Russian revolutionary history, for, apart from spreading Fourierist ideas, it marked a reversal in the movement which began in the most oppressive years of Nicholas I's régime: 'a practical movement', as Herzen put it, which 'driven into the book, was [through Petrashevsky] venturing out of the book into the world of practical action.' Indeed, the two were interconnected, for, to quote Herzen again,

le fouriérisme plus que le saint-simonisme convient à la jeunesse de Pétersbourg. Le fouriérisme, qui ne tendait qu'à une réalisation immédiate, qui voulait l'application pratique, qui rêvait, lui aussi, mais qui appuyait ses rêves sur des calculs arithmétiques, qui cachait sa poésie sous le titre d'industrie et son amour de liberté sous l'embrigadement des ouvriers, le fouriérisme devait trouver un écho à Pétersbourg. Le phalanstère n'est autre chose qu'une commune russe. . . .[182]

Although the conflicting evidence about Petrashevsky makes it difficult to form a precise picture of his personality, he appears to have been something of a knight-errant and an indefatigable eccentric given to somewhat desiccated cerebrations. No one disputes, however, his extraordinary courage and self-dedication. He was especially devoted to Fourier. 'On reading his works for the first time', he said, 'I seemed to be reborn. I worshipped the greatness of his genius. I destroyed all my other idols and made him my sole god, as a pagan does on becoming a Christian.'[183] He looked for and found in Fourier a solution not only of social and political but also of personal spiritual problems. He also made an abortive attempt to set up a phalanstery on his own estate (he was a small landowner but worked as a clerk in the Foreign Ministry). Politically, Petrashevsky's ideas were an uneven mixture of reformism and revolutionism, with an emphasis on the former. Like Diderot before him, he expressed his views in a book of reference—'A Pocket Dictionary of Foreign Words Adopted in the Russian Language' (*Karmannyi slovar' inostrannykh slov, voshedshikh v sostav russkogo yazyka*).

It was a tract for the times and was designed to plant dangerous thoughts in the reader while saying the unexceptional and the far-fetched. Thus, under 'Negrophil' he advocated the liberation of the serfs, under 'novation'—the benefits of revolution, under 'odalisque'—the rights of women, under 'opposition'—civil liberty and the jury system. The 'Dictionary' defeated its aim, for, though Petrashevsky (together with his collaborator Maikov) successfully hoodwinked the censor, the police saw through it and the book was confiscated. In 1849 Petrashevsky and his followers, who used to meet once a week in his scrubby Petersburg flat, were rounded up—about a hundred in all. Twenty-one of these were condemned to death, but the Tsar commuted the sentence to various terms of hard labour in Siberia. A macabre farce was enacted in which the condemned men were taken through all the preparatory motions of public execution and then reprieved at the very last moment. The story is familiar from Dostoevsky, one of the victims. The fact that Fourier's post-humous career in Russia helped to send Dostoevsky to the House of the Dead may well be his greatest claim to fame today.

Chernyshevsky was not a member of the Petrashevsky circle, although he said that he was looking forward to 'getting involved with them.'[184] He was, however, in touch with at least two leading 'left-wing' members of this rather ill-assorted group—Alexander Khanykov and Nikolai Speshnev. Khanykov introduced Chernyshevsky to Fourierism and 'sowed the seeds of revolution' in him. The meeting with Speshnev seems to have taken place later, on Speshnev's return from Siberia in 1856.[185] Apart from Dostoevsky, who belonged to the moderate section of the group, Speshnev was perhaps the most remarkable figure among the Petrashevkists. It is customary to regard him as the model for Stavrogin, the main character in Dostoevsky's *The Possessed*, although Bakunin has a similar claim to the title. What appears to have escaped literary historians is that—to judge at least from the internal evidence—he has undoubtedly also provided the prototype for Rakhmetov, the elusive revolutionary hero of Chernyshevsky's novel *What Is to Be Done?* Speshnev was known as 'the aristocratic revolutionary', whose excellent taste went hand in hand with personal austerity and complete devotion to his political cause. He was physically beautiful, oddly feminine, icy-cold and remorseless. He had doubts about the wisdom of the mob and was impatient of mediocrity. His friends were constantly intimidated by his intellectual brilliance and disdainful if unobtrusive pride. But he also had a tremendous personal magnetism and the 'demonic' power to make hearts dance, minds burn, and people respond to his call to sinister and violent revolutionary action. Many of these traits, as well as some important biographical details, are to be found in Rakhmetov—the revolutionary at his most 'uncanny', 'terrible', and 'titanic', 'the sombre monster', in the words of the novel's heroine, Vera Pavlovna.[186]

Although Speshnev always called himself a communist and was in reality a follower of Blanqui and Babeuf, who insisted that the revolution must be made by a trained *élite* before the masses had been brought to its side, he embodies some characteristic features of the circle's genius, Fourier—a combination of the 'utopian' and fantastic with the cerebral and calculated. And this, in part is true of Chernyshevsky himself.[187]

4. *Of Beauty, Art, and Reality*

If historical periods were to be defined by the form of literature that they nourished most abundantly, then the sixties in Russia would undoubtedly be known as the decade of criticism. This does not mean that it was the decade of the best criticism, or that the best literature developed in dependence on it. But during this time criticism as well as literature proved of more importance to the intellectual and social evolution of Russia than did criticism or literature to the evolution of any other country.

In England [Chernyshevsky observed in his essay on Lessing], which can pride itself on the greatest poet in Christendom and on a number of superb writers unequalled perhaps by all the literatures of the rest of Europe taken together, in England the fate of the people never depended on its literature. It depended on religious, political and economic relations, on parliamentary debates and private controversy, whilst literature strictly so called had a secondary influence on the country's historical development. The same place must be assigned to literature in the life of almost every other European country.

In Russia, though she suffered a greater estrangement of the mass of the people from cultural life than England, the reverse is true. There culture, and more particularly literary culture, had a profound bearing on political life, and literature and criticism were largely responsible for bringing men into groups and stimulating them to political activity.

When this has been understood it is clearly impossible to read the Russian critics as simple commentators and judge their worth on the accuracy of their assessment of individual authors. They were no connoisseurs savouring the artistic past and present. What they sought was art that was not deprived of its purpose: to evaluate, to praise, to glorify, as well as to reveal that which is ugly, hard, and questionable in life. And what one must look for in their work is the value of their generalizations, which for them were not generalizations made with an easy sweep of the hand, but were the most precise statements possible about life that has acquired or lost meaning in passing through the artistic medium.

It is possible that one of the prime dangers of all literary criticism and all aesthetic discourse is that in attempting to explain the value and function of art or the condition of the artist's mind, they may explain away all knowledge of the artist and his work. When, moreover, a critic is compelled or chooses to be a prophet, intent on saying what art should or should not be, and using it as the field in which to judge the present and build his vision of the future, his activity may conceal the confusion and excitement of the creative act. The Russian critics of the sixties, receiving and tightening as they did the stern heritage of Belinsky, were then and still are today accused of just such concealment, of having swamped literature with theory and stifled in the process their own and their readers' aesthetic sensibility.

As regards literary criticism in the special sense of the word, the justice or otherwise of this accusation can best be discussed in the subsequent chapters devoted to Dobrolyubov and Pisarev. Although Chernyshevsky was by training a literary historian and began his journalistic career with works of literary criticism, and although he had a remarkable awareness of literary activity in Russia, his professional interest in literature soon gave way to preoccupation with political and economic questions, and, as had been noted, it was Dobrolyubov who took over from him the literary section of the 'Contemporary'. Their approach, their tastes, and their method of dealing with literature were essentially alike. Chernyshevsky's most important contribution in this connexion lies not so much in his discussion of writers as in his aesthetic generalizations, which he expounded mainly in the treatise on the 'Aesthetic Relations of Art to Reality'.[188]

Now it is odd to find that this work gives no support to the view that Chernyshevsky turned art into a vehicle of propaganda, made didacticism an artistic—or unartistic—dogma, and dealt a death-blow to all aesthetics, as Pisarev insisted with acclamation. Admittedly, its style seems on occasion to emulate the manner of an assiduous, hortative schoolmaster; there is a touch of ponderousness and rationalist bluntness, which could have been the reverse side of the author's uncompromising intellectual honesty. All this grated on Turgenev, for whom thought, too, had an appropriate beauty, a grace the lack of which caused him acute discomfort. But he failed to see that behind the flat and brittle manner was an account of great interest and permanent value. This was duly acknowledged even by Vladimir Soloviev—a man who did not yield to Turgenev in subtlety and taste and whose intellectual sensitivity was greater than his.[189] At any rate, Chernyshevsky considered that his primary purpose in writing the book was an aesthetic one, as indeed is indicated by the very title.

His purpose was formulated in terms of Feuerbach's 'anthropological' ideas and in avowed opposition to Hegel, although in view of the ban by the censorship Feuerbach's name does not appear in the first published version. The view prevailing among a number of prominent contemporary Russian critics and literary historians was that art could make more use of idealist than of any other thought, because, in their view, artistic insight came from supernatural illumination rather than from an experience of the world of sense, and that a proper account of art and artistic pleasure could be made only from the standpoint of the ultimate norms of art, in terms of 'ideal', 'timeless', 'universal' Beauty and its 'pale reflections in the world'.[190] They used habitually the romantic category of the Sublime in their estimate of artistic works, for sublimity was considered grander, more awe-inspiring and more likely to

convey the Absolute than even Beauty. They insisted on the
poetic value of the infinite in what is represented, because this
quality was supposed to set the mind free to expand its inner
powers unconditioned by the actuality of things, and to sustain
the divine glow of fancy. To use a modern term, it was the
eminently 'uncommitted' approach to art—'art for art's sake',
the ineffable subjectivism of 'pure poetry', the ideal of man's
mind as a *tabula rasa* unpolluted by insinuating influences, and
of artistic meaning as painless illumination by 'the radiance of
Beauty itself'. Whether at its 'noble-emotion' stage of older
times, or at its later, 'technical' stage in which emotion and
experience could be any emotion or experience about anything,
it remained the attitude of a bystander, astounded, fearful and
possibly pleased, but essentially 'disinterested'. As is known, the
chaste philosophers of the Sublime could look at naked females
'without interest', and even Pygmalion was an unaesthetic
man to them.

In regard to this ticklish point Chernyshevsky did not
perhaps differ much from the idealists who incurred his blame;
but in all other respects he considered artistic experience to be
eminently 'interested'. In full accord with his fundamental
philosophical position and attitude to life, he was determined to
do away with large abstractions in aesthetic discourse.

It is not by chance that Plato, to whom the world owes a
persistent faith in absolute Beauty throned above the earth,
also brought as complete an accusation as could be against art,
as a pursuit unworthy of man's intellectual dignity and entirely
vicious in its effect. Reality was too insistent, too crude, and its
artistic reproduction only served to remind one of it: so, in his
panic lest his world be endangered, the idealist had to invent
a system that left his ideal intact and to deny reality even at
an artistic remove. But Chernyshevsky believed in art precisely
because it was a way of identifying reality—through intimacy,
through awareness of the immediate, through contact with the
particular. Instead of seeking in art an improper or harmless
or perfect means of apprehending an ideal supernatural order
of things, he sought a real presence. To the habit of concentrating on the lofty, the allegorical, and the oblique he opposed the
literal sense, the direct meaning, the historical actuality. He
looked not for what words do to the literary artist's material,

but for what the material does to the words. The true artistic attitude, Chernyshevsky says, is 'respect for real life': 'beauty is life'; 'that in which we perceive life is beautiful'; 'an object is beautiful inasmuch as it reveals life or awakens the awareness of life'. 'The living man does not care for things that never move in life. He can never look long enough at living beauty, but very quickly tires of the *tableau vivant* which the devotees of exclusive art prefer to the portrayal of life.' The artist for Chernyshevsky is primarily an explorer of 'sensible reality', extolled by Feuerbach, who regarded every imaginary world as a mere counterfeit, a pale, delusive simulation of actuality. He puts his images at the mercy of the true, observable world.

There was something Tolstoyan in this aesthetic fidelity to truth. Indeed Chernyshevsky valued Tolstoy and was able to predict with remarkable insight his characteristic contribution as a novelist because he felt that Tolstoy had a gift of truthfulness, of making every item of experience grist to his mill, of preserving the realistic illusion by which, like life, a story tells itself.[191] Ingenuity, sophistication, distinction of style left Chernyshevsky with the impression of frivolity. They were a flaw in the mirror of reality, distracting from what is being presented. This was also Tolstoy's attitude. But whereas Chernyshevsky had no need to cultivate anti-stylishness, because his natural manner of writing had no trace of elegance or eccentricity, Tolstoy is known to have made his sentences deliberately inelegant so as not to intervene between his work and the life depicted in it.

The visible world, in Chernyshevsky's view, the changing reality of time and place, is the artist's chief inspiration. They are the tablet on which the cipher of beauty is written every hour, and he brings to the surface its pleasure and enchantment. From this it followed that there were no absolute standards in art persisting independently of time, place, social condition and, presumably, subjective taste. 'Beauty in itself' or any generality embracing all arts would appear to have been an impossibility to Chernyshevsky, although he did not say, as some have done on similar premises, that art is the only self-justifying activity man knows. His aesthetic relativism did not in any way inhibit his pursuit of aesthetic values, perhaps with no more reason than that which enables people almost always and everywhere to distinguish Botticelli's *Primavera* from a postcard of fat women on sale at sea-side resorts. In any case, Chernyshevsky knew what he was talking about, while never claiming that aesthetics could make men produce beautiful things or even satisfy the desire for beauty, whatever these may mean—only the modest desire to understand human experience.

'Life [Chernyshevsky writes] presses forward and carries away in its course the beauty of things', so we are told by Hegel. True enough. But along with life pass our desires. It is absurd, therefore, to regret the vanishing spectacles of beauty: they go, having fulfilled their purpose, having afforded as much pleasure as a given moment can contain. To-morrow will be another day and with it other needs to be satisfied by other, novel things of beauty.

In this respect, Chernyshevsky appears to have been almost at one with the worldly aesthetes: 'the beneficial value of art', he said, '. . . lies almost exclusively in that art gives pleasure.' But he quickly added that art also serves 'to edify', for, naturally, he did not share either their belief in aesthetic values existing in a universe of their own, or their treatment of art as a mere comfort and amenity. The artist's first aim was, after all, not delight, not superior or private amusement, but truth. 'Without truth there is no poetry'; and what is expressed must be made objective in order that it may be true. 'Truth is only in concrete realization', in the raw presence of life.

It is not difficult to see the limitations of this 'objective', 'realist' approach to art. It may induce not only an interest in things said or represented at the expense of the way in which they are said or represented. It may cause, above all, an underestimation of sensibility and imagination. We need the contrasts of absolute and relative values, of idea and reality, fantasy and result, poetry and action, detachment and intimacy. They supply the element of tension in art as in life, allowing things and people to be mysterious and surprising, as, in fact, they mostly are. 'L'art est fait pour troubler: la science rassure.' To demand insistently the reproduction of a more real and solid universe, to magnify the presence of things and people in their appearance and behaviour inhibits the artist's interest in the different levels of existence, in the state of mind, in the impact of personal experience on one's awareness of the external world, and cramps his imaginative insight.

With a genius realism may and does produce masterpieces. Chernyshevsky was not a genius either as a novelist or as an aesthetic philosopher, and he did not avoid the pitfalls of the realistic approach, which would have made nonsense of his aesthetic enterprise had he not had the courage to be inconsistent. His inconsistencies in this respect are the inconsistencies —or perhaps no more than the already familiar divergent but cognate elements—of his essential philosophical outlook, which, indeed, could be studied almost exclusively on the basis of the 'Aesthetic Relations of Art to Reality'. As regards art, there is no doubt that, for all his concern with literature and aesthetic value, Chernyshevsky's appreciation of imagination was deficient. He has even been made responsible for preparing the the ground for Stalin prize novels about pig-breeding and tractors.

The power of imagination [he says] is exceedingly limited, and its creations are very pale and weak as compared with those offered by reality. . . . The most perfect paintings of Raphael are known to have been portraits of existing people; the ugliest creations of mythology and popular superstition have proved not at all unlike . . . the prehistoric monsters discovered by the scientists. History and careful observation of contemporary life show that existing people, not even those who are arrant fiends or paragons of virtue, commit crimes more terrible or feats more heroic than anything invented by the poets. Fantasy was compelled to stoop before reality. Even more: it was compelled to admit that its imaginary creatures are but copies of the things found in reality.

'A real apple', runs Chernyshevsky's well-known and unprofitable dictum, 'is more beautiful than a painted one.'

Chernyshevsky scarcely recognized that ambiguity in art which Aristotle called 'the skilful lie', and of which Baudelaire said more strikingly—apropos of Delacroix's paintings—that things, because they are false, are infinitely closer to the truth, whereas 'the majority of our painters are liars precisely because they have neglected to lie'. In other words, it is only by exaggeration and distortion that the artist begins to express those intangible qualities which lie outside mere appearance. The use of untransmuted lumps of reality is aesthetically speaking unrealistic, and this kind of reality can be made to contribute to art only if it has passed through the fire of creative imagination, and been tempered by it. Objects cannot be tied down to any one sort of reality: in fact, they do not exist for the artist at all except in so far as a relationship exists between them, and between them and himself. Chernyshevsky might have qualified his approach in an age in which artistic ideals had not been affected by the invention of photography. Before this invention it was admitted that painting at any rate, whatever else it may become, was in the first place an art of imitation. Nowadays, painting has abandoned literalness, and if Picasso's *Guernica* succeeds, as perhaps no other painter has succeeded, in depicting the human condition, in fragmentary images of terrifying distortion, one reason is that this is something the camera could not do. But even Raphael's *Madonna del Granduca* tells something which no photographic copy of his lady sitters could have expressed. Nor is *War and Peace* an imitation of reality resembling that of an academic picture.

It would, nevertheless, be misleading to attribute to Chernyshevsky, as is currently done, a mere naturalism of the kind advocated and practised by Zola, whose voracious materialism would have been as suffocating to him as it was to Zola's fastidious critics. In fact, as Kagan rightly observes, 'Chernyshevsky disavowed not only the idealistic claims for the independence of art from life, but also the notion of art as "imitation of nature" which dominated all previous materialistic aesthetics'.[192]

Aristotle called poetry an art of imitation (*mimesis*), which accorded with the Greek habit of thinking about all art, just as it accords with our way of calling art a mode of 'expression'. The argument was that art imitates nature, that it is a skilled copying or mimicry of known objects in the world. Together with his theory of ideas, it provided Plato with an apparently plausible reason for his disparagement of art, for if art imitates things, and things represent ideas, and ideas are the true reality, then art deals with reality at third-hand and it might just as well not be there. In an article on Aristotle's *Poetics* (published for the first time in Russian in 1855), Chernyshevsky tried to show the importance of Aristotle's critique of Plato's imitative fallacy.[193] Putting aside Plato's *a priori* considerations, Aristotle produced the familiar argument from experience that if poetry merely mirrored nature it could give no more than nature gives us; but in fact we enjoy poetry precisely because it gives something which nature does not give. More significantly still, if some arts, such as painting, may suggest imitation in the sense of mimicry, others, such as music, show that whatever imitation may mean, it does not mean mimicry.

To this extent Chernyshevsky agrees with Aristotle and, by substituting 'reproduction' (*vosproizvedenie*) for 'imitation' (*podrazhanie*), which was the accepted but inaccurate translation of the word *mimesis*, he shows the flaws in the naturalistic approach to art.[194] 'To imitate', he says, 'means to copy external appearance, senselessly . . . and without understanding its essential character. . . .' 'It is an empty and wasted pastime', which serves 'to deceive feeling.' True art 'reproduces the essential features of the original', 'the typical', as Chernyshevsky calls it, following Belinsky; it depends on the artist's understanding of life, and ultimately upon his purpose in producing the work at all.[195] In fact, it is a creative rather than an imitative activity, in which, after all, even fantasy is restored to its rightful place. For, as Chernyshevsky remarks, in apparent contradiction to his previous statements, it is through fantasy that 'the poet transforms the seen and heard . . ., re-makes that which has been received by the senses and creates something new'.[196]

This is further supported by Chernyshevsky's view that the artist's search for the real, the objective, the given, and straightforward must not obscure for him the subjective experience. For it is the interaction of subjective experience and external events which constitutes life, and without it there is no art: the tension between conscious will and unconscious response, between creation and acceptance is a basic paradox of artistic activity. Just as 'to register life as it is' failed to meet Chernyshevsky's epistemological requirements, so now mere transcription from nature failed to meet his aesthetic needs. What we want and what the artist aims at is not transcription but an imaginative reconstruction of the possibilities of nature. Beauty, Chernyshevsky says, is not only 'life exactly as it is', but also 'life as we mean it to be'—'all that makes manifest the ideal, the purpose and object of our aspirations and our love', and yet cannot express them in abstraction from the situations which realize them. Imagination may do no more than heighten

or concentrate these situations by omitting all that is insignificant. But that will be enough to make the artistic work something quite different from that aping or raping of the world
which current materialistic and idealistic aesthetics alike assumed it to be.

Inasmuch as the measure of art remained for Chernyshevsky its reference to real life, he was concerned not so much
with things happening in nature as with things happening in
human nature, in facts and events embodied in human life.
This was also Aristotle's idea: as Chernyshevsky observes,
'Aristotle's *Poetics* has nothing to say about nature; he speaks of
men, of their actions, of events happening to people as the object
of poetic representation.' Elsewhere, apropos of Lessing's
Laokoon, Chernyshevsky says that 'human life provided the sole
basic element, the essential component of poetry. The dramatic
was its main stimulus and power. Poetry must eschew all that is
immobile, all that is lifeless and abstracted. It speaks only of the
way in which environment acts on man and man acts on the
world surrounding him. Poetry is the drama of human life.'
But even 'landscapes are significant inasmuch as they provide
the setting for the manifestation of human life, or suggest and
prefigure such manifestation'.[197]

This sense of the importance and eloquence of the human
meaning in art is perhaps the most valuable element of Chernyshevsky's aesthetics, although its relevance is more obvious in
literature than in other forms of artistic expression. It was part
of his deliberate attempt to discard the general and to assert
the particular, to stand for existing changing reality with its
untidy peculiarities, against the classical rejection of it, and in
so doing to collide with the reigning aesthetic dogma. Not that
he wished to be exclusive: but it was the human position, the
essential humanity of a work of art which appeared to him as
far more interesting than anything else any one else might be
able to find in it. It was the human reference that, for Chernyshevsky, gave a work of art its universal, which is not its average
but its 'typical', significance—that which reveals life at its
highest and most intense. Every artist proceeds from some
particular experience, on which he seizes, which he isolates out
of the flux of things and maintains as an inspiration: it provides
unity and meaning to his work. For Chernyshevsky nothing

enlarged the artist's experience, nothing deepened that unity and meaning so much as 'the voice human and profane'. In this, he continued the main tradition of Russian art, at any rate of Russian literary art, whose chief concern is the nature and destiny of man. Whether in its attempts to provide a documentation of reality and to interpret or satirize contemporary life, or in its adventures in the sphere of ultimate spiritual quest, Russian literature is seen to have been almost exclusively employed in the exploration of man, and no poetic proliferations could ever deflect it from its function of illuminating human existence. While many of Chernyshevsky's western European contemporaries who concerned themselves with questions of aesthetics—Spencer, Taine, Zola—strove to eliminate the 'pathetic fallacy' and to universalize artistic ideas by bringing them to a scientific standard and often overweighting them with scientific pretensions, Chernyshevsky sought for interchange between the artist—not merely his tastes, his intellect and his social conscience but the whole of his being—and the world of men to which he belongs.[198]

Now an artist, or for that matter an aesthetic philosopher, who wishes to be a humanist, is involved in a kind of infinite regression with a finite sum of which perhaps only the artist has the formula. For men are in situations, situations are in history, history is in society, society is in politics and economics, and so on. The stages of this regression are not a mere succession of extraneous circumstances. A man quite alone may have his own depth of courage, passion, honesty, self-knowledge; but it remains true that even while facing a remote, alien, or hostile world outside, he must know it to be his own. The artist gives new force to the statement *nihil humanum mihi alienum est*; and his humanity is measured by his awareness of the real world, even when he denies it and seeks the creation of new realities. There can be no divorce between art and life, because every situation implies the extremities of human existence. For this reason, it was not possible for Chernyshevsky to judge a work of art without assessing the living link between it and the complex of historical and social factors in which or out of which it had grown. If the artist eschewed this identification in favour of detachment, or 'inner experience', or formal experimentation, he was neglecting an essential responsibility of art. Indeed, it is this sense of responsibility which, in Cherny-shevsky's case, produced a tension between him and the age in which he lived, and made him a rebel.

The argument in favour of 'committed art' is old by now, although it has more recently been given new currency by existentialist doctrine, as well as by the school of 'socialist realism' in Soviet Russia. It has been so mulled over that its effect tends to be one of weariness. But seeing that the history of art gives repeated evidence of accepting society, probing or questioning society, rejecting society and accepting it again, the argument has lost none of its relevance; and in Cherny-shevsky's time it was refreshingly new.

Chernyshevsky felt no inclination to retreat into an ivory tower. He was quite incapable of doing so, and he considered the pursuit of mere aesthetic comforts to be a parochial and trivial as well as an inhuman affair. The separation of art from politics (in the widest sense of the word) appeared to him, there-fore, to be a major aesthetic falsehood. He not only rejected 'art for art's sake', but could not believe that such a thing was possible. In refusing to admit involvement in human deeds and values, in being neutral, in playing safe, in concentrating on technique, the artist, in his view, became a debtor by default—an agent of the social myths and pressures around him. In the last resort, the aesthete had to defend his purity against the same force as that against which the tyrant has to defend his privileges.[199] What Chernyshevsky thought a peculiarly nauseat-ing flavour in this attitude was its infinite possibilities for deception, whereby a smart or, as he called it, an 'Epicurean aristocracy' and its hangers-on claimed artistic value for their 'detached', 'charming trivialities'.

Chernyshevsky could scarcely be blamed for rejecting the idea of 'art for art's sake', if this means, as it nearly always does, that art has no function in life. Manifestly, it has a function, for it is a mode of communication or, more, a dialogue, the means whereby the artist overcomes his isolation and imparts his discovery, and in so doing affects other people. (In this broad sense, by the way, Chernyshevsky held that the engineer, the bootmaker, or the journalist are as truly artists as the poet, and the fine arts are special in their 'fineness', not in their 'artistry'.) As Aristotle had already stated (borrowing his idiom from his favourite science, biology), to know what poetry is, we must examine not only its 'organism' but also what this organism does in the lives of human beings. For him the essence of the poet's art was to give pleasure; for Homer, to make men glad; for Longinus, to 'elevate' or arouse ecstasy; for Walter Pater, to titillate. For Chernyshevsky, the primary function of art was to create an awareness of the human situation and to put a valuation on it, thereby enriching life as well as literature. Any writer who did not do this in one way or another he tended to regard as frivolous, a humbug, or a coward. The secret of this attitude was *not* to deal with literature or art in general as if it were something else: it was a mere refusal to regard art as a snake biting its own tail. To say that Gogol's *Dead Souls* belonged to Gogol's *Dead Souls* was as meaningless to Chernyshevsky as to say that his shoes belonged to his shoes. Each belonged, in a special way, to man, because man had need of it. And Chernyshevsky, alike as aesthetic philosopher and literary critic, wished to know what the need was and how it was satisfied.

Such was the celebrated aesthetic 'utilitarianism' and 'didacticism' of Chernyshevsky which he passed on to his literary successors and which turned the enchanted garden of art, where everybody wanders aimlessly, into a battlefield. A great many disparaging generalizations have acquired currency on this account, and many of them have served to falsify Chernyshevsky's real position. Even Plekhanov, seizing on a phrase of Chernyshevsky that art is a 'textbook for life', declared him an '"enlightener" of the purest water' intent on turning literature into an exercise of rational persuasion. Others complained that Chernyshevsky was determined to debar readers from the pleasure of 'losing themselves' in a work of art, and robbed them of the satisfaction of being entertained. That Chernyshevsky was not a *littérateur* at leisure, a dilettante with a taste and the resources for an infinite variety of aesthetic delights, and vibrating on all wave-lengths with equal liberality and urbanity is quite true. More than this, such delights, however exquisite, were in his opinion, largely symptoms of snobbishness and isolation, proper to the upper classes who imagined themselves to be outside the battle. He believed in the needs and the potentialities of 'the common people'; and he was too conscious of the deep alienation and disorder in Russian society not to seek the widening rather than the refining of culture.[200] The assertion often encountered that the two processes are incompatible or even mutually destructive was to him an evasion, not a solution. Since culture is mixed with its age and immersed in its interests, artistic activity, he insisted again and again, could not escape being involved in the passionate and ferocious movements of society at large. He expected that the social and economic ascent of the masses, in the changed conditions of a future society and guided by a 'conscious intelligentsia', would also produce an appetite for higher values: a popular movement, he believed, must want the highest. This view became fairly widespread among the later populists; it seems to prevail in modern post-revolutionary Russia; and it is largely responsible for the wide prestige which culture now enjoys in Russia.

But all this does not add up to the idea, attributed to Chernyshevsky, that the arts, and literature in particular, are a mere code of behaviour for the people. Nothing could be further from the truth. Not only did he believe that artistic effect can only be achieved by working through particular and intimate experiences, but that didacticism and moralizing turn art into an abstraction. He was completely opposed to every kind of rigidity. He laid stress on Belinsky's resistance to preaching in literature and assailed any tendency among writers to reduce art as well as life to a system.[201] 'An artist', he observed, 'must strive to eliminate from his work as much as possible all that is abstract, to achieve concreteness, in images that are alive and individualized.' 'We yield to none in our concern for the reflection of social life in fiction', he wrote in a review of Tolstoy's *Childhood and Adolescence*. 'But surely, not every poetic image can tolerate the intrusion of social questions. We must not forget that artistic quality consists in the inner unity of a work of art and that in portraying "Childhood" one must portray precisely it and not something else: neither social matters nor scenes of war, neither Peter the Great nor Faust, neither Indiana nor Rudin, but a child, with the feelings and attitudes peculiar to it alone.' And Chernyshevsky commended Thackeray to the readers of the 'Contemporary' for his gift of 'entering joyfully into the feelings of his characters', and for 'not having written a single cold page . . . or spoken a single dead word'.[202]

Chernyshevsky was a 'committed' thinker and critic, a 'critical realist' whose gaze was constantly directed towards the new forms into which society was evolving. Yet neither his commitment nor his realism entailed the confusion that arises when the terms 'critical-realistic literature' and 'tendentious literature' are used as if they were interchangeable. He did not rely on theorems postulated in advance and then demonstrated in quasi-artistic terms, and he realized that at the level where a work of art becomes worth considering form and content are inseparable. He wished the writer to make a choice and use his powers of observation and insight in a certain direction, and literature to have a moral and social bearing—but as literature, not as a system of beliefs tricked out in fancy language, from which the fancy can and must be removed if one wants to get down to brass tacks.[203]

It is a known fact that many books generally taken as seminal for a given time, because they embodied the conscience of the age or because they had acquired some other value as human documents, proved indifferent as literature. *Télémaque*, *La Nouvelle Héloïse*, *Uncle Tom's Cabin* were, *1984* or *Dr. Zhivago* are important books, but the former are already and the latter may come to be esteemed but deciduous literary remainders. Their influence may be a factor in assessing the artistic achievement, but the achievement is very much less than the influence. Such was also Chernyshevsky's *What Is to Be Done?*, one of the first in a long succession of radical novels in Russia—a novel which by no stretch of imagination could be considered great art and which yet is as significant to the historian of literary, social, and political ideas as any great art could be. It was at the very centre of the artistic as well as the social movement of the sixties, and even later. Strictly proscribed by the censorship, which dubbed it as 'highly dangerous' and 'devoid of all artistic value', decried by the reviewers of the official and semi-official press as 'demoralizing rubbish', it spread clandestinely through Russia, borrowed or sold on the literary black market. '*What Is to Be Done?*' the painter Ilya Repin recalled, 'fired the minds of a whole generation: it was read with passion, in tattered, printed or hand-written copies and preserved, together with other prohibited literature and pictures of "the

politicals".'[204] It was produced by the prosecution at many
political trials as an important piece of evidence found in the
possession of the accused. Young people discussed interminably
and vehemently the novel's meaning and implications. It
became their confession of faith and code of behaviour. Many
of these discussions among women students, Repin writes,
'ended in a brief ceremony. One had to answer three questions.
First question: Do you renounce the old order? Answer: I do.
Second question: Do you curse Katkov? Answer: I curse him.
Third question: Do you believe in Vera Pavlovna's third
dream (the heroine's fantastic dream about future society in
Chernyshevsky's novel *What Is to Be Done?*)? Answer: I do. A
pair of sharp scissors then produced their harsh, energetic click
and down went the luxuriant plait of hair.'[205]

Never has the new trend . . . [wrote Pisarev] declared itself so
resolutely and strongly. All those who are nourished by routine or
stew in it are, therefore, enraged by [Chernyshevsky's novel].
And, no doubt, they have reason to be: the novel mocks their aesthetics, destroys their morality, demonstrates the fraudulence of their
chastity and does not conceal its contempt for its own judges. This,
however, constitutes but a small portion of the novel's failings: the
major sin is that it should have become a banner for the hateful
trend, showing this trend its proximate aims and gathering round
them all that is young and alive.[206]

But even Nekrasov admired Chernyshevsky's novel. That he
should have admired it for what it is was perfectly natural;
that he should have equated this, though not unreservedly,
with artistic worth is surprising. Chernyshevsky himself had no
delusions on that score, for he stated conclusively in a letter
from Siberia: 'I have not a trace of artistic talent . . ., and all
its [the novel's] merit consists merely in its truthfulness.'[207]
'Truth' here, it would seem, was meant to denote an honest
reflection of life as he saw it, and a will not to allow himself to be
deceived and not to deceive others; but also something less
fixed or final, namely, that which suggests and inspires more
genuine human relations. None of Chernyshevsky's detractors
needed to be convinced of the first part of his unassuming statement and they denied even the validity of its second part. His
admirers, on the contrary, while applauding the second part,
resolutely denied the first.[208] But there is no reason, why

the statement should not be taken at its face value and accepted as a criterion for judging Chernyshevsky's performance.

What strikes one in particular is that, because he was not suitably endowed as a writer of fiction, Chernyshevsky not only wrote his novel on a fairly low imaginative plane, but also failed to live up to his own aesthetic standards—the standards of realism. The plot of the novel has already been roughly outlined: it provides the necessary framework for the socialism, or 'co-operative socialism' of the tale and for the disclosure of the contemporary moral problems. But one misses that kind of concreteness which Chernyshevsky advocated as the hallmark of true literary art. There is no sense of the physical presence of his characters, except, remotely, in Rakhmetov, who, although an essential element in the structure of the novel, takes very little part in the story itself. There is no compound of their manner of speech, their ideas and their behaviour. They all speak with the same voice, men and women alike. The author uses them all the time, without leaving them free for a moment, and in using them deprives them of life and credible motivations. There are some vivid scenes, particularly at the beginning, in the descriptions of the heroine's early life in her parental home and of the first meeting with her rescuer and first lover Lopukhov, but they coexist with a number of feeble inventions and implausible situations. The dialogue consists of a confrontation of views rather than of people. And there is a great deal of it, for Chernyshevsky's heroes and heroines are always explaining themselves. Chemistry, physiology, sociology are massively directed by the characters upon each other, and even declarations of love are infused with scientific considerations, somewhat reminiscent of the author's own relations with the young Olga Sokratovna.

And yet there remains a great deal in the novel that has enduring value. Chernyshevsky felt his characters deeply. He felt their love, their refusals, and their hopes. What he felt even more was their problems and the tasks which faced them in a hostile world. The problems are not just driven home painstakingly but are experienced with the truthfulness characteristic of Chernyshevsky's own attitude to life. This gives the novel a peculiar moral texture and moral force. It succeeded in gripping the imagination of his contemporaries because the events and characters shown in it appealed not only to the understanding, but to the feelings as well, at any rate to their moral feelings. Faulty and bare as a work of art though it is, the novel proved an inspiring monument to their search and a testimony, almost unique in Russian literature, of a writer's concern for the fate of his fellowmen. Chernyshevsky might have anticipated the words of the hero in a modern play (Sartre's *Le Diable et le Bon Dieu*): 'I have taken my century upon my shoulders and have said: I will answer for it even while I rebel against it.'

IV

NIKOLAI DOBROLYUBOV
1836–1861

1. *A Compassionate Outsider*

'A POVERTY-STRICKEN childhood in the home of a poor priest; half-starved and meagrely educated; then four years of feverish, relentless work; finally, a year abroad, spent in presentiment of death—that is all there is to say of Dobrolyubov's biography.' This summary from an obituary by Nekrasov correctly conveys the eventless pattern of Dobrolyubov's brief life. He was born on 24 January 1836 and died of consumption on 17 November 1861. The eventlessness and brevity contrasts with his prominence in the intellectual history of Russia. At the age of twenty-one Dobrolyubov was already an influence, a power, a person of dominant intelligence, who both embodied and clearly saw the characteristic currents of his time. Even Strakhov, the *pochvennik* philosopher and Dobrolyubov's literary enemy, said that 'to dismiss Dobrolyubov as an ephemeral, incidental figure is to dismiss literature as ephemeral and incidental'.

There is a great similarity between Dobrolyubov's and Chernyshevsky's early life. Both were sons of priests; both were educated in torpid provincial seminaries, although Dobrolyubov's home town, Nizhny-Novgorod, was less of a cultural backwater than Chernyshevsky's Saratov; both absorbed the atmosphere of religion and, in youth, actively sought religion; both were obedient sons of their parents and of their Church, diligent, prim, and orderly in their ways; both were drawn from a distinctly conformist environment into opposition and revolt. And yet, with Dobrolyubov, we are in another, more troubled world, and it is hard to think of two men more different in their psychological make-up. Unlike Chernyshevsky, Dobrolyubov was not a product of idyllic family life, nor a serene and balanced personality. His personal relationships were unhappy, and he had no gift for them. Those who meant most to him were his kind and sensible mother and, later, Nekrasov and Chernyshevsky. His father was an intelligent but high-handed and prickly man whose life and work consisted largely in efforts to creep into the good graces of the local aristocracy, in order to be different from the rest of the lower clergy who lived in obscurity and were received through the back door. He was not as poor as Nekrasov made him out to be. The son was more intelligent and poorer than the father, almost as high-handed and irascible, and prone to a tortured sense of his own inadequacy.

There exists a legend about Dobrolyubov for which Chernyshevsky is in a measure responsible and in which Dobrolyubov, together with his family, appears as a paragon of virtue, delicacy, and ascetic self-abnegation. Chernyshevsky was Dobrolyubov's first biographer, and the extensive biographical material which he collected is still one of the most important sources for the study of his young friend's life. But, guided by a sense of discretion and a belief that, as he says, 'in a society where vulgarity reigns supreme' one must 'remain secretive', he deliberately withheld some of the evidence.[1]

Fortunately, Dobrolyubov kept a diary, which is more important for his biography and the climate of his inner life than any similar documents are for the interior biography of any other Russian nineteenth-century writer.[2] In fact, it is one of the most outspoken diaries in Russian nineteenth-century literature. Like Tolstoy he is pitiless in his self-analysis and appallingly intimate. Nothing that concerns himself is held back behind a veil of good taste, or sensibility, or protestations of innocence. There is even a touch of masochism, or of irony that has the masochist's vanity in it, although he did state explicitly that he meant his confidences to be kept secret. The effect is slightly repulsive, even if the honesty cannot but attract. But Dobrolyubov never pretended to be an amiable character. Instead of the essential charm of Chernyshevsky which his curious roughness projected, Dobrolyubov's Diary leaves the impression of bitterness, if often of noble bitterness, and of arrogance that hides a deep-rooted unease. Yet it is also happily free from Chernyshevsky's pedestrian discursive thoroughness. While subscribing to many of the principles of the Enlightenment—reason, nature, science, progress, and the rest—and, later, scoffing at all the 'deeper' things in life, the Diary reveals a dark, mutinous undercurrent in Dobrolyubov, and an unassuaged craving for life. This, as well as Dobrolyubov's passionate moral convictions, consort badly with his somewhat cold-blooded analytical mind or, for that matter, with his outer imperturbable self. At times the Diary reads like the case-history of a resentful, sore, and stubborn youth who adopts defiant attitudes because he is profoundly vulnerable, whose lack of self-assurance makes him pliant and arrogant in turn, and who is tough with himself and even tougher with almost everyone else. The toughness was largely a mask, concealing, as we shall see again and again, a morally sensitive man with a deeply wounded conscience and an effective and grim kind of humour.

Some entries, nevertheless, are depressingly humourless. Of these a section entitled 'Psychotorium' deserves special attention, for it shows Dobrolyubov at his most religious. It is a long confession of sins which would have been even longer had Chernyshevsky not torn out and destroyed most of the pages. That he has done so is understandable, for even in its truncated form it is a tedious record of a tormented Christian of the gloomy variety. Chernyshevsky was sickened by its interminable biblical and other pious phrases, by the wearisome religious plaints, the self-scourging and compunctious macerations for every thought and spoon of jam or glass of tea that seemed to divert him from the minute attention to personal salvation. In all this there was much more of the religious temperament than in Chernyshevsky's account of his own early spiritual life. According to one of his teachers, Kostrov, Dobrolyubov was known as 'the most pious man in Nizhny-Novgorod'. His reputation at the theological seminary, which he left at the age of seventeen against the wishes of his father, was of the most devout, reliable, and studious, if unpopular, pupil, destined for the career of a godly and successful ecclesiastic.

Yet, even at his most devout, he gives the impression of having deliberately, even desperately, attuned himself to an uncongenial exalted mood. The attitude has certain affinities with Gogol's state of mind when he lashed himself into religious frenzy and produced his lamentable 'Correspondence with Friends', which, incidentally, Dobrolyubov admired greatly at first but later disclaimed as a betrayal by 'a novelist turned bigot'. Dobrolyubov took refuge in religion from uncertainties and a sense of personal inadequacy: religion remained with him, while it remained, as something to hang on to rather than as a deep conviction; and the overwrought belief in immortality seems like a mere version of trying desperately to live. On his own admission, it was his private, lonely half, the half which kept him a stranger in his world and made him unfit for human relationships, that moved him to cling to religion. 'We are all the more ready', he concluded, 'to look with reverence at everything sacred, the more distant it is from us.'

But the more he tried to live the religious life and draw strength from it, the greater his sense of unreality became; and, as time went on, even the emotional value of the religious imagery and observance, to which he continued to adhere with an almost cruel honesty, faded away. He began to feel that by immersing himself in devotion he was losing the taste, the need for and the love of reality: the narrow gate was leading not to fuller life, for which he owns 'an irresistible longing', but to emptiness and death. He suspected that he had become the victim of a tragi-comedy, in which his rich supply of guilt-feeling was being traded on and exploited. In addition, he suffered increasingly from his environment. Almost everything in it combined to stifle thought and to atrophy the imagination. Tenacity, judicious study, and subservience to his superiors were alternating in him with revolt against what he considered to be the empty rhetoric of his teachers and the 'deluding rigmarole' invented by bigots in order 'to subdue the free spirit of man'. 'I am condemned to wallow in this dirty pool,' he wrote of his seminary, '. . . in this suffocating atmosphere of pedantic freaks, rude ways and vulgar hilarity. . . . There is not a single ray of light or nobility or feeling in this vale of ignorance and coarseness, not a day of relief . . . from tedium and mental suffering.'[3] The whole ecclesiastical world, with which he had voluntarily and involuntarily identified himself, turned in his mind into a huge instrument of stagnation, 'oriental time-lessness', and obscurantism.

Still, as can be seen from a great many Diary entries for 1853–4, the process of accommodating himself to loss of faith was very distressing and evidently concerned not merely intellectual ideas but deeper loyalites and motivations. He continued to seek for some sign of God, some trace of divine providence, but found nothing. 'I believe,' he wrote at the beginning of 1854, 'I believe, I believe—with all my strength, with love and prayer . . . Lord, help Thou my unbelief!' Then suddenly he realized that he was living in a fool's paradise—or hell.

The realization came with the death of his parents, especially of his mother—the only human being in his life to whom he was really and deeply attached. The event made him remember God's hand in the way one remembers a whip, and wrung from him the complaint as old as the world, that God has deserted man. 'It has convinced me of the truth of my resolve, of the non-existence of those phantoms conceived by oriental fancy. . . . It has embittered me against that mysterious power which we dare to call good and merciful, without noticing the evil pervading the world and the cruel blows which this power deals at its own worshippers.'[4] Evil in the world was connected for Dobrolyubov with early experience of a godless world.

For a time he submerged himself in fearful introspective prayers addressed to God, to his mother, and mostly to his own wretchedness. There is a moving and somewhat macabre account of this in the Diary which contrasts with the self-controlled, almost coldly off-hand manner with which he seemed to treat his loss in the eyes of the outside world. The prayer remained a mere deliverance to a void. There was no answer beyond the pain—except the suffering of others and compassion with the misfortunes of others. This is important, for Dobrolyubov had in abundance that gift for suffering—a Russian gift perhaps—which does not narrow, which overcomes isolation and intensifies solidarity. The story of his inner life as recorded in his Diary is, in a sense, a story of how the thought of others or, in his own words, 'the fate of the people and of the world which I tried to quit', transformed his private sorrows into a creative achievement. On the other hand, his struggles and afflictions were not his alone, but those of the society in which he lived. 'Our unwashed seminarists', as Turgenev fastidiously referred to the younger generation of the sixties, recognized in Dobrolyubov their own anxiety and struggle, and that is why he, as well as Chernyshevsky, became archetypal.

Later, Dobrolyubov wrote to a friend that 'for the course of two years I kept on battling against old enemies within and without. . . . I looked that enigmatic life straight in the face and saw that it was very different from what Father Paisy [a teacher at the seminary] and the Right Reverend Jeremy [Archbishop of Nizhny-Novgorod] claimed it to be.'[5] The collapse of the religious system resulted in the liberation of uncommitted emotion and intellectual curiosity. He began reading avidly the forbidden champions of emancipation—Feuerbach and the other left Hegelians, Proudhon, Belinsky and, above all, Herzen, whom he admired most of all. The new experience also led to cynicism, or to what was regarded as such by Dobrolyubov's later literary enemies.[6] The 'cynicism' was, he said, his liberated capacity for laughter, suppressed by the 'phantoms of oriental fancy'. From now on his convictions were firmly set: even Chernyshevsky, to his own avowed regret, was not as unflinching as Dobrolyubov. What had vanished was the torment, the fearful introspection, the longing for the living or the dead gods. There remained the more obvious satire, the invective, and the moral conscience. Having lost his faith, Dobrolyubov became more high-minded than ever: indeed, the loss proved a painful beginning to moral advance, for it gave an alert independence to his conscience, and a sense of personal responsibility.

There was still much to contend with: poverty, precarious health, social humiliations, distracted unrequited passions and indignities, the hopes and corruptions of his age and Dobrolyubov's own unwieldy nature, and, later, the continuous, wearing struggle with the censorship. All this goes further to explain his gnawing sense of unhappiness and his fierce and sardonic protests than mere 'biliousness', which Herzen held to be characteristic of the species—the men of the sixties.

Poverty became grinding when, with the death of his parents, Dobrolyubov was left to provide—by private lessons and by journalism—for two younger brothers and five sisters as well as for himself. By this time he had already left Nizhny-Novgorod for the capital, where, lacking the necessary funds to study at the University, he had entered the Teachers' Training Institute.

The passions and indignities of love were part of the most poignant and sombre moments in Dobrolyubov's life. He was continuously in love all his life, with one woman after another, but there are no signs that his loves were much more than obsessive hallucinations known to himself alone: when disclosed they drove every woman to flight. Dobrolyubov was uncommonly ugly and sexually unattractive. He had himself in mind when he wrote, apropos of Turgenev's *On the Eve*, that 'every decent and sensible girl would flee from [him], crying *"quelle horreur!"*'. A private pupil of his called Nataliya Tatarina, who loathed her teacher, even while finding him interesting to listen to when she was able to take her mind off his physical frame, left this description of her teacher: '. . . a fairly tall, lanky young man with a hollow chest and narrow shoulders . . . "What a sight!", I thought to myself. A fat nose, fat shapeless lips—like two round, thick pieces of flesh—a greyish-green face and thin, stringy ginger hair.'[7] To this must be added a large protruding forehead, minute but penetrating myopic eyes, extreme awkwardness in demeanour, and a flaccid, sweaty handshake.

Dobrolyubov's hopeless infatuations began when, at the age of fourteen or fifteen, he fell in love with a little girl of twelve, who belonged to the inaccessible aristocracy of Nizhny-Novgorod. The later objects of his love cannot be enumerated: they included actresses, wives of his best friends, Chernyshevsky's sister-in-law (Anyuta Vasilieva), Parisian *can can* girls, and Italians from Messina (one of whom he intended to marry). Eventually he got himself involved with prostitutes. The story of these activities and experiences, which, abandoning every comforting reticence, Dobrolyubov minutely recorded in his Diary (although the virginal Chernyshevsky tried to prune it as best he could), is a story of sudden flarings-up of love in the midst of stale and sordid squalor, until his half-tragic half-ludicrous passions petered out into nothing. But he was no egotist who uses woman as a mere mirror of his desire and gets away with any number of liaisons, for the simple reason that he never loses his head and is never in love. His attitude to these women was quite free from cynicism and vulgarity, and even quaintly inspired his advocacy of women's rights. He was like a Saint Augustine who robbed orchards as a boy and kept mistresses as a young man but cried *peccavi* and was never vile, cruel, or mean. Indeed, he considered marrying one of the prostitutes (Masha) and, but for Chernyshevsky's objections, would have married another one (a German girl called Theresa Grunwald). 'And why', he asked, 'should their business be considered lower than . . ., for example, our business of teaching in which we sell ourselves to teach things we don't know and propagate ideas we don't believe in?'—which reminds one of a similar remark by Rozanov, to the effect that 'lawyers, scholars, professors and writers are all like prostitutes, *prostitués prêcheurs* . . .: the others are infinitely, metaphysically preferable'. Dobrolyubov's dreams of 'entering the stage of social activity in the manner of Cato Sapiens or Zeno the Stoic', were succeeded by declarations that 'love is my only desire now. It is the centre of all my powers, of all my life, and the consciousness of its defeats and lasting non-fulfilment weighs on me, torments me, fills me with anguish, resentment, envy, with all that is hideous and wretched in human nature.'[8]

All this was proof of more than mere sexual compulsion in an *amoureux manqué* too ugly to find a partner. It showed Dobrolyubov's essential innocence and grief, his secret aspiration towards happiness, and his intense and restless desire for life and respect for it. He never rationalized immorality, in the manner of his contemporary, Leontiev, who acquiesced in the pagan pleasures of the body and talked of a 'full and beautiful life'; and his promiscuity tells of a continuous, and ultimately a romantic, effort to reconcile mundane love with his ideal. Hence, perhaps, his early captivation by Lermontov, whose discontented, in part 'demonic', in part supercilious, but deeply poetic hero, Pechorin, became for a time Dobrolyubov's model.[9]

Disappointments in love were not Dobrolyubov's only besetting worry. He also suffered from humiliations at the hand of a caste-ridden society. He despised the ill-bred clerical milieu to which he belonged, and he hankered after the 'free and easy ways' of people enjoying superior social status. 'To-night [2 November 1853] I was prepared to sacrifice intelligence, knowledge, nobility, the loftiest convictions for superficial urbanity, vulgar fluency and the glib manners of a mundane fop. . . .' His vain attempts in this direction met with 'painful pin-pricks' and 'offensive snubs'. Such avowals naturally evoke the image

of a man suffering from what is today referred to as an
inferiority complex. And Dobrolyubov's later violent diatribes
against the liberal gentry who flew their culture like a
banner could, no doubt, be interpreted as a sign of snobbery of
the inverted kind. Indeed, Turgenev, Annenkov, Katkov, and
even Tolstoy saw in Dobrolyubov, at best a wronged child
pursuing an all-out vendetta, at worst a truculent 'rude brat'
(*nakhalnyi malchishka*), with all the prickles of one who is not out
of the top drawer and refuses ever to allow himself to forget the
fact. That Dobrolyubov's sardonic postures were to some extent
a reply to humiliations undergone—the reply of pride—cannot
be denied. What strikes one, however, more forcefully is that
he had none of the barren temper of an envious climber. The
hurts of pride were transformed in him into an understanding
of the misfortunes of other people and a respect for their
human dignity. He strove, in the first place, after sincerity.
The 'snobbery', inverted or otherwise, was, as it were, the
chastity of the perfectionist hunting for shams and impostors
and driven by a passion for truth and justice in his own conduct
as well as in that of others. He also knew how to laugh, even at
himself; and he knew how to love and to hate. His hatred did
not concern wounded vanity, or any other outward, superficial thing. It was more like Belinsky's, if without his ardour
and generosity: it was a form of moral refusal, thoroughgoing
and lasting—the hatred of an idealist who is too honest to
revenge himself by knavery. Even Dostoevsky, Dobrolyubov's
foremost castigator, said that it was 'imbued with a just and
sacred thought', and that Dobrolyubov himself was 'a great
fighter for truth'.[10]

When Dobrolyubov became a recognized literary critic he
had plenty of occasions to attend salons: it in no way tendered
to his self-esteem. On the contrary, he experienced unease, but
on moral, not on social grounds, and because he felt he was
wasting his time. He knew that his mind was his only fortune,
and he turned himself consciously, almost conscientiously, into
an intellectual tough, or a tough intellectual. He was not
insensitive, but his sensitivity was mainly exposed to the phoney
and the lofty, and at the least suspicion of these he turned
tough. Few if any of his generation had such an unerringly
merciless eye for the bogus, such a capacity for seeing through

moral, political, and cultural shams. Some believed that this served as a screen, and that he had invented the mask of a satirist, of a down-to-earth critic, in order to compensate for the absence of feeling. Even Chernyshevsky, or rather Levitsky of the *Prologue*, said that Dobrolyubov was 'as frigid as a fish'. There are passages in the Diary where Dobrolyubov himself laments his atrophy of feeling, or confesses that his mind is cold. In context, however, this appears more like a natural suspicion of heart-strings, of things that are all sentiment and sensibility, and a proneness to tear down the romantic halo from life. He may have seen human beings with a lack of warmth, but he also saw them with a peculiar intensity and longed for true human relationships. He was shy, and like most shy people, he confided himself most readily and spontaneously when he was in love. We have seen that far from evading experience he craved for it, with passion and compassion. 'Life presses on', he wrote with surprising artlessness, 'in all its fullness and energy, with its love and disquiet, its joys and sorrows. It takes one's breath away. I wait for it impatiently, feverishly, excitedly. . . .' And still more naïvely: 'What a strange thing! A few days ago I felt I could really fall in love; and last night I had a sudden urge to learn to dance. What the dickens! It must be the beginning of reconciliation with society. I only hope I shan't yield to this silly mood. I must make no concessions to my society; I must keep my distance and feed my bile.'[11]

The seeming heartlessness was no more than an assumed intransigence of the mind which contrasted with his curiously feminine and vulnerable appearance. One cannot dislike him, even though by all the laws of what appeals to us we ought perhaps to do so.

Chernyshevsky liked him enormously, almost inordinately, although by temperament—not by conviction—he was quite uncongenial to him. They met in 1856, through an ex-pupil of Chernyshevsky's, when Dobrolyubov was still a student at the Teachers' Institute, and the meeting marked the beginning of a remarkable partnership. In the same year Dobrolyubov wrote his first contribution to the 'Contemporary' (no. 8)—an essay on Russian eighteenth-century literature. Most of his previous writings consisted of bitty and bitter topical poems with a revolutionary bent. They were published in the Institute's

handwritten magazine *Slukhi* (Rumours) and distributed clandestinely in the capital and even in some provincial university
towns.[12] One of these poems was intercepted by his superiors.
Dobrolyubov got into serious trouble, gave in—for the last
time—and finally established his reputation as 'a politically
unreliable element'. This reputation was enhanced by the
activities of a small student circle, known as the 'Dobrolyubov
gang' (*dobrolyubovskaya shaika*), which engaged in 'subversion',
in 'fostering among ourselves', as one active member of the
group, Stsiborsky, put it, 'the ability to respond with all
our minds to the challenge of the times, in the promotion of an
understanding of contemporary issues, and in an attempt to
apply our acquired knowledge to life'. Dobrolyubov, the ringleader, was regarded by his associates as a kind of literary
surgeon, sharpening his knife to probe the maladies of the times
and impatient of all knowledge that lacked relevance to life and
action. 'In place of God and humanity he put man, and assured
us that life is the only criterion of all existing things.' To this
must be added Dobrolyubov's early profession of 'unflinching
socialism', however ill-defined it may have been then. 'I am a
determined socialist', he declared in the Diary (15 January
1857). 'I am prepared . . . to join the society of the dispossessed, with equal rights and common ownership for all. . . .
There is no ideal on earth, unless it be the democratic community prefigured by Herzen in London in 1855.'[13] A friend
recalls that on being told by a fellow-student that 'a precipitate
liberation of the serfs might prove unwise', Dobrolyubov turned
pale and, shouting 'Scoundrel!', threw him out of the room.

Chernyshevsky recognized in Dobrolyubov the quintessential
raznochinets who had the courage of his insights and his
beliefs, who knew how to create a sense of reality, and who
besides, possessed an uncommonly sharp wit and incisive
manner. 'What a remarkable force of intellect!', Chernyshevsky
(Volgin) said in 'Prologue' of his first impression of Dobrolyubov
(Levitsky). 'His writing is excellent, unlike mine: it is concise,
buoyant, scintillating. . . . Above all, what an understanding
. . ., what a clear view of things and what independence of mind
—at the age of twenty-one!' This was an excessive tribute, as were
nearly all Chernyshevsky's references to Dobrolyubov. At any
rate, none of Dobrolyubov's writings can be considered brilliant.

On the other hand, he cannot be fairly saddled with that polemical manner which was devised by some of his radical contemporaries, notably by Antonovich, as well as by their opponents, and in which all pretence of style is abandoned and long tirades are interrupted by passages of low abuse. Just as his character was at the same time sensitive and tough, humane and bluntly dismissive, so his writings could be both discriminating and coarse. But it suited Chernyshevsky, and it suited Nekrasov, who appreciated, and knew how to exploit, not only Dobrolyubov's quick and trenchant mind but also his enormous capacity for work and powers of application. In 1858 Dobrolyubov became co-editor of the 'Contemporary'. From then on nearly every issue contained some signed or unsigned contribution by him. His frequent Bibliographical Notes on a variety of social and literary themes became one of the most exciting features of the review. They are masterpieces of summary exposition, bristling with abrupt transitions from derisive gaiety to discursive gravity, from the sublime to the ridiculous and back again.

On joining the 'Contemporary' Dobrolyubov found himself in the midst of the keen controversy that divided the 'fathers' and the 'sons', and he showed himself in no mood to pour oil on the troubled waters. I have described the situation in some detail elsewhere in this book. But a quotation from Panaev, referring specifically to Dobrolyubov, will complete the picture.

Realizing [Panaev wrote in the 'Contemporary'] that the new generation has embarked on the ridiculing of our smoothness and debility, our romantic fads and lyrical effusions, that it is fast gaining ground on us . . ., that it is forcing its new and harsher way . . ., we, or at any rate some of us, took offence. . . . Our resentment was aimed, in the first place, at Dobrolyubov. From long standing, or because we had acquitted ourselves well in the heyday of our youth, we all, or rather some of us, had learnt to enjoy authority, or some little authority. We . . . would have found it agreeable if someone representing the younger generation had shown us that respect in which we ourselves held those whom we considered authoritative in our younger days. . . . But Dobrolyubov not only failed to entertain any respect for us, but refused to pay attention to us. . . . We could not help feeling mortified. We concluded that the younger generation, for all its undoubted intelligence, was arid, cold, flat, heartless, captious, and the victim of that awful doctrine—nihilism. Nihilists! Even if we did not go as far as to stigmatize the whole generation by this terrible name, we assured ourselves that Dobrolyubov at any rate was a nihilist of nihilists.[14]

There is nothing new or unusual in that old men resent being told that they have seen their day; although in Russia, where fashion or *Zeitgeist* proved a particularly cruel master, devouring a generation in ten years instead of the usual twenty, the resentment was more pronounced than elsewhere. Old men are always shocked to discover that, having fought for an ideal, the young merely take it for granted, or push it aside, or deride it, and they conclude that the young are going to the dogs. What was new in this context was the imputation of nihilism. Indeed, it was suggested that Turgenev's Bazarov—the 'nihilistic' hero of the novel *Fathers and Sons*—was drawn from Dobrolyubov. As has been noted already, the novel, which appeared in 1861, roused the anger of the young radicals because at first they took it to be a deliberate caricature of Dobrolyubov and of themselves. There is little evidence to prove the suggestion, and Turgenev denied it. In any case, he created his hero with unmistakable love and admiration, whereas he loathed Dobrolyubov, as he frankly admitted to Chernyshevsky. Later, it is true, he declared, as he often did in such cases, that he 'esteemed him greatly, both as a man and as a writer'; but at the time in question Dobrolyubov was for him nothing but a 'hard and intolerant blusterer', 'a literary Robespierre', and 'a rattlesnake' (Chernyshevsky being a mere 'snake'—not the other way round, as Antonovich suggests). And it is of course difficult for the tolerant to tolerate the intolerant, difficult for the soft to be soft towards the hard.

Dobrolyubov, for his part, did exactly what Panaev said: he studiedly ignored Turgenev. Politeness was not his forte; because it is often at war with sincerity, or because those who think they have discovered the truth will make little impression if they murmur it so as to offend nobody, Dobrolyubov inclined to treat politeness as a system of stock responses and pharisaical obligations. There is an often-quoted account by Chernyshevsky of a famous occasion on which Turgenev met his 'adversary' at one of Nekrasov's literary dinners. Being naturally civil, but also self-consciously concerned to remain on good terms with the young and not to miss the boat, Turgenev tried, despite repeated rebuffs, to engage him in conversation. 'Ivan

Sergeevich', Dobrolyubov blurted out at last, 'your talk bores me, and if you don't mind we'd better stop talking to one another altogether.'[15]

His reactions to Turgenev were similar to those of Chernyshevsky, but without the latter's courtesy. Indeed, Chernyshevsky even tried, with little conviction it is true, to impress on his friend that one ought not to repudiate out of hand someone who, like Turgenev, was 'more or less capable of sympathizing with something that is not dishonest'. While admitting Turgenev's aptitude for 'approaching contemporary life with acumen', and paying a number of other literary tributes, Dobrolyubov remained unmoved. Turgenev, the eminent bystander, who registers amused astonishment and turns the perfect phrase; Turgenev, who tries hard to by-pass doctrinaire arguments and always manages to get the best of both worlds; Turgenev, who 'raises us above surrounding reality' and drifts into antiseptic liberalism—stood for all the things which, in Dobrolyubov's view, were not an affair of living people, or rather, could survive, whether in life or literature, only at the price of a terrifying inhumanity. As for Chernyshevsky but more so, for Dobrolyubov 'liberalism' was the touchstone by which current moral, social and literary attitudes were to be tested. 'His voice', Chernyshevsky (Volgin) said of Dobrolyubov (Levitsky), 'was like a discord in the sweet concert of the Russian liberals.'

The conflict came to a head with the publication of a review by Dobrolyubov of Turgenev's novel *On the Eve*: it bore the challenging title 'When Will the Real Day Come?' (*Kogda-zhe pridyot nastoyashchii den'?*). It represents one of the most extreme statements of Dobrolyubov's radical creed. *On the Eve* was to be welcomed as a reminder of the 'real day' to come, as the opening of 'a real heroic epic', 'a Russian Iliad and Odyssey', and not the story of a mere 'sojourn on Calypso's island', as Turgenev seemed to intimate in his increasing uneasiness at the prospect of reaching the ultimate. When, through the good offices of the censor (Beketov), and before its appearance in the 'Contemporary', the article came to the notice of Turgenev he was horrified. His horror was due not only to the article's mordant tone, but to its implied suggestion that his novel could, paradoxically enough, be interpreted as an omen, however indirect, of the revolution to come, whereas, in fact, his political moderation was known to everybody. '*I urge you*, my dear N[ekrasov],' he wrote hastily to the editor of the review, '*not to publish this article*: it will bring nothing but trouble for me; it is unjust and caustic; and I wouldn't know where to run away to if it appeared in print. Please accede to my request. I'll drop in.— Yours, I. T.'[16] None the less, the article did appear in the 'Contemporary' (1860, no. 3), in a censored version, and it contributed decisively to the great divorce.

Most of Dobrolyubov's important work was written before the final break became apparent. It shows his capacity for precise statement and cogent argument; but it also displays a sweeping animosity for his opponents and a defiance which testified to his growing sense of dissatisfaction with himself and with life around him. In consequence, he suffered more from the censorship than any other contributor to the 'Contemporary', and most of his articles were returned by the censor with the sting drawn, thereby rendering the author more impatient than ever.

What especially raised Dobrolyubov above the prominent men [of the sixties], what constituted his characteristic trait . . . [Antonovich writes in his reminiscences], was this remarkable force, this irresistible energy and irrepressible passion of his convictions. His whole being seemed electrified by them, ready at any moment to burst out and shower sparks . . . on anything that barred the way to the realization of his convictions. Indeed, he was prepared to give his life for their realization. Every one of his thoughts and words strained to become action, which, as yet, was impossible in the prevailing conditions. And this impossibility became a source of continuous mental and moral agony. . . . It is not surprising, therefore, that during the brief term of his literary activity this man turned into a true sufferer, a martyr; that all the time he was burning as in a fever, from frustration, outrage and even despair.[17]

As far as his public life was concerned, Dobrolyubov found vent for these in two ways—by using his satirical pen, and by trying to encourage the little revolutionary activity that was in progress at the time. Since direct satire exposed him to the rigours of the censorship, he wrote oblique satirical verse under such pseudonyms as Konrad Lilienschwager, Yakov Kham (Jack the

Blackguard), D. Svirishelev (the Whistler), and similar fancy names. With this in view, he founded in 1859, together with Nekrasov, a Supplement to the 'Contemporary' which he called, apparently after an Italian magazine of the same name *Fischietto* (not *Diritto*, as Nekrasov, in his ignorance of any foreign language, believed), 'The Whistle' (*Svistok*), which Herzen described as 'the buffoon show attached to the big theatre' (*balaganchik pri bolshom teatre*).[18] The aim was 'to finish off the old world with laughter', and those most hit were 'the smugly complacent, grandiloquent, supine, and soulless gentry (*bary*)'. In fact, no Russian publication, not even Shchedrin's satire, served so much to discredit the liberalism of the gentry as 'The Whistle'. The Supplement won Dobrolyubov the reputation of the greatest literary master of gibes and flouts and jeers. The poems, as also the occasional pieces of satirical circumlocution in prose, have little literary value; but they are spirited, deft, and sharply observant, and show his ever-growing awareness not only of social evils but also of the causes from which they sprang. Those who were affronted by its shrill and discordant whistling read the magazine with almost as much eagerness as those who rejoiced in it.

It has been noted earlier on that up to the winter of 1861 (the generally accepted date for the beginning of 'Land and Freedom') there were no organized political groups engaged in revolutionary activities during Alexander II's reign. Dobrolyubov could not, therefore, have been associated with any such activities. But we have also seen that even before this date there existed a number of loose circles of young radicals, 'without centre or leadership' (Shelgunov), united only by a common concern for 'a complete transformation of Russian society'. Of these, the most important was the group around Chernyshevsky and the 'Contemporary', and one of its most active members was Dobrolyubov. In point of fact, by temperament and inclination, he was more activist than Chernyshevsky who, though undoubtedly an inspiration for them all, remained, as we have seen, somewhat aloof. Chernyshevsky himself is alleged to have admitted that he was unsuited for the role of a 'practical politician: not so Dobrolyubov, for he is an excellent organizer'.[19] Since there was as yet nothing to organize, Dobrolyubov confined himself to incitement, and held out the alternative of revolution. 'Until now', he wrote to his friend Shemanovsky in 1859, 'there was no . . . activity open to honourable and decent men in Russia: that's why we sour and fall into decay. But we must *bring about* this activity. All our energy . . . should be directed towards it. I firmly believe that, even if there are no more than one hundred such people as you and me . . ., if we set our heart upon it and make the final choice, such action will happen despite all the villainy of the obscurantists. . . . We can take control of the present and capture the future.' Another correspondent was summoned 'to plunge into the seething cauldron . . .: I could put it more briefly, but you know what I mean. . . .' 'As for me, I seem to be deliberately marked by fate for the great cause of total revolution.'[20] Some of these utterances were not more than expressions of adolescent non-conformity; others testified to Dobrolyubov's moral and social awareness, which led him to understand the conflicts of his society and to resolve to change it, to make it freer and more alive.

In 1858 Dobrolyubov was taken ill with scrofula, brought on by dissolute life, overwork, and continuous tension and restlessness. It was soon followed by consumption. In 1860 Nekrasov and Panaev persuaded him to go to Switzerland for a cure. But this proved too late. For a year he wandered through France and Italy, and then returned to Russia when reaction was setting in, when some of his friends had already been arrested, and Chernyshevsky had hinted in his letters at the end of the 'thaw'. Like Belinsky before him, Dobrolyubov died just in time. 'It is not work that killed him', Chernyshevsky wrote in a tribute to his friend, '—he worked with uncommon ease. He was destroyed by his social grief (*grazhdanskaya skorb'*). At times he promised that he would rest, but could never resist the feverish impulse to work. He could never stand aloof. He felt that his work was hastening the march of our history and he perpetually hurried time.'[21]

2. *In Succum et Sanguinem*

Speaking of Chernyshevsky's persistent attempt to belittle himself before Dobrolyubov, Antonovich noted that the latter 'did exactly the same in regard to Chernyshevsky: he always compared himself with Chernyshevsky to his own disadvantage, put him above himself, and considered him his guide and mentor. It must be said . . . that in these mutual compliments Dobrolyubov was nearer the truth.'[22] Most of Dobrolyubov's philosophical, and all his social and political ideas were, indeed, unoriginal. In addition, he is fairly typical of those whose rejection of error is more convincing and more meaningful than the positive formula in which they try to define what they believe. The philosophy was inherited from Chernyshevsky, and, beyond him, from Belinsky, Herzen, and their common vade-mecum, Feuerbach, although the tone and accent are Dobrolyubov's own.[23] As a thinker he was much more lightly equipped than Chernyshevsky: he was less painstaking and erudite, more personal and impromptu.

Like Chernyshevsky, Dobrolyubov sought, in the first place, to bridge the Platonic or the Cartesian gulf. He believed the process of life to be unitary in the sense that it comprises physical as well as mental and spiritual processes; that the peak of the process is man; that the process itself indicates and gives moral authority to the personal qualities which are needed to promote it and which are also roughly identical with those required for the fulfilment of ideal society. It was part of his intellectual capital to think of all mystical and metaphysical thinking as dishonest. Writing of Polonsky, he complained that the poet 'saw in everything some special occult meaning: his world is populated by strange, miracle-working phantoms, driving him far beyond existing reality. One must admit that such a mood . . . in no way favours, and even endangers, a poet. It can degenerate into meaningless mystery-mongering and fade into strained allegorism and conventionality.' 'It is time', Dobrolyubov writes elsewhere, 'to abandon abstract ideas which are supposed to shape life, just as we have abandoned the teleological dreams of the scholastics: they derive from a dualism which divides the world into mind and appearance and assures us that only pure ideas possess true reality, whilst all . . . visible things are merely their reflection.' Yet 'all our efforts to conceive the spirit in the abstract, as devoid of material properties, or to define its "essence" have always been and will be entirely fruitless'. 'Since the now familiar truth that energy is an inherent quality of matter, and that matter exists for us only to the extent to which it reveals some kind of force—since this truth has become common knowledge, we have found all Ormuzds and Arimans wholly superfluous notions.'[24]

Having done away with 'Ormuzd' and 'Ariman', however, Dobrolyubov proceeded to argue that

the claims of vulgar materialism, which debases the significance of man's spiritual nature by reducing his soul to some kind of rarefied matter, are pathetic and ridiculous. The poverty of such ideas has been irrefutably exposed a long time ago. They are untenable even from the scientific point of view, and only a benighted ignoramus could possibly pursue such materialist reasoning. We do not, therefore, profess that physical activity is more important than spiritual activity, or that physical contentment is the aim of human life.[25]

And yet, Dobrolyubov suggests, who can deny the rightness of materialism in a world of the dispossessed, 'cured', he says, 'of the habit to eat'? And how right it is to realize that the belly comes before the soul, not in the scale of value but in point of time.

The attempt to discover a unity beneath or within man's double nature had its epistemological implications, similar to those found in Chernyshevsky. These were clearly present to Dobrolyubov's mind, although he never considered them *au fond*. As there is no gap between spirit and matter, subjective mind and objective nature, bodily events always accompany and are accompanied by mental experiences. Knowledge ceases to be the apprehension of reality by a transcendental mind and becomes the fusion of subject and object into the reality of human experience.[26] It makes just as much sense to talk of the world being in our heads as it does to talk of our heads being in the world, for both views are based on what Dobrolyubov considered to be a cardinal fallacy, namely, the assumption of two abstract entities.

In what way is the spirit united with the body . . ., and where does it reside in the body? What agency transmits physical pain to the soul? Through what medium do thoughts and volitions pass to the body? . . . In asking all these questions the schoolmen failed to realize that this way of talking presupposes the existence of an ideal entity—the soul—mechanically inserted in the body, and results in gross materialism. If the soul occupies a particular spot in the body it must of necessity be material itself, and the same must be inferred in regard to its connection with the body, seen in this extraneous fashion.

Yet knowledge is concerned with 'real life' and has for its principle a 'total living being'—man.[27]

While Dobrolyubov was even less inclined than Chernyshevsky to think that the universe is perfectly contrived and that everything in it happens for the best, he was also more aware than Chernyshevsky that the first steps in human knowledge are man's growing consciousness of himself as separate from nature which enables him to step out of his environment or have power over it. Discarding though he did all notions of 'Ormuzd' and 'Ariman', Dobrolyubov entertained the idea of a struggle of conflicting forces, affecting in equal measure life in nature and the thought and behaviour of human beings. This idea is central to his most interesting work 'The Reign of Darkness' (*Tyomnoe tsarstvo*), about which more will be said in another connexion. None the less, the conflicting forces are ultimately— Hegelian-wise—'raised to a natural unity', in which nothing is compulsive or imposed from outside and yet no experience is complete until it has been related to its opposite.[28] Dobrolyubov did not go beyond such largely declarative statements, which are interesting as far as they go, but do not dispose of intellectual difficulties. He had neither the gift nor the taste for speculative thinking.

Three basic elements may be detected in Dobrolyubov's materialistic outlook: an implaccable realism; a concern with man as the measure of all things; and a preoccupation with moral value.

The very word 'matter' seemed to satisfy Dobrolyubov's deep-seated need to find something real, solid, undisguised in a world of dissolving abstractions and dissimulation. He had a kind of instinctive horror of ideas that were not lived or living, that were dummies concealing man's uneasiness about his ability to cope with real situations and serving as a means of protection against their frightening possibilities. The relevant conflict was not between matter and spirit, whatever these may be, but between fact and abstraction, between life and theory, between *succus et sanguis*, which Feuerbach wished to restore to the plundered victims of abstract principle, and the pale extensions of that principle.

They [the idealists of the thirties and forties, Dobrolyubov wrote], were moved by lofty but . . . dissociated strivings. They sought truth; they desired the good; they took pleasure in beauty; and they valued *principle* above everything else. *Principle* was the name for a general philosophical idea which they put at the basis of all their logic and morality. They had acquired their principle at the price of tormenting doubts and abnegations, but they were never able to free themselves from its crushing, deadly weight. There was something pantheistic in their pervasive clinging to principle. Life became a service to principle and man a slave to it. Every action at variance with principle was a crime. . . . Masters of abstract logic, they remained ignorant of the logic of life and found no difficulty in dealing with life by means of logical constructions. . . . Facts, facts, that's where we must begin! . . .[29]

Although many claim to be interested in facts, Dobrolyubov contends, the interest languishes as the facts can no longer be fitted into ideal patterns, and men continue to manipulate them as counters, to deal with the reality of impermanence by creating the fantasy of changelessness, to turn simple experience into pretentious myth, and ordinary thoughts into irrelevant word-spinning. In this respect, and despite his advocacy of the procedures of natural science even where they were inappropriate, Dobrolyubov believed 'caste-ridden scientists', engaged in 'hair-splitting investigations of dead things', to be no better off than metaphysicians speculating about man's ideas. They all alike took their orders from the sciences of death. 'To wrench a fact from its living context and put it on a shelf beside dust-covered folios, or to classify . . . it according to the logical divisions of the schoolmen is to destroy that living quality whereby a fact becomes what it is—an event within the real context of life.'[30] For Dobrolyubov deductive reasoning was like an unpardonable luxury—the only intellectual activity which was perfectly suited to a gentleman respectably poised over the gulf of the real world with its evil and injustice. To this he opposed the intellectual and moral attitude of the men belonging to the younger generation, in whom he found an 'intense feeling for reality' and, following from this, 'a holy disquietude'.[31]

'In place of the woolly abstractions . . . of past generations',

Dobrolyubov wrote, 'they [the men of the sixties] looked at the world and saw men of flesh and blood. . . . Principles gave way to a consciousness of deep affinity with other men, and to an awareness of complete solidarity between all human beings.' The proof of the prodigious errors of abstraction was man's humanity, seen not against the background of vast impersonal systems, or, as Dobrolyubov said, 'the general run of things', but as evidence of itself, of the variable causes and matter of life. As for Herzen, man for Dobrolyubov was a creature circumscribed by nothing but the laws of his own being, and passionately engaged in his particular destiny. But there was none of Herzen's generous, imaginative insight into human behaviour which made him quiver in response to the variety of life. Dobrolyubov saw man bereft of 'mood' or individual sentiment, and stripped of all aesthetic trimmings, of all that is poetic and bizarre.[32] But he had a greater sense than Herzen of confident human energy fulfilling itself in action, and this gave his humanism a more strictly practical bias. He insisted not on the importance and elusiveness of *who* man is, but on *what* he is and what he does. Hence his interest in human 'types'. It was a novel feature in the outlook of the radicals which became dominant with Pisarev but which they both failed to bring into full play or to explore, because they were deficient in psychological insight, and possibly also in psychological interest. As a theme, however, the search for a new image of man, capable of taking a fresh look at reality, has as much claim to the attention of the historian of Russian thought as the current concern with the creation of a new society.

The search lent support to, and in a measure explains, Dobrolyubov's incessant attempts to drive a wedge between the 'fathers' and 'sons', to see breaks, which were real enough, and not to see the no less real continuities. We have seen how tempting it is to reduce this to a suitably rationalized reflex action in a young man with a chip on the shoulder. In point of fact, Dobrolyubov genuinely felt that there are experiences in history which change the image of man; that often among men who seem contemporaries little contemporaneity exists; that the danger for society lay not only in its evasions and betrayals, its illusions and complacencies, but in the impoverishment of its types of men, of which these crimes were only symptoms; and that its regeneration could only occur through the creation of a new kind of man. He resented the 'type' of a liberal for what he described, in mounting epithets, as his 'mean and passionless existence', his 'moral smoothness', his 'refusal to take risks', his 'connivance' and 'smearing over cracks (*zamazyvanie treshchin*)'. The resentment expressed a deeply felt anger at the condition of contemporary man. But more than this, it testified to his realization that when a society or an individual declines the experiences which present themselves to passionate minds, they are automatically excluded from the realm of history.

Although Dobrolyubov's 'typological' method was not productive of feeling for individual human character, it did sharpen his eye for people's generalized attitudes and manners, especially for their undesirable attitudes and manners. This did not, however, require for its foundation a doctrine of man in the abstract, who lies behind the attributes of real men and women —a doctrine which Dobrolyubov himself imputed to his opponents among the liberal Westerners. On the contrary, he wished to preserve the concrete human person. He held up an image of man, embodying, as he says, 'independence and the fullness of individual being'. His ideal 'type' was someone 'ready to doubt and question again and again', someone who does not cringe to authority or reel back before danger, who 'defies the enslaving necessities and conformities of life', and who is yet capable of identifying himself with other men and of seeking a common world where free people can act. 'It is better to suffer shipwreck', he said, 'than to get stuck in the mud'; and a mind that was not uneasy irritated and bored him.[33]

Like most of his radical contemporaries, Dobrolyubov was a democrat by instinct and conviction, and he opposed the elevation of private behaviour to the most important role; but like them, he also continuously protested against the humiliation of the individual and the degradation of human dignity. He protested, as has been noted, against the threat to the individual from impersonal systems and the 'pretensions of abstract thought'. He protested against the treatment of men as things or objects, and against the levelling of human activities to a common denominator. Above all, he exposed that form of abandonment of individuality which consists in the inner, socialized slavishness of man, in 'slavery of the spirit', of which he gave a remarkably penetrating analysis in 'The Reign of Darkness'. The last stage of dehumanization is here described as the dazed acquiescence of man, stable, well-adjusted, and submerged in an anonymous mass, in which 'the more individuality is effaced, indistinguishable and dim, the more it approximates to the ideal of a perfect human being'. Dobrolyubov is reported by his friends to have declared to his shocked superiors at the Teachers' Institute that 'it is an error to call every two-legged animal a man'.

A true ethic despises ethics: this might be a fitting summary of Dobrolyubov's moral convictions. The driving force of all his speculations was an intense moral feeling. It may be said that while Chernyshevsky tried to work out the principles underlying the intellectual outlook of the men of the sixties, Dobrolyubov gave expression to their moral aspirations. Yet, in spite or because of this moral sensitivity, he was quite unable to bow before the ethics of others. Besides being continually at war with prevailing moral shams, he repudiated all moral law. He considered it an affair of 'experts in morality' (*rutinyory morali*), who, secure in their righteousness, could and for ever would punish those who refuse to obey it. True morality for him was a peculiarly human affair: he sought to identify it in a given human context and subject-matter, rather than in relation to a set of principles or 'soothingly changeless truth'. 'Even virtue', he said, 'can assume a vile and savage form', if it is unrelated to the living image of man. He described as 'ridiculous' any moral discipline whose quality lies in its remoteness from the world, or in imitation of some abstract reality. Value, in the last resort, could be known only in concrete instances, in the individual case, historically; and all morality was seen by him as historically and even individually conditioned. In a static, hidebound, conventional world man has simply to imitate moral character, and he is, in fact, 'moral' in proportion to his dissolution in conformity and vulgarity, that is, to his own degradation; but in a changing, forward-looking world he has to invent moral character, and he is moral in proportion to his creative independence.[34]

With the disappearance of moral absolutes, ethical obligation presented itself to Dobrolyubov in terms of man's self-affirmation as an individual and as a member of the human community: hence the utilitarianism, which he shared with and took over from Chernyshevsky.[35] Like Chernyshevsky, Dobrolyubov set down a hedonistic vision of the free life, or 'rational egotism'; but it was even less Benthamite than Chernyshevsky's utilitarianism. It was 'rational' because it claimed to take nothing for granted and used reason to criticize and expurgate morality that was an emanation of fixed law or established custom. It was 'egotistic' or self-regarding only because it concerned itself with the recovery of personal identity, and suggested the desirability of life and a response to it. It was aimed, in Dobrolyubov's words, against '. . . abdication of individuality and the subjection of man's personal impulse to abstract, lifeless principle'.[36] But it had none of the confident implications of classical utilitarianism that the pursuit of one's private interest is conducive to the good of all, or that in an open discussion between truth and error truth will always prevail.

Dobrolyubov drew his ideal 'type' of moral man in an essay devoted to Stankevich, one of the chief leaders of the 'remarkable decade' and a friend of Belinsky, Bakunin, and Herzen.[37] He was attracted by Stankevich's capacity for 'being always true to himself . . ., which imbued all his actions with a peculiar inner freedom (*prostor vsekh ego deystvii*)'. He contrasts, on the one hand, the 'noble egotism' of Stankevich which consisted in moral and intellectual independence and originality, in freedom of judgement and 'wholeness of character', as well as in a willingness to share or in 'self-surrender for others', and, on the other, the 'narrow egotism' of those who defend their material and spiritual privileges, who look upon the world and other men as instruments for their service, who hide from contact with the world or take refuge in alleged superiority and thereby reveal their essential weakness.

Elsewhere Dobrolyubov commends the common-sense virtues of honesty, justice, and integrity, which he regarded as 'self-sustaining'. Anything that was mere devotion to custom, habits divorced from conviction, unquestioning acceptance of authority; any behaviour that was compatible with bowing and scraping before divine and human majesty; any moral or political cant and decorous airs—all this evoked in him instant and instinctive dissent.

Most of Dobrolyubov's views on morality were expressed in articles of literary criticism. But his journalistic career coincided with the liberal first years of Alexander II's reign, when certain current issues were fairly widely discussed in the press, and this enabled him to speak up on a number of occasions. Of these two may be singled out as particularly memorable. One was the appeal made in 1858 by a reactionary magazine, *Illustratsiya* (Illustration), against any measure designed to ease the known disabilities of the Jews who lived in western and southern Russia. The appeal, which received widespread support in ecclesiastical circles, caused a stir among the liberal intelligentsia. Some 150 men of letters, academics, and others issued a document protesting the undesirability of racial discrimination: it was written in the language of most contemporary liberal journalism, which abounded in such phrases as —'though much may be said on both sides . . . nowadays, when society has received a moral stimulus from the Throne . . .', or 'in these days of progress . . .', or 'at a time when a few forceful words have been uttered concerning certain welcome changes in the police force. . .'. Dobrolyubov felt an almost greater moral revulsion from the protest than from the appeal. The first issue of 'The Whistle' contained a sarcastic diatribe against anti-Semitism in which the phobia appears in its true light, as a form of degrading sub-humanity, the resentment of the spiritual slave, and the fear of the alien in the herd. But the 'protest' by 150 men—'the pride and adornment of our literature', as Dobrolyubov calls them—was no better. Dobrolyubov found it vague to the point of meaninglessness, and tame and trivial to the point of comicality—an instance of his familiar *bête noire*, of 'well-meaning', 'insipid liberal cant'.[38]

The other occasion was provided by the educational theories of the celebrated pedagogue Nikolai Pirogov (1810–81), whose work 'Questions of Life' (*Voprosy zhizni*) subjected the prevailing system of education to vigorous criticism. Dobrolyubov, who had a special interest in education, welcomed the book as a first step away from 'obtuse pedagogical officialdom' towards an education that will help a young person 'to acquire sincere convictions, and an understanding of what he and his purpose in life are. . .'. 'Such convictions', Dobrolyubov argued, 'cannot be ready-made: only he can possess them who has been taught from early youth to look into himself, . . . to love truth with sincerity, to stand up for it fearlessly, and to be free and candid with his teachers as well as with other children.'[39]

Unfortunately, Pirogov soon showed signs of deviation from these enlightened principles. He became involved in the composition of a widely propagated document known as 'Rules Concerning the Transgressions and Punishment of High School Pupils in the Kiev Educational Region' (*Pravila o prostupkakh i nakazaniyakh uchenikov gimnazii Kievskogo uchebnogo okruga*), which recommended flogging or even slaps in the face as an essential method of education. Dobrolyubov was dumbfounded by Pirogov's conversion and proceeded to attack him and his followers in two articles ('Contemporary', 1860, no. 1, and 1861, no. 8) entitled 'Pan-Russian Illusions Destroyed by Flogging' (*Vserossyiskie illyuzii razrushaemye rozgami*) and 'From the Frying Pan into the Fire' (*Ot dozhdya da v vodu*). These depict Pirogov and his collaborators as obsessional disciplinarians, at times homely and endearing, but liable to turn nasty at short notice, and containing deep in their psyche the policeman's complex. The enemies of education, for Dobrolyubov, are authority armed with a birch, and virtue flagellating vice. He denounces the straining at the gnats of non-observance and immodesty and the swallowing of the camels of obsequiousness, insincerity, and injustice. Behind all this he detected, though he could say it only by allusion, an early attempt to force the child into a system in which everyone was content to remain in the station to which it had pleased providence to place him, and which enabled authority to call good the same kind of acts for which he receives punishment and to practise them with a good conscience. The villains, indeed the enemies, turned out to be not only individual pedagogues who 'muffle up their follies in the pompous garments of religion and morality', but the whole hierarchy of the social order, everything that made it what it was.

3. *Revolution in a Moral Key*

Durkheim has said that socialism is not a science, a 'miniature sociology': it is a cry of pain, sometimes of rage. It is debatable

how far this can be said of Marxian and post-Marxian socialism; but it is largely true of pre-Marxian socialism, whose
springs have been more moral or even emotional than scientific.
It is undoubtedly true of Dobrolyubov, for whom all social and
political issues appeared in uncompromising moral terms. In a
sense, Dobrolyubov was not 'political' at all, although he had a
great deal in him of what Byron called 'the poetry of politics',
characteristic of many Russian social thinkers: it was embedded
in such words as 'justice', 'freedom', 'human dignity', and so
on, and expressed itself in a partiality for action and opposition,
against mere thinking or talking or even publicizing.

This left a marked impression on Dobrolyubov's view of
history, which was materialist and determinist up to a point,
but very much less so than is sometimes suggested, notably
by Polyansky. It was quite free from that inflexible,
'scientific' determinism propagated by Dobrolyubov's older
western European contemporaries Auguste Comte and Thomas
Buckle, according to which events occur with undeviating
regularity, and history develops in obedience to fixed laws.
'History', Dobrolyubov said, 'represents the same variety . . .
and confusion of different elements as we observe in life itself.
You may find in it anything you look for; you may find confirmation for any theory. And even untruth is not easily detectable, for we have not discovered any common denominator
whereby to test even the simple facts of history. . . .' 'Obliging
people', he wrote metaphorically of historians with a teleological bias, 'are satisfied that if the Volga flows into the Caspian
Sea, this could not happen but for the peculiar, unsubstantial,
ideal sympathy which the river entertains for the sea, and that
it must as a matter of necessity have reached the Caspian by
virtue of this irresistible purpose, even though its way may have
been barred by an entire Alpine range.'[40] History, and
the world as a whole, Dobrolyubov saw as a creative process in
which persons, their ideas and moral endeavour played a
leading role. Matter and spirit, society and knowledge were
only aspects of this process, which at once embodied and
justified human effort.

Admittedly, Dobrolyubov was even less consistent than
Chernyshevsky in his view of who or what is paramount in
history. On the whole his attitude was more voluntaristic than

Chernyshevsky's. He tended to stress human initiative at the expense of impersonal historical agencies, and 'the impact of great historical actors on the course and development of history'.[41] But this was more an expression of his desire to break with recognized habits, to oppose certain routine methods of acting, feeling, and thinking, as well as of his interest in human 'types', rather than an invitation to hero-worship. 'The story of Peter [the Great]', he says, 'offers more proof than anything else of how a complete renunciation of the past, a total and instantaneous transformation could come about by the will of one man over against popular habits and instincts. . . . The chronicler of Peter's work will, therefore, understandably tend to appeal to the fortuitousness of history. And yet, even here, such an appeal would not be justified.'[42] There are not, and certainly there should not be, sovereign individuals in history. The idea of sovereignty, according to Dobrolyubov, belongs to the 'reign of darkness': it is a snare and a delusion, maintained by idolatry and by terror, which increases in proportion as its hold over human beings declines.

In addition, Dobrolyubov repeated Chernyshevsky's criticism of the traditional school of history-writing, which wants to know first and foremost whether an individual historical agent is a 'good thing' or not, and refuses to see that the individual may be moral while society is very immoral indeed; in other words, it fails to show the complex web of factors and circumstances which constitute history. In a reference to the historian Karamzin, Dobrolyubov suggested that, instead of inquiring how administrative decrees and the squabbles and private victories of the princes contrived to bring about the Russian State, historians would be more profitably employed in discovering the nature of the material and spiritual life of the people that was expressed or betrayed in its making.[43]

In spite of his moral bias and non-philosophical bent, Dobrolyubov was, no doubt, greatly influenced by the general intellectual climate in Europe, where the idea of progress had become something like an article of faith. He had a vague belief in progress, both in its eighteenth-century sense of progress towards rationality and in its nineteenth-century sense of man's increasing mastery over nature by means of scientific knowledge. He looked forward to the day when perfect knowledge would be made possible by a perfect society or, vice versa, when a perfect society would be made possible by perfect knowledge. 'Every villainy', he declared in his Diary, with a measure of justification, 'is perpetrated by men from sheer stupidity.' Elsewhere he says that two kinds of ideas operate in history—rational progressive and irrational reactionary ones— and that their continual alternation and conflict makes it what it is. A new and better future could be brought about by means of popular enlightenment and an increase in human knowledge. 'Parasites reign supreme, but they are on the decline wherever education spreads.' As far as Russia was concerned, Dobrolyubov expected the intelligentsia to promote such a spread, provided it succeeded in abandoning its 'flabby ways', its 'idyllic Oblomovism', and stopped indulging in 'empty exhortations' unconnected with the facts of social life.[44]

Although the idea of progress offered some basis for Dobrolyubov's hope of general improvement, his interest in it owed very little to confidence in the beneficent and largely compromised kindliness of the laws of nature and society. He chose progress, as he said himself, 'in opposition to stagnation'[45]: because it meant for him a realization of the effects of human action, of a future not predictable and therefore alive and liberating, a possibility of movement and renewal in an entrenched, obtuse society living on the rumbling volcano of a subject race—the peasantry. It may be said that Dobrolyubov used a basically optimistic, non-tragic social creed to provide an instrument for an essentially tragic view of life. He was not easily deceived about human realities, and to his mind most of the things that his society taught one to respect and reverence did not deserve anything but cynicism. To 'improve' this society was, in point of fact, impossible: it was a jejune occupation which produced an optimistic, bovine frame of mind and had no relevance in a 'reign of darkness', at a time when so much was happening and the foundations of life and thought were slifting. We have seen already what Dobrolyubov's reactions were to the rule of moderation, which, in spite of the difficulty or, on the contrary, of the confidence human beings have always experienced in keeping to it, he steadfastly refused to regard as a counsel of perfection. In the end, even enlightenment proved to be an illusion, for 'where and when', Dobrolyubov

asks incredulously, 'has real improvement in the life of the
people come about simply as a result of convictions held by
clever people, and without being wrung from [established
society] by the claims of the people themselves?' 'We can
expect nothing from the beneficent spread of education and
sound principles . . . without the impact of special, extraordinary circumstances.'[46]

Dobrolyubov could not, of course, spell out the precise nature
of these extraordinary circumstances, and, perhaps for the same
reasons of precaution, even his statements to this effect in
private correspondence remained similarly vague.[47] There can
be no doubt, however, that what he meant was revolution. In
this he was even more extreme—to be precise, more determined
than Chernyshevsky. He had no capacity whatsoever for the
smallest measure of that instinctive accommodation by which
societies are said to survive. To his mind it was enough for the
common beliefs to be the articulate expression of the habits
upon which society rests, of the 'status quo', as he says, for them
to be exposed to challenge and rejection. Antonovich writes
that 'Dobrolyubov dreamt . . ., like Father Gavazzi . . ., of
thundering against society, stirring it, setting it on fire, and
leading it into action.' There exists, indeed, a lengthy tribute
by Dobrolyubov to Gavazzi in which he praises the Italian
romantic revolutionary for setting at naught 'any good that is
done without the slightest risk to oneself'.[48] He had something of
Bakunin's *schaffende Lust der Zerstörung*, although it was a harder,
a more astringent, moralistic version of it, and it did not turn
into anarchistic, metaphysical revolt against the very notion of
organized society. In any case, for a man like Dobrolyubov, who
put such a high price on truth and justice, the existing order
was uninhabitable. The claim, for instance, made by the
liberals, that the peasant reforms, which reached their sad
climax when Dobrolyubov was already a dying man, were the
beginning of human liberation and of democratic practice in
an absolutist State, was for him the greatest fraud in contemporary Russian history. In Chernyshevsky's 'Prologue' he (Levitsky) is made to declare to Volgin (Chernyshevsky) that, in the
circumstances, even the abolition of serfdom is 'a mere trifle'.
All the then current slogans—'promising vistas', 'swimming
with the hopeful current', 'a bird in the hand is worth two in

PLATE 3

b. Dobrolyubov, aged 24

a. Dobrolyubov, father and son (aged 18)

the bush', and the rest—he regarded as the platitudinous, the glib, and the phoney in pretentious disguise.[49]

There was a time [Dobrolyubov wrote, early on in his journalistic career] when people sang songs of praise to the love of woman; female readers wept tears and male readers mused melancholically over the misfortunes of platonic lovers. Subsequently, platonic love became an object of mockery, and platonic sorrows failed to evoke any great sympathy. Then, strange though it may seem, people began to concern themselves with social matters, and for twenty years we have been reading stories and novels in which praises were sung to the platonic love of social activity, to platonic liberalism and platonic nobility. Many tears were shed and dreams dreamt over this new Platonism. But it is high time to recover from the dreams. If platonic love of woman is ridiculous, a thousand times more ridiculous is platonic love of country, people, truth, and so on.

And again:

When will the real day come? [Dobrolyubov asked in the celebrated article of this title]. What has our society done in the last twenty to thirty years? Until now—nothing. It has educated itself, it has developed, it has stood aloof listening to the Rudins [hero of Turgenev's novel of that name] and has mourned their nugatory if noble fight for ideals. It has prepared itself for action, and has done nothing. . . . Having *recognized* an idea, one must go on making it real.

Later, Dobrolyubov expressed his astonishment that 'learned men could defend the benefits of half-measures for the future advance of [even] western Europe, and repudiate radical and decisive changes as a danger to her well-being'.[50] In Russia, at any rate, no changes could be expected until the social apparatus was affected at its root, and no justice could be done nor democracy work without a social revolution. It is this conviction which moved Dobrolyubov, as it moved Chernyshevsky, to challenge Herzen whom he reproached—unfairly, as we have seen—with betraying his role of the critic of society apart from its abuses. 'For goodness sake!', he noted in his Diary (5 June 1859),'What is our advance guard coming to.They have already succeeded in dulling their sensitivity, which previously enabled them to understand a call to revolution wherever it was heard and whatever its expression.'[51]

Not much can be said of Dobrolyubov's precise social ideals.

At any rate, they cannot be defined in terms of any known economic and political theory. In this he preferred to be advised by Chernyshevsky, who, he claimed, had said all that could be said on such matters. He seemed to have an instinctive feeling that economic or political definition would inhibit his appeal to the moral impulse of his readers. The very form of this appeal was not conducive to steady analysis or technical elaboration: 'I call', he said, 'not to coxcombs, not to advertisers of modern frippery, not to pedants and walking automata, but to those who still have a spark of the sacred fire of love and freedom left in them. . . .'

All that I saw [we read in 'When Will the Real Day Come?'], all that I heard made me grow heavy with a feeling of discontent. From very early on, one question impressed itself on me: why, why was there so much suffering? Was there no means of taking away the sorrow that seemed to weigh everybody down? . . . My mind was overcome with these thoughts and I found no rest within or without. But after much reflection I came to realize that the very foundations of human life could be imperfect, that they have no more than relative, accidental, ephemeral value and are subject to change. . . . From the abstract law of justice I moved on to the exigencies of . . . real man, and eventually reduced my search to one formula: man and his happiness.[52]

The message is simple enough. Its moral value, if not its novelty, lies in that it was a stand for humanism against a repressive society, for freedom against organized cruelty and organized stupidity, for social responsibility against parasitic privilege.

The moral bias is evident even where Dobrolyubov tackles specific social problems. His case against feudalism and capitalism is made not on the grounds that they are or are not efficient, but that they are 'a flagrant violation of humanity', and that in them the mass of mankind is dependent to a degree incompatible with humanity on the will of others. 'Despite their ostensible disparity', he said, 'there is a secret, unspoken alliance between outright oppression and enlightened capitalism. As a result, they are for ever engaged in making delicate and moving concessions to each other and forgive each others's offences with one end in view: together to oppose the labouring classes and prevent them from gaining their human rights.'[53] In a society where *bourgeois* virtues and *bourgeois* vices are encouraged history impresses itself as a story of thriving prosperity. For Dobrolyubov, the story was a common and sordid affair—a story of parasitism and exploitation: 'only the actors change, but it is always the same play that is being acted.' 'The only things that deserve the attention of the historian are the rights of the labouring men, on the one hand, and, on the other, parasitism in all its guises: in the dismal taboos of Oceanian savages and in Indian Brahmanism, in Persian satrapy and in the Roman patriciate, in medieval tithes and in feudalism; or, today, in redemption fees, bribery, peculation, privateering, flunkeyism, dronishness, serfdom, marriages of convenience, *dames aux camélias*, and all the rest . . .' And the only way of stemming this tide of degradation is to recover the image of man who 'disposes of nothing but his labour'. Because his life hems him in among his circumstances few choices are left to him, but his very predicament contains a promise of liberation, for it is not natural for him to strive to preserve the order into which he was born, and he will perish with it or overthrow it.[54]

While depending on the intelligentsia for educating 'the people', for Dobrolyubov the operative factor was the people themselves, because they alone could turn words into deeds and overcome the glaring contradiction between the principles that were being preached and the things that were being done. '. . . Among these people there is a force for good, which in any case does not exist in that corrupt and half-demented society which claims to be educated. . . . The masses are inarticulate: they cannot, therefore, and do not want to, rely upon words, or delight in the sound of their voice as it carries into the distance. What they say is no empty talk. Their speech is an appeal to facts on the condition of immediate action.' Mazzini, Dobrolyubov observes, appealed to 'God and the people': this is a half-truth, or one truth too many. 'Remove "God", there remains "the people".'[55]

Some have blamed Dobrolyubov for expecting too much from 'the people', and even for being a crypto-Slavophil or crypto-*pochvennik*. Others, on the contrary, maintained that he had no populist leanings at all. Still others regarded him as standing in the main tradition of populist thought. The label is of no importance. The evidence shows that in fact he shared some of the characteristic tenets of populism, such as Russia's

relative exemption from certain western European economic
developments, the importance of the communal system, the
value attached to the human person as well as the responsibilities of the intelligentsia *vis-à-vis* 'the people', and the latter's
latent revolutionary capacities—all of which can be traced to
Chernyshevsky.[56] It is of some interest that for a time, while
still at the seminary, Dobrolyubov was an avid reader of
Pogodin's extreme Slavophil journal *Moskvityanin* (The Muscovite) and, as has been noted, of Gogol at his most Slavophil. It
was a passing infatuation from which he was soon cured by the
reading of Belinsky. But some of his later critical essays (e.g.
the review article on the works of S. Aksakov) still have a
distant Slavophil ring. He believed that a human community
takes on a character and temperament of its own which is more
than merely the sum of the characters and temperaments of its
members, and that when this 'communal type' is most definite
and purposive it 'follows its own historic ways', and is a source
of strength and inspiration to all who participate in it.

On the other hand, he saw tradition as turning easily into
'stagnation' and 'reliance on immutable principles', national self-
confidence degenerating into isolationism and superiority, and
complacency hardening into tyranny. His sympathy for the
'simple people' was largely due to the fact that he believed them
to be less settled, less tied to traditions, more exposed to and
ready for change and social upheaval. He loved Russia neither
as a patriot who turns to tribal and religious chauvinism in
order to cover up reality, nor as an expatriate who covers up
his escape from it. His love was part of a spontaneous committal
to the world around him, of a sense of being in that world with
others and an inability to sunder himself from them, either by
extolling or by denigrating them. He was a fierce enemy of all
self-conscious and self-righteous national as well as social
apartness. He fought the Anglophobia prevalent in Russia in his
time and believed that to talk of Russia's mission during the
Napoleonic wars was understandable, but under and after
Nicholas I such talk began to sound hollow in the extreme.

In essence [Dobrolyubov said] our history was never interrupted. . . . However abrupt and violent the upheaval produced . . . by
Peter's reforms may seem to be, on closer examination it will appear
as a much less radical breach with old Russia than . . . the

Slavophils imagine it to be. Old Russia could not disappear with the shaven beards. It is too close to us to be turned into an imaginary earthly paradise inhabited by near-angels. 'Man has wept before now, and rivers of blood have swamped him.' And after us he will go on weeping and blood will continue to flow. . . . No antiquated illusions will save us from this sad reality.[57]

4. 'A Literary Robespierre'

The accepted view of Dobrolyubov as a literary critic is that, although most of his writings were about imaginative litera-ture, he looked for social meaning in everything as perverted puritans look for sin, and never went beyond using literary texts to illustrate sermons on contemporary Russian life. Even Zaitsev, a fellow *raznochinets* and a collaborator in the 'Russian Word', maintained that Dobrolyubov was 'a judge of society rather than of literature'; and Ivanov-Razumnik claimed to sum up Dobrolyubov's and Chernyshevsky's ideas on art by declaring that, while the latter thought that 'a real apple is more beautiful than a painted one', the former believed that 'a real apple is more useful than a painted one'.[58] Since such and similar aesthetic or antiaesthetic views attributed to Dobrolyubov are not often found at the base of enduring literature or literary criticism, he came to be dismissed as a tendentious pamphleteer and a mischief-maker who must, even more than Belinsky before him, be held responsible for the decline of literature in Russia. His only contribution was to have provided unwitting evidence that art and social and moral sympathies or antipathies go ill together.

The verdict is undeserved and merely shows what strange tricks the writing of literary history plays with the mood of a generation or an age. As a matter of fact, Russian literature was alive and kicking, and no one knew better than Dobrolyubov that it was important. Nor can one deny the positive value of Dobrolyubov's own contribution. Despite his twenty-one years he carried enough interest to obtain authority for his 'tendency' among a great many contemporaries, readers and writers alike; and, above all, the tendency proved invigorating and led to the formulation of important truths.

Dobrolyubov, it is true, had an intensely irritable side,

especially when his essential beliefs were offended. His criticism abounds in the exhortations, the rancours, and the biased valuations of a *littérature engagée*. What he represented with uncompromising conviction was perhaps even less a literary trend than a literary conspiracy, in which the role of the critic acquired an almost greater influence than that of the creative artist. Moreover, with Dobrolyubov the critic turned into a prophet of radical change that was necessary if the cultural barriers were to be broken down and literature to become an effective and meaningful communication between men. He threw literature out of the library and the drawing-room into the street. He sought to overhaul, to revalue, and to reverse the canons traditionally used in the practice and appreciation of the arts; and he stampeded writers and the reading public all over Russia in pursuit of these aims.

There were few important writers in Russia who regarded themselves as a rarefied minority; and, until at any rate the beginning of the twentieth century, there was no literary *élite* cultivating attitudes of posed detachment and coterie facetiousness. But, as has been noted in connexion with Chernyshevsky, there were a number of literary critics—Grigorovich, Pisemsky, Druzhinin, Dudyshkin, and others—who sought to 'deflect the writer and reader from the real world', and whose work could have no meaning at all for the vast majority of the Russian people. Their position was clearly formulated by Druzhinin: 'the artistic theory which we uphold', he wrote, 'seeks to make art serve its own exclusive purpose. . . . The poet lives in his own exalted sphere and comes down to earth as the Olympian dwellers used to do, mindful that their true home is the Olympus above.'[59] In addition, there was Turgenev, who distinguished himself by his sensitive and agile evasiveness and his straining to explore and discuss political issues, while retaining the freedom to retreat. And there were a host of minor 'Parnassian' poets, of whom Aleksey Tolstoy (1817–75), Yakov Polonsky (1819–98), and especially Afanasy Fet (1820–92) were the most outstanding. Their reactionary politics went hand in hand with ingenuity in the tesselation of airy poetic images and the capitalization of private dreams. For Dobrolyubov all this spelt intolerable escapism, and may also have offended his humble rugged origins.

The only thing that could reconcile us with literature [he wrote in 1859 in the already-quoted 'Literary Miscellanea'] is the wail of despair in which there rings a sombre discontent, a sharp reproach and the piercing call to a truer and more active life. Such a call would have to bear not on literature alone but on society as a whole. It will come from a realization that there is no time for sterile elegance in the face of so many living issues. We are choked by effete, idle speech that makes one sink into drowsy complacency and fills the heart with delectable dreams. . . .

At another time and in other circumstances one might have expected from a critic more pleasantness, more playful interest, and a preference for half-truths to whole ones, although this, too, is hardly sufficient for the creation of literature, even a critical one. Dobrolyubov was not in the least interested in being merely interesting, nor pleased to be regarded as merely pleasing. '"Aesthetic interest"', he wrote apropos of Turgenev's *On the Eve*, 'has long become the province of young females fainting on sofas.' He refused to take works of art at their face value until he saw them as symptoms of the condition of men, and only after having discovered their core of truth relevant to men. The 'living issues' of which he spoke were the known issues of his society, which had no shortage of anger and inhumanity. They were brutally simple in their consequences and their causes, and it was Dobrolyubov's sensitivity that made him view them as the aesthetic no less than the moral catalysts of his literary work. Instead of carefully probing the minutiae of individual sentiment, or analysing the intricacies of literary technique, he sought to uncover the clash between irreconcilable extremes, between good and evil, justice and oppression, light and darkness. Where he lacked such a purpose he tended to write lifelessly. But even when pure poetic inspiration laid its claim on him as a critic, he was unable to turn his back upon the malady and alienation he had observed.

Dobrolyubov never bothered to elaborate an aesthetic theory. He admitted, in his first essay on Ostrovsky, that he felt no need 'to cultivate the aesthetic tastes of the public. I would be bored stiff with attempts to lay down the rules in this matter and with lengthy and profound disquisitions on the subtle refinements of art.' He believed with Chernyshevsky that art should be 'true to life' in the literal sense, that literal truth is better than contrivance, and that a true artist should proceed *ab realibus ad realiora*. He repeated Chernyshevsky's argument in favour of 'particularization' or 'typification' as an essential function of the arts: the function, that is, of reviving our mind for the perception of things rather than generalizations, especially of things that are based on a human truth, and discovers the universal in particular, concrete experiences.[60] He could not admit any divorce between art and life, and, although he was able to gauge as well as any the artistic effectiveness of a literary work, what he looked for was always the link between the finished product and the complex of human and social factors out of which it had grown. His aesthetic was intimacy with life and a sense of its values. 'In regarding literature as an illumination of things in life', he said, 'we expect it to have one quality without which it has no merit, namely truthfulness.'[61] He saw no need for detachment, except in so far as he remained critical in his very intimacy with life. Nor did he attach any great importance to the distinction between art and craftsmanship, and any effort at communicating life he regarded for the purposes of this argument as art. He even suggested that there is an underlying identity between literature, philosophy, and science, inasmuch as they all are concerned with 'reality'. Only their approach, method and 'temper' differ. Science is 'analytic', while literature is 'synthetic'. The philosopher and scientist analyse, collate, abstract, infer, prove. The artist is 'impressed and surprised'. He thinks in terms of concrete images which, if successful, convey universal significance.[62] Above all, 'form' for the artist is not something deliberately created, but springs from his personality and from his material. 'Nothing in nature and life that assumes artistic form can have any value at all', Dobrolyubov noted in his Diary (8 February 1857), 'unless it is illumined by the artist's vision and insight, unless it has passed through his soul—not like a daguerreotype on glass, but in a fusion with his inner life—and has reappeared in verse, in sound, in imagery that comes from his temper and spiritual awareness.'

There is no question, therefore, of mere 'imitation of reality'. Art, and in particular literature, reflects the artist's understanding, it seeks to teach through the exercise of imagination and, in fact, it mostly does teach, even if it lacks understanding and imagination, because he is a man speaking to men, because art is not self-sufficient or set apart from the social and ethical context. 'What makes art significant?', Dobrolyubov asks: 'A picture of rippling brooklets and of dales in relation to hillocks, or a portrayal of the course of man's life, of life's diverse conflicts and social interests? . . . You deem it proper to call the partisans of the social trend mudlarks. Let it stand! We shall not quarrel; we shall even express our gratitude to you and our astonishment at your aesthetic wisdom. . . .'[63]

And yet Dobrolyubov did not wish to advocate a doctrinaire approach. He even assailed the tendency to reduce literature to an 'abstract and logically watertight system', to a substitute for propaganda or a lecture hall.

According to literary pundits, [he wrote] a work of art does not tolerate any fortuitousness: everything in it is expected to be strictly measured and to proceed uniformly from a given point, following a natural pattern and the rules of logical necessity. But what if the natural pattern demands logical inconsistency? From the pundit's point of view, one ought not to choose subjects in which fortuitous-ness is not amenable to the demands of logical necessity. We, on the contrary, believe that a work of art can incorporate any and every matter, however fortuitous, and that in such cases abstract logic must give way to real experience. We are convinced that life and nature have their own 'logic', and that this logic may prove very much superior to the one which is often imposed upon them.

Elsewhere, he objected to the idea that 'every writer must create under the pressure of some theory. In fact, he may pro-fess any opinion he likes, provided he has a talent that is truthful and sensitive to life. A real work of art embodies an idea not because the author aimed at it while creating his work, but because he was struck by those facts out of which the idea flows and of which it is the natural corollary.'[64] Even where Dobrolyu-bov showed a preference for a literature that exemplified the beliefs and attitudes he already accepted, he insisted that to succeed such literature must overcome 'cankered factionalism and the party spirit', and, in any case, must have a recogniz-able relationship to events and people as we know them. In a discussion of Ivan Nikitin's 'The Divorce of Mind and Feeling' [*Raspad uma i chuvstva*], whose realistic poems of the life of the poor could not but appeal to Dobrolyubov, he, nevertheless, severely criticized the poet's work because it was conceived in the brain and never brought down into the heart, because it was made at the desk and, in the process, lost all impact and sincerity. There was a deeper sense of feeling for Dobrolyubov in many an inarticulate and bawdy phrase than in high-lit sophistication or dramatic postures; and nothing worth while in literature could replace for him simplicity of feeling and directness of expression based on men's day-to-day experience of one another.[65]

. . . . .

Chernyshevsky, following Belinsky, had expressed the view that since the eighteenth century satire was 'the most vital, or rather the only vital, element in our literature'.[66] For Dobrolyubov this became something like a dogma which he professed in an essay entitled 'Russian Satire in the Age of Catherine'(*Russkaya satira v vek Ekateriny*). Indeed, he went further than Belinsky and Chernyshevsky and became an advocate of satire at its most savagely destructive. Satire is a subversive art. As Dobrolyubov asserts, it does not, or should not, merely deprecate abuses and aberrations, but aims at the foundations of life.[67] Being subversive, it is militant, and the purpose of its exaggerations is to demonstrate that in the complex world of human actions nothing is invulnerable. It is not surprising, therefore, that in choosing satire as the main object of his literary criticism, Dobrolyubov was accused of holding nothing sacred and of disseminating nihilism. The accusation is far more to the point than the charge of not being able to appreciate literature. His obsession with satire was in a sense a symptom of 'bad taste', for bad taste is often what offends against decorum, creates embarrassment and speaks lightly of things considered holy. Good taste in Dobrolyubov's society was the taste of the people he was pledged to oppose, and implied an avoidance of the very subjects he was most anxious to bring up. But, although preoccupation with satire may have turned Dobrolyubov into a nihilist and impeded the cultivation of good taste, it in no way weakened his moral sense. His very addiction to satire prevented him from witholding moral judgement and merely enjoying or mocking or even pitying humanity: it made him take sides, and induce his readers to take sides, for or against existing people, ideas or institutions. His laughter was founded on the moral dignity of resistance, when common sense would have urged a man to conform. In a tired society that has reached stability and judges by common-sense standards people can afford not to take sides, and not to take themselves or their surroundings seriously enough to be worth serious humour. Their laughter is associated with the tame, civilized habit of adjustment to environment. Dobrolyubov carried his humour like a burden or curse that had tipped the scale against life as he knew it. He was in perpetual opposition, for ever scraping the whitewash off alleged sepulchres.

Dobrolyubov reviewed a phalanx of writers and books, great and small, some memorable, others long forgotten and not worth remembering. He wrote about all of them, partly because it was his duty as literary editor, partly because they provided suitable occasions for dealing with topical, cultural and social questions of interest to himself and to his public, whatever the differences in their terms of reference may have been. The criticism which resulted was uneven in quality, although it threw light, if not always on the work under discussion, then on the aspect of life of which the work was an indication. One does not find in it romantic feeling or high drama or subtle overtones, and Chernyshevsky's painstakingness is replaced by wit, impatience, and vivid scorn. But in at least three important cases Dobrolyubov rose to surprising heights of critical perception and evocative power, and two of them concerned works of satire, or of what he chose to interpret as such. These were his discussion of Ostrovsky's plays, to which he devoted two long essays ('The Reign of Darkness' and 'Ray of Light in the Reign of Darkness'—*Luch sveta v tyomnom tsarstve*) and one on Goncharov's novel *Oblomov* (*Chto takoe oblomovshchina?*—'What is Oblomovism?').

Alexander Ostrovsky (1823–86), as has been noted already, was a member of an important group of writers, the *pochvenniki*. The association remained ambiguous for, apart from sharing with them, and with Grigoriev in particular, a fondness for wild living and the 'Russian soul', his moral and social sympathies lent themselves to a variety of contradictory interpretations. To Dobrolyubov's great annoyance, he was frequently referred to as 'our merchant Shakespeare'. He is the author of some fifty comedies, the most important of which were written and produced in the face of formidable obstructions by the censorship during Dobrolyubov's brief literary career. They were responsible, more even than the plays of Griboedov and Gogol, for the establishment of the school of Russian realistic drama (*bytovoy teatr*) which dominated the theatre before Chekhov and Stanislavsky. They deal in the main with the narrow life lived by the mid-nineteenth-century Russian lower middle class, especially the merchants and minor civil servants, of whom Ostrovsky had a first-hand knowledge.[68] It was a torpid, bucolic, cosy world, yet full of rapaciousness, meanness and stereotyped religiosity, and it typified for Dobrolyubov parasitic Russian society dragging along in a moral and spiritual vacuum. In exposing this 'reign of darkness', however, he went beyond the ostensible purpose of Ostrovsky's plays and created pictures of great symbolic significance. He seemed to perceive, even beyond their social theme, a hinterland of Dostoevskian darkness, a doomed humanity wriggling in infernal circles from which it could not or would not escape.

As a rule, Dobrolyubov's criticism displays few signs of psychological dimension, but in this case he surpasses himself, especially when he attempts to show the insidious spiritual enslavement of Ostrovsky's world, where, in addition to the more obvious external pressures and submissions, nothing is allowed to grow from within. 'Ostrovsky', he says, 'is able to look into the depth of the human heart, to distinguish the essence from all extraneously accrued hideousness and malignancy. This explains why external oppression, the heavy weight of all his environment pressing upon man, is felt much more acutely in his plays than in many other writings which may be equally unendurable in matter, but which conceal the inner condition of man behind an outer, public aspect.'[69]

Actually, Ostrovsky was even less of a psychologist than Dobrolyubov. His remarkable evocation of life derived not from any insight into inner man, but was built up out of a thousand points of detail, remembered and conveyed with extraordinary realism; and, with a few exceptions, his characters are not individualized human beings but adroitly manœuvred types, people seen in their social behaviour and interrelations. It is also doubtful if Ostrovsky ever meant his plays to be mere parables of darkness. Apart from his central interest in the scenic and dramatic effect of this harsh and primitive land, he may even have wished to make his readers and viewers understand it on its own terms, while himself looking on with forbearance and only a dash of disapproval, to appease the conscience. Indeed, his other great critic, the *pochvennik* Grigoriev, claimed to be able to 'see through' the grimness of these plays, to discover in them the broad expanse of Russia and 'the organic forces of pristine national life'. Some of Ostrovsky's comedies may provide evidence for this view.[70] But the important ones, such as 'A Hang-over from Other Men's Wine' (*V chuzhom piru pokhmelie* (1856)), 'The Ward' (*Vospitannitsa* (1859)), and especially his masterpiece, 'Thunderstorm' (*Groza* (1860)) —the only Ostrovsky play familiar to western European readers —offer no such evidence. They present, on the contrary, a stream of characters that seem like the embodiment of major horrors combined with the small vices of a corrupt and callous society. And Dobrolyubov was undoubtedly right in treating them as symbolic figures of a ghastly realm, with, as he says, 'the dreary pallor of death upon it', figures that conduct us through Russia at its darkest.[71]

The 'ray of light' in the darkness was Katerina Kabanova, the heroine of the comedy *Thunderstorm* and victim of the claustrophobic terrors and stale boredom of the Kabanov family. Katerina was Dobrolyubov's favourite literary character, because he saw in her a unique combination of love, poetry, and generosity with boldness of spirit. He attaches particular importance to the tragic outcome of the play, which, instead of the customary victory of virtue over vice of traditional comedy, ends in Katerina's suicide. Grigoriev believed that her fate served to redeem the surrounding oppressive world and enabled one's rage to die down in humility and surrender. For Dobrolyubov, on the contrary, Katerina's end spelt that world's final damnation, and an evocation of a wholly other world, prefigured, as he believed, in the life of the Russian people. Hers was not the path of a virtuous, acquiescent young virgin, willing victim of divinely ordained circumstances, as even Pisarev seemed to think, but of the woman who dared, and challenged even, and especially, in her death. Unlike the *pochvennik* apologists of meekness, Dobrolyubov could see nothing redeeming or noble or even pleasant in this quality, whether it occurred in women, children, peasants, or house serfs.

Dobrolyubov's other important contribution to critical literature was his essay on *Oblomov* by Alexander Goncharov (1812–91). Nothing of great interest attaches to Goncharov personally, except that he wrote this one remarkable novel, which has become a classic, despite its vapid and slovenly style; that he was an overworked and somewhat strait-laced Director of the official literary censorship; that he was an inveterate bachelor; and that he suffered from persecution mania, as a result of which he accused a number of Russian and foreign writers, amongst them Turgenev and Flaubert, of having plagiarized him. Dobrolyubov did not deal with these personal trifles, but with the novel, which appeared in 1858. As in the case of Ostrovsky's characters, he was responsible for turning Oblomov into a symbol. Oblomov, the 'superfluous man' *par excellence*, the unattached *rêveur* living on self-induced experiences, noble ideas, and chronic irresolution, personified the weary and futile 'Russian reality', with its privileged monstrosities and sleepy, affectionate idyll. 'The idyll, that is the enemy.'[72] Dobrolyubov viewed Oblomov with a kind of fascinated revulsion, like a true satirist in search of uncomfortable truths: when he finds them, the people discomfited become almost his friends. No other critical work by Dobrolyubov gives the impression of such mastery of his theme and sense of discrimination; and, despite the all too apparent partiality, it shows him at his intellectually and aesthetically least restricted. Among the relatively uninspired literature on Goncharov it is, after a century, still one of the most illuminating works on him, or rather on the characteristic attitudes of his self-projected hero.

The last essay in literary criticism which deserves attention and which was also the last Dobrolyubov ever wrote (it appeared in the 'Contemporary' in 1861, no. 9, under the title 'The Downtrodden People'—*Zabitye lyudi*) is devoted to Dostoevsky's novel *The Humiliated and Insulted*, published in the same year. Neither this nor the previous novels by Dostoevsky with which Dobrolyubov deals in this essay reveal the later and essential Dostoevsky. None the less, Dobrolyubov succeeded in bringing to light, with more sympathy than even Belinsky, some important features in his work. The most surprising thing is that Dobrolyubov, who always found it easier to understand the literature of the human environment than the literature of the human mind, was able to respond to such an apparently uncongenial theme as the split personality, the thwarted and yet rebellious man—Golyadkin in Dostoevsky's *The Double*—who struggles not against external circumstances alone but against the monsters of his own disintegrating mind. Admittedly this too presented itself to Dobrolyubov as in a sense a symptom of society's state of health; but he commends Dostoevsky for showing the horror and grotesqueness of this human predicament, 'without thinking at all whom it would benefit or for what idea it will prove useful'. Above all, he shares Dostoevsky's optimism as regards man, or compassion with man—the belief and the hope that for all their absurdity, humiliation and degradation men preserve, as Dobrolyubov says, 'the spark of God'.

He was apprehensive, however, lest this hope should lead, as it seemed to have led Dostoevsky, to sentimentalism or evasion of reality. The last thing Dobrolyubov wished to do was to preach humility to the 'humiliated and insulted'. To the myth of the suffering Russian turning the other cheek and leaving a noble example behind he opposed the threatening peasant rebel, who snorts his indignation, who attacks the enemy where he is weak, who sacks and burns mansions and does not cringe or promise it will never happen again. Dobrolyubov suspected that Dostoevsky's 'ideal of the golden age ... consisted in that everyone would be pleased with his station, acknowledging the ... profound justice of his position and obeying with the same alacrity with which others commanded. . .'. This, Dobrolyubov observes, is the saddest version of the sad idea of the 'heavenly kingdom', where 'there are many grades of bliss, but people in the lower grades will fraternally sympathize with those in the upper ones and delight in that reflection of upper bliss to which the elect are entitled'.[73] Such 'golden hopes', to his mind, could only distract and distort, and must ultimately crumble; but hope itself gave rise to a deeper understanding of the nature of man and put one's enlightened will against human degradation.

V

DIMITRY PISAREV

1840–1868

1. *A Defeated Egotist*

THE death of Dobrolyubov and the disappearance of
Chernyshevsky from the literary stage coincided with a
perceptible change in the political and intellectual climate
in Russia. After the agrarian reforms, the abortive peasant
risings, the liquidation of the student disturbances, and the
suppression of the Polish rebellion of 1863 the forces of reaction
had regrouped. As has been shown in the first chapters of this
study, a kind of stealthy counter-reformation was taking place
and steadily gaining strength. The penalties for speaking out
became more severe than they had been before 1861 and the
rewards of subservience were correspondingly greater. The
administrative reforms, it is true, went on, but, unlike the
peasant question, they proved a tranquillizer rather than a
stimulant. As a contemporary put it, 'the Petersburg of Chernyshevsky turned into a city of *cafés chantants* and dancing classes,
of good intentions and rapacity'.[1] Moral turpitude, defection,
treachery became a habit even among some erstwhile radicals,
while others were driven to social despair or shut themselves up
in a world of private pursuits. The situation caused a shift in
the dissenting attitudes which many accounts of the sixties tend
to ignore in their concern with likeness rather than with
difference; or which they try to reduce to 'irrelevant household
squabbles' among the radical intelligentsia. The new trend
found its most pervasive inspiration in Dimitry Pisarev, the
most prominent of the Russian 'nihilists'.

Pisarev was born on 2 October 1840 in Znamenskoe, the
ancestral home of the Pisarevs, in the province of Orel.[2] Although
Znamenskoé was a fairly typical 'nest of gentlefolk', hospitable
and lavish, his father was no more than an impoverished scion
of the lower nobility who succeeded in squandering the family's

already diminishing fortune. The centre of the crowded home, with its numerous related and unrelated hangers-on, was Pisarev's mother. Madame Pisareva was an overwhelming mother, selfishly clung to by her only son and selfishly clinging to him. She watched him, spoiled him, and mortified him. The coddling and fussing went so far that the boy soon came to think the world was made of pink cotton wool and *marrons glacés*. For a long time Pisarev persisted in the habit of crying every day: it became part of his taste for ritual, common to most young children. He was a naughty but, at the same time, a very obedient boy, especially when he had *maman* in the same room to make him feel secure. He would never eat a sweet without permission, and when offered one by a stranger would keep it in his mouth without swallowing it until *maman* appeared on the scene. Throughout his life he oscillated between a longing for the rest and passive pleasure of lying in his mother's arms and irritable disaffection. His early education took place at home and, as his mother decreed, its aim was to produce 'un jeune homme correct et bien élevé'. It consisted of innumerable French and fewer German lessons, 'un peu de musique', and a little history. According to his eldest sister, Vera, Pisarev grew up a pale, sickly, refined, and conceited *bébé*. His favourite nickname was 'little crystal box' (*khrustalnaya korobochka*).

In 1851 a family council was convened to consider the boy's future and, despite the protestations of his mother, it was decided that Dimitry should continue his education not at home but in St. Petersburg, where he was to live with well-placed relations. He was duly sent off 'to the accompaniment of bitter tears, exhortations, fervent prayers, and copy-books with French and German vocabularies'. At school he remained as delicate as ever, and his part-Russian part-French letters during this time contain, besides occasional *vignettes* of school life, interminable accounts of his own scholastic achievements, marked by an unrelieved string of *alphas*. The letters are seasoned with declarations of unbounded filial devotion, especially to his mother, and with sugared religiosity; but, though trivial, they provide early proofs of his verbal talent. 'At school', Pisarev himself wrote, 'I belonged to the category of the sheep.'

The appearance of a submissive milksop, however, was

largely superficial and stemmed more from the peculiarities of Pisarev's upbringing than from his essential character. As he grew up he showed increasing signs of loneliness and homelessness—the lot of many members of the intelligentsia from the gentry, and one of the sources of their rebellious and passionate one-sidedness. The experience which added to, and in part explains, this tendency in Pisarev was his distracted infatuation with his cousin Raisa Koreneva. The relationship, intense, often tormenting but inspiring, was to dominate most of the rest of his life.[3] It had begun already in Znamenskoe where Raisa, an orphan, spent her childhood, and it continued until and even after her marriage to a certain Evgeny Gardner, a perfectly eligible young man of German extraction, whom Pisarev referred to as 'that valetudinarian nincompoop'. Pisarev's sister says that the girl was very pretty but incorrigibly fickle. Madame Pisareva, not surprisingly, believed her to be utterly unworthy of her son's love and, indeed, would scarcely have consented to any marriage unless it might help to restore the rapidly declining prosperity of the Pisarev family. She was as quick to perceive and exploit disillusion in her son as she was to interfere with the growth of passion and affection. But this did not apparently affect Pisarev's deep feeling for his mother.

Even as a student, and despite increasing financial difficulties, Pisarev did not give up the habits of his walled-in and cherished childhood. The heated social and political controversies which followed the death of Nicholas I left him largely untouched, and he seemed unaware that around him the settled world was breaking up. He was not interested in anything but philology—the subject he chose for his university course. One of the reasons he gave for this choice was 'the attraction of the blue collar and dazzling gold of the sword-hilt' worn by the students of the Philological Faculty. His fellow students knew him as 'the chirping cherubim', as a bright-eyed young thing who copied lectures on pink paper with assiduity but little understanding. Miscellaneous company meant little to him, and even later, when he acquired greater social confidence, he always preferred the company of women. His only close male friend was a fellow student called Treskin, who in turn was passionately attached to Pisarev. A timid and priggish young man, 'continually undergoing spiritual crises and contemplating mysteries', Treskin, nevertheless, held complete sway over his friend, as well as over a number of other students whose temperaments and minds, according to another fellow student, Skabichevsky, 'were averted from reality'. Much later, in an autobiographical essay entitled 'Our Academic Learning' (*Nasha universitetskaya nauka*), in which he criticized the Russian university system, Pisarev wrote: 'We called ourselves men of thought, although we had no right at all to describe ourselves in this way. While the new students considered Dobrolyubov their teacher, we looked down on him, and on the 'Contemporary' in general, with the sovereign contempt peculiar to our caste. We did not read them and were proud of it: they were not worth the pains.'⁴ In Skabichevsky's words, the members of this student group were 'gradualists and mortal enemies of all zealous and extreme ideas'. 'They denied satire and expected poets to concern themselves solely with the bright side of life. . . . In their studies, they showed a marked preference for specialization and for minute elaboration of small isolated facts.'⁵ These preoccupations prompted Pisarev to spend a great part of his university studies in what he came to regard as fruitless work on Humboldt's biography. He dreamt of a brilliant academic career, and saw himself as a dedicated pundit, rightly contemptuous of anything or anybody who fell short of his own scholarly standards. A certain intellectual snobbery remained with Pisarev throughout his life, although he was never able to assert himself to the end or harden himself against others.

'In the winter of '58', Pisarev wrote in the autobiographical essay quoted above, 'I succeeded in finding work in a journal for young women (*Dawn*). . . . I was put in charge of the bibliographical section, that is to say, I had to draw the attention of the young readers to those books and magazine articles which were supposed to enrich their minds without damaging the spotless purity of their hearts. The journal's character was treacly but not dishonest. . . .'⁶ 'Pisarev's contributions dwelt with relish on 'the development of womanhood', on 'aesthetic education' and 'moral harmony', on science that 'does not lead to a denial of either the moral law or the truths of religion', and even, in a manner of vague benevolence, on the undesirability of serfdom. But side by side with these comforting exhortations adapted to the least exigent of his female readers, he published a number of reviews on Goncharov, Turgenev, and Tolstoy which showed considerable literary and critical perception.

I wrote my jejune and innocuous little pieces [Pisarev says] with an enthusiasm which I never experienced while working on Humboldt's biography. . . . I said nothing that was new or startling, but for me it was both new and startling. My book notices forced me out of an unventilated cell into the fresh air; and this change gave me a wicked pleasure which I was unable to conceal either from myself or from others. . . . One year of journalism proved more useful for my mental development than two years of assiduous hackwork at the university and in the library.[7]

The change affected even Pisarev's appearance. The soft-faced adolescent, looking like the lightest of *soufflés*, became almost within a year a sparse and wiry figure, charged with nervous energy, with sharp features and the forehead of a keen intellect. But the eyes retained a weak expression. Most of his portraits and photographs fail to do him justice, for he is said, for instance by Shelgunov, who met him for the first time in 1861, to have been very good-looking, in spite of a large head and disproportionately small ears. His external manner conformed entirely to his mother's ideal of 'un jeune homme correct et bien élevé'. He dressed extremely well and with taste; he was polite, urbane, communicative and, in life, determined to charm away enmity, which he treated with such disdain on paper. Of all the men of the sixties, Pisarev was certainly the most brilliant, the most amusing and the wittiest, although, confronted with a real problem or psychological situation, he was often inclined to fall back on unconcern, or on rhetoric and mock-sententious epigram. At any rate, he was incapable of being dull. To judge by his own account of student life in St. Petersburg, the university seems to have brought out in him a tendency to the whimsical, the irresponsible, and the irreverent. With these qualities he could not allow himself to be confined in any system or academic discipline, nor was it possible to occupy a professorial chair.

While Pisarev's Petersburg relations complained that 'Dimitri a mal tourné et devient un Saint-Just en miniature', Treskin warned him against becoming 'the same kind of chatterbox as Dobrolyubov' and charged him with having 'sold his soul to the devil'. This did not prevent Treskin from becoming himself

a contributor to *Dawn*, although he confined himself to translations of Merovingian tales in which he tried, as Pisarev observed,
to convey 'the spirit of the original with the same thoroughness
with which monkeys catch fleas'. Pisarev became increasingly
uneasy in the company of stuffy and pedantic schoolmen. To his
mother's horror he announced that he did not believe in God
any more. The chocolate-box religion of his early youth turned,
without any sense of loss or discomfort, into a conviction that
religious faith was nothing but a morbid desire to set up a fetish
and adore it, to fall down and worship something. The latter
attitude was more in character, for Pisarev strikes one as a man
who lacked anything remotely approaching religious experience,
even though, to judge from his letters, in boyhood his eyes
turned continuously and somewhat unctuously to heaven.[8] What
he had to say later about religion was never more than the
ironical preliminaries. But there was intellectual disquietude.
He felt a growing desire to live in a world of discoveries, of multiple interests and devouring curiosity, and he was both intoxicated and perplexed by his newly discovered powers.

> The summer of '59 [he wrote] was for me a time of mental crisis.
> All the notions ingrained in me since my childhood, all the ready-
> made judgments which I considered the inviolable foundation of my
> existence . . . all this began to founder almost of its own accord,
> revealing its complete worthlessness. . . . Once awakened, the readi-
> ness to analyse and scrutinize could not be lulled at will. . . . The
> mind pokes fun at phantoms and dispels them, and man is left
> looking at the destruction of old certainties. In the end, he ceases to
> look and a new life begins in which he learns to employ his mind's
> limitless powers against all obstacles and resistance. . . . But
> the transition is difficult and agonizing. . . . In my case it was so
> painful that it shook my whole being.[9]

The intellectual fever drove Pisarev into what he himself
described as a 'Promethean mood'—a mood that proved more
spirited and wanton than mere obstreperousness in a sensitive
and selfish young man who had spent his childhood in swad-
dling clothes. It appears to have brought him face to face with
some terrifying isolation, the sense of which overwhelmed him
from time to time throughout his life.

If Pisarev was the wittiest, he was also the most solitary
amongst the leading men of the sixties—a man who lived in the

intellectual paradise and personal hell of egotism. At times he turned his solitude outward, as it were, on ideological enemies: he adopted violent opinions, scored off everybody, from the deity downwards, and was wilful and destructive. It is this that prompted some fairly intelligent critics, such as Ivanov and Volynsky, to represent Pisarev as a 'conceited wrangler', suffering from the 'intrusive pretentiousness of a pseudo-genius', whose views 'were formed in a delirium' and whose reputation owed everything to the 'cultural primitiveness of the Russian public'.[10] But, though he undoubtedly held the palm of haughtiness among the 'sons', treating his paternal victims with a cruelty they hardly deserved and regarding even some of the 'sons' as premature dotards, Pisarev was never rude. On the contrary, he was polite and sophisticated. The haughtiness originated partly in a desire, which he shared with Dobrolyubov, to arouse a sense of reality and break through the veil of familiar and lethargic notions, partly in naïve satisfaction in being clever at the expense of the less quick-witted. His presumption had a note of amused vengeance and of pleasure in shocking, but none of the sour smell of fanaticism typical of some minor nihilists. He was also extremely honest and sincere, but without the staggering heroism and spiritual tenacity of a Chernyshevsky or a Dobrolyubov. 'I say what I think', he wrote from prison, 'I say what I have suffered, what I have acquired by personal effort and experience.'

The sense of isolation, however, which at times pressed so hard on him, owed at the beginning as much to a breakdown in his love-affair with Raisa as to a breakdown of old beliefs, about which he wrote in 'Our Academic Learning'. Raisa, who liked to play all the tricks in the game of romantic love and drive her admirer frantic with frustration, encouraging him all along the line, suddenly declared that she loved another. On receiving the news Pisarev collapsed completely. His letters to his mother at this time (November–December 1859) are uncontrolled outbursts of despair, mingled with morbid fancies, tormented self-assertion, and filial abandonment. He revelled in his solitude and yet yearned to sink into the arms of his managing and possessive mother: she served as a kind of missing superiority which was to cure him of his illusion but in which he never really believed. Madame Pisareva, for her part, poured

PLATE 4

b. Pisarev, aged 26

a. Pisarev in the Peter and Paul Fortress

boundless affection and solicitude on her unhappy son, while
scarcely able to conceal her pleasure at the unexpected reward
for her surreptitious labours to separate the lovers.

Yet Pisarev's condition deteriorated, until madness came
upon him. It was a form of depressive mania in which weariness
and/or a frenzy of self-destruction alternated with fantastic
presumption. Twice he attempted suicide. He was put into a
mental home, where he spent four months and whence he fled
by jumping out of the window. Although he recovered temporarily from the nightmare, the experience undergone left a dark
residue of ambiguities in his outlook as well as in his mental
condition, all the more remarkable in someone who had come
to regard himself as a confident rationalist, a sturdy progressive,
a believer in the omnipotence of science, and a utilitarian.

On regaining strength, Pisarev retired to Grunets, his impoverished parents' only remaining country property. Petu-
lance and megalomania gave way to the desire for a self-contained peace of mind. He now wished to become an 'Epicurean'
and a 'hedonist', 'harmoniously enjoying', as he said, 'the
different possibilities of life', turning from one thing to another,
seeking aesthetic pleasure, not edification. He read a great
deal of poetry, especially his favourite poet, Heine, and translated *Atta Troll*. Raisa suddenly changed her mind and even
promised to marry him, and Pisarev threw himself at her feet.
Like so many Russian men, and despite the aura of self-assertion
in his philosophy of life, he was emotionally weak and passive,
and in the affairs of the heart, felt it natural for life not to be in
his own hands.

In 1860 Pisarev returned to the capital to continue the interrupted university course. But this could no longer engage his real
interest. Financial difficulties were to some extent but not altogether responsible for his decision to embark in earnest on a
journalistic career. It is significant that the journal on which he
sought employment was not the 'Contemporary' but the
'Russian Word'—a review with a much less remarkable, brief,
but curious history.[11] It was launched in 1856 by a self-willed
Maecenas, a certain Count Kushelev-Bezborodko, described by
Turgenev as 'a perfect imbecile. . ., but rich and therefore
useful'. Its first editors were the poets Polonsky and Grigoriev,
and it nearly turned into a mouthpiece of Grigoriev's *pochvennik*

creed. But these were soon replaced by quite a different person, Grigory Blagosvetlov, to whom Bezborodko, for somewhat obscure reasons, offered the journal as virtually a free gift. Blagosvetlov (1824–80) was a *raznochinets* and an ex-seminarist: he attended the same seminary as Chernyshevsky, but spent some years abroad where Herzen employed him for a time as a tutor to his children. Later he showed himself an able literary impresario in the manner of Nekrasov. He combined the outlook of an enlightened if somewhat antiquated rationalist with a taste for drudgery and business acumen. But he also had the reputation, partly justified, of an ill-mannered scribbler whose editorial activity consisted, amongst other disagreeable things, in inserting poisonous words and malicious quips into the manuscripts of his contributors.

Blagosvetlov received Pisarev with condescension, but soon realized that his talent could be exceptionally useful in promoting the cause of the journal, and during the six or so years in which Pisarev worked for the 'Russian Word' Blagosvetlov's attitude to him oscillated between extravagant flattery and concentrated unpleasantness, according to the needs of the moment. Still, with Blagosvetlov's uncertain support and under his largely unsolicited guidance, Pisarev soon acquired a leading position in the journal and in the Russian literary world at large.

The 'Russian Word' differed from the 'Contemporary' in a number of ways. Between them they had made, moulded, or sometimes inflated radical opinion and the careers of many writers. Both represented an outlook that was enlightened, unstuffy, and adventurous. But, while mostly combining against a common enemy, they also fought battles against each other, in which a clash between different personalities and different points of view played an almost equal part. Despite Blagosvetlov's heavy hand, Pisarev introduced into the 'Russian Word' an air of ironical high spirits which marked it off from the more deliberate, reflective character of the 'Contemporary'. Compared with the latter, the 'Russian Word' leaves the impression of almost deliberate frivolity, although its editors resented the reputation of a light-minded adjunct to the more solid journal of Nekrasov and Chernyshevsky. It tended to diverge, at least during the first years of Blagosvetlov's editorship, from political and economic thinking to a rationalism which had more of the Enlightenment in it, and its large scientific section sought to train a searchlight on the intellectual rather than the social darkness of Russian life. The difference has been summed up by Shelgunov in the following comparison between Dobrolyubov and Pisarev:

Dobrolyubov and Pisarev alike [he says] are essentially popularisers; but Dobrolyubov speaks with a sterner accent. . . . whilst Pisarev is more specious and facile. . . . In Dobrolyubov's manner there is, perhaps, something of Boerne [a contemporary radical and critic of Heine], whom he resembled in his political outlook. Pisarev, on the other hand, has more of Heine's dissipation and diversity. Dobrolyubov often writes as though the moment for action is at hand; Pisarev thinks that no [direct] action is possible and, therefore, popularises. Dobrolyubov shows the way to social deeds, Pisarev concerns himself with individual behaviour; Dobrolyubov seeks to rouse our energy, Pisarev to make us think. Dobrolyubov stirs passion: he incites, fires, provokes. Pisarev believes that passions . . . are futile. Dobrolyubov relies on the progressive forces of society; Pisarev . . . believes primarily in the need to cultivate the faculty of judgment and to teach people to think.[12]

When the 'Contemporary' and the 'Russian Word' resumed publication in 1863 the difference turned into an open conflict. 'The schism among the nihilists', as Dostoevsky called it, lasted for nearly two years and amounted to a public scandal.[13] The Government and the conservative section of the public, with Dostoevsky in the vanguard, viewed this with uninhibited *Schadenfreude*; some of the older radicals were dismayed by what they considered to be a tragic misunderstanding; the young took sides eagerly and vehemently, and, being in a mood to enjoy great things and great ideas deflated, they mostly took Pisarev's side as the more deflationary. Among the chief protagonists were Shchedrin and Antonovich, who appeared for the 'Contemporary', and Pisarev and Zaitsev, who spoke for the 'Russian Word'.

The name of Shchedrin (pseudonym of Mikhail Saltykov [1826–89]) has appeared on a number of occasions in the preceding pages. He was a satirical novelist of great talent whose most important work belongs to the period after the sixties. No other writer depicted with such frightening authenticity as well as in such repulsive caricature the world of mid-nineteenth-century provincial Russia. For Dostoevsky, whose relations with him were those of lasting and reciprocated enmity, Shchedrin's satire was nothing but an allegory of his rage and disgust with human beings as such. In fact, he was a wonderful comedian, a mimic and a parodist, able to show the reality behind his own distortions; and his most important creations, such as 'The Golovlev Family'—*Semeystvo Golovlevykh* (1872–6), are, in the words of a modern critic, 'the greatest *monumentum odiosum* erected to the memory of the Russian provincial gentry'.[14] At the time in question, however, Shchedrin was known mainly as a semi-journalist, a practitioner of 'applied literature', speaking in anecdotal riddles and rather baffling Aesopian allusions.

Shchedrin's partner, Maxim Antonovich, had none of his creative talent and a considerable measure of that spitefulness which defaced the stories of some minor radicals in the sixties and, for that matter, of their adversaries.[15] Around Antonovich cluster disagreeable memories of the most virulent reviews in the 'Contemporary'. He was capable and versatile but rude, and his favourite weapon was the sneer. He also suffered from a suspicious turn of mind, as a result of which he continually took offence, looked for offence, and gave offence. No radical journalist equalled him in offensiveness, except perhaps his opponent in the 'Russian Word', Varfolomey Zaitsev (1842–82), a brash and discourteous 'son', but a more attractive person than Antonovich. The venom of these and a few lesser men left a rancour from which the most vehement impeachments of a Chernyshevsky, a Dobrolyubov, or a Pisarev were quite exempt. In addition, they, and Antonovich in particular, were largely responsible for turning radicalism into a new orthodoxy, which, like the orthodoxies which they overthrew, tended in the course of time to become rigid and hidebound, and exposed itself to the challenge of a new generation of innovators.

Pisarev's leading part in the controversy between the two reviews calls for some elaboration of this interesting if not altogether edifying episode in the history of Russian radicalism.[16] Apart from the difference in emphasis already mentioned, they disagreed on a variety of concrete questions, on Bazarov in Turgenev's *Fathers and Sons* and Katerina Kabanova in Ostrovsky's *Thunderstorm*, on the worth or futility of art, on the political maturity or immaturity of the black races, on the philosophy of Schopenhauer and the economics of Mill, and on other matters. The gaily destructive and assiduously provocative manner in which Pisarev and Zaitsev discussed these questions seemed especially designed to enlist the enmity of their fellow radicals on the 'Contemporary'.[17] It was Shchedrin who made the first considered attempt to repulse the sharp-shooting of the 'nihilists' from the 'Russian Word'. In an article entitled 'Our Social Life' (*Nasha obshchestvennaya zhizn'* ['Contemporary', 1864, no. 1]), he ridiculed the 'senseless ravings' of Zaitsev and the 'emancipated lady-nihilists' who 'dissect human corpses with a fearless hand ... to the accompaniment of singing and dancing'. This was an ironic allusion to Pisarev's favourite literary hero, Bazarov, who advocates the 'scientific dissection of frogs' as the highest human ideal, and to Chernyshevsky's promise of 'joyful labour' in the novel 'What Is to Be Done?'. According to Shchedrin, the nihilists 'were nothing but unrepentant servants of the Establishment, and the servants of the Establishment were mere unrepentant nihilists'. 'Every party,' Shchedrin continued in his arraignment ('Contemporary', 1864, no. 3), 'every cause has its *enfants terribles* who can be tolerated ... until they turn into lop-eared bawlers playing the fool.' Their frivolity prevented them from 'penetrating below the surface, or, worse, made them take the surface for the heart of the matter and propagate it with vociferousness, conceit and impetuousity'. Having got hold of a 'shibboleth invented by Turgenev [nihilism]', 'devoid of meaning as it is and quite uncharacteristic of the true aspirations of the younger generation ... these lilliputians from a certain ... blustering press organ of nihilistic trash ... proceed to don it [nihilism] as if it were a gold-brocaded robe, and to make a banner for themselves from a piece of nonsense'. Although Shchedrin was too perceptive to dismiss out of hand the challenge of Pisarev's ideas, however nihilistic, and eventually even came to change his attitude to nihilism itself, the words had the force of blows delivered with harmful intent and in the full expectation of being repaid in his own coin.[18] The repayment marked an appalling decline in the level of discussion which some took to be also a decline in intellectual vitality. Yet no one, neither Pisarev nor Zaitsev, nor even the envenomed Blagosvetlov and Sokolov, another expert in gutter-snipe abuse, could compete with Antonovich in baseless vituperation. He set the example by blackguarding the contributors of the 'Russian Word' as 'rascals', 'swine', 'rotten sandwiches' (!), 'Blagosvetlov's abortions', 'Pisarevian lack-wits', and so on.

It is, of course, regrettable that Pisarev should have expended his talent in dealing with this kind of disparagement, and particularly in taking part in it; but among all the disputants, including even Shchedrin, he stood out by the astringency and verve of his invective. Though truculent at times, it was often subtle and always effective. Instead of Antonovich's cudgel he used a rapier and achieved a rare mastery of it, as can be seen in such polemical essays as 'Flowers of Innocent Humour' (*Tsvety nevinnogo yumora* [1864]) and 'We Will See!' (*Posmotrim!* [1865]), directed against Shchedrin and Antonovich respectively. Moreover, unlike many of the disputants and especially their detractors, Pisarev realized that behind this quarrel there were more important issues than either the apparent subjects of it or the manner in which it was conducted. For him, the fascination of the controversy, however unseemly and dependent on the clash of personalities, was due to the fact that there was something to quarrel about. There was an assumption of common aims and the controversy, therefore, could have become a real disputation; whereas the division with the other camp—'the opponents of inquiry and change'—was so wide that it was impossible to make any words carry across it.

The common aim was formulated by Pisarev himself in his last rejoinder to Antonovich as 'the great question of the hungry and the disinherited', and it will be discussed at greater length in another connexion. As for the disagreements, these owed much to the growing populist tendency of the 'Contemporary'. It was most conspicuous in the contributions of Grigory Eliseev, a co-editor of the review. Eliseev (1821–91) was a man who lacked definite principles, or who waited for events before declaring them. He represented populism at its most soothing and 'sheepish': it was Turgenev who about the same time advised Herzen to stop doing what the latter in fact never did— 'prostrating himself before the Russian sheepskin'. Pisarev instinctively resisted the guilty, at times frugal quixotry of certain populist attitudes which, in his view, were reflected in the editorial policy of the 'Contemporary' after Chernyshevsky's removal. But even Dobrolyubov's admiration for Katerina Kabanova, whose suicide he believed to be the supreme protest against the 'realm of darkness', a tragic gesture, revealing the force of life inherent in the Russian people, was considered by Pisarev a piece of idyllic romanticism. 'Russian life', he said, 'contains no independent source of renewal; it provides nothing but raw material to be moulded and re-created by men's ideas.' He detested emotionalism, not least in the form of 'genuflexions before popular wisdom and popular truths', and one of the few emotions he could not control was his revulsion against emotionalism in any form.[19] In the last resort, man was thrown back upon himself, even if this involved a hatred of the vulgar crowd. The theme was inseparable from Pisarev's whole attitude to life, with its underlying sense of conflict between self and others. It meant a certain bias for the 'classical', the discriminating and discursive. It also meant a distinctive 'towniness', a heightened sense of social differentiation, which characterizes urban society and renders its members rootless, mobile, and atomistic. Pisarev himself contrasted this with primitive communities whose 'ideas are as uniform as their material productions'. We shall see that all these tendencies influenced Pisarev's view of social development in Russia and his pronounced Westernism. They enabled him to appreciate the impact of economic and industrial growth on Russian society; and they made him suspicious of spontaneous popular revolution. Unlike Chernyshevsky and Dobrolyubov, Pisarev was an intellectual and a dissenter rather than a class-fighter, a moral prophet or even a revolutionary, although they were all alike confronted with the same basic social problems and concerned themselves with the same maladies of their age.

Strange as it may be, Pisarev conducted his polemic against the 'Contemporary' not from a study, nor from the editorial office of the 'Russian Word', but from prison. He was arrested in July 1862 and spent four and a half years in solitary confinement in the Peter and Paul Fortress. But we must complete his life story before dealing with the circumstances of this imprisonment.

Having recovered from his physical and mental breakdown, Pisarev, as has been noted, returned to St. Petersburg. He emerged from the illness with a harder shell and a desire for 'harmony', yet still determined to assist the work of destruction. He wished to maintain a kind of healthy state of nothingness, an attitude of negation to everything outside himself which, however, had a core of moral and social conviction. The negation was aimed especially at tenets, beliefs, and settled habits of thought. It found its most vivid expression in the essay—one of the first written for the 'Russian Word'—entitled 'The Scholasticism of the Nineteenth Century' (*Skholastika XIX veka*); and it bears all the marks of his mature writing: clarity of thought and eloquent special pleading, spiced with incisive asides and flashes of epigrammatic wit. He sought 'to do away with the fog of contemporary metaphysics and mysticism'. He also claimed to show the sole aim of literature: '. . . to liberate the human person from all constrictions.' These, he wrote, 'result in timid thinking, in caste prejudices, in authoritarian traditionalism and the pursuit of universally valid ideals; they serve to protect time-honoured lumber and prevent man from breathing freely and developing all his faculties'.[20] In his own words, Pisarev followed 'wantonly and gaily . . . the slippery path of journalistic demolition'. This does not seem to have interfered with his university studies, for he succeeded in preparing at the same time a work on the neo-Pythagorean philosopher Apollonius of Tyana which he submitted as a magisterial thesis.[21] It was written without a rough copy and, on his own admission, 'in a happy-go-lucky fashion, with sweeping views and risky generalizations'. But the Faculty Board declared the work worthy of distinction, although it noted its 'lack of thoroughness and solid learning'. The thesis was published in the 'Russian Word' and Blagosvetlov, overcoming his customary parsimoniousness, paid Pisarev the considerable sum of 600 roubles in fees.

The romance with Raisa continued. 'If she has lovers', Pisarev wrote to his mother, 'neither you nor I have any right to interfere. It is my conviction that woman is free in spirit and body and can dispose of her life as she wishes, without giving account to anybody, including her husband. For all the world I cannot see any virtue in a woman capable of enjoying life who yet fails to enjoy it. Such behaviour is a fruit of mass prejudice.'[22] Nevertheless, when Raisa finally decided to marry Gardner, Pisarev, despite his libertarianism, was ready to challenge his rival to a duel. He even appeared, masked and

armed with a whip, at the railway station when the newly
married couple were on the way to their honeymoon. Gardner
had no difficulty in tackling his somewhat feeble assailant.
The situation was comic as well as humiliating in the extreme,
but it is not certain whether Pisarev, avowed egotist that he was,
did not feel more mortified by the humiliation of his vanity and
the wound to integrity from being in love at all than by the
beating suffered at the hands of his rival. As an avenger he was,
in any case, more impressive with pen and paper than with
cloak, dagger, or whip. There is a letter of his to Gardner,
written at the critical time, which catches Pisarev's living voice
and the typical sardonic twist which he used when dealing with
his victims.[23] It well-nigh finished off Raisa's husband—or
so Pisarev believed.

The collapse of the love-dream did not bring about a re-
currence of illness: it only disabused him of the idea that things
were held together as securely as his enlightened rationalism
implied, although it did not disabuse him of the idea that women
were angels and his mother a demigoddess. In fact, it is at this
time that Pisarev displayed most of the symptoms of intellectual
excitement and took an uninhibited pride in his achievement
as a writer and as the real force behind the 'Russian Word'. This,
as he put it to his mother, proved 'an excellent substitute for
Raisa'. The achievement was considerable, for even Chernyshevsky, despite Pisarev's apparent anti-Dobrolyubov bias, tried,
unsuccessfully, to tempt him to join the 'Contemporary'. But in
1862 both reviews were suspended: the obsession with security
which disfigured Alexander II's régime after the peasant risings
and student disturbances prevented the authorities from drawing any important distinction between the two reviews and they
justly regarded them as equally dangerous. Shortly before the
suspension Pisarev made the acquaintance of an expelled
university student, Pyotr Ballod, who had recently set up one
of the first illegal pocket printing-presses. The press did not live
long, for in the middle of June of that year Ballod was arrested
for issuing a proclamation against a government agent, a
certain Baron Fyodor Firks, who wrote under the pen-name of
D. K. Shedo-Ferroti ('The Russian Government under the
Protection of Shedo-Ferroti'—*Russkoe pravitelstvo pod pokrovitel-
stvom Shedo-Ferroti*). The baron was the author of a highly

disingenuous pamphlet aimed at discrediting Herzen among the many readers of the *Bell* in Russia.[24] The pamphlet seems to have enjoyed a *succès de scandale*, which roused Pisarev, too, to write a rejoinder. This was to be published in the 'Russian Word', but the censor, not unexpectedly, disallowed publication. Soon the review itself was stopped and Ballod offered to use the article, or rather a more pugnacious version of it, as part of his proclamation. Pisarev's sense of frustration at his forcibly interrupted journalistic activity accounts to some extent for his eager acceptance of the offer. It is this document, found by the secret police among Ballod's papers and supported by Pisarev's reputation as an outspoken free-thinker, which was responsible for his arrest and long imprisonment.[25]

The article is important for being his only explicit political statement; but as an attack on the citadels of sovereign power and property it differs from similar pronouncements by Chernyshevsky and Dobrolyubov. It consists of an ardent defence of Herzen, and itself sounds like Herzen at his politically most eloquent. Pisarev reminded his prospective readers of the motto to Herzen's *Polar Star* taken from Pushkin, in which he hails the dawn of Reason. 'May Reason', Pisarev wrote, 'spell the undoing of the decrepit despotism, of decrepit religion, of the decrepit stronghold of the official morality of to-day!' He charged Alexander II with deceitfulness and 'Nicolaian manners' (*nikolaevskie zamashki*). He called him to account for 'the Polish blood' and 'the blood of the martyr Anton Petrov', for 'the absurd solution of the peasant question', for 'the ruined lives of a host of students', and the suppression of all creative thought.

To prevent his [the Tsar's] subjects from discovering their natural rights [Pisarev continued], it is necessary to keep them unconscious. Knowledge fosters insubordination, and they must be compelled to remain in darkness lest they rear their heads. This is a crime against the spirit of man. . . . A crime which Alexander would not dare commit as a decent individual is readily perpetrated by him in his capacity of autocrat of all Russia. It is a case of the office that corrupts the man, rather than of the man who corrupts the office.

In the face of this, 'to liberalize (*liberalnichat'*) by leave of the censorship' will not do; what is needed is revolutionary propaganda. In conclusion, Pisarev declared that to overthrow the snugly reigning dynasty constitutes the sole aim and hope of all honest critizens. Not to seek revolution in the present state of affairs, one must be either infinitely dense or infinitely bribable in the service of the reigning evil. . . . Only scoundrels side with the Government—those who have been bought with the money taken from poverty-stricken people by means of fraud and compulsion. Beside the people stand those who are young and willing to innovate, all those capable of thinking and acting. . . . As for the dead and the decaying, they will collapse into the grave of their own accord. Our business is merely to give the last push and throw mud on their putrid corpses.

It is not easy to decide how far this outburst should be taken at its face value. Some students of Pisarev (for instance, Kirpotin and Coquart) regard it as an isolated incident in the development of his political convictions, followed by a 'realistic' period, which showed him in a much milder mood, and, still later, by a new would-be revolutionary phase or at least a more resolute preoccupation with social and political questions. Others (Plotkin among them), while not denying certain vacillations in Pisarev, maintain that the document expressed his essential outlook and that, in the words of a contemporary, Shelgunov, 'Pisarev never betrayed the trend which started with Belinsky and was continued by Dobrolyubov'.[26] The former view suffers from the schematism peculiar to all attempts to periodize the thought of individuals and thus to stretch it on the bed of Procrustes. Though hardly a typical revolutionary, Pisarev was inconsistent, in this as in other respects. He was not only subject to sudden changes of mood but delighted, to the point of whimsicality, in what he himself called 'the inconsistencies and deviations from the norm' and 'the felicitous mistakes of genius'. These admitted, irrespective of all chronology, the meeting of conflicting attitudes without necessarily rendering Pisarev guilty of self-betrayal. But he was also weaker and more vulnerable than either Chernyshevsky or Dobrolyubov, and hence succumbed more easily—in his behaviour if not in his convictions—to vacillation and anxieties.

This, in a measure, explains his conduct in the Fortress which had none of the courage and strength displayed by Chernyshevsky. There was a great deal of beating of the heart, tears and repentance, mingled with occasional peevish contrariness.

At first Pisarev denied any complicity in the proclamation against Shedo-Ferroti. But when Ballod as well as his own letters had given him away, and especially when he had realized that the secret police deliberately kept him in a state of uncertainty about his fate, he broke down: he admitted his 'error', invoked his youth and 'nervous disposition' and asked for forgiveness. This saved him from Ballod's fate—fifteen (later reduced to seven) years forced labour and deportation for life in Siberia.

Despite frantic *démarches* by Madame Pisareva and by other better-connected relatives, the Emperor consistently refused to shorten the term of imprisonment. Pisarev's own plaintive declarations to the effect that he loved his fatherland and its sovereign, that he was an exemplary prisoner, that he 'bore [his] cross like a Christian' and was a regular communicant of the Orthodox Church were similarly ineffective.[27]

It is strange, however, that he allowed himself few if any such plaints and evasions in the letters to his mother, his chief correspondent during the years of imprisonment.[28] He complains about 'time dragging on tediously', but shows no signs of feeling sorry for himself. Some of the letters are, indeed, surprisingly cheerful or even flippant. 'Life in the Fortress is cheap', he reports to his mother: 'it gives me pleasure to think that it compares so favourably with life in the capital where prices are so high.' He thanks his sister for

taking [his] equanimity for what it is: there is nothing artificial about it. In fact, it is peculiar to my egotistic temperament. Last spring, when Raisa was about to marry, I felt more miserable than I thought I could ever be. But I did not scream my head off, I did not weep, I did not spend sleepless nights, I did not surrender to the empty ache of longing, and I did not lose my capacity for work. This alone should prove to you, my dear friends, that there is not the slightest reason why you should pity me and that I am almost incapable of suffering.[29]

There is also this characteristic reply to a letter from Raisa, which I quote at length:

Mia cara! [he wrote] in your last letter you are tilting against windmills. There is not the slightest reason why you should think I am your chronic suitor. In order to convince you of the contrary, I give you a constitutional charter in respect of our future relations. Once I am again master of my movements, I shall suggest to you by letter post the following question: 'Do you or do you not wish to see me?' If you reply simply and clearly 'I do not', then you will not see me any more. Should we, nevertheless, meet again, there will, of course, be no word about love from me, unless you choose to have it. I am not condemning myself to celibacy, but I intend to marry only if and when a suitable person succeeds in making me love her to distraction. At the moment I have no time to concern myself with such trivialities, because (1) I am Government property, (2) we are beset by a punitive censorship to which I have to adjust all my mental processes. Generally speaking, life is grand, and its bowels conceal a number of wonderful pearls. I do not in the least object to enjoying them, but I am not going to look for them: I have to work and have no time to waste playing the fool. If a pearl should come my way I shan't let it go. Are you satisfied, my rabid Lady Macbeth and fierce fighter of windmills? If so, don't dare to suggest that I solicit your friendship. I happen to be your childhood friend and there is no question of seeking to obtain it. But I am in no mood to solicit you for anything. I have danced attendance on you more than enough. I am heartily sick of this stupid occupation. . . . I shall probably love you always, but to try to obtain your love—no. enough of that! . . . Good bye.[30]

However, Pisarev appeared to belie these epistolary declarations to Raisa by his curious correspondence with a provincial lady, a certain Lydiya Tsvileneva, who was an acquaintance of his mother and sister but whom he never met before or after.[31] He proposed marriage *in absentia*. 'Accidental circumstances', he announced to her, 'are detaining me in the capital. . . . But why should this be an impediment? You do not know me? Surely, life cannot be all ecstasies of love. Women are often condemned to boredom for ten years with the man who, for a few weeks, has been an object of the most insane passion. No intelligent woman will be bored with me . . . I'll teach her German and English!' This 'love affair' looks rather like a practical joke on Pisarev's part, due to an instinct which had spurred him to naughtiness in his childhood and left him later with an occasional urge to put his tongue out, even from prison.

For most of the first year of imprisonment Pisarev was not allowed any visitors or any books, and he seems to have gladly fed on his thoughts. After a number of attempts, however, his mother succeeded in obtaining permission not only to visit him but also to supply him with books and, above all, with paper 'in order', as she claimed in her petitions, 'to enable him to support his family by writing articles'. Most of his well-known essays, including his contributions to the controversy with the 'Contemporary,' were written during this time, and the third year of solitary confinement proved particularly fruitful. He said himself that he wrote best in periods of enforced calm. Boredom, of which he still complained from time to time, no less than fame, stimulated his imagination, and these moments brought out the pungency and verve reflected in his writings. The articles passed through an intricate and lengthy process of mutilation or sequestration by various censorship departments, and some were, together with many letters, smuggled out in the shoe-soles of Madame Pisareva, who, by the way, became her son's very efficient if rather fussy literary agent. But most of the articles duly appeared over his signature in the 'Russian Word', thus putting Pisarev in the position of the freest political prisoner in Russia. The authorities may have vaguely suspected that, politically, he was the least revolutionary of the leading Russian radicals.

The 'freedom' lasted until 1866, when, after Karakozov's attempt on the life of the Tsar and the inauguration of Mura- viev's and Katkov's régime of terror, conditions in the Fortress changed drastically. The sympathetic Suvorov, Governor- General of St. Petersburg, was removed from his post. All visits to prisoners were forbidden. Even before this, Pisarev's mental state began to deteriorate, and Blagosvetlov's callous treatment of his collaborators, and especially of Pisarev, contributed to it, for he exploited Pisarev's isolation and dependence on him to the full and paid little or nothing. Even Madame Pisareva's relentless management of her son's literary affairs was not equal to Blagosvetlov's sharp editorial practice.

When, on the occasion of the Tsarevich's marriage in November 1866, Pisarev had been released from prison he was, despite his mere twenty-six years, nearly a broken man—in the loving hands of his mother. For a while he lived, depressed and idle, in her exclusive company. He clung to her now more than ever before, he wept with her, he kissed her hands and, at times, detested her. But soon he found himself again drawn into journalism, and again in the grip of Blagosvetlov.

After the suppression of the 'Russian Word' Blagosvetlov

became editor of a periodical called 'Action' (*Delo*), which survived many vicissitudes by dint of his skilful editorial opportunism, based on the belief that, as he himself admitted, 'anything nowadays might pass for socialism'. He succeeded in enlisting the support of some of his previous collaborators still enjoying freedom; but the partnership proved short-lived. Blagosvetlov's despotic attitude to Pisarev became quite intolerable, although he in turn complained of the 'haughty bearing of my friend from the gentry' and declared that Pisarev was 'finished as a writer'. Pisarev, at any rate, parted company with him as much, or more, for personal reasons as for reasons of principle. The only opening left for Pisarev now was the 'Annals of the Fatherland'.[32] Nekrasov, whose business acumen matched Blagosvetlov's but who also possessed some of the qualities of a gentleman, had bought the review from Kraevsky, with the avowed if unpublicized aim of turning it into a revived 'Contemporary'. In fact, it became the most important organ of populism or, to be more precise, of the later populism as expounded and interpreted by Mikhailovsky.

It was not easy for Pisarev to work on the 'Annals of the Fatherland'. Nekrasov, though sympathetic, kept him in the background, despite Pisarev's recognized status as a brilliant literary critic who enjoyed the added and unique honour of having had his collected works published during his lifetime (in a heavily censored edition). The strong contingent from the suppressed 'Contemporary', including the mawkish Eliseev and the mighty Shchedrin with whom he had joined issue in the past, did not contribute to Pisarev's comfort. In addition, Blagosvetlov was not entirely wrong in suggesting that he had lost his previous vigour as a writer. Pisarev's articles at this time undoubtedly lack their customary lustre and in part appear almost jaded.

But they struck a new note. Hitherto his *leitmotif* had been egotism, if often in the sense in which egotism and integrity are one. The egotistic mood lay close to the tragic, and even had an air of doom. After all, Pisarev became mad largely because he felt himself the only self in the world. But even at his most sane he was apt to use intellectual devices to protest, gaily and recklessly, his self-sufficiency. And this tended to deprive his thought of relevance, to make him handle it like an instrument of mere pleasure and with too much ease. Had he been just a gifted, neurotic egotist, however, it is possible that he would not have earned so prominent a place in the Russian movement of liberation. He would have remained what he appeared to be in the eyes of his detractors: a frivolous and unbalanced figure, a moral and literary lightweight whose voice in the cause of ideals never rang quite true. In reality, he had a very different side, which could be detected even during his early intellectual development, but which came properly to life only later, during his third year in prison. Solitary confinement moved him to abandon mere solitary pleasures and to feel the shock of the misery of others—'the hungry and the disinherited'. And this brought a new urgency into his moral and intellectual world. 'I have begun to feel a love for other people', he wrote to his family on 17 January 1865. 'Before, and even quite recently, I had no concern for them whatsoever. Previously I wrote partly for money, partly to please myself. . . . My work ceases to be a mere intellectual game. It involves my feeling.' Later, in an impressive letter to Turgenev, whom he met for the first time in 1867, he stated apropos of Bazarov that the supreme moral question is 'Cain, where is thy brother Abel?'[33] Indeed, Pisa-rev's life may be summed up as a continuous effort to maintain and yet to break down his isolation.

But on emerging from prison he felt deserted, in a cold and menacing world. In the same letter to Turgenev he spoke of his inability to adjust himself to it and to the newly gained freedom. 'I hate all fools in general,' he wrote, 'and especially those fools who pretend to be my friends, my helpers and my allies.' He was ill at ease with other people and sometimes behaved oddly in their company. Some of his actions (such as mixing dishes at table or attempts to undress in public) were unmistakable symptoms of a renewed clouding of his mind. This was accompanied by more or less frequent alternations, such as he experienced during his previous mental illness, between dejection and elation, technically known as cyclothymia.

In a lucid interval he had a last, very tempestuous and very pathetic love-affair. The woman in this case was his mother's second cousin, Maria Markovich. She had been married before and was five years his senior. A *femme fatale*, with some literary gifts and even greater literary ambitions (she wrote under the name Marko-Vovchok and is mainly known as the author of a number of quite impressive Ukranian folk-tales), she exerted a fascination on many, including Herzen and Turgenev, but as a person was little more than an attractive *intrigante*, relying on chance and intent on being both independent and tempting.[34] She did not share Pisarev's passion, which made him exclaim that he had 'no luck with [his] cousins'. But she was intrigued, flattered, and apparently frightened by it. In a way, Pisarev found himself in the position of the lover-son. His mother was horrified. She had by then become a faintly ludicrous figure, exhausted but still strenuously engaged in sheltering her ailing son from the world and, not least, from women. She was happiest when she had him all to herself—in prison. The flimsy pretexts which she threw up to wrench him from this attachment, however, could not withstand his uncontrolled amorous ardour. Indeed, to please him and to keep him she finished by imploring the hateful cousin (in a curious letter written in French) to become his mistress. We do not know if Maria embraced the offer, but soon afterwards she joined the exhilarated Pisarev in Dubbeln, a Baltic sea-side resort, where he arranged to spend the summer with her. It is here that Pisarev met with his tragic end: he was drowned on 4 July 1868. There is some evidence that this was another, successful, attempt at suicide. It could have been the result of sudden depression merging into the death-wish; or, in the manner of Pisarev's French contemporary, Jules Lequier, a gesture of revolt, darkened and dignified by the counsels of madness; or just a capricious challenge to his unwilling mistress.[35]

2. *The Splendour and Misery of Reason*

Some four years after the death of Pisarev a puzzled official of the Censorship Department wrote that 'of all the Russian socialist writers, Pisarev seems to be the most popular among the younger generation: their immaturity is such that they not only read his works but study them, and every line serves as an occasion for heated and passionate debate'.[36] The impression was correct, at any rate as regards those of the younger generation who were in their twenties at the time of the Karakozov affair. But Pisarev's popularity was due to the fact that he was

—more than Chernyshevsky or even Dobrolyubov—a crystal-
lizer of thought rather than an original thinker; and the crystal-
lizers of thought often achieve a greater fame and influence
than the initiators of new ideas. He said himself, in a letter to his
mother, that his main task was 'to acquaint the public with the
best in European scientific knowledge': 'I assimilate with great
ease the thought of others and have a gift for passing it on in a
completely intelligible manner.' He was himself a fairly typical
representative of European scientific culture, which he, though
a literary critic by profession and inclination, deliberately set
against the literary, aesthetic, and philosophical trend of
traditional culture.

In nineteenth-century Russia, where science had not yet the
strength of a social force behind it, the scientific attitude was
bound to be more self-assertive than in western Europe. It was
hard on the rigidity and ossification, real and imagined, of
traditional cultural habits. It was expansive, impatient, and
destructive. Whereas the resentment which the spokesmen of
traditional culture felt for the scientific was pervaded with fear,
the resentment from the other side was brimming over with
irritation. The claim to scientific detachment wore rather thin,
not least with Pisarev. Unlike Chernyshevsky who, except in
cases of acute disagreement, displayed a remarkable ability to
converse with his readers, Pisarev trounced them and told them
sharply of the mistakes they made and the time they had wasted.
His manner resembled somewhat the procedure of certain
modern philosophers who disprove propositions by making the
person who utters them look foolish, and who claim that what
looked like philosophical argument was only a battle in the
clouds about verbal confusions.

But Pisarev was not 'philosophical' at all. Although pre-
eminently a man of ideas, he not only rejected all intellectual
systems but wished to write off philosophy altogether, as 'logo-
machy' and 'kite-flying', and substitute for it a scientific account
of the world and of human faculties and feelings.[37] Not many
of his contemporaries were so prone to use the expression
'scientific' in a flatly laudatory sense and make its absence
a matter of abuse, on the assumption that only the things we
can see and touch are 'really' real. There was no need any
longer to puzzle over the elaborate probings and inquiries of his

predecessors. Pisarev was eager to ask questions, but he demanded that they should be downright questions which are the concern of every human being, and that the answers should be simple and understood by all. Statements should be tested by a rigorous pragmatic standard. This was also to help to track down and to dispose of the various forms of 'scholasticism', which 'petrifies life into concepts', and of obscurantism, which was 'exploited by those who deceived others and protected themselves'. As often happens with people who adopt an anti-philosophical attitude, Pisarev failed to persuade either himself or others that he had no philosophy. But since he yielded deliberately and without the slightest embarrassment to intellectual contradictions, he nearly got away with his anti-philosophy. He prided himself on being 'a mere human being, with living ideas, full of declared sympathies and antipathies, which I have no wish to conceal'; he even criticized thinkers (Lavrov, for example) for their 'absence of subjectivity'.[38] It is this intellectual candour that made his ideas not just a beaten track of thought or codification of the opinions of others, but a personal experience, even where he appeared to be merely 'playing' with them.

Generally speaking, Pisarev accepted the idiom common to the men of the sixties; but he never showed any susceptibility to Hegelian influences, whether of the right or the left, and his outlook was more clearly marked by some of the characteristic traits of the Enlightenment at its most spirited and life-affirming. He sought a positive attitude to nature, 'disclosed, divined, opening up its laws to the perceiving human mind'. He wished man to take an interest in the world around by observation and reasoning, to concentrate on the down-to-earth elements of life, and to rescue man from the sickly cult of Platonic *Weltschmerz*. Mystics, seers, and metaphysicians were 'spinners of fairy-tales': searching anxiously for some magic formula, some metaphor or equation that would express the universe, they were quickly satisfied, and faded out into 'beatific stagnation'. In an article on 'Plato's Idealism' (*Idealizm Platona*), one of Pisarev's most stimulating early contributions to the 'Russian Word', he repudiated Platonism on the grounds that it was 'not even a philosophy, but a religion—which accounts for its tremendous success during the mystic period of the decline of paganism'. Plato was an 'authoritarian aristocrat' preaching to a select company of erotic intellectuals, a religious poet who 'abandoned the fragrant world of pictures and images for the lofty but frigid sphere of abstract thought, of phantoms and hallucinations'. He blinded men to 'the richness of life, to the tangible reality of matter, the play of line and colour, the kaleidoscopic variety of phenomena, and to all the things that make our life full and rich'.[39]

Like Chernyshevsky and Dobrolyubov, Pisarev reacted strongly against dematerialized spirit, but unlike them he did not bother to argue at length that man is not bifurcated into a mind and a body, and does not engage in some acts which are thought to be mental and others physical. He refutes idealism by jubilantly affirming the living world, no longer a dim shadow of reality but 'nature's dance', to which man sets the tune. It was partly his dilettantism but partly also the measure of his talent that he could, by such asides, suddenly remove a problem from its traditional context and place it in a fresh one, or at least look at it differently. Among the Russian nine-teenth-century radical thinkers only Herzen possessed—to a much greater extent—this ability to break up mental habits and look at familiar problems through glasses of a different colour.[40]

As a matter of fact, Pisarev's early essays, especially 'The Scholasticism of the Nineteenth Century' and the essay just mentioned on Plato, strike some characteristic notes of Herzen. He shared Herzen's idea of a life force, irreducible to any normative and teleological principles. Each moment for him had its own veracity, and man's self-engagement in it was truthful because it was transitory and undetermined by any-thing outside itself. 'I shall not set any goal before myself, nor any preconceived idea. I do not know what results I shall arrive at and do not in the least worry about what I shall achieve in life. I am absorbed in the process of living.' And again: 'I know nothing of goals and ideals, but only of the flux, of which man seeks to possess himself and in which he delights.'[41] Later, when Pisarev became immersed in Darwin, he was continuously trying to relieve the concept of biological purpose from the oppressive undertones of 'final' causation, from 'goal-seeking', which had been detected as miraculously manifest in the growth and development of living things. Life just happens to have developed as it did and as it is. All that we can do is to observe the facts, to assimilate change and share in its creative process without expecting to find meaning elsewhere, and thus forget that man cannot be anything but himself. There is but one necessity, Pisarev said, 'the blessed necessity of being oneself'.

With the sense of the immediacy of life went an insistence on the value of the human person, deciding his own actions for himself and taking the consequences of them. Many people, Pisarev complained, positively desire automatism and regimentation in their lives and themselves 'turn into automata, into desiccated, torpid, flabby creatures...following the dictates of the prevailing state of affairs and the taste of the crowd'.[42] The lament about the destruction of independent thinking, the abolition of will, the elimination of initiative and the erosion of personality is Pisarev's constant refrain, and it will be necessary to refer to it in other connexions.

But side by side with this he persisted in explaining man as wholly a phenomenon of nature, and hence as a mere mechanism responding to stimuli, a puppet to be twitched into whatever it does by impersonal natural forces. It has been shown that Chernyshevsky and Dobrolyubov found themselves involved in the same *non sequitur*. The contradiction reflects the perennial mind-matter dilemma, which becomes particularly acute in periods of questioning and transition. But whereas in Chernyshevsky and Dobrolyubov the discrepancy could be reduced to statements each emphasizing different aspects of a complex truth, Pisarev ran almost deliberately into self-contradictions, revealing under the most reasonable exterior a kind of reckless passion of unreason. Few provide a more striking example of the *splendeurs et misères* of reasonable men.

Most of Pisarev's scientific knowledge was second- or third-hand, derived, in the first place, from Vogt, Büchner, and Moleschott. Of these only Moleschott could be considered a scientist in his own right; the other two were, like Pisarev, popularizers. But, in their time, all three enjoyed the reputation of being the highest mountains of 'scientific materialism', since dwindled to something more like molehills. Strictly speaking, they were not materialists in the classical manner of a Holbach, Helvétius, or La Mettrie: rather, they approached the half-way house familiar from the German intellectual scene—a physiological or biological philosophy, a *Lebensphilosophie*.[43] In any case, Vogt's *Physiologische Briefe*, Büchner's *Kraft und Stoff*, and Moleschott's *Physiologisches Skizzenbuch* were treated by Pisarev as indispensable textbooks of knowledge, and he wrote a number of articles, expounding and defending their materialism. In his interpretation, conveyed in the usual roundabout way to escape the censor, this meant that human beings were physiological or chemical mechanisms, and that human behaviour was explicable in terms of glandular secretions. It was then, and may still be, possible to claim scientific authority for such a view; but with Pisarev it became a proposition with which he had started out, and which appeared to be as binding as the universals of the schoolmen whom he attacked. One suspects that the analysis recommended by Pisarev, had he ever come to it himself, would not have shaken him.[44] The redeeming feature of this apparent finality lay in the vigour and intellectual fluency with which he tried to defend it: they carried the reader along and prevented inconvenient questions arising.

The other scientific and would-be-scientific writers who produced a great impression on Pisarev were Darwin, Comte, and Buckle. His long essay on Darwin's *Origin of Species* ('Progress in the Animal and Vegetable World'—*Progres v mire zhivotnykh i rastenii*), written in prison in 1864, is a first-class work of *haute vulgarisation* which was largely responsible for acquainting the Russian public with Darwinism. It is also one of the most reliable of his scientific writings, least affected of all by the distortions and simplifications peculiar to many of his other works of popularization. In it Pisarev, for once, modestly admits his limitations in dealing with scientific matters. His admiration for Darwin had no bounds. Philosophically, the significance of Darwin lay in the fact that he encouraged Pisarev's materialism. The conception of a struggle for existence and the survival of the fittest by natural selection appeared to present a complete challenge to the idea of purpose and design in life, or rather, referred purpose and design to life itself and thus offered a biological explanation in a region which was considered a stronghold of idealistic philosophy and religion. Pisarev introduces Darwin as 'a thinker of genius', a man whose 'approach to the life of nature reflected a breadth of vision and depth of insight that made his discoveries an unparalleled event in the history of science'.[45] The admiration for Comte and Buckle was more qualified, but both attracted him by their investigation of the effects of science on society and civilization and by their treatment of it in the context of human activity at large. They were, as Plotkin observes, his 'anti-Hegelian weapons'. But he espoused Buckle more readily—not, so it seems, for any intrinsic reasons but because of a marked preference for anything English to everything French.[46]

Pisarev revelled in *réductions à la baisse*, in explaining, and explaining away, the higher by the lower. The idea that all the higher forms of life are more refined and complex equivalents of the lower forms appears to have exercised an irrational fascination on him. He believed that if all the lower laws of force and life are inviolable they cannot revoke their constitution when they issue out of the region of physiology into that of moral life. The meaning of the universe, if we must ask about it, is, therefore, not different in kind from the meaning of twitches in frog legs: hence Pisarev's well-known injunction (which he never attempted to carry out in life) that there is no more worthwhile pursuit than dissecting frogs, as Turgenev's Bazarov did in defiance of the dreaming, loquacious 'fathers'. Strangely enough, Pisarev never stopped to think that his argument, presented with apparent seriousness, to the effect that in dissecting bodies one did not come across a soul, defeated its aim, since the discovery of a soul by this means would have been, of course, an excellent reason for adopting his materialism. Yet 'it is precisely here, in the dissected frog,' Pisarev declared, 'that lies the salvation and the renovation of the Russian people". 'The new philosophy . . . attempts to explain, and indeed does explain, all that occurs in the world order through the agency of those mechanical, physical and other forces which are subject to an unlimited variety of observations and experiments.'[47] Life consists in stimulus, response, and rationalization; and life progresses as the stimuli, the responses and the rationalizations become richer and more satisfactory. 'We cannot either believe or doubt *ad libitum*', Pisarev wrote; 'our thoughts unfold themselves in a certain order, independently of our volition. Even the process of our thinking is subject to the conditions of our physical organization and the circumstances of our development.' Life is produced by the conditions which produce life.[48]

However, as in the case of his older radical contemporaries who made similar declarations, Pisarev's insistence on physical reality did not arise from a sense of loss, or because he felt that bodies were all men had. On the contrary, materialism gave him soul and determinism freed his will. They enabled him to assert man's power to act and move and think. Materialism seemed to promote a new consciousness in man engaged in making his world, whereas for the idealist in whatever shape he was only important as ground for other aims. It was to be a kind of 'gay knowledge', *gaia scienza* (in a would-be Nietzschean sense), which reawakens human life whenever it has spent itself. 'It is gayer to live,' Pisarev wrote, 'it is easier to breathe when, instead of the looming phantoms and abstractions, one sees tangible phenomena, when one becomes aware as much of one's dependence on them as of one's domination over them': 'illusions vanish, facts remain!'[49] In 'The Scholasticism of the Nineteenth Century' he asserted that 'a fresh and healthy materialism' is congenial to the Russian. And when Lavrov objected that, on the contrary, the Russian prefers a sceptical agnosticism and considers materialism just another piece of metaphysics as dusty and old-fashioned as the theories which Pisarev opposed to it, Pisarev replied that Lavrov was merely covering up his inability to commit himself: timid, adaptable agnosticism only served to sap life and did not differ from idealism, which dangles the carrot of hope in front of the human donkey. They spelled, alike, 'the moral castration of the human person' and the 'enslavement of the Russian people'.[50]

Whereas Chernyshevsky combined his materialism, fairly consistently, with a 'realistic' theory of knowledge, Pisarev derived knowledge from subjective sensations. He continually appealed to 'facts', but these lacked for him the independent authority which they had initially for Chernyshevsky. True facts were verifiable facts, and verifiable meant one's own experience through the senses. The external world was a construction from changing sensations, and any inquiry into the nature of reality independent of experience was, in Pisarev's view, impossible.

I know only what I see [he wrote], or, in general, that of which the evidence of my senses can convince me. . . When I see an object, I need no deductive proof of its existence: self-evidence is the best guarantee of reality. When I am told of an object which I do not see or perceive with my senses, I say and think that it does not exist for me. The impossibility of manifest evidence precludes real existence. . . . Such are the canons of materialism, and philosophers of all times . . . would have saved a lot of time and effort, and in many cases would have spared their assiduous admirers fruitless efforts to understand the non-existent, if in their investigations they had not stepped beyond the limits of that which is open to immediate observation. . . . We wish to know what is; we do not wish to know what might be.[51]

Discussions about the soul or self, the meaning of life, beauty, goodness, and so on, proved, therefore, to be mere 'juggling with words', and, in the manner of a thoroughgoing positivist, Pisarev relegated to thinkers the sole task of analysing the verifiable presuppositions and propositions of science. Why, he asked Antonovich, who made a ponderous attack in the 'Contemporary' on a Philosophical Lexicon compiled by a professor of philosophy at the Kiev Theological Academy—why 'tilt against windmills?' The professor's 'metaphysical senilia' are 'dangerous to nobody, if only because of the antediluvian language in which they have been presented'. It is quite enough 'to warn the public not to waste their money'.[52]

Of all the problems from which the principle of verification or verifiability released Pisarev, those of ethics had particular importance for him. Since the only proper judgements are judgements of fact as this is understood in the laboratory, to assess the worth of human actions was a vain pursuit. There was no valid means of telling other people what to do. Moral judgements, according to Pisarev, were merely intimations that we liked or approved of certain things and disliked or disapproved of others. All moral certainties were, therefore, of their nature impermanent and relative, and there was no way of relating the relative to anything that did not incur change. The following statement by Pisarev, facetious as it is, can be considered typical:

If one gourmet likes to have sherry for dinner and another prefers port, there will hardly be a critic in the world able to prove conclusively that one of the two is right and the other wrong. Logically speaking, it is possible that Mr. A's preference for sherry and Mr. B's for port come either from physiological causes, i.e. from the peculiarities of their palate, throat and stomach, or from historical causes, i.e. from acquired habit. Mr. A's penchant for sherry and Mr. B's for port may subject these gentlemen to various inconveniences and ordeals. If Mr. A happens to find himself in some small provincial town with no drinkable sherry, he will be faced with the sad necessity of choosing between giving up his favourite beverage and taking some other wine, and remaining true to himself and standing up to the trial with becoming fortitude. In Mr. A's predicament some will follow one path, some the other, but I venture to suggest that neither side will be held up to public praise or contumely because of the choice made. The trouble is that, when it is a matter of choosing between sherry and port, we remain cool and calm, and argue with simplicity, common sense and a certain skill. . . . When it is a matter of lofty problems we at once assume a sour countenance and begin to speak in a high-pitched voice. . . . We will allow a fellow to cultivate his own taste with regard to his dessert and *zakuski*, but heaven forbid if he voices an independent opinion on morality. . . .[53]

This being so, decisions can be made either by each individual according to his own feeling and preference, or by authority and in obedience to norms. Authority and norms Pisarev rejected. There remained a frank pursuit of one's inclinations. The 'self' or ego, unreal though it may have appeared to Pisarev as a metaphysical entity, was the ultimate measure of moral as of any other experience. And when he analysed the actual motives which made men take a certain course of action he usually discovered—*à la* Bazarov—self-interest and ambition; he did not discover a desire to promote principles and ideals, in which, in any case, he did not believe. Coquart explains Pisarev's moral solipsism as 'l'égotisme éternel de la vingtième année'. This may account for declarations such as Pisarev made to his mother: 'For me', he wrote, 'each person exists only to the extent to which he causes satisfaction in me. This is not a theory, not a figure of speech, but a frank avowal. A person I don't see does not exist for me . . .'; or for saying about his mother that he 'would not hesitate to kill her if that should serve his purpose'.[54]

In a more considered version 'egotism' for Pisarev denoted the 'emancipation of the human person' or 'absence of all moral constraint'. 'To do what one pleases is to act in such a way as to be oneself at each and every moment, even while surrendering to others. The difference of one man's behaviour from another man's behaviour is a difference of temperaments. Freedom consists precisely in this. The social question is a question of personal morality. . . .'[55] The goal, if any, of moral life was the immediate heightened sense of personal experience. As we shall see, this did not prevent Pisarev from making strong moral protests and even having urges to make a better world for others to live in. But he had an extreme dislike of universally valid morality, whose function seemed to him to be, as it were, the reverse of alchemy, the depreciation of living things, the transubstantiation of wine into water. All that he said about the familiar deadly sins, about conventional virtue, respectability, obedience, devotion, compliance, and the rest, fell in with this mood, and it had a ready hearing among his young contemporaries.

Still, it was typical at any rate of the later Pisarev to assert the egotism of others, especially of the underprivileged others, as well as his own. And this implied, naturally, a limitation on the self-seeking nature of man, at least to the extent to which it interfered with the self-seeking nature of other men. He was thus impelled to embrace utilitarianism, which claimed to reconcile conflicting egotisms.[56] The propagation of utilitarianism—at its most Benthamite—was a distinctive feature of the 'Russian Word' for which Blagosvetlov was even more responsible than Pisarev. It explains, perhaps, the review's frequent strictures on Rousseau and on all abstract moral and social gospels, such as social contracts, national rights, the well-being of society, as distinct from the individuals who compose it, and the rest. The question 'How far does this or that thing enhance the happiness of the human individual?' was also Pisarev's chief moral preoccupation. But Blagosvetlov, following Bentham, postulated as the end of politics 'the greatest good of the greatest number': Pisarev, on the contrary, cared more for the good of the individual, for the maximum fulfilment of man's personality, in a life obedient to oneself and pursuing pleasure, not profit or interest. In his letters between 1861 and 1862 he even referred to profit as a source of slavery. He said that there was some baseness in holding nothing but profitable opinions, and that truth was by no means always profitable.[57] Things are called good because we desire them, and not the other way round, i.e. we desire things because they are good or profitable, or because others suppose them to be good or profitable. In the last resort, Pisarev suggested apropos of Bazarov, the only remaining useful thing was the promotion of moral and mental health, and the support of the sheer dynamism of personal living. At the same time, Pisarev resisted the tendency of utilitarianism to assume harmonies or identities of interest where there were none, or where they entailed conformity with the governing social influences. More than any other Russian radical, he used utilitarian notions to support his attitude of individual protest. In doing so, he continually failed to distinguish between what belongs to the definition of a social situation and what belongs to individual motivation. He was, indeed, no more able than anybody else to solve the problem of conflicting value judgements between different individuals or, for that matter, the whole ancient paradox of the 'subjective' and the 'objective', of saving one's life by losing it.

In one respect, however, Pisarev appeared to offer something fresh. Instead of trying to work out the relation of individual to social behaviour, he sought the transformation of human nature and the creation of a new type of man. The idea will be discussed in the next section. It shifted the whole problem of morality from what men do or ought to do to what they are or ought to be, and appealed to psychology rather than ethics.

But side by side with all these views which eschewed norms and obligations in human conduct, Pisarev made incredible claims for natural science; and this involved him in further contradiction. His confidence in the beneficent results of scientific knowledge led him to believe in the possibility of a science of morals as exact as physics or physiology. He almost succeeded in persuading himself that the dissection of frogs had elucidated the whole truth about man. Science was to have a bearing on all human values; and the familiar admonitions about its limits and limitations merely evoked his irritation. In addition, he expected science to be not only knowledge, but also communication of knowledge: not an esoteric pursuit, cultivated by a special, scientific priesthood, but 'popularization', concerned with bringing enlightenment and promoting human progress. It entailed a way of thinking about life, a way of forming attitudes of behaviour as well as of thought; and it admitted, therefore, of the possibility of a rational and scientific basis of human morality. This explains Pisarev's optimism, which affected to believe that human behaviour will improve at least proportionately to the increase in scientific knowledge.

Yet, in Pisarev's context, the very appeal to science begged the whole question. Following the dominant nineteenth-century view, he held that science dealt with what was measurable and predictable, with 'twitches', with empirical generalizations and observable regularities. If the physical universe could be reduced to ordered rules, then man, too, could be brought within a single pattern. An ethic based on such reduction implied the immutability of human nature and the predictability of human conduct, which excludes the exercise of freedom. A man, Pisarev maintained, can no more be punished for having an inefficient conscience than for having an inefficient leg. True, this restriction of freedom was Pisarev's paradoxical way (which he shared with Chernyshevsky) of safeguarding it. For if human actions are the result of physical conditions it becomes difficult to hold people responsible for what they do, and society is bereft of its most powerful sanction for securing good behaviour and thereby keeping man in bondage. But to manufacture moral ideas out of the materials of physical necessity also implied a claim to universal validity and an obligation to conform. It is here that Pisarev came to grief.

The trouble with such ideas is not that they are wrong, but that they could become true, that they actually are the best possible rationalization of certain existing attitudes, in which man appears as a function of something else or is submerged in the impersonal life-process of the species, and ends up in the deadliest and most sterile passivity. With characteristic inconsistency, Pisarev held on to the theory but repudiated its implications. Though virtue and vice were reduced to 'chemical products', he invariably approved of actions not because they exemplified scientific rules but because they originated in exceptional experiences and in personal conviction. As has been seen, he preached egotism as the most powerful of all the instincts, and the love of self as the most powerful of all the passions. He advocated the right to live as fully as possible, to take all the risks of one's freedom and reject all outward checks on one's choices. He attacked his society for having succeeded in killing the mind in the surviving body; and the thing he dreaded most was that 'boring chimera'—the average man, who behaves and thinks according to circumstances. He could not even help feeling slightly ironical about the prudent positivist Buckle, for whom the fierce and unpredictable were conducive to superstition; and who regarded the fortuitousness of events, from the unobtainability of fresh bread to earthquakes, as a sign of the primitive.[58] Among the men of the sixties, Pisarev belonged to the extreme champions of the human person against the encroachments of the environment, of that very objective world of phenomena, conditioned, caused, determined, in which his frogs moved and had their being. It is this world that stood in danger from Pisarev's plea for the human world of 'free subjectivity'. Indeed, it stood in danger from his own acute rationalistic mind, assailed by the sinister charms of untrammelled human existence, even while producing the mechanistic conviction that it was nothing but an elaborate calculating machine.

In a later essay on the conflict between Church and State in medieval Europe Pisarev wrote: 'Despite my respect for general causes, I must state categorically that the major conflict between the emperors and the popes which had such far-reaching consequences was brought about by the personality of the monk Hildebrand. And it seems to me that his personality was not only the occasion but the actual cause of the conflict.' Without its impact 'the conflict might not have arisen at all, and the whole history of European civilization would have taken another, unknown course'. The shape of Cleopatra's nose, after all, influenced not only wars but civilizations. And Pisarev proceeds to insert a question mark against the cast-iron determinism of the scientific evolution of mankind that he held in such high esteem: 'How far', he asks, 'does the impact of man's individual spirit and character impinge on the general course of historical events? The question is of the utmost importance and difficulty: it has not been solved and cannot be solved with monolithic simplicity.'[59]

It is true that such questions arose in Pisarev's mind chiefly when dealing with matters of history. 'The natural sciences', he wrote, 'must not be on any account identified with history, although Buckle attempts to reduce both to a common denominator. In history everything is in the idea, everything is in the person. . . . In natural science everything is in the fact. . . .' And this led him to an insistence on the priority of ideas and intellectual attitudes in a historian's account of human affairs.[60] Yet even here Pisarev failed to be consistent. His frequent protests against the cultivation of science divorced from human ends made him push historical causes, like everything else, into the sphere of material facts. 'Cold and hunger!', he exclaims. 'It is these two simple causes which explain all the real sufferings of mankind, all the vicissitudes of history, all the crimes of individuals and all the immorality of social relations.'[61] It was the business of science to deal with these material facts and to deduce valid action from their analysis. But, by the same token, science and the work of scientists were not, for Pisarev, something apart from their conduct as human beings. He realized that the clash and combination of human agencies were not so dispassionate a matter as the combination of chemical substances. In the end, it proved blasphemous to bottle the infinite variety of life even in scientific jars, prepared by professionals claiming 'a monopoly of learning and oracular authority'. True, the value of science remained unimpaired, but primarily as a means of fostering 'the cold criticism of the sceptical mind', as an abrogation of pre-scientific wisdom and humility, of intellectual passivity and wonder. Apart from this, science, too, turned into a 'beautiful anachronism'.[62] Even Comte, whom Pisarev admired, is urged to watch the spectacle of science with less of the reverence appropriate to a Church and with more of the freedom of the spirit appropriate to those who promote 'the cause of denial', from which Comte and Buckle alike were as far removed as possible, and whose object could not in any case be scientific in the sense of 'undeniable'.[63] 'Denial', 'nihilism' was perhaps the only cause in which Pisarev found complete self-expression and where his mind did not wander into a kind of universal schizophrenia.

.   .   .   .   .

The term 'nihilism', though applied to some rationalists in the Middle Ages, and later to various 'negative' trends among the French Encyclopædists, has become a term of abuse. A French dictionary published in the latter half of the last century defined a nihilist as 'une personne non civilisée'; an English dictionary about the same time preferred the description 'a worldly, dissipated, riotous person'; while Bismarck announced in the German *Reichstag* in 1884 that 'der russische Nihilismus ist eine klimatische Abart des Fortschritts'. In Russia, Pushkin had already been nicknamed 'nihilist' by his adversaries. To judge from the caricatures of the official Russian press of the sixties, a nihilist represented something akin to a contemporary version of a 'beatnik'. A report of the Third Section gave the following description of the species, or rather of its female representative: 'She has cropped hair, wears blue glasses, is slovenly in her dress, rejects the use of comb and soap, and lives in civil matrimony with an equally repellent individual of the male sex or with several such.' The Russian promoters of the terror of established moral and political principle saw this appearance as leading in some obscure way to the established principle of terror itself, and 'nihilism' became the shibboleth attached to Russian revolutionaries, especially, though quite improperly, to those of the terrorist wing.[64]

In literature, as has already been noted, the term was first introduced by Turgenev in *Fathers and Sons*, to describe a new type among the intelligentsia—men who, in the words of one of the novel's characters (Arkady), 'bow before no authority of any kind, and accept no faith, no principle, whatever veneration surrounds it'. But few among Pisarev's contemporaries understood the significance of nihilism better than Herzen, although some nihilists, particularly the nihilistic *émigrés* in Geneva who spent their time in badgering him, roused his resentment. 'What a pity', Herzen wrote to Ogarev at the beginning of 1868, 'that I have come to know properly this Maccabaeus of Petersburg nihilism [Pisarev] so late. This is where true awareness and vindication of oneself lies—spoken out not by a fool or a wretch, but by a keen-sighted young man.'[65] Earlier on, he wrote that 'nihilism is a remarkable phenomenon in the intellectual history of Russia':

'Nihilism' is force of logic without restraint; it is science without dogma; it is unconditional allegiance to experience and a ready acceptance of all consequences, wherever they may lead. . . . Nihilism does not turn 'something' into 'nothing', but shows that 'nothing' that has been taken for 'something' is an optical illusion, and that every truth, however it contradicts our comfortable notions, is more wholesome than they are. Whether the name be appropriate or not does not matter. We are accustomed to it. It is accepted by friend and foe, it has become a police label, it has become a denunciation, an insult with some, a word of praise with others. . . . When Belinsky, on hearing a friend's lengthy explanation to the effect that 'Mind' attains self-consciousness in man, indignantly replied: 'So, I am not supposed to be conscious on my own behalf but on behalf of 'Mind'! . . . But why should I be taken advantage of? I'd better not be conscious at all. What do I care for the 'Mind's' consciousness?'—when he said this, he spoke as a *nihilist*. When Bakunin convicted the Berlin professors of being frightened by negation, and the Parisian revolutionaries of conservatism, he was a *nihilist* in the fullest sense. . . . When the Petrashevskists went to forced labour for seeking, in the words of their sentence, 'to overthrow all divine and human laws and destroy the foundations of society' . . . they were *nihilists*.[66]

This may also be taken as a summary of Pisarev's position. But his nihilism had an accent of its own, and its moral and intellectual setting was a personal one. It contained, broadly speaking, three elements. In his early writings, particularly in 'The Scholasticism of the Nineteenth Century', but also in the later 'Our Academic Learning', nihilism was predominantly intellectual and critical. It was a form of scepticism carried to the point of iconoclasm, in his attitude to axioms, dogmas, and to everything that had been taken for granted. The troubles of man were analysed by him in this connexion mainly as under-education, starved imagination, privation of light, and so on. This was linked with an open-mindedness that verged on naïve credulity towards new concepts, especially scientific concepts, which seemed to hold out a promise to Pisarev's search for new forms of life. The credulity served to enhance the force of denial: it involved a regression to a more primitive level, quite unknown to Herzen, a new innocence of perception liberated from the cataract of all traditional ideas, a kind of 'drawing back to take a better leap'. At this point, Pisarev showed none of that sense of the hopeless suffering of the people which filled Chernyshevsky and Dobrolyubov with an urge for destruction; and it had little in common with the moral convictions in which their rebellion was set. But it was also devoid of any note of disillusionment of the kind which makes a creed out of necessity and accuses life of nothingness, from ceaseless brooding on man's terrible fate. Pisarev intellectualized: hence the contempt for fluff and flurry, the acid manner, the urge to expose authoritative ideas and utterances to intellectual ignominy. Frequently, an imp of youthful mischief broke out from the spirit of denial, although his personal biography shows that underneath there ran a dark stream of unrest and self-searching to the point of self-destruction. As mental revolt against all kinds of intellectual values his nihilism threatened not so much the prevailing social and political order as this order's balance of mind. But in this Pisarev went further than any of his contemporaries.

If authority proves mendacious [he wrote in a celebrated passage], doubt will destroy it, and this will do immense good. If it should prove indispensable or useful, doubt will subject it to radical criticism and re-instate it. In a word, here is our ultimatum: what can be smashed, must be smashed. What stands the blow is good; what flies into smithereens is rubbish. In any case, hit out right and left: no harm will or can come of it.[67]

It is a mystery how the 'ultimatum' could have passed the censor. It caused jubilation among the young radicals whose mood it reflected, and extreme confusion in the Censorship Department. The liberal censor Nikitenko was beside himself. His *démarche* against the 'Russian Word', and Pisarev in particular, provoked the latter's biting remark that his opponents sought 'to make literature a department of the police'. He also wrote about reactions in the Moscow press: 'It pleases me that my ideas displease the Muscovite pundits, and I am sure that many writers wish, as I do, to provide the 'Russian Messenger' [Katkov's paper] with as many opportunities as possible to display its peevishness.' However, he added a plea for the negators, and for the reasons that drove them to negate: they were, he said, up against 'the tragic enthralment of Russian thought'.[68]

The other elements of nihilism appear in Pisarev's examination of two literary characters—Turgenev's Bazarov and Chernyshevsky's Rakhmetov—and in his 'destruction of aesthetics'. Both topics will be discussed in the next two sections. But it will be convenient to isolate here from his treatment of the two literary characters the specifically nihilistic features.

In his essay on 'Bazarov', written in 1862, Pisarev deliberately presented nihilism without regard to any sensibilities. The Bazarovs 'lend themselves to no compromise and no hopes of any kind'. They are 'strangers', not because they are victims of circumstances, but because they are men who have consciously expelled themselves from their surroundings and circumstances and whose isolation is evidence of freedom. They are 'lonely individuals', deprived of the support of the multitude, deprived even of much pride in the existence of the self, but sticking stubbornly, none the less, to their independence. Their nihilism excludes every attitude that is likely to serve as a prop to confidence. Even denial is denied if it is sustained by love of the image which it destroys, or if it becomes a satisfying edifice to dwell in. Their pursuit of scientific knowledge is a form of 'hygiene', directed towards the elimination of any odd entity which can be found cumbering man's free thought and his ability to see reality as it is. 'Nature', Pisarev says, 'must be explored. Instead, we enter into pathetic relations with her, we lose time in wonder, we obfuscate our minds with all sorts of illusory images, in which some claim to discover beauty, others consolation, still others even meaning and logic.'[69]

Bazarov's free-thinking, as Pisarev presents it, is remote from the secure and balanced rationalism of the eighteenth century. He lacks the optimistic belief of the men of the Enlightenment in their own age and civilization, their historical self-satisfaction, their sense of prestige and status. And, though Pisarev commended Voltaire and Diderot for not having felt 'the slightest pity or sympathy for the things they negated and destroyed', he ascribed to them a nihilism that would have filled them with despondency. True, Pisarev's nihilism did not at this stage amount to a doctrine of social and political revolt. But instead of being, as before, merely or mainly an extreme form of scepticism, it became a kind of denuded amoral morality, in which human acts appear as arbitrary gestures: Bazarov 'thinks what he wills to think' and 'does what he chooses to do'. He is completely independent even of the few things he believes in. He deliberately suppresses his moral imagination; he is tough and matter-of-fact; and the daring defiance of any real or imaginary gods is replaced by the habit of doing without either the gods or the stimulus of defying them.[70]

Pisarev was anxious not to turn nihilism into a romantic posture, which is often only a form of dramatized opportunism.

He examined it with simple exactitude and a remarkable absence of emotion. 'Denial', he said, 'is a hard, tedious and deadly task.'[71] The earnestness as well as the vigour with which he denied saved Pisarev from being just an iconoclast swinging a sword at respectable opinions. As it was, his nihilism even became a heroic creed, an exhortation to live with one's ailments, to master one's plight in an imperfect world by being aware of it. It could not heal wounds, nor, as the fate of Turgenev's Bazarov showed, remove the bitterness of death. It was, in Pisarev's words, nothing more than 'stark realism'. Its only apparent moral or social reference consisted in that it marked a turning inside out of falsehoods which had lasted for centuries and on which it took revenge through Bazarovian extremes of discourtesy: 'a malady, perhaps', Pisarev said, 'but a malady of our time which we must live through', 'a pathological phenomenon, as pathological as the world which [the nihilist] denies'.[72] But even the exposure of falsehood entailed no sense of tragedy, which, to be absorbed, calls for pity, terror, and forgiveness. 'Much may change with time', Pisarev concluded, 'but . . . we have, meanwhile, to console ourselves with the supremely fruitless realization that we do to a certain extent comprehend the incongruity of life.' '"And that is nihilism?"', he ends by asking in the words of Bazarov's outraged interlocutor. '"That is nihilism", Bazarov [and Pisarev] repeated, this time with pointed insolence.'

The conclusion suggests a moral and social wasteland—the nemesis perhaps of an inveterate rationalist at the end of his tether, grasping nothing at all and ignorant of what he is to do. In point of fact, Pisarev was more or less confident and more or less successful in grasping reality, and he claimed that nihilism leads in the end to a discovery of true humanity and even of true social relations. The connexion was never properly worked out by him: paradox continued to have its arresting effect on him. Broadly speaking, the connexion was indicated by a shift of emphasis from nihilism to revolution, from a feeling that the old world was doomed to a realization that it must be changed. Revolutionary elements can be found in Pisarev's early writings, notably in the document which was responsible for his imprisonment. Admittedly, such elements referred in the main to his concern for the liberation of the human mind. They owed little to any positive examination of contemporary social problems. But even those who pursue, as Pisarev pursued, destruction by 'hitting right and left' cannot fail to create: it suffices to create new words and new valuations in order in the long run to create new things. In any case, the new things were already emerging; the settled habits of thought and behaviour against which Pisarev maintained an incessant protest had begun already to be shaken by the rapid differentiation and disintegration of post-Reform Russian society. The function of the rebel was becoming significantly different by being more self-controlled and less arbitrary. Furthermore, Pisarev could not eliminate in himself the moral fervour which he condemned in others but which impelled him to seek a reconciliation between 'egotism and altruism'. Even his ambivalent attitude to the impersonal forces at work in life, in which, none the less, man remained conscious of his own free will and rationality and ability to change it, had obvious moral and social implications. Even science to him was not so much research as application of research to purposes which were moral, a way of behaviour taking place in human society, rather than a mere method of understanding the mechanics of the world.

All this prepared the transition from nihilism to social revolution, and it found its symbolic expression in that Pisarev turned his attention from Bazarov to Rakhmetov. There is some evidence that Chernyshevsky himself conceived his novel *What Is to Be Done?* as a kind of counterblast to Turgenev's *Fathers and Sons*. It will be remembered that the latter caused surprise and indignation to some radicals, particularly those around the 'Contemporary', for Bazarov was taken to be a deliberate caricature of the 'sons' precisely on account of those extreme nihilistic and egotistic features with which Turgenev endowed him and which Pisarev extolled. Chernyshevsky's Rakhmetov, who does not stand artistic comparison with Turgenev's hero, shares some of the latter's characteristics. But, unlike Bazarov, he is first and foremost a revolutionary, dedicated to the subversion of the existing order: he is a man without a private past, present, or future, without emotional needs and satisfactions; he is completely and selflessly identified with the fate of his fellow men. Pisarev tried to draw a kind of composite portrait, combining the nihilism and individualistic non-conformity of

Bazarov with the revolutionary socialism and sense of solidarity
of Rakhmetov. He did this in an essay entitled 'The New Type'
(*Novyi tip*) or 'The Thinking Proletariat' (*Myslyashchii proletariat*) and written in prison in 1865. Its ostensible aim was to
examine and commend Chernyshevsky's novel, but it can be
regarded as a definitive statement of his own beliefs.

3. 'The Thinking Proletariat'

It is significant for Pisarev's general approach to the problems
which occupied him as a man and a writer that his profession
of faith took the form of a psychological study. He seldom
showed any interest in ideas or systems of thought as such, but
always wished to discover the man who adopted them. When
he discussed human behaviour he did not discuss its goodness or
badness, or even the goodness and badness of the arguments by
which behaviour was justified or blamed, but the human being
himself, and why he should do what he does or think as he thinks.
He applauded or denigrated human gestures, the 'ethos' or
'character' of man, rather than his thoughts: 'the only thing of
interest to me', he stated, 'is man's living individuality.' The
quotation is from an essay written in 1865 on the Slavophil
Ivan Kireevsky ('A Russian Don Quixote'—*Russky Donkikhot*),
where this attitude is clearly set out. 'Nothing can be vaguer or
more vapid', Pisarev wrote at the beginning of this essay, 'than
the loose terms "obscurantist", "progressive", "liberal", "conservative", "Slavophil", "Westerner", and the like. Such labels
in no way characterize the man to whom they are applied, but
impose a uniform on his intellectual personality, and instead of
a man who lives, thinks and feels in his own way we get a stiff
signboard of cut and dried conviction.' Pisarev objected to the
treatment of Kireevsky by the 'Contemporary': 'Instead of considering the development of Kireevsky, Khomyakov and the
other Slavophils,' he said, 'instead of examining the characteristic features which moved these men to reject rational enquiry,
instead of elucidating Slavophilism as a psychological phenomenon, the critic from the 'Contemporary' plunges into a sterile
polemic against the propositions of the Slavophil theories.'[73]
Nothing in these theories was remotely congenial to Pisarev, and
the writings of the Slavophils appeared to him, in his own words,

as not much more than 'incoherent speech' and 'a staccato of ejaculations'. Nevertheless, he was interested in the Slavophil mind, and he succeeded in drawing a brilliant portrait of Kireevsky the man—'the Russian Knight of the Rueful Countenance', as he called him.

This psychological or typological method, familiar already in a less-developed form from Dobrolyubov, provided Pisarev with a much more effective instrument for impressing his contemporaries than a theory would have done. For it did not act on the conscious mind alone, but penetrated that deeper level which is indifferent to theoretical constructions and which he experienced as real even while his own rationalism and scientism were doing their deadly work. He influenced his contemporaries above all by his search for a new man, whose moral and intellectual attitudes rather than reflected principles would lead to spontaneous morality and who would therefore serve as a model. Man could not, in Pisarev's view, remain as he was and yet be the inhabitant of a world different from and better than the world he actually lived in. The world he lived in was a consequence and a projection of what he was. If men continued to be as they were and had been in the past, it was obvious to him that the world they lived in could not change. What was needed was not a change of hearts, as the cant phrase goes, nor even a change of heads, although this was better, but the creation of a new human type. If it were not for Pisarev's radicalism and nihilism, the idea might seem to carry an echo of Matthew Arnold of Rugby. But a comparison with Heraclitus' 'ethos of man which is his demon', or Aristotle's '$\chi\alpha\rho\alpha\kappa\tau\dot{\eta}s$', or, even more, with Rousseau's 'homme nouveau' 'qui n'a de rapport qu'à lui-même ou à son semblable', would be more appropriate. To achieve this end, Pisarev put his trust not in the operation of grace, for which Rousseau called without believing in its possibility, but in man's conscious effort and in knowledge of oneself and of the world around. At all events, the supreme question was 'What kind of man are you?'[74]

The interest in 'type' expressed itself on a number of levels. At the lowest level it referred to all the reactions that living organisms make against surrounding difficulties and limitations. This explains in part the attraction of Darwin for Pisarev. For Darwin's principle claimed to account for the selection of improved types and for the extinction of deteriorated types, and to show that of an indefinite number of individual variations in the type, that one which gives advantage to the individual in the struggle for life in any particular place, tends also to be perpetuated in that place. 'Victory is on the side of the strongest,' Pisarev writes approvingly of Darwinian struggle and selection, 'and consequently the qualities of the strong victor are made lasting in the offspring. . . . Nature annihilates all that is weak and fragile, and supports all that is vigorous and lasting.' 'Every species constantly operates for itself alone and complete selfishness is the basic law of life in the whole organic world.' While criticizing Malthus on Chernyshevskian lines, he declared, with customary inconsequence, that 'suffering is indestructible because . . . life is founded on an incessant mutual extermination of living and sentient beings'.[75]

But the process of sifting and winnowing that goes on in nature had its counterpart on the higher and specifically human level. Pisarev's need and search for a new species of man became a need and a search for a new Prometheus, whom he endowed with some of the distinctive qualities of the Nietzschean superman.[76] It is difficult to see how this could coexist with twitching frogs and registering apparatuses with cold entrails. But coexist they did. Like Nietzsche, Pisarev thought that the criterion of true humanity was mental and bodily health, creative power and a will to self-fulfilment. Like Nietzsche, he delighted in 'outstanding individuality', in man who is diverse, animated, precise, touched with the ardour of life and capable of imparting these qualities to his environment. At times he believed indulgently that life depended merely on the art of making it palatable, and attributed the symptoms of illness in the species man to a diet of ideas—religious, philosophical, and artistic—which disguise the flavour of reality. As a cure for this he prescribed a Stendhalian mixture of Epicureanism and the cultivation of unrestrained energy which would bring out the wildest and the bitterest in life.[77] But the Epicureans are said to have been gentle, accommodating, and unenterprising people who wanted a quiet existence and a minimum of metaphysics. Pisarev, their Russian disciple, took greater risks and aimed at greater satisfactions. He talked of man's 'Promethean','Titanic' nature, of the 'Titans of thought', 'of love', and 'of imagination'.

There were no gods left to be robbed of their fire, but he took a light from man who is a law unto himself and kindled with it the flame of nihilism. This was Pisarev's hubris. As in Nietzsche there existed a link between the exaltation of the self and nihilism; and, significantly, both became insane at the moment of fusion between self-deification and negation.

It would, however, be wrong to represent Pisarev as a Russian Nietzsche: what is suggested is an analogy, not an identity. He felt no need to turn man's will to self-fulfilment into mere repugnance from society, and into a lust for domination, whatever biological extravagances he may have allowed himself when talking of Darwin. 'Our life', he wrote, '. . . has no need of mighty individuals: we have more than enough of these. What we need . . . is awareness of reality.'[78] His hero was not a posturing, mystagogical Zarathustra, whom he would have repudiated with vehemence had he lived to know him, but the pragmatic Bazarov, who inclines to action rather than to dream, who leans on the intellect rather than on emotion, who is tragic but never plays himself up, and appears almost insensitive.

From the very first moment [Pisarev wrote], Bazarov conquered my imagination. . . . For a long time I could not account for this exclusive attachment. But now I understand it perfectly well. No other character has ever found himself in such a tragic situation. . . . It reduces itself to his stark solitude among all those who surround him. Everywhere he creates brutal disharmony; everybody suffers by his presence, by his very existence. He is perfectly conscious of it. What is more, he understands with painful clarity the fatal cause and the inescapability of these sufferings.

They are the conditions in which the veil is torn away from all intellectual and moral imposture and man's true identity is revealed. 'But his situation is all the worse for that, all the more painful and insoluble.'[79] Pisarev's hedonism and utilitarianism did not prevent him even from declaring in this connexion that 'without illness there is no pathology', that happiness and creativity go ill together, and that pain is resourceful in springing new surprises, never the same for any two of its victims, whilst well-being blurs into featureless satiety.

Man, as seen by Pisarev, is caught in a conflict between life with other human beings and life in dissent. He knows, as Bazarov knew, that even love no longer binds life, that he cannot conjure fate, that he must defer to pain and death, extracting his grain of significance from his solitary defiance. But, once again, this was far removed from the Nietzschean complex of 'power-wielders'. It never occurred to Pisarev to confer on man the frantic quality of Nietzschean 'artist-tyrant' Neros who sublimate cruelty because they have no other means of asserting themselves, and who dominate their fellows because they fear them. He expressed horror at the way in which

man's most precious gift—his personal independence—is continually sacrificed for all kinds of vast and sublime aims nurtured in the minds of the great; while we, simple mortals, are driven to renounce all initiative. Heroes, sages, and geniuses would charge themselves with thinking, feeling, and living on our behalf! This might serve to introduce into our lives an order such as never existed before; it might bring about unimaginable harmony. But what boredom, what oppression for those other puny creatures, atoms, insects, who are reduced to a perfectly regulated, measured, commonplace existence![80]

The latter sentiment shows that Pisarev refused to accept a tyrannical society as much as tyrannical individuals. He deplored the transformation of men into impoverished things, depending on powers outside themselves, whether they be idols of their own making or the vast authority of individual rulers and the invisible authority of present or future social schemes. Hence his pronounced dislike of the State. Like many anarchistically inclined nineteenth-century Russian thinkers, he held that the State existed for the purpose of legitimizing the pressure of society against the individual; and that it took upon itself to represent all human activities by fostering a sense of belongingness as the ultimate need of man: as he said, it 'owes everything to its rapaciousness'. In addition—and this was especially characteristic of Pisarev—he viewed the State as the main organ for the promotion of humbug and stupidity. 'Mental darkness', he observed, 'is essential for the tranquillity and collective well-being' of the political bee-hive. Far from proving their wisdom and intelligence, the so-called great statesmen have shown that they were rarely endowed with imagination and possessed commonplace minds.[81] 'There can be no question of progress in the State', Pisarev maintained in his thesis on Apollonius of Tyana. Being primarily concerned with the behaviour of individual persons, he believed that 'changes in the existing order [were] due to progress based on the development of the individual human being'. He expected great things for society at large from such development. His confidence, however, was tempered by a conviction that 'what has been hallowed by the flattering name of historical progress is but transition from one kind of war to another, and from one kind of slavery to another . . . slavery has a habit of concealing itself under different guises'.[82] The notion that men serve as platoons in the mighty battalions of history, marching towards a goal to be attained by distant posterity, offered no more satisfaction to him than the notion of man's crushed bones serving as material for the erection of mighty social edifices.[83]

In a remarkable allegorical essay on 'Bees' (*Pchely*), which was considered by some of Pisarev's detractors to have been a more dangerous attack on the existing order than 'all the revolutionary proclamations taken together', he described the prevailing social condition of man on the analogy of 'drones dancing in honour of the majesty, benevolence and political wisdom of their sovereign lady'; while 'the worker-bees live to provide the rubble and foundation for the social structure. Some naturalists are moved to tears by the spectacle of wisdom displayed by the bees and of their enviable capacity for social cohabitation. For my part, on the contrary, I cannot help wondering at their monstrous subjection. It goes so far that, maimed though they are themselves, they go on systematically maiming others and thus become insensible victims and insane victimizers at one and the same time.'[84] Men in the herd are shown to be subject to delusions and self-delusions, which turn them into units in an undifferentiated and soulless mass. Removed from primary satisfactions, working without joy in work and relying on substitute pleasures, with their mental furniture supplied at tenth hand or not at all, they become infantile, dull, and submissive, as though they had undergone a spiritual truncation. Unless they revolt, they are saved for life not worth living—a lifeless life of obedience, huddled into a safe, warm crowd.

In this Pisarev took revolt further than most of his radical contemporaries, for he made a stand not only against the privileged classes but also against the mass of the people. He envisaged a new group altogether—an intellectual *élite*, a 'thinking proletariat', or 'thinking realists', whose thoughts enable them to control their environment in a scientific manner. His belief in the essentially rational nature of man made him regard reasoning and reasonable men as the salt of the earth.[85] This accounts for the fact that, as a rule, Pisarev is read and judged within the exclusive framework of the rationalist Enlightenment—an approach which we have seen to be prevalent also among some students of Chernyshevsky. True, Pisarev inclined to write off the irrational side of human life and history as a manifestation of stupidity, or at least to believe as long as possible that it was too unreasonable to be true. He also inclined to think that ideas, however 'typologically' interpreted, rather than social forces, determine the course of events. This gave his historical essays a certain air of timelessness. He lacked the sense of history which was so strong in Chernyshevsky and which was not weakened by Chernyshevsky's own occasional leanings to rationalism. He often treated history as a stage of mere intellectual debate, and the past as an ammunition dump from which he selected shells to fire at intellectual opponents.

We have seen, however, that some of Pisarev's strongest impulses served to baffle his rationalism, to say nothing of the contradiction involved in believing human life to be controlled by reason, while constantly appealing, as Pisarev did, to men's rationality. Similarly, he upheld the ideal of the 'thinking proletariat' for reasons that had little in common with those for which he held his rationalistic and scientific beliefs.

The prototype of such a 'proletariat' was Chernyshevsky's Rakhmetov, and Pisarev saw in *What Is to Be Done?* a living commentary on it. Rakhmetov appears as a Bazarov with a social conscience whose 'love of other men', Pisarev tells us, 'stands in direct proportion to the depth of his egotism'. He embodies both self-affirmation and self-surrender. He at once scorns the mob and yet lives by dedicating himself to others. He is the opposite of the mean, the weak, and the frustrated. Like a true aristocrat, he is courageous, honest, unselfish; he is also hard-working, which a true aristocrat is not. He approaches 'Caesar with the heart of Christ', who does not refuse to serve the underdog and is all the more noble for not refusing to do so. Only one thing in Rakhmetov grated on Pisarev: his ascetic bent and the apparent inability or unwillingness to suffer or feel desire. Pisarev distrusted the puritanism which has been the curse of so much progressive thought, stunting the senses and killing the capacity for enjoyment. But he acclaimed Rakhmetov's passion for freedom which stood in the way of remaining at peace with his environment. This carried an invitation to revolution: first, by bringing man to his senses and making him see himself and the world as they really are; second, by destroying the existing world as effectively as possible; and lastly, as a consequence of such destruction, by precipitating the course of history. At this point Pisarev even turns into an advocate of 'utopianism', to counteract the complacency and caution of those who live under the domination of the everyday world, and to let in air where everything is enclosed and preordained. 'My dream', he wrote, 'can outrun the natural course of events or it can fly off at a tangent. . . . In the first case, it can do no harm: in fact, it may sustain and intensify the force of human enterprise. . . .' Rakhmetov does not concern himself with order and proportion. His 'strength cannot be applied to petty deeds'; it 'cannot be employed in times when routine reigns undisturbed, when long, humdrum, wearying historical intervals seem to go on for ever'.[86] He is the *reductio ad absurdum* of the normal world, and he consciously and conscientiously plans its undoing.

Inasmuch as this entailed the destruction of established habits in thought and behaviour, Pisarev stuck at nothing. But he was less unequivocal when he came to apply it to political matters. Sometimes he seems to side with the advocates of extreme revolutionary measures. His proclamation against Shedo-Ferroti contained an open appeal to revolutionary action. Writing about the French Revolution, he spoke of the monumental simplicity of those who try to reduce it to the schemes of wicked or misguided demagogues, inciting the mob to dark and wicked deeds; and he acclaimed 'the inexhaustible resources of burning, fearless and relentless negation that accumulated in the mind and heart of the French people. . .'. But, he adds, revolution in France had been betrayed by the substitution of the aristocracy of money for the aristocracy of birth, and only the Jacobins understood this 'tragi-comic paradox' of revolutionary history. When a revolution becomes a 'historical reality', Pisarev concluded, it is no use stopping half-way or 'blinking at it', or pretending that it is of no account.[87]

With the revolutionary mood went a pointed anti-liberalism. Like the fictional Bazarov and Rakhmetov, and like most of Pisarev's actual fellow radicals, he was repelled by the vaguely eclectic, adjustable attitude of the liberal 'fathers', who, of course, in turn abhorred his violent negations. He disliked their cautious empiricism and their habit of 'sprinkling *eau de Cologne* in fetid stables'. He described the Gironde, in the manner of Belinsky, as a 'putrid corpse', and he thought the tragedy of his beloved poet Heine lay in that he had tied himself to that corpse.

In all our towns and nearly all our villages [Pisarev wrote of Russia] there languish, pine, mumble, simper and suffer in aromatic pain thousands of timorous individuals, in whom all the respectable European liberals from Lord Russell to Julian Schmidt would be bound to recognize their younger brothers. They may still be quailing and inexperienced, but their thin descants already catch the familiar melodies of liberal miauling. The part of a liberal is beset by such enormous difficulties, his exertions are so irksome, his path is strewn with so many and such sharp thorns, that ten years would not suffice to reach the wondrous clarity and imperturbability of vision, the unimpeachable solidity of behaviour, which are the hallmark of an experienced liberal, matured in the great school of stabilization, mystification and confident dropping of buckets into empty wells.

But whether mature or immature, the liberal has 'a physiognomy of his own . . ., which betrays his unceasing concern for lofty ideals and pursuits which [in real life] cause in him the same sort of sensation that insect powder does in a bug'.[88]

These strictures on liberalism, however, owed more to psychological incompatibility than to clearly defined political considerations. Similarly, Pisarev's revolutionary ideas never received definite political expression either in word or in deed. As a matter of fact, at times he even showed a marked preference for peaceful changes in society and for what he called the 'chemical way' of political development. This was particularly pronounced throughout his early journalistic career. Thus, he commended Apollonius of Tyana for refusing to sow the seeds of revolution: 'his [Apollonius's] aim', Pisarev wrote, 'had been wider and deeper, as well as more worthy of a thinking human being', for revolution and communism 'are offensive to the dignity of man'. The evidence shows that the events preceding, and culminating in, the Polish rebellion of 1863 had given rise in Pisarev to scepticism in regard to forcible political action, and he himself observed that 'a feeling of exhaustion inevitably succeeds periods of great tension' in history.[89]

But, alike in his revolutionary and evolutionary moods, Pisarev saw the moving force of history not in the people, who can be duped, but in a conscious intelligentsia, inspired by a radical, scientific humanism. Even in admitting the legitimacy of popular revolutions where these could help to hasten the course of history, he insisted that 'no one could mould [them] except men of thought'. To extend the influence of the intelligentsia was, therefore, 'the *alpha* and *omega* of . . . social development'. 'The fate of the people', runs his famous dictum, 'is decided . . . not in popular schools but in the universities.'[90] No one would have been less at home in the villages of Russia than Pisarev. He regarded the peasants as pre-civilized people, 'passive material', 'machines that differ from [ordinary] machines . . . by their unfavourable capacity for feeling exhaustion, hunger and pain.' He did not believe that the intelligentsia 'could extract anything of importance from popular wisdom'.[91] Nor did he believe in the claim to genius of the Russian popular masses, whether based on the discovery of a Russian soul, in the manner of the Slavophils, or on the premise that Russia was exempt from the normal rigours of social development, in the manner of the populists. The Slavophil attacks on those new historical elements which seemed responsible for the corruption of the old way of life and its solid values appeared to him as a piece of mere naïvety; and he attributed 'the turgid, nebulous ravings about the spirit of the people, about Russian civilization and Russia's future influence on the mental life of Europe' to a Quixotic complex.[92] In his view, the 'ages of faith' provided examples not of 'moral beauty' but of widespread darkness, inhumanity, and corruption which it would be difficult to match; and the myth of 'national purity' produced in him a feeling of claustrophobia. It is impossible to find a single instance in Pisarev's writings where Russia is compared favourably with western Europe. He never went further than to say that 'our civilization is neither better nor worse than all the rest'. More often than not, he maintained that Russia had everything to learn from the West.[93]

Similarly, the populist belief in the peculiar ways of social development in Russia, and in the saving power of pre-industrial or any other communalism, struck him as a naïve simplification.[94] He not only acknowledged the rupture of 'organic society' but, unlike the populists, saw in this a beginning of liberation, because, in his view, it had brought on a thaw in the frozen, static Russian world. It seemed to augur an expanding universe, divergent, variegated, and rich in texture, and to dispel the reassuring feeling of stability, rest and order.

Pisarev's attitude lacked the warmth of the Slavophils and populists whose hearts lay in the farm-house, but it had a more direct bearing on conditions in post-Reform Russia, which had begun to be seriously dislocated by a money economy and had become erratic through industrialization. And it was undoubtedly of more use to men who had to grapple with her real problems. In this respect, Pisarev represented a closer link between the sixties and Marxism than Dobrolyubov or even Chernyshevsky. He wanted Russia to stop being a society of landlords and peasants, of usurers and beggars, a society held back from progress by ancient taboos, bigotry, and sloth: he wanted her to sever all cosy relations and to develop those internal strains which make a country a social volcano. Hence he preferred industrial economy to the rural economy advocated by many populists.[95] A dynamic society called for the full utilization of the scientific industrial revolution; and, in his view, the artistic culture that failed to comprehend this was bound to be inhuman in the long run. He knew that there was a great deal wrong with industrial society, but the thing to do was to find ways of putting that right, rather than dream oneself into religious or social myths which had no connexion with reality. He inclined to give the middle classes an active part in the social life of the nation such as had hitherto been confined to the gentry. At times Pisarev almost leaves the impression of being more disturbed by the brutish dullness, the triviality and meddlesomeness of Russian autocracy than by its moral and social evil. The presence of an active *bourgeoisie*, to his mind, could serve as a possible antidote to the 'power-ridden bone-headedness' of the Russian State. But he thought of this *bourgeoisie* in terms of a managerial aristocracy of talent, an *élite* consisting of industrialists and thinkers, rather than one of privilege and class, one which combines liberty with property and makes man into a perfect competitor or a perfect market.[96]

In any case, it was not for the intelligentsia, whether cultural or industrial, to ally itself with vaguely imagined forces like the masses, but for the masses to rise above their amorphous, anonymous collectivity and become partners in the common-wealth of 'thinking proletarians'. Pisarev's friend Skabichevsky reproached him for dealing with the people in the same way in which medieval knights treated their underlings, by demanding their complete surrender and admiration; while Pisarev's opponent Antonovich impressed upon him that 'the simple people, with undeveloped minds and ignorant of Buckle and electricity, are not less capable of feeling oppression . . . and of protesting against it than those who . . . rave about Buckle, stand high above prejudices and are acquainted with the natural sciences.' Indeed, 'a protest based on Buckle and [Pisarev's] articles', Antonovich asserted, was of less relevance than 'a protest coming from [the people's] own understanding and sentiment'.[97]

The complaints were not altogether fair. Pisarev's 'intellectual *élite*' in no way resembled a sect snobbishly holding itself out-side the battle. Skabichevsky and Antonovich must have known that a large part of Pisarev's journalistic work consisted in militating against the occult preserve of esoteric cliques—artistic, social, and scientific—which he considered sterile precisely because of their remoteness and failure to communicate with their fellows.[98] Sometimes, though seldom, he even fell back on the masses, stirring behind the scenes.[99] At any rate, the 'thinkers' were meant to be 'proletarians', not landowners or even stock-holders, although these last were a product of the highly differentiated society welcomed by Pisarev. He sought to en-large, not to restrict, the 'thinking proletariat', until it became conterminous with society itself—a process of levelling up. As a matter of fact, he was not greatly interested in class as such—except in the broad sense that landowners and capitalists tend to behave differently in the social sense from peasants and workers—but in human beings before they are converted into generalized groups and, thereby, often lose their identity.

Above all—and this is more important than any views Pisarev may have entertained about who or what influences the course of history—he felt bitterly about social injustice, and the poverty and misery of men. His 'ferocious egotism', instinctive or intentional, could not disguise an inability to turn his back on men, weighed down by pain and hunger, turned into slaves and deprived of personality. He may have felt at times akin to Stendhal, who desired the happiness of the people with all his heart but preferred to spend a fortnight of each month in prison to having to live 'with shopkeepers'. But unlike Stendhal he could not close his eyes contentedly and accept the pleasures of life in face of the frustrated humanity of others. In this respect he did not differ much from the conscience-stricken 'fathers' who, he thought, had nourished themselves on the milk of benevolence which did not cost them anything and whose sincerity he was disposed to question. 'When all is said and done,' he wrote in the celebrated passage already referred to, 'the ultimate aim of man's entire thinking and acting is to solve once for all the pressing question of the hungry and the disinherited. Apart from this question there exists nothing that deserves our reflection, concern, or anxiety.'[100]

His own remedy contained the familiar rationalist ingredients. In one sense, he believed that it is only when people cease to be hungry for food that they begin to be hungry for knowledge and culture. [101] But, at the same time, he ascribed the prevalence of hunger to intellectual paralysis: 'Our predicament', he said, 'consists in that we are poor because we are stupid, and we are stupid because we are poor. To become prosperous we must become intelligent, but we cannot become intelligent because our poverty does not allow us to breathe.' In order to break the vicious circle Pisarev suggested an extreme 'concentration' or 'economy of intellectual forces', enabling men to turn to 'ever more intelligent action', while in the process mental power supersedes physical. With greater control over nature man's control over other men declines, and equality becomes diffuse throughout society, culminating in a harmonious order of things.[102]

The most or only interesting element in this optimistic scheme was Pisarev's idea of equality. He knew from Russian life, even more than from reading Tocqueville or Proudhon or Herzen, the nature of an inegalitarian society, with its vulgar irrelevancies of class and status, its intellectual poverty and moral disablement. He concluded that the 'aristocracy of money' as well as the 'aristocracy of birth' created differences which, besides the waste in human resources they both produced, degraded the quality of man. In his view, they destroyed creative relationships between men, while conveniently safeguarding those between the ruler and the ruled, between the exploiter and the exploited. The centre of Pisarev's social thinking was not the issue of what man has but of what he is. And it is this that led him into the socialist ranks.

4. *'The Destruction of Aesthetics'*

'No artist tolerates reality', said Nietzsche. Pisarev's attitude to art could be expressed by reversing this statement. It was already implicit in Belinsky and more so in Chernyshevsky. But whereas these latter chose for their motto 'Reality is higher than art', Pisarev launched a campaign against art iself and the culture which has produced it. He did not confine himself to treating art as an instrument for conveying the artist's view of man and of human society: he proclaimed the deposition of aesthetic values, and he used or misused Chernyshevsky's treatise on aesthetics as a weapon for destroying them. His motto was 'no reality tolerates the artist', or rather 'no reality tolerates art'. He demonstrated his anti-aestheticism in at least three essays (all written in 1865, during the latter part of his imprisonment), of which 'The Destruction of Aesthetics' (*Razrushenie estetiki*) is the most outspoken.[103] But none of them lend themselves to a uniform interpretation, because he could not always make up his mind whether he was attacking the idealist notion of beauty, or all art, or merely the primacy of 'form' over 'matter' in a work of art. This explains why some of his commentators tried to isolate one or other of these facets, while ignoring or minimizing the rest. Yet, essentially, it was an all-out attack in all three directions. Pisarev's treatment of aesthetic problems can best of all be discussed under these three heads.

At the outset, his general philosophical position left no room at all for any ultimate ideals or norms of art. 'Beauty in itself', 'true beauty', 'ideal' or 'universal' beauty, for him as much as for Chernyshevsky, were just words—'a mumbo-jumbo of indefinite Platonic and Hegelian notions'. Nothing, in his view, was more relative than our sense of the beautiful, and any attempt to divorce it from the concrete experience of the beautiful had no meaning. He could see no other choice except that between immutable aesthetic standards, remote and inapplicable to anything in particular, and aesthetic thrills, where one man's sense is another man's nonsense and which are closely linked with the outward aspects of life, with immediate sensation and the physical awareness of the here and now. 'Personal impressions . . .', he said, 'are the sole criterion of beauty.'[104] This antipathy to the idea that art could be the means of apprehending an ideal, unseen, or supernatural order need not detain us any longer, for it merely echoed Chernyshevsky's already familiar views on the matter. Pisarev lacked even more than Chernyshevsky, or pretended to lack, a proper appreciation, to say nothing of a theory, of imagination; and he took a perverse pleasure in not having, or in pretending not to have, these things. He was remarkable only for the boldness with which he stated his position and for his almost alarming facility, which makes one wonder whether, even to his own mind, the problem was really as simple as he made it out to be.

The opposition to art itself has earned Pisarev the greatest obloquy and has largely contributed to his reputation of an arrogant, malicious iconoclast, with no regard for sensibilities and bleakly deriding what he could not or would not understand.[105] In actual fact, it was imbued with a moral urgency and sincerity of purpose which make him a remarkable figure in Russian intellectual history, although he often concealed this purpose behind an avowed worldliness and an Epicureanism *quand même*. It also represents one of the aspects of his outlook which has least suffered from the passage of time.

Aesthetic nihilism is a characteristically Russian attitude. It is shown in the views of many Russian writers pursued by a feeling of guilt at being writers at all. No one expressed this more intensely than Tolstoy—the only force, as Gorki said, 'powerful enough to overcome the influence of Greece', that is, to challenge the prestige of culture in the world. The experience sprang from an acutely felt conflict—*pace* Rousseau, almost unknown in western Europe—between culture and life. Pisarev's reflection on this conflict impelled him to expose the myths and idols of culture to which men have become enslaved, and for the creation and maintenance of which they have enslaved others. He asked himself the blunt, tactless, yet still relevant question about culture: it is all very beautiful, but can it possibly be true, that is, does it fit the condition of man? He was led to believe that culture, even or especially at its greatest and most exquisite, does not survive unshaken in the face of the human suffering that sustains, pervades, or surrounds it. It is, he said, 'a parasitical plant which feeds continually on the sap of human toil'. It is perishable, or, more, it must be destroyed, because it is a treasure of which 'the hungry and the disinherited' have been deprived and which has thereby ceased to serve a human purpose. Nothing appeared to Pisarev more banal as well as more inhuman than the plea for 'spiritual values', the spirit of which had long ago evaporated, or the defence of the blessings of civilization by those who regard them as their apanage and enjoy them as their special preserve.[106]

The tilting at culture exposed Pisarev to the same charge of self-mortification which he made against the dedicated radical. He seemed himself to go off with relish into the austerities of radicalism, strenuously disparaging art as 'useless' and ridiculing the cultivated man as an anachronism. Believing as he did that art was a 'citadel of arbitrary private taste', he found himself rejecting it for the very reasons which earlier on served to bolster up his case for aesthetic egotism.[107] There was something of the revenge of a pleasure-seeker in this—a form of angry anti-cultural snobbery, in the manner of Lucky Jim who pounces on 'filthy Mozart' and 'all those rotten old churches, museums, and art galleries'. Pisarev's more enlightened detractors were tempted to regard his iconoclastic leanings as philistinism of the kind which has been endemic in obscurantist secular and ecclesiastical society in Russia. The criticism missed the point. Pisarev was, on the contrary, a very cultivated man. In his early journalistic career, as a contributor to 'Dawn', he even showed signs of being a consummate aesthete.[108] According to Turgenev, who appears to have drawn Nezhdanov, the hero of his novel *Virgin Soil* (1876), from Pisarev, the latter's 'plebeian' anti-aestheticism went hand in hand with a remarkable sense of aesthetic values, elegance and aristocratic distinction.[109]

Others similarly speak of his sense of neatness and beauty, of his distinctly aesthetic qualities, and nowhere more than when denying aesthetics. Far from being a philistine who had never attained culture, he despised it with a peculiar personal superiority and the conviction that he had seen through it. He was, in fact, repeating the experience and under-going the disillusionment of the intellectual who has noticed that the culture he has acquired is neither admired nor even demanded by those who have been forcibly deprived of it. The art galleries and museums may be rotten, but what really mattered was that it was better to starve them of treasures than human beings of food. The attitude amounted to a deli-berate self-divestment, to a rejection of stone images. Once more, it suggests a comparison with Tolstoy, whose search for truth urged him, with all his great novels behind him, to look at art as a husk to be discarded—an impediment, not a help to the attainment of the perfect life.

.   .   .   .   .

The disappearance of culture, in Pisarev's view, was to be succeeded by the emergence of a 'non-cultural', scientific culture, whose ideal was neither invented nor abstracted but found and left where alone it could be represented, 'in actual and living phenomena'. It was to be a culture which reflected man's changing and unimpeded vision of the universe, free especially from all the burdens of the past, and with none of the hot air of exalted places. Its 'temples' would be 'the workshops of human thought'. It would eschew the artist as a sacred monomaniac, misunderstood and misinterpreted, and ensure his status as simply a human being, endowed with a special gift of articulation and free from somnolence and escapism. His business would be, roughly, to articulate on behalf of the inarticulate, to express for those who are unable to express them-selves what is conducive to their growth as human persons and 'thinking proletarians'. He would be a spokesman for others and the despair of aesthetes yearning for elegant elaboration.

With this in mind, Pisarev embarked on his destructive 'promenade through the gardens of Russian literature' and of art in general. He showed no forbearance of any kind, brow-beat the ignorant, decried the extraordinary waves of the spirit, and seemingly enjoyed the Pyrrhic victories of his sardonic intellect over his deliberately restricted imagination. He compared addiction to art with the 'sickly attachment of an aged spinster to cats, parrots and pug-dogs'. He declared that the results of scientific labour were of greater importance than any work by Shakespeare or Pushkin, that writers would be best employed in popularizing scientific propositions, and that he himself 'would rather be a Russian shoemaker than a Russian Raphael'. This neither prevented him from continuing to read Shakespeare and Pushkin, nor led him to any visible inclination to make shoes. There was, of course, no reason to assume the incompatibility of Raphael and a shoemaker, and the fact that Pisarev made the assumption merely provided evidence that, without knowing it, he was involved in a vicious circle: for had culture and science in Russia or elsewhere been more widespread and more assimilated they would have encouraged, not inhibited each other. As it was, he could see no salvation from the social estrangement of culture other than by destroying culture in the name of the shoemaker—the least guilty and least conspicuous partner in the contest.

Some of Pisarev's onslaughts look like exercises in concealing the shallowness of thought by the brilliance of shock tactics. He himself regarded them, with a degree of justification, as 'salubrious' and 'hygienic'. The assertions of music, painting, and sculpture came in for particular strictures.[110] They seemed to him specifically designed to hinder the process of sweeping oneself as bare of the expected artistic emotions as possible, and of freeing oneself from all illusions, notably those which delight and elevate. He admitted prose as the most 'useful' medium and the least beset by 'thinness and implausibility', provided it did not itself turn into an instrument of romantic passion, easy charm, and gracious affectation. The exemption was significant, not only because prose literature could be legitimately considered the most adequate means for bringing the creative artist within the scale of human comprehension, but also because Pisarev's imagination was overwhelmed by his intellect. As often happens in such cases, he gives the impression of having been made of words. He had a great sense of the meaning of words and a great gift for them, but he was tone-deaf and had no visual perception. He confessed that he was 'deeply indifferent' to music and painting and unable to distinguish between 'the great Beethoven', 'the great Raphael' and 'the great chef Dussault'.[111]

Pisarev's aesthetic nihilism entitled him to ignore technical questions about the nature of art. Since, however, he was perfectly capable of artistic, or, to be more precise, of literary artistic appreciation, and, in fact, derived great pleasure from literature, we find him holding strong views about the problem of form and content in art. According to some, these views were the only recognizable symptom of his anti-aesthetic creed. In reality, they owe more to his intellectualism and to the current pre-occupation among Russian literary critics with the substitution of relevance to human life for technical elaboration. The quality of a work of art, for Pisarev, was determined by its subject-matter: what had meaning were the facts and the words which conveyed them. What failed to give an authentic sensation of life was wholly dispensable. Pisarev began by professing that if anything was to be derived from literature it was derivable by the individual rather than by society, and in terms of pleasure rather than profit. He finished by rejecting all literature that was in any way likely to serve uncheckable interior fantasies and the soft centre of inward experience: everything in fact that required the suspension of shared experience and the acceptance of a scale of private values. A writer, he said, 'cannot by-pass the immense world of unfeigned human suffering which surrounds us like a dark, impenetrable wall'. 'A poet has to choose between being a titan shattering mountains of age-old evil or an insect rummaging in flower dust.'[112] Pisarev was convinced that a writer writing in a vacuum was reflecting the prevailing philosophical abstractions and social myths. Chernyshevsky thought the same and added that such a writer invariably became an understrapper of those in power.

A writer's function was to teach, to make people think rather than feel. As has been noted earlier on, Pisarev reacted violently to emotionalism, to everything that was 'great', 'deep', 'sensitive', and obscure, which prompted many to think, or deceived them into thinking, that he wanted to do away with feeling altogether. Even the erotic attributes of literature—'the sighs of dainty damsels', as he put it, and 'the quaverings of enamoured nightingales'—seemed to him to be tedious and to receive an amount of attention and a degree of respect out of all proportion to their importance. He was most scathing when dealing with poetry, especially lyrical poetry. He preferred foreign poets, above all Shakespeare, Goethe, and especially Heine, to Russian poets; and he preferred almost all Russian poets to Pushkin, whom, significantly enough, he persisted in identifying with Onegin. 'You like Pushkin?', he asked in 'The Realists': 'if you please, just look at him!'—'our nice, pretty-pretty Pushkin', 'the drowsy figure of a lounging lizard', 'the mountebank addicted to pretty juggling tricks', 'the soul of Russian manorial wit', and so on.[113]

It is tempting to dismiss all this as the shouting down of genius by a flamboyant pigmy, although one might also feel some satisfaction in seeing an arrow discharged at the great, even if it hits them in the wrong place. But there was more to this than meets the eye. Pisarev himself possessed a great measure of Pushkin's love of life and, in a sense, could not help feeling at home in his transparent and rational poetic universe. He recognized these traits in Pushkin and, especially in his early criticism, applauded him because of them.[114] But he was too deeply impressed by the existing contradiction between art and life not to recoil from Pushkin's playful, intoxicating dissipation, ubiquitousness, exuberance, and all the other things that failed to conform to his self-imposed, etiolated standards.

Few if any of Pisarev's numerous literary essays contain any discussion of the style and the beauty or ugliness of the works examined. He deliberately avoided such discussion.[115] He realized, of course, that there is a difference between meaning as it can be tracked down and detached in a simple paraphrase, and meaning as it is transformed or embodied in a work of art.[116] But his overriding concern was with what a work does to a reader and how it is made intelligible to him. He viewed it as a means to an end, not an end in itself; as an instrument through which the artist conveys his vision of the world and of man to the reader, not a diversion or relaxation.[117] A novelist failed if blindness prevented him from seeing an essential part of life, or if his dullness of mind rendered him unaware of the ideas that had gone to the making of the world he inhabited. His task was to produce not a finished object, however pleasing, nor a piece of decoration or even edification, but something that stimulated new ways of seeing and thinking, something that showed the way of danger, doubt, and denial.

It has been said that on Pisarev's terms literary analysis had little or no chance. Similar doubts were expressed about Chernyshevsky and Dobrolyubov. Pisarev's intellectual and moral exigence, it is true, slackened to some extent when he immersed himself into a literary work and moved into a world looser, more elusive or more powerful than his own will to define and delimit it. But even his ideas, far from destroying, encouraged the critic in him. At least they did not make him ignore what was of real value or to over-estimate doubtful talents.[118] His criticism profited by his conviction that literature should be part of life, by his hatred of humbug, literary as well as moral and political, by his humanism, which shunned compulsion and stupidity as much as sentimentalism and pomposity, and even by his polemical talent and stinging humour. But he did not rack literary subjects on a Procrustes' bed of theory. Writing of Turgenev, he paid tribute to his 'extraordinary artistic sincerity':

his characters [he observed] live by virtue of their inherent vitality. He cares for them; he is carried away by them; he feels their irresistible attraction in the very process of creating them. This saves him from attending merely to his own reactions, from disposing of his characters at will, from turning the image of life into an allegory with a moral purpose and a virtuous solution. . . . The power of the artist [sic] asserts itself, breaks down theoretical fences, triumphs over the errors of the mind and, in the end, redeems everything. . . .[119]

Much of Pisarev's criticism took the form of a psychological analysis of literary characters and an anatomy of their intellectual and moral attitudes. Here as elsewhere he was interested in typology rather than in plot, narrative, structure, style, or formal pattern. Even Heine is discussed as a human type rather than a poet.[120] The gallery of portraits comprises many familiar Russian literary heroes, often in conjunction with their feminine companions: Pushkin's Onegin and Lermontov's Pechorin, Turgenev's Rudin and Herzen's Beltov, Goncharov's Oblomov and Dostoevsky's Raskolnikov, and others, with Bazarov and Rakhmetov dominating the scene.

When Pisarev's essential sympathy was engaged he showed

evidence of penetrating observation and understanding, as can be seen in his discussion of the last two characters. Where he detested the ideas of a writer, or where the works under review conveyed a faith in all that lay atrophied under the lid of custom and morality, he confined himself to derision and expressions of sweeping animosity. He did this, for example, in the case of Klyushnikov, Krestovsky, and Leskov. Since most of their works known to him happened to be worthless from the artistic point of view, Pisarev unexpectedly veered off into aestheticism and dismissed them on artistic as well as on ideological grounds.[121]

Where he did not feel particularly committed in his convictions, his criticism was uneven and erratic: he could be discerning as well as short-sighted, or both together. His estimate of Tolstoy and Dostoevsky is a case in point. He was the first to draw attention to what Leontiev called Tolstoy's method of 'psychological eavesdropping': the mastery in recognizing 'the inception of human thoughts and experiences' before man himself becomes aware of them.[122] But Dostoevsky remained largely recalcitrant to Pisarev. Pisarev could not admit horror and the grotesque, or respond to submerged fantasies and the language of darkness. His long essay on *Crime and Punishment*, though dealing at length with the character of Raskolnikov, stops as a rule at those parts which are concerned with poverty, slums, money-lending, and murder, and overlooks the different and contradictory levels on which Raskolnikov, or for that matter all the other characters of Dostoevsky, exist.[123] The ostensibly cool, rational, worldly spirit of Pisarev was repelled by Dostoevsky's idea that suffering cleanses the soul. For him, no less than for all his fellow radicals, the characters of those who suffered were not cured but distorted by suffering. He could scarcely think otherwise, because his ultimate concern was not with his own sufferings but with those of others.

And yet, Pisarev's sister reports that he read Dostoevsky's novel in a state of anguish, soon after leaving prison, that he wept when he was reading it, and that the reading nearly finished him. The idea of a super-man turning into a sub-man inevitably struck a chord, for it epitomized in some ways his own personal tragedy. In the essay on *Crime and Punishment* he reverts on several occasions to Raskolnikov's experience of 'infinite, tormenting isolation and estrangement'. Pisarev and

Raskolnikov alike lived in the mania of human solitude, asserting their ego and defying society; both made themselves by their isolation not more but less human; both were haunted by the call 'Cain, where is thy brother Abel?'; and both reflected a society that had lost its bearings and threatened to disintegrate.

ABBREVIATIONS

H.	A. Herzen, Complete Works in 30 vols., Academy of Sciences, Moscow, 1954–64
IV.	*Istoricheskii vestnik* (Historical Messenger)
IZ.	*Istoricheskie zapiski* (Notes on History)
KA.	*Krasnyi arkhiv* (Red Archive)
KS.	*Katorga i ssylka* (Penal Servitude and Exile)
L.	Leningrad
LN.	*Literaturnoe nasledstvo* (Literary Heritage)
M.	Moscow
P.	St. Petersburg, Petrograd
RA.	*Russkii arkhiv* (Russian Archive)
VI.	*Voprosy istorii* (Questions of History)

NOTES

CHAPTERS I–II

1. See, for example, S. Tatishchev, *Imperator Aleksandr II, ego zhizn' i tsarstvovanie* (The Emperor Alexander II, His Life and Reign), 2 vols., P., 1900; and I. Shumaker, *Imperator Aleksandr II. Istoricheskii ocherk ego zhizni i tsarstvovaniya* (The Emperor Alexander II. A Historical Essay on His Life and Reign), P., 1905.

2. H., vol. xv, p. 198. Herzen's verdict is shared by most historians. See, for example, A. Presnyakov, *Samoderzhavie Aleksandra II* (The Autocracy of Alexander II), *Russkoe proshloe* (The Russian Past), 1923, vol. iv; or S. Graham, *Alexander II, Tsar of Russia*, London, 1935; also the interesting account by Anna Tyutcheva, daughter of the poet Tyutchev and for more than twelve years the Tsarina's lady-in-waiting, in her reminiscences and diaries, *Pri dvore dvukh imperatorov* (At the Court of Two Emperors), 2 issues, M., 1928.

3. This is true of some of the most important works on this period: G. Dzhanshiev, *Epokha velikikh reform* (The Time of the Great Reforms), P., 1907; *Istoriya Rossii v XIX veke* (The History of Russia in the Nineteenth Century], 'Granat', vol. iv; Hugh Seton-Watson, *The Decline of Imperial Russia*, London, 1952; M. Florinsky, *Russia. A History and an Interpretation*, 2 vols., New York, 1955, vol. ii. It is also true of the large standard work on the subject edited by A. Dzhivelegov, S. Melgunov, and V. Picheta, *Velikaya reforma: russkoe obshchestvo i krest'yanskii vopros v proshlom i nastoyashchem* (The Great Reform: Russian Society and the Peasant Question in the Past and Present), 6 vols., M., 1911. This work is of general interest for the study of Alexander's reign, but, as regards the peasant question, it has been superseded by P. Zaionchkovsky's *Otmena krepostnogo sostoyaniya v Rossii* (The Abolition of the Servile Estate in Russia), M., 1954. Zaionchkovsky's book also contains a valuable bibliography on the peasant reform.

4. The term 'obligation' is used here in a general sense. More specifically, it was applied by Kiselev, one of Nicholas I's few outstanding advisers, who was appointed Minister for Imperial Domains in 1837, to peasants whom he intended to enter into 'voluntary' agreements with their owners concerning the allotment of land and compensation for using it.

According to the tenth census (*reviziya*) of 1857–8, the strictly Russian inhabitants of the Empire numbered approximately 60 million, of whom about 50 million were peasants. Of these roughly 20 million belonged to the land-owning aristocracy and gentry, and just under 20 million were State peasants, euphemistically known as the 'free rural estate' (*svobodnoe selskoe sostoyanie*). The remaining 10 million were in other states of 'obligation' (in particular, the apanage peasants [*udelnye krest'yane*] owned by members of the imperial family), and a few were unattached. All these peasants held about 105 million *desyatin* of land (1 *desyatina* = 2·7 acres). The land-owning class numbered in the same period over 100,000, with 30·6 per cent. of the territory of European Russia (about 100 million *desyatin*) in its possession, although many estates had less than 100 male serfs. I quote round figures throughout, for all contemporary statistics are only approximately correct. See V. Semevsky, 'Krest'yanskii vopros v Rossii v XVIII veke i pervoi polovine XIX veka' (The Peasant Question in Russia in the Eighteenth and in the First Half of the Nineteenth Centuries) in *Krest'yanskii stroi* (*The Structure of Peasantry*), P., 1888, vol. ii, p. 570; and P. Lyashchenko, *Krest'yanskoe delo i poreformennaya zemleustroitelnaya politika* (The Peasant Question and Post-Reform Agrarian Policy), P., 1913, part 1, pp. 6 ff.

5. The literature on the status of, and the conditions of life among, the peasantry before the emancipation is extensive. One of the most important sources is *Zapiski Alexandra Ivanovicha Kosheleva (1812–1883)* (The Notes of Alexander Ivanovich Koshelev [1812–1883]), Berlin, 1884. Koshelev was a well-known Slavophil expert on agrarian Russia. Equally important are: A. Zablotsky-Desyatovsky, *Graf P. D. Kiselev i ego vremya* (Count P. D. Kiselev and His Times), 4 vols., P., 1882; and N. Druzhinin, *Gosudarstvennye krest'yane i reforma P. D. Kiseleva* (The State Peasants and the Reform of P. D. Kiselev), 2 vols., M.-P., 1946; also the standard work by Semevsky, cited above, and I. Ignatovich, *Pomeshchich'i krest'yane nakanune osvobozhdeniya* (The Landowners' Peasants on the Eve of the Emancipation), 3rd ed., L., 1925. The standard works in English are G. T. Robinson's *Rural Russia under the Old Régime*, London, 1923, and J. Blum, *Lord and Peasant in Russia*, Princeton, 1961. On the gentry, see A. Romanovich-Slavatinsky, *Dvoryanstvo v Rossii ot nachala XVIII veka do otmeny krepostnogo prava* (The Gentry in Russia from the beginning of the Eighteenth Century to the Abolition of Serfdom), 2nd ed., Kiev, 1912.

6. M. Pogodin, *Istoriko-politicheskie pis'ma i zapiski v prodolzhenii krimskoi voiny* (Historico-Political Letters and Notes during the Crimean War), M., 1874, pp. 262 ff.; Y. Samarin, *Works*, vols. i–ix, xii, M., 1900, vol. ii, p. 33. See also *Krest'yanskoe dvizhenie 1827–1869 gg.* (The Peasant Movement between 1827 and 1869), ed. by E. Morokhovets, M., 1931, First Collection, consisting chiefly of extracts from the annual reports of the Third Section.

7. The national debt in the second quarter of the nineteenth century was rising rapidly, and under the strain of the Crimean War it reached the astronomical figure of 1,759 million silver roubles in 1858. See L. Khodsky, *Osnovy gosudarstvennogo khozyaistva* (The Foundations of State Economy), P., 1901, pp. 431 ff.

8. See, for example, the often-quoted official memorandum of Zablotsky-Desyatovsky, 'O krepostnom sostoyanii v Rossii' (On the Servile Estate in Russia) in his book on Kiselev, vol. iv. Kavelin's 'Letters from a Village' (*Pis'ma iz derevni*), written shortly before the emancipation, give a revealing picture of the position of the labour market in the grain-exporting regions. In the province of Samara, described by Kavelin, there was a free fight for surplus labour, and landowners with insufficient 'souls' used to kidnap peasants so as to be able to compete with their neighbours in wheat production (Kavelin's *Works*, 4 vols., P., 1897–1900, vol. ii, p. 667).

9. There exist three versions of this famous speech. The quotation is taken from the text revised by the Tsar himself (*Golos minuvshego* [The Voice of the Past], 1916, nos. 5–6, p. 393).

10. See *Materyaly dlya istorii uprazdnenya krepostnogo sostoyanya pomeshchich'ikh krest'yan v Rossii v tsarstvovanie Alexandra II* (Documents on the History of the Abolition of the Servile Estate of the Landowners' Peasants in Russia during the Reign of Alexander II), 3 vols., Berlin, 1860–2, vol. i, hereafter referred to as *Documents*. This important collection of evidence, the first of its kind, was compiled and published anonymously by Dimitry Khrushchev, Assistant Minister of Imperial Domains from 1856 to 1857 and later a member of the Senate.

11. See A. Kornilov, 'Gubernskie komitety po krest'yanskomu delu' in *Ocherki po istorii obshchestvennogo dvizhenya i krest'yanskogo dela v Rossii* ('The Provincial Committees on the Peasant Affair' in 'Essays on the History of the Social Movement and the Peasant Affair in Russia'), P., 1905 also.

According to an imperial rescript, originally issued to the Governor-General of the Lithuanian provinces and subsequently sent 'for information and guidance' to other regions, the terms of reference were the following: (a) the landowners were to retain legal title to the land, but peasants were to be given personal freedom, and a cottage and garden (homesteads) to be paid for by themselves within a specified time; they were also to occupy other land in return for annual dues (*obrok*) or corvée (*barshchina*); (b) peasants were to be organized into village communities (*obshchina, mir*) with police supervision by the landlords; (c) arrangements were to be made for the collection of taxes and other obligations *vis-à-vis* the State.

12. This has been a source of disquiet even to much earlier students of rural Russia. A well-known advocate of serfdom at the time of Catherine II, the historian and economist Prince Shcherbatov, devoted a whole book to the subject (*O povrezhdenii nravov v Rossii* [On the Deterioration of Morals in Russia]): 'The basic evil in Russia', he suggested, 'lies in that in many regions a great number of peasants abandon agriculture and become addicted to other trades. Previously the peasants applied themselves to tilling the soil; they were poor but satisfied. But now, having abandoned agriculture, the peasants proceed to other work and become indeed richer in money, while agriculture is declining' (London, 1858, p. 92).

13. For a fuller analysis, see Kornilov, op. cit., p. 253; also T. Emmons, *The Russian Landed Gentry and the Peasant Emancipation*, Cambridge, 1968. It should be pointed out, however, that there were a few places where the emancipation entailed no profit, or even positively harmed the landowner. In such cases the latter insisted on and received prohibitive compensation in money for the peasant homesteads: up to 1,200 roubles per *desyatina*, i.e. much more than the price of land in the two capitals.

14. On Unkovsky see G. Dzhanshiev, *A. M. Unkovsky i osvobozhdenie krest'yan* (A. M. Unkovsky and the Emancipation of the Peasants), M., 1894.

15. This is what Herzen wrote, in the form of an obituary notice, apropos of Panin's appointment: 'The incredible news of *Panin's* appointment in place of *Rostovtsev* has been confirmed. The protagonist of the most violent and uncompromising reaction is in charge of the emancipation of the

peasants. The news has filled us with deep sorrow. But it is not enough to mourn, the times are too critical. This is a challenge, this is impudence, this is a deliberate insult to public opinion, a concession to the party of slave-drivers. The temper of the government has changed, and in consequence all relations with the government must also change. . . .' H., vol. xiv, p. 247.

16. Although out of date and not reliable in all respects, the most important and interesting study of Milyutin is still *Un Homme d'État russe d'après sa correspondance inédite. Étude sur la Russie et la Pologne pendant le règne d'Alexandre II*, Paris, 1884, by A. Leroy-Beaulieu. See also *Documents*, vol. ii, p. 22.

17. The prevailing atmosphere at the time is described by N. Semenov, *Osvobozhdenie krest'yan v tsarstvovanie Aleksandra II* (The Emancipation of the Peasants in the Reign of Alexander II), 2 vols., P., 1890, vol. i, pp. 603 ff. The bulk of this work consists of the minutes of the drafting commissions. See also *Documents*, vol. ii, pp. 122 ff.

18. See Semenov, op. cit., vol. ii, pp. 770 f., for examples of how the original allotment of land to the peasants was reduced on the insistence of some landowners and with the support of Panin. Kavelin's work *Zapiska ob osvobozhdenii krest'yan v Rossii* (Memorandum on the Emancipation of the Peasants in Russia), from which the first quotation is taken (*Works*, vol. ii, p. 48 and pp. 111 f., 128 for the other quotations) is one of the most important contributions to the land-reform debate by a spokesman of progressive Government circles. He contends that servile labour 'deprives the serf of the incentive to work hard' and thereby directly and indirectly thwarts the economic growth of the country (ibid., pp. 13, 17, 25). He insists on the need to free the peasants with land, provided the landowner is indemnified for the loss of free labour, 'because they [the peasants] constitute as much the property of the landowner as his land' (p. 46).

19. The document itself, repeatedly amended in subsequent years, contains two distinct elements: an outline of the regulations proposed by the various provincial committees, systematized by the central committee and approved by the State Council, and an ordinance prescribing the establishment of special courts and magistrates to arbitrate between the landowners and the serfs, and of 'communal administrations' (*obshchinnye upravlenya*) to register the appointment and title of lands. See *Polozhenya 19-go fevralya 1861 g. o krest'yanakh vyshedshikh iz krepostnoi zavisimosti* (The Statutes of 19 February 1861 about the Peasants Who Have Passed out of Servile Dependence), M., 1916; also *Otmena krepostnogo prava. Doklady ministrov vnutrennikh del o provedenii krest'yanskoi reformy* (The Abolition of Serfdom. Reports of the Ministers of the Interior on the Execution of the Reform, 1861–1862), M.–L., 1950. The latter publication contains much hitherto unknown material and is an indispensable compendium to the study of the statutes as they were applied and received throughout Russia. The first systematic examination of the Emancipation Act (*Razbor novogo krepostnogo prava* [An Examination of the New Serfdom]) was carried out by Ogarev, and it is still valid in all essentials. See N. Ogarev, *Izbrannye sotsialno-politicheskie i filosofskie proizvedeniya* (Selected Social, Political and Philosophical Works), 2 vols., M., 1952, vol. i.

20. It is impossible to give here a comprehensive account of the complex

economic and financial arrangement. See A. Lositsky, *Vykupnaya operatsiya* (The Redemption Operation), P., 1906, particularly pp. 16 ff.; and 'Vykupnye platezhi' (The Redemption Payments) by D. Shakhovskoi in the already quoted symposium, 'The Great Reform', vol. vi. The extent to which the Emancipation Act robbed the peasants of the means of their livelihood can only be estimated by an examination of the 'inventories' (*ustavnye gramoty*) and 'redemption deals' (*vykupnye sdelki*) which defined the economic relations between landowner and liberated serf and which varied according to region, i.e. according to the quality of the soil and/or the needs of industry. Such a study has recently been carried out by Zaionchkovsky (*Provedenie v zhizn' krest'yanskoi reformy 1861 g.* [The Implementation of the Peasant Reform of 1861], M., 1958). The author presents a thorough analysis of no fewer than 2,457 'inventories' and 2,896 'redemption deals'. The resulting picture is depressing, and it is not surprising that one of the chief means of resisting the Emancipation Act on the part of the peasants was to refuse to approve the 'inventories'.

By 1877, when more reliable statistics for the distribution of land in European Russia after the reform became available, 166·3 million *desyatin* belonged to the State and other public bodies (including crown and church lands); and 94 million *desyatin* were owned privately, of which 73·2 million *desyatiny* belonged to the gentry. The landholdings of the peasants were in fact so restricted that, to use a then current expression, 'land hunger' ensued, with real hunger often close upon it, especially when the crops failed. The peasants were eventually compelled to take leases of additional land from the landowners, paying huge rents and thereby increasing their already onerous obligations. The state of affairs turned into a vicious circle, which became increasingly vicious with the rapid increase in population. For a statistical picture of land distribution among the peasants, see the large coloured map attached to Zaionchkovsky's *The Abolition of Serfdom in Russia*, and *The Great Reform* (table on pp. 92 f). On the insoluble difficulties experienced by the peasants, see the old work by Skaldin (F. Elenev), *V zakholust'i i v stolitse* (In the Deep Provinces and in the Capital), P., 1870, pp. 46, 94, 213; and Zaionchkovsky, *The Implementation of the Peasant Reform of 1861'*, *passim*. Their position also depended on the number of adult males in each household, women being discounted in the distribution of land. According to the statutes, the peasants were entitled to so-called 'gratuitous' or 'beggarly' allotments (*darstvennye* or *nishchenskie nadely*), for which no payments were to be made and the size of which amounted to one quarter of the average redeemable allotments (about 1 *desyatina* or 2.7 acres per male serf). There were approximately two-thirds of a million peasants who availed themselves of the offer.

The position of the State and apanage peasants (most of them lived in Siberia and in the north of European Russia) was more favourable. It was fixed by special decrees (in 1866–7 and 1863, respectively) which extended to them the statute of 1861, although the apanage peasants were released from personal servitude in 1858. The State peasants in particular received more land (between 5 and 8 *desyatin* per male peasant as compared with the average of 3¾ *desyatiny* for the landowners' peasants). But

NOTES

later they were bound by law, not merely encouraged, to redeem their landholdings. The new obligations proved ruinous and opposition to them was in some cases more determined than among the other peasants. Revolts among State peasants, however, occurred mainly in industrial—especially mining—districts, where State peasants supplied the bulk of the labour force. See P. Lyashchenko, *Ocherki agrarnoi evolyutsii Rossii* (Essays in the Agrarian Evolution of Russia), 2 vols., L., 1925, vol. i, pp. 187 ff., 299 ff.

21. Thus even in the late eighties and early nineties up to 40 per cent. (according to district) of all the estates in the province of Tambov had no equipment or livestock of their own and the land was cultivated by the primitive implements of the peasants. Similar conditions prevailed in the provinces of Orel, Saratov, Nizhnii, and a few others.

22. The essays appeared regularly between 1872 and 1882 in *Otechestvennye zapiski* (Annals of the Fatherland). Separate edition, M., 1937.

23. The injustice of the new system impinged on the peasant all the more tangibly as many individual disabilities remained in force and, as before, he was deprived of fundamental human rights: the ex-serf was still subject to corporal punishment (about which the angry Herzen had some terrible things to say); the ex-serf provided recruits for the army; the ex-serf was obliged to mend the roads; the ex-serf paid the poll-tax (*podushnye*); the ex-serf was unable to move or travel in Russia without an internal passport, and so on. Some of these disabilities were abolished before the end of the century, others (such as corporal punishment and passport restrictions) —in theory if not in practice—immediately before and after the revolution of 1905; others still came to an end only in 1917.

24. See the Second Collection compiled by Morokhovets (*Krest'yanskie dvizheniya v 1861 g. posle otmeny krepostnogo prava* [Peasant Movements in 1861 after the Abolition of Serfdom], M., 1949), consisting mainly of reports by aides-de-camp and other persons about their missions in the respective regions (p. 3); and P. Zaionchkovsky, 'Iz istorii obnarodovaniya Polozheniya 19 fevralya 1861 g.' (From the History of the Publication of the Statute of 19 February 1861) in *IZ.*, 1955, no. 54, pp. 271 ff. The panic in Government circles and among landowners was such that, despite careful planning, considerable disorganization ensued. In some places the news of the reform was withheld until the beginning of April or even later; elsewhere only disjointed fragments of the statute were available, which served only to confuse the peasants and increase their mistrust.

25. Some of the most interesting are: *Epokha osvobozhdeniya krest'yan (1857–1861) v vospominaniyakh P. G. Semenova-Tyan-Shanskogo* (The Time of the Emancipation of the Peasants in the Recollections of P. G. Semenov-Tyan-Shansky), 4 vols. P., 1911–16; *Dnevnik D. A. Milyutina* (The Diary of D. A. Milyutin), 4 vols., M., 1947–50; Koshelev's 'Notes . . .' cited above; P. Boborykin, *Za polveka* (Half a Century Later), M.–L., 1929; *Iz vospominanii 1859–91 godov* (From Recollections of the Years 1859–91), iv, 1907, nos. 10–11, by F. Solovtsev, who was for many years an 'arbitrator'; and 'Epizody pri vvedenii Polozheniya 19-go fevr. 1861 goda' (Episodes during the Implementation of the Statute of 19 February 1861) by N. Reshetov, *RA.*, 1885, no. 10.

26. It appeared for the first time in *KA*. iii. 16, pp. 118 ff.

27. The appellation is not entirely inappropriate if one remembers that the generals in question were some of the chief evil geniuses of Alexander's reign: Count Vladimir Adlerberg, Minister of the Imperial Court and member of the Central Committee (responsible for the new legislation on the peasantry), Nikolai Sukhozanet, Minister of War and a prominent leader of the suppression of the Polish insurrection, Prince Vasily Dolgoruky, Head of the Third Section and a member of the Central Committee, Konstantin Chevkin, Minister of Transport and member of the Central Committee, and the most sinister of all, Count Mikhail Muraviev, 'The Hangman' (*Veshatel*).

28. 'Oh, what will happen to-night?' one Grand Duchess is made to exclaim, 'how can one give freedom to such barbarous people? What if they kill us all?'—to which a lady-in-waiting replied reassuringly: 'Don't be frightened, your Highness, nothing will happen, except a new dress for you, as always happens on great feast days.' There is no corroborating evidence for this not improbable story, but see Anna Tyutcheva, op. cit., for a description of the prevailing atmosphere in court circles.

29. The printing of the edict took place under military guard, at night, in strictly imposed silence and behind sealed doors. The compositors had to take an oath under threat of forced labour in Siberia that they would not read what they were setting up! But there was a great shortage of copies, for thousands were sold clandestinely by those very officials from whom the thick fog of mystification emanated. Pertsov, whose informant was his brother Vladimir, an important official in the Ministry of the Interior, says that the mystification may have been a device for promoting the paper black market of the bureaucracy.

30. For this and similar manifestations, see, for example, *Documents*, vol. iii, pp. 247 ff.

31. The more humourously inclined officials in the capital had a good laugh at Tuchkov's telegraphic report, for by a mistake the preposition and the first syllable of the following participle at the beginning of the sentence in question ('Pri prinyatykh mnoyu merakh . . .') were joined together into one word, *pripri*, which means, vulgarly, 'driving someone into a tight corner'. Tuchkov explained the precautionary measures by the fact that 'the working people, of which there are about 140,000 in the province, represent a class morally unstable and, therefore, special attention must be drawn to the need of applying police measures to them' (quoted by Zaionchkovsky, *The Implementation of the Peasant Reform . . .*', p. 61). In St. Petersburg the 'working people' (i.e. serfs) constituted more than half of the population —260,000 out of 494,000.

32. The most complete evidence for the movement will be found in the publications of Morokhovets (Collections I and II), cited above. See also F. Venturi, *Il populismo russo*, 2 vols., Turin, 1953, vol. i, ch. 7. For the later period, see Y. Yuferov, 'Krest'yanskoe dvizhenie v Rossii v kontse 70-kh i v 80-ye gody XIX veka' (The Peasant Movement in Russia at the End of the Seventies and in the Eighties of the Nineteenth Century), *Uchenye zapiski Sverdlovskogo gosudarstvennogo pedagogicheskogo instituta* (Scientific Reports of the State Pedagogical Institute of Sverdlovsk), second issue, Sverdlovsk, 1939.

The Government was bombarded with reports not only of active opposition but also of peasants just looking on 'idly, obstinately and contentedly' at the destruction of their masters' property. In a very few cases the ex-serfs helped out without payment, or even with payment refused. Somewhat later the evasion of 'obligations' took the form of a curious Russian method of 'working to rule': the peasant, ordinarily very hard-working, would go to work on the master's land at nine or ten in the morning, have an interesting conversation about his breakfast, go home to have his breakfast, return to the field, lie down, get up, scratch the ground, lie down again, dine, sleep after dinner, and only wake up to find that it was so near sunset that to begin to scratch the ground again was scarcely worth while and that he might as well go home.

A member of the secret police reported to the Head of the Third Section (Dolgoruky) on 15 April 1861 that 'the animosity of the peasants of Kandeevka [centre of some of the most serious disturbances in the provinces of Penza and Tambov] . . . against the landowners springs from the oppressive rule of the latter. [The peasants] have some grounds for saying that they have already worked off all they owe to the landowner, because ever since there existed a three-day *corvée* [i.e. since Paul I] they did not take advantage of the privilege but went on working for six days a week' (*KA*. i. 92, pp. 101 f.). Koshelev reports that when his peasants were informed that it would take them half a century to redeem their land 'they just laughed derisively'. For a description of such and similar reactions of the peasants to the provisions of the Emancipation Act, see the letters from various private correspondents seized by the Third Section, and published in *KA*. i, 74, pp. 8 ff.

33. There is evidence to this effect in the work of the commissions which prepared the land reform, as also in the subsequent history of the *zemstva* and in the bureaucracy's resistance (at any rate until the inefficiency and obsolescence of the army forced on the Government the conscription laws of 1874) to universal military service as conducive to 'dangerous proximity between the lower and upper classes of society'.

34. H., vol. xv, pp. 90, 107. 'Polish blood' alludes to the execution of Polish demonstrators in Warsaw in April 1861 under Alexander II's viceroy Prince Mikhail Gorchakov.

35. In his subsequent report Apraksin observed that 'the peasants were about to fetch their cudgels'.

36. One landowner, a member of the Kazan local government board, however, declined to participate because, as he said, 'it's somewhat embarrassing to pour champagne over blood' (*kak-to nelovko krov' zalivat' shampanskim*).

The most trustworthy account of all these happenings is by the staff adjutant of the military governor of Kazan, F. Polovtsev, who took a direct part in the suppression of the uprising. See his 'Reminiscences' (*Vospominaniya*) published in *IV.*, 1907, nos. 10–11. There is a complete collection of all the relevant documents, edited by A. Yampolskaya and D. Gutman (*Bezdnenskoe vosstanie* [The Bezdna Uprising] *1861*, Kazan, 1948). Some important letters by Polovtsev have been published in *KA*. i. 74.

37. H., vol. xv, pp. 173 ff.

38. See Khodsky, op. cit., pp. 217 f.

39. Tolstoy was merely perpetuating the tradition of his obscurantist predecessors Uvarov, Shirinsky-Shikhmatov, and Putyatin. After fourteen years in office he was succeeded by a further series of actively reactionary ministers, such as Delyanov, Shvarts, and Kasso. Only Ignatiev, appointed Minister of Education in 1915 and dismissed in 1916, made real attempts to foster education, but this proved already too late. See P. Ferlyudin, *Istoricheskii obzor mer po vysshemu obrazovaniyu v Rossii* (A Historical Survey of Measures Concerning Higher Education in Russia), first issue: *Akademiya nauk i universitety* (The Academy of Sciences and the Universities), Saratov, 1893.

40. See N. Chekhov, *Narodnoe obrazovanie v Rossii s 60-kh godov XIX veka* (Popular Education in Russia from the Sixties of the Nineteenth Century), M., 1912; and Sh. Ganelin, *Ocherki po istorii srednei shkoly v Rossii vtoroi poloviny XIX veka* (Essays in the History of Secondary Schools in Russia in the Second Half of the Nineteenth Century), M., 1954.

41. Historians dwell at length on the progressive role of the gentry of Tver in this connexion. But Moscow, though less 'liberal' and more 'feudalistic' or 'oligarchic', did not lag far behind in its 'most and entirely loyal' addresses, as when she suggested to the Government in 1865 'to crown . . . the State edifice by summoning a general assembly of the elected people from the Russian land for the consideration of the needs common to the whole state'. This, incidentally, marked the virtual end of political agitation among the gentry for a long time to come. 'What did you mean by this scurvy trick?', Alexander asked the Marshal of the Zvenigorod nobility apropos of the address. 'What exactly were you driving at? A constitutional form of Government?' And on receiving a qualified affirmative reply, he rejoined: 'You think perhaps that I don't wish to waive my rights from petty vanity! I give you my word that I am prepared to sign on this table any constitution if I were convinced that it would be of any use to Russia. But I know that if I do this today, tomorrow Russia will break up into fragments' (quoted by A. Kornilov, *Obshchestvennoe dvizhenie pri Aleksandre II. 1855–1881* [The Social Movement during the Time of Alexander II. 1855–1881], M., 1909, p. 134). It is easy to be wise after the event: but Alexander has been throughout singularly inept in his prognostications. In addition, he was pulling wool over the Marshal's eyes, for there is no evidence that he envisaged at any time a constitution for Russia, not even when he approved a few hours before his tragic end the so-called Loris-Melikov constitution. This was, in point of fact, no constitution at all, but at most a hasty expedient, a plan for a mere commission with a few chosen representatives from the *zemstvos* and urban municipalities to advise on certain measures within their competence before they came up to the State Council, which in turn was only advising someone else (the Tsar) (see 'Konstitutsionnye proekty 80-kh godov XIX veka' [Constitutional Projects at the Beginning of the Eighteen Eighties], *KA.*, 1928, vi). Florinsky calls it 'a jejune version of a proposal made by Valuev [the successor of Lanskoi] in 1863' to placate the liberals for their support of the Government's suppression of the Polish rising in the same year.

Alexander's attitude to any limitation of his political power remained throughout basically the same as that expressed in his own handwriting on the margins of an often-quoted, exceedingly mild and loyal address to him on the matter by his Chamberlain, Mikhail Bezobrazov: 'irrelevant and highly impudent', he commented, 'unheard of effrontery', 'nonsense'. As for the equally loyal, though less mild liberals from Tver (Unkovsky, Aleksey Bakunin, Petrunkevich, and others) their fate at the hands of Alexander offers poor evidence of his constitutional intentions.

Inasmuch as the 'Loris-Melikov constitution' can be considered a step in the right direction, it was taken by Alexander with his back to the wall, and in his usual perplexed and aimless fashion. The atmosphere in the capital at the end of the seventies was tense in the extreme. The cumulative effect of terrorism against the Crown and its servants produced panic, which spread even to the population. People expected a large-scale revolutionary upheaval on the twenty-fifth anniversary of the Tsar's reign and began to leave the capital. 'It seems to me', Valuev wrote at the time, 'that everything is crumbling. Only a supernatural power can arrest the landslide.' The 'frightened, pitiful, played-out Tsar' (as a French diplomat described Alexander at the time) had to do something, anything, short of limiting his basic absolute power to which he clung obsessively, in order to divert attention from the threat, and he called upon Loris-Melikov. The latter instituted his ephemeral, tragi-comic 'dictatorship of the heart', which issued in the celebrated constitution, with the ubiquitous secret police (now under the Ministry of the Interior) continuing its ubiquitous activities and the desperate terrorists continuing their desperate terrorism.

The main work on the practical aspect of the *zemstvo* activities is B. Veselovsky's *Istoriya zemstva za 40 let* (History of the *Zemstvo* during Forty Years), 4 vols., P., 1909–11. The political significance of the *zemstvo* movement is discussed by A. Golovachev, *Desyat' let reform, 1861–1871 gg.* (Ten Years of Reform, 1861–1871), P., 1872; by I. Belokonsky, *Zemskoe dvizhenie* (The *Zemstvo* Movement), M., 1914; and V. Gamiza, *Podgotovka zemskoi reformy 1864 goda* (The Preparation of the *Zemstvo* Reform of 1864), M., 1957. Equally important are the two works by Witte and Lenin from which the two quotations in the text are taken: *Samoderzhavie i zemstvo* (Autocracy and the *Zemstvo*), Stuttgart, 1901, and *Goniteli zemstva i Annibaly liberalizma* (The Persecutors of the *Zemstvo* and the Hannibals of Liberalism) *Complete Works*, 30 vols., M., 1929–37, vol. v, respectively.

42. In accordance with Pahlen's policy, and as a result of the acquittal by a jury of the political criminal Vera Zasulich, political crimes after 1878 were not subject to civil courts and trial by jury (introduced by the legal reform of 1864) but to administrative law. Moreover, even the normal functioning of civil law could be and was suspended in favour of martial law by the arbitrary decision of the Crown. As for the jury, which Alexander frankly considered 'a western tomfoolery' (*zapadnoe durachestvo*), only those were eligible who owned not less than 100 *desyatin* of land, or real property valued at 5,000 roubles or more, which effectively excluded the vast majority of the Russian people. It is characteristic, however, that capital punishment was reserved for serious political offences. The normal punishment

for ordinary wilful murder was penal servitude, often to terms as short as eight years. See *Sudebnaya reforma* (The Legal Reform), M., 1915, edited by N. Davydov and N. Polyansky; and I. Yushkov, *Istoriya gosudarstva i prava* (History of the State and the Law), part 1, M., 1950. See also the section on the legal reform in 'Granat's' *History of Russia*, vol. vi, part v.

43. Quoted by Florinsky, op. cit., p. 1112. On the law governing the censorship, see K. Arseniev, *Zakonodatelstvo o pechati* (Legislation on the Press), P., 1903, and especially M. Lemke, *Epokha tsenzurnykh reform 1859–1865* (The Time of the Censorship Reforms, 1859–1865), P., 1904.

44. See the already quoted 'Diary of D. A. Milyutin', which contains material for the study of the whole period and a valuable introductory essay by P. Zaionchkovsky; also the latter's *Voennye reformy 1860–1870 godov v Rossii* (Military Reforms in Russia between 1860 and 1870), M., 1952.

45. H., vol. xvi, p. 199. 'Saint Annenkov of Petersburg'—Ivan Annenkov, Chief of the St. Petersburg police; 'Saint Paul Gagarin'—Prince Pavel Gagarin, reactionary chairman and member of a number of State commissions and committees; on Philaret, see below, p. 68.

46. At the end of the Crimean war there were 650 miles of railway in the whole of Russia. When Alexander died there were nearly 15,000 in operation. But the problem of communication was not only one of railway construction (which proceeded at a slow pace) but of building or at least *draining* Russian roadways. A Governor-General is said to have been drowned in the street 'puddles' of the large provincial city in his charge. An official similarly drowned in another place was suspected of having committed suicide. But an inquest settled the matter by announcing that 'the above-mentioned dead body, suspected of forcible aquatic self-strangulation (*nasilstvennoe vodyanoe samooudushenie*) on the preceding night, was merely hiding in the afore-named puddle (*skryvalos' v vyshepoimennovannoi luzhe*)'.

47. See A. Shestakov ('Nikodim'), *Ocherki po istorii naemnogo truda v selskom khozyaistve Rossii* (Essays on the History of Hired Labour in the Russian Agrarian Economy), 2 parts, M., 1924; and M. Naidenov, *Klassovaya bor'ba v poreformennoy derevne (1861–1863)*), (Class Struggle in the Post-Reform Village [1861–1863]), M., 1955.

48. See A. Rashin, *Formirovanie promyshlennogo proletariata v Rossii. Statistiko-ekonomicheskie ocherki* (The Formation of the Industrial Proletariat in Russia. Essays in Statistical Economy), M., 1940; also N. Rozhkov, *Gorod i derevnya v russkoy istorii* (Town and Country in Russian History), 3rd ed., P., 1913, and especially the standard work by Lenin, *Razvitie kapitalizma v Rossii* (The Development of Capitalism in Russia), *Complete Works*, vol. iii. It is of some significance that, as proletarianization proceeded, Russian economy came to be seriously affected by western European foreign expansion and investment. It was a typical case of cheap labour attracting foreign capital.

49. Industrial strikes in Russia (prohibited by the penal code as 'rebellion against lawful authorities' and punishable with forced labour) were a relatively unknown phenomenon even in the late sixties, although they grew in extent and intensity after that (see B. Koz'min, *Rabochee dvizhenie v Rossii do revolyutsii 1905 g.* [The Working Class Movement in Russia before the Revolution of 1905] M., 1925). This moved the populists, who in any case

and above all looked to the peasants in rural districts for revolution, to regard the urban proletariat as conservative, anti-revolutionary, and entirely subservient to their *bourgeois* environment. See, for example, P. Tkachev, *Publichnye chteniya v Zheneve* (Public Lectures in Geneva), *Selected Works*, 4 vols., M., 1933, vol. iii, p. 260.

50. Apart from the unfit living conditions in unfurnished filthy cattle-sheds, where men, women, and children were herded together, the hours of work as often as not exceeded human endurance (up to eighteen or even more hours a day). More extensive use than anywhere else in Europe was made of female and child labour. As a rule, wages were paid four, three, or two times a year (on great church feasts) or not at all, owing to an elaborate system of fines for the flimsiest transgressions, absence for any reason, or defects in production, and to compulsory purchasing in factory shops, where a variety of goods were sold to the workers at above the normal retail prices.

The first book that drew the attention of the public to the plight of the Russian industrial and rural proletariat was *Polozhenie rabochego klassa v Rossii* (The Situation of the Working Class in Russia) by V. Bervi, who wrote under the pseudonym of Flerovsky and whom the Government committed to a mad-house and eventually deported to Siberia. It is a largely descriptive, very chaotic and very moving book, which provides a wealth of information, based on first-hand experience, and a patient and detailed presentation of all the then available evidence. It is still one of the most valuable studies on the subject. It was originally published in 1869, but there is a new edition in Bervi's *Selected Economic Writings*, 2 vols., M., 1958, vol. i. See also the better organized *Russkaya fabrika v proshlom i nastoyashchem* (The Russian Factory in the Past and Present), P., 1907, by M. Tugan-Baranovsky (the original appeared in German, Berlin, 1900); also N. Blagoveshchensky, *Semidesyatye gody na fabrikakh i zavodakh* (In the Factories and Plants of the Seventies), M.–L., 1929, which conveys vividly the atmosphere of Russian factory life. Equally important is the testimony at their trials of the weaver Pyotr Alekseev, the carpenter Stepan Khalturin, the fitter Vasily Obnorsky, and other peasant workers implicated in revolutionary activities. Alekseev's speech at the famous Trial of the Fifty in 1877, depicting the plight of the workers, was, together with the speech of his fellow-accused Sofia Bardina, cut out from the court records, but was published and distributed clandestinely. See also *Zhizn' russkogo rabochego pol veka tomu nazad* (The Life of a Russian Worker Half a Century Ago), M., 1929, by V. Gerasimov, a factory worker.

51. One of the chief forums for the defence of the existing industrial system was the congresses of the influential Society of Industrialists and Manufacturers under the presidency of K. Skalkovsky. Its principal and most respectable press organ was *Ekonomicheskii ukazatel* (Economic Guide), edited by Professor I. Vernadsky, an advocate of the Manchester School of Economics.

52. The quotation is a translation from the original French version published confidentially in a hundred copies under the title *Chronique du mouvement socialiste en Russie, 1878–1887*, P., 1890, pp. 712, 718.

53. This and the above quotations from contemporary newspapers are taken from A. Reuel's *Russkaya ekonomicheskaya mysl 60–70-kh godov XIX*

veka i marksizm (Russian Economic Thought in the Sixties and Seventies of the Nineteenth Century and Marxism), M., 1956, pp. 166 ff. See also B. Koz'min, *Ot 'devyatnatsatogo fevralya' k 'pervomu marta'. Ocherki po istorii narodnichestva* (From the 'Nineteenth of February' to the 'First of March'. Essays in the History of Populism), M., 1933.

54. Elaborately presented historical assumptions, alleged to become true by being made, die hard: they turn into unassailable myths and historians expend their gifts and energy on trying to fit things into their narrow pattern. Russia's exemption from the ardours and agonies of social and economic conflict is one such myth, upheld even now by some social historians: see, for example, F. Stepun who, in an essay on the Russian intelligentsia and Bolshevism (*Russian Review*, Harvard, October 1958), argues that the Russians were not attached to their possessions, that, as a consequence, 'most of the great landowners of the province of Tver waived [?] ownership of their land when they set the peasants free', and that there were no economic conflicts, no proletariat and no *bourgeoisie* in Russia. The actual state of affairs, as has been shown, bears no relation to Stepun's picture. See also the evidence in the already cited works by Dzanshiev on Unkovsky (pp. 63 f., 67) and by Semenov (vol. ii, pp. 935 f.).

55. Apart from the previously mentioned general works, the two classics dealing with this development are A. Kornilov, op. cit. (Note 41), and M. Lemke, *Ocherki osvoboditelnogo dvizheniya 60-kh godov* (Essays on the Liberation Movement of the Sixties), P., 1908.

56. Apart from the previously mentioned newspapers, conservatism was represented by such influential organs as Katkov's *Russkii vestnik* (Russian Messenger) and *Moskovskie novosti* (Moscow News), Meshchersky's *Grazhdanin* (The Citizen) and, later, *Novoe vremya* (The New Time), edited by Aleksey Suvorin and known as 'the weather-cock'.

57. The inclusion of Cherkassky among the Slavophils needs qualification, for he did not care much for the Slavophil beliefs. But he sympathized with practical Slavophilism and was a fairly faithful ally of Samarin.

The other Slavophil journals of the late fifties and early sixties were the short-lived *Molva* (Rumour) and *Parus* (Sail), edited by the brothers Aksakov, and *Den'* (Day), edited by Ivan Aksakov. These were followed by *Moskva* (Moscow) (1867–8) and *Rus'* (Russia) (1880–6).

58. *I. S. Aksakov v ego pis'makh* (I. S. Aksakov in His Letters), 3 vols., M., 1888–92. The letter is dated 20 October 1861.

Urusov was a reactionary Assistant Minister of War; Askochensky was an equally reactionary editor of *Domashnyaya beseda dlya narodnogo chteniya* (Home Conversation for Popular Reading). I was unable to identify Barkov, but he is apparently not to be identified with the eighteenth-century pornographic poet and translator of the same name.

Apart from occasional mild rebuke about certain abuses, 'The Day', in fact, did not, and in the circumstances could not, contain any such attacks on the Synod or on Tolstoy. But similar feelings can be found in some of Aksakov's earlier letters, where he says, for instance, that 'the words "nationality", "Orthodoxy", "Russian spirit" give me the shudders' (7 March 1856); or: 'For goodness' sake be reasonable and impartial, and

stop foisting on people unnatural sympathies for things with which
one can't sympathise, for pre-Petrine Russia, for ritualistic Orthodoxy,
for monks (as our late Ivan Vasilievich [Kireevsky] used to do)'
(17 September 1856).

59. This has, in fact, been enthusiastically claimed by the last of the
Slavophils, Baron M. Taube, in a curious and almost unintelligible book
bearing no less a title than *Poznanievedenie sobornogo vostochnogo prosveshche-
niya po lyubomudriyu slavyanofilov* (The Science of Knowledge of the Eastern
Catholic Enlightenment According to the Slavophil Love of Wisdom),
P., 1912. For Aksakov's anti-Semitic ideas, see his *Works*, 8 vols., M.,
1886–91, vol. iii, pp. 685 f. On the later Slavophilism and Panslavism, see
the old study by A. Pypin, *Panslavizm v proshlom i nastoyashchem* (Panslavism
in the Past and Present), P., 1913; and M. Boro Petrovich, *The Emergence of
Russian Panslavism 1856–1870*, Columbia, 1956. The best study in English on
Slavophilism is N. Riasanovsky's *Russia and the West in the Teaching of the
Slavophils*, Harvard, 1952.

60. It should be noted, however, that the loyal traditionalism and
devoted, if not wholly consistent, service of the Slavophils did not altogether
save them, or for that matter many other perfectly safe public men in Russia,
from the inconveniences and suspicions of the autocratic régime, even at its
most liberal. Thus in 1858 the Governor of Moscow sent a secret memorandum to Prince Dolgorukii, Chief of the Third Section, with a list of 'ill-
intentioned' people, specifying in each case in inimitable *non-sequitur* the
reason of their unreliability. The list contained Katkov (then, admittedly,
still hovering between liberalism and reaction), Samarin and Koshelev
('Slavophil—dangerous'), Evgeny Yakushkin ('son of a Decembrist—
dangerous'), the millionaire brewer Vasilii Kokorev ('a Westerner—recalcitrant disposition'), and the liberal censor Nikolai von Krause ('a friend of
all the Westerners and all the Slavophils—capable of anything and wants
all kinds of revolutions'). Lemke, op. cit., p. 8.

61. The few existing works on Grigoriev are very much less interesting
than his own unfinished autobiography, written a few months before his
death: *Moi literaturnye i nravstvennye skitalchestva* (My Literary and Moral
Wanderings), M., 1915; see also *LN.*, vols. 11–12.

62. Nikolai Leskov (1831–95), whose important work belongs to a later
period, was in fact 'discovered' by Grigoriev, just as Grigoriev was 'discovered' by Ostrovsky. The beginning of Leskov's literary career had been
marked by persistent attacks on the radical intelligentsia, as a consequence
of which he became involved with extreme reactionary groups and turned
into a favourite protégé of the Court circles. This circumstance prevented
Leskov from gaining proper, not merely 'official', recognition, although the
radical 'Contemporary' was one of the first to recognize his remarkable literary
gifts. His later development showed him less conformist and traditionally
minded than his protectors hoped. Eventually he shifted his allegiance to
the radicals and finished as a devout Tolstoyan. The extreme vehemence
with which he came to repudiate his early conservative associations presents
the sad picture of a man of intelligent good will and talent who finds himself
continuously in a false position.

The same cannot be said of another member of the conservative group, Fyodr Tyutchev (1803–73)—one of the greatest Russian poets and a determined panslavist. Ironically, he always preferred to speak French rather than Russian and to live abroad (especially in Germany) rather than in Russia. He was a very brilliant, original, inexhaustibly seductive man and a celebrated conversationalist. But he is weightier and more profound when studied in his poetry. As a poet he was a visionary, haunted by cosmic forces and daemonical dreams and full of ceaseless questionings. By the time he began to express his conventional panslavist views in verse (most of this belongs to the last ten years of his life), he was already largely spent as a poet. See K. Pigarev, *Zhizn' i tvorchestvo Tyutcheva* (Tyutchev's Life and Work), M., 1962—the most important recent monograph on the poet.

63. On Strakhov, see the excellent discussion in Chizhevsky's *Gegel v Rossii* (Hegel in Russia), Paris, 1939, ch. iii. 2; and V. Rozanov, *Literaturnye izgnanniki* (Literary Exiles), P., 1913.

64. Soloviev, in a polemic with Strakhov, one of Danilevsky's outspoken advocates, traces the main argument of this book to a work by the German historian Heinrich Rueckert, *Lehrbuch der Weltgeschichte in organischer Darstellung*, Leipzig, 1857. The full title of Danilevsky's book is *Rossiya i Evropa: Vzglyad na kulturnye i politicheskie otnosheniya slavyanskogo mira k germano-romanskomu* (Russia and Europe: A View on the Cultural and Political Relations between the Slav and the Germano-Roman Worlds). It became a bestseller in the eighties and later went through a number of editions, of which one (1888) is prefaced by Strakhov's examination of Danilevsky's life and work.

65. On Danilevsky, see Boro Petrovich, op. cit., *passim*; and P. Sorokin, *Social Philosophies of an Age of Crisis*, Boston, 1950, ch. iii. The best study on Leontiev is by N. Berdyaev, *Leontiev*, London, 1940 (Engl. trsl.).

66. V. Zenkovsky, *Istoriya russkoi filosofii* (History of Russian Philosophy), 2 vols., Paris, 1948, *passim*.

67. These ideas received wide publicity in the ecclesiastical press of the official variety, such as *Tserkovnye vedomosti* (Church Gazette), but particularly in such semi-official, more popular periodicals as *Kolokol* (Bell, not to be confused, of course, with Herzen's *Bell*), *Russkii palomnik* (Russian Pilgrim), *Khrist'yanin* (The Christian), *Khrist'yanskoe chtenie* (Christian Reading), *Domashnyaya beseda* (Home Conversation), *Dushepoleznoe chtenie* (Reading Useful for the Soul), the somewhat more sophisticated *Pravoslavnoe obozrenie* (Orthodox Review), and many others. The majority were published in the two capitals, but some, and by no means the worst, appeared in the large provincial towns.

68. *Sobranie mnenii i otzyvov Filareta, Mitropolita moskovskogo* (Collection of Views and Reviews of Philaret, Metropolitan of Moscow), 5 vols., M., 1887, vol. iv, pp. 17, 131. Philaret (1782–1867), it should be noted, was a man of great intelligence and conviction. Unlike most of the higher clergy who were remarkable chiefly for their wealth and ostentation, he was, in addition, outspoken, imperious, and independent, whenever he considered it necessary to be so (as, for example, in the question of the Bible Society in Russia).

He also made a contribution to theological thought. See G. Florovsky, *Puti russkogo bogosloviya* (The Ways of Russian Theology), Paris, 1937.

69. Theophan, successively bishop of Tambov and Vladimir, abandoned his episcopal see and became a hermit. See his *Pis'ma k raznym litsam o raznykh predmetakh very i zhizni* (Letters to Various Persons on Various Matters of Faith and Life), M., 1892. Nicholas Berdyaev who, much later, tried hard to assimilate Theophan's writings on 'matters of life' came to the sad conclusion that they are 'the quintessence of platitude, servility and obscurantism' (*Dream and Reality*, London, 1950, p. 190).

John Sergiev, parish priest of the naval base of Kronstadt, was a man of devotion and pastoral gifts as well as a convinced anti-Semite and an active supporter of Tolstoy's excommunication by the Russian Church in 1901. His diary, *My Life in Christ* (*Moya zhizn' vo Khriste*), which exists in several English translations (e.g. by E. Goulaieff, London, 1897), contains pages of insight side by side with musings stamped with the depressing air of panegyrical sycophancy. All these men were, needless to say, staunch advocates of flogging and capital punishment.

70. Some of the relevant material has been published in *RA*. v, 1935, pp. 189 f. See also *Documents*, vol. iii, pp. 265 f.

71. A comprehensive account of the fate of religious dissent in Russia will be found in S. Melgunov's *Iz istorii religiozno-obshchestvennykh dvizhenii v Rossii XIX v.* (From the History of Socio-Religious Movements in Nineteenth Century Russia), M., 1919; and *Tserkov' i gosudarstvo v Rossii* (Church and State in Russia), 2 vols., M., 1907–9; also in A. Prugavin's *Monastyrskie tyurmy v bor'be s sektantstvom* (Monastic Prisons in the Struggle against Sectarianism), M., 1905.

72. This and the whole depressing way of life in seminaries is brilliantly conveyed in the well-known *Ocherki bursy* (Seminary Sketches) by Nikolai Pomyalovsky (1835–63), who himself received a seminary education and drank himself to death at the age of twenty-eight. The sense of constriction affected even those who merely wished to pursue their scholarly work. The painful story of Klyuchevsky's attempted escape is a case in point. For documentary evidence about life in the seminaries and among the lower clergy, see I. Belyustin, *Opisanie selskogo dukhovenstva* (A Description of the Rural Clergy), published anonymously in London in 1858. See also Dobrolyubov's article about the critics of this book *Complete Works*, M., 1934–9, vol. iv, pp. 343 ff.

73. S. Soloviev, *Collected Works*, P., 1895, vol. iii, p. 36. For evidence about the activities of the ecclesiastical censorship, see A. Kotovich, *Dukhovnaya tsenzura v Rossii* (Ecclesiastical Censorship in Russia), P., 1909; but it covers only the first half of the nineteenth century. See also M. Reisner, *Dukhovnaya politsiya v Rossii* (The Ecclesiastical Police in Russia), P., 1907. Klyuchevsky, who went to a university after his early education at a seminary but later taught at a theological Academy, was dismissed for propounding unconventional views on history. Golubinsky and Bolotov were unable to publish their works for similar reasons.

74. As far as the academic periodical publications are concerned, only *Pravoslavnyi sobesednik* (The Orthodox Interlocutor) of the Kazan Academy

showed any signs of independence, until the purge of the editorial board by the Synod (to be more precise, by the Moscow Censorship Board) in 1859–60.

75. Apart from Florovsky's highly critical estimate of Bukharev (op. cit., pp. 344 ff.), the most interesting account is by V. Rozanov, *Okolo tserkovnykh sten* (By the Walls of the Church), 2 vols., P., 1906, vol. ii, and by A. Karpov in *Put'* (The Way), Paris, 1930, nos. xxii and xxiii. See also the biographical account in P. Znamensky's *Istoriya Kazanskoy dukhovnoi akademii* (The History of the Kazan Theological Academy), Kazan, 1891, pp. 124 ff.

76. See my *Studies in Rebellion*, London, 1957, ch. i. 2–4.

77. Frankfurt-am-Main, 1957.

78. The further implication is that, had this march not been interrupted by irresponsible revolutionary dreamers, there would never have been the calamity of a revolution in Russia—a view which appears to have as much to do with history as fairy tales.

79. For the above quotations, see Chicherin's *Vospominaniya* (Reminiscences), 4 vols., M., 1929–34, vol. iv, pp. 169 ff.; vol. i, p. 12. His political views and general outlook are sufficiently reflected in his Reminiscences, but see also *Neskolko sovremennykh voprosov* (Some Contemporary Questions), M., 1862; and *O narodnom predstavitelstve* (On Popular Representation), M., 1899. His attitude to Russian economic problems on the eve of the emancipation is expressed in the essay 'O nastoyashchem i budushchem polozhenii pomeshchich'ikh krest'yan' (On the Present and Future Position of the Landowners' Peasants), *Atenei* (Atheneum), January–February 1858. For an excellent analysis of Chicherin's economic views, see N. Tsagolov, *Ocherki russkoy ekonomicheskoi mysli perioda padeniya krepostnogo prava* (Essays in Russian Economic Thought at the Time of the Abolition of Serfdom), M., 1956, part ii, ch. 7.

It should be noted that most Russian economists who reflected the views of the Government were protectionist, although Chicherin was not entirely consistent in this and occasionally adduced arguments in favour of free trade. One of the leading protectionists was Chicherin's fellow-traveller Babst, a professional economist and editor of two economic journals (*Vestnik promyshlennosti* [The Messenger of Industry] and *Aktsioner* [The Shareholder]). Protectionist theory and practice were fairly widespread in continental Europe, especially after the unification of Germany. They were a frequent accompaniment of initial capitalist development or, as Marx put it, 'an artificial means for the manufacture of manufacturers'. In Russia, protectionism was endemic and spreading all the time: tariff walls and other protective measures increased customs revenue and helped to palliate the chronic financial insolvency of the State; they took care of many industries in which the Government had direct and indirect vested interests; and they accorded with the dominant view that, since the State was the only source of social and political organization, it was natural that the advancement, control, and protection of the nation's productive powers should be the Government's responsibility. Even Witte maintained that Russian financial administration must be based on the 'traditional belief' that every action affecting Russian society emanates from the Tsar. See M. Sobolev,

Tamozhennaya politika Rossii vo vtoroi polovine XIX veka (The Customs Policy of Russia in the Second Half of the Nineteenth Century), Tomsk, 1911, pp. 35, 39 ff., 58 ff., 150 ff.

80. Op. cit., vol. i, p. 136.

81. This is to invert in a sense the order indicated by these terms, for 'small deeds' usually denotes the social and political apathy which characterized the attitude of the bulk of the Russian public in the eighties, while 'senseless dreams' is the famous dictum of Nicholas II apropos of certain constitutional demands made by the progressive members of the *zemstva* shortly before the revolution of 1905.

An interesting account of these and other liberal trends and ventures will be found in George Fisher's *Russian Liberalism* (From Gentry to Intelligentsia), Harvard, 1958, which deals in the main with a later period. It is a more readable book than Leontovich's *Geschichte des Liberalismus in Rußland*, and it contains an excellent bibliography. While admitting the traditional mistrust of the Russian gentry towards the tsarist bureaucracy, I find it difficult, none the less, to accept Fisher's contention that the whole nobility resented 'revolutions from above' (see, for example, p. 31). In any case, the nobility always sought to make such 'revolutions' serve their economic interests, and the land reform shows that in important matters its efforts were not unsuccessful.

82. This view has been upheld, for instance, by A. Kizevetter in his *Bor'ba za zemstvo pri ego vozniknovenii* (The Struggle for the *Zemstvo* at its Inception). M., 1914. For a more balanced estimate of liberal trends in the *zemstva* during the sixties, see M. Dragomanov, *Liberalizm i zemstvo v Rossii, 1858–1883* (Liberalism and the *Zemstvo* in Russia, 1858–1883), Geneva, 1889. See also Fisher, op. cit., ch. 1.

83. H., vol. xvi, p. 86.

84. The other distinguished names with which this group is ordinarily associated are the ex-Decembrist Nikolai Turgenev, the novelist Ivan Turgenev, the literary historian and one-time censor Alexander Nikitenko, the memoirist and critic Pavel Annenkov, the historians Sergei Soloviev and Konstantin Arseniev, and others, including a number of moderate populists who contributed to the 'Annals of the Fatherland'.

85. See the illuminating *Pis'ma K. Dm. Kavelina i Iv. S. Turgeneva k Al. Iv. Gertsenu* (The Letters of K. Dm. Kavelin and Iv. S. Turgenev to Al. Iv. Herzen), edit. by M. Dragomanov, Geneva, 1892.

86. Kavelin's *Works*, vol. ii, pp. 5 f., 17, 26 ff., 43. For Kavelin's economic views, which were more concerned with practical application than with theory, see Tsagalov, op. cit., part ii, ch. 8.

87. 'Letters . . .', p. 57. It is easy to imagine what reactions this kind of language evoked in Herzen or, for that matter, in Chernyshevsky, who also knew Kavelin personally.

88. Kavelin's *Works*, vol. ii, pp. 1001 f. Chicherin, too, wrote about Marx, but, lacking Kavelin's commodious mind, he viewed Marx with unmitigated antipathy.

89. On Kavelin's philosophical views, see Zenkovsky, op. cit., vol. i, pp. 351 ff.

90. As has already been noted, a considerable number were of clerical origin. Until the sixties, their future was decided for them before they could

know if they had any vocation. They were, as a rule, precluded from entering any secular profession or place of learning, and automatically continued their fathers' ecclesiastical career—a circumstance described by one of its victims as an oblique tribute to the doctrine of apostolic succession. To the belated regret of the secular and ecclesiastical authorities, the reforms helped to remove these disabilities, and masses of emancipated seminarists swarmed into the large and small cities of Russia in search of new educational facilities and new forms of activity.

91. It is not possible to discuss here the populist doctrine and movement, which originated in Herzen and Bakunin, was developed by some of the radical thinkers of the sixties, and received systematic expression in the works of Lavrov and Mikhailovsky. Any attempted contribution to the literature on populism would have to be a separate undertaking; and after the monumental study by Venturi (op. cit.) and, in part, the book on Mikhailovsky by H. Billington (*Mikhailovsky and Russian Populism*, Oxford, 1958), to say nothing of the many studies in Russian, such an undertaking might be considered redundant. Certain aspects of populism, however, have already been touched upon and will also be treated in connexion with Chernyshevsky and Dobrolyubov.

92. See, for example, Chizhevsky, op. cit., pp. 246 f.; and N. Berdyaev, *The Russian Idea*, London, 1947, ch. v.

93. H., vol. xvi, p. 204.

CHAPTER III

1. Most of the relevant material has been recently collected from various sources in *N. G. Chernyshevsky v vospominaniyakh sovremennikov* (N. G. Chernyshevsky in the Recollections of His Contemporaries), ed. by Y. Oksman, 2 vols., Saratov, 1958 (hereafter referred to as *Ch.*), vol. i. An important source is Alexander Pypin's *Moi zapiski* (My Notes), published separately in 1910 (Moscow). Pypin (1833–1904), a historian of Russian literature and social thought, was a cousin of Chernyshevsky and his faithful friend. During Chernyshevsky's deportation he took charge of his children and saved most of his papers from the police. Chernyshevsky's own reminiscences (*Iz avtobiografii* [From an Autobiography]) are included in his *Complete Works*, ed. by B. Koz'min, V. Kirpotin, P. Lebedev-Polyansky, N. Meshcheryakov, I. Udaltsov, E. Tsekher, and N. Chernyshevskaya, 16 vols., M., 1939–53 (hereafter referred to as *Works*), vol. i, pp. 566 ff. The *Complete Works* are provided with extensive commentaries, which are invaluable for the study of Chernyshevsky and his time and show Soviet scholarship at its most impressive. See also *Letopis' zhizni i deyatelnosti N. G. Chernyshevskogo* (A Chronicle of. N. G. Chernyshevsky's Life and Work), M., 1953, by N. Chernyshevskaya; *N. G. Chernyshevsky. Literaturnoe nasledie* (N. G. Chernyshevsky. Literary Heritage), ed. by N. Alekseev and N. Chernyshevskaya, 3 vols., M.–L., 1930; and the collection of essays by V. Cheshikhin-Vetrinsky, *N. G. Chernyshevsky, 1828–1889*, P., 1923.

2. E. Lyatsky, 'N. G. Chernyshevsky i [and] I. I. Vvedensky' in *Sovremennyi mir* (Contemporary World), 1910, no. 6. See also Vvedensky's

impressions of Chernyshevsky as a student in *Ch.*, vol. i, pp. 295 ff. On Petrashevsky and his group, see below, section 3.

3. Kostomarov's autobiography, published in *Biblioteka memuarov* (Library of Memoirs), M., 1922, throws much light on the early Chernyshevsky. For the above quotation, see pp. 326 f.

4. These impressions belong to G. Shaposhnikov, who himself left no written testimony: they were conveyed orally to Cheshikhin-Vetrinsky (op. cit., p. 73). Many other pupils of Chernyshevsky were similarly impressed. See, for example, the anonymous portrait of him as a teacher in M. Voronov's autobiographical novel *Boloto* (The Bog), P., 1870.

5. *Ch.*, ibid., p. 113.

6. The text of the speech appeared in *Severnaya pochta* (Northern Post), the official paper of the Ministry of the Interior, on 13 September 1866 (see *Ch.*, ibid., p. 115).

7. *Works*, vol. xiv, pp. 359 f.

8. Since Tolstoy was an exact contemporary of Chernyshevsky and they started their respective Diaries almost at the same time, it may be interesting to compare them in this connexion, even though Chernyshevsky has no real claim to such comparison. The earliest and most trivial of Tolstoy's entries display to the full the keenness and individuality of his psychological understanding; and yet they shared an intense need for a rational and moral justification of life.

9. *Ch.*, vol. ii, pp. 161 f.

10. V. Pypina, *Lyubov' v zhizni Chernyshevskogo (Po materiyalam semeynogo arkhiva)* (Love in the Life of Chernyshevsky [Based on Family Archives]), P., 1923; and the articles of A. Lebedev, incorporating unpublished letters, in *Russkaya starina* (Russian Antiquity), 1910–12, particularly 1912, no. 4. Only those with whom Olga Sokratovna maintained amorous friendships and who were under the sway of her youthful charms have expressed favourable views about her. Amongst these were Dobrolyubov, Mikhailov, and to some extent Nekrasov.

11. Pypina, op. cit., p. 33.

12. Op. cit., pp. 13, 16, 17.

13. These are recurring phrases throughout the second part of the Diary devoted to Chernyshevsky's relations with Olga Sokratovna. *Works*, vol. i, pp. 454 ff.

14. Pypina, op. cit., pp. 32 f.

15. 'Contemporary', 1859, no. 1; nos. 4, 5, 8. These articles were later collected in one volume and published under the title *Zhenshchiny* (Women) by P. Kartavov, P., 1903. Mikhailov (1825–65) was a bad poet (though an excellent translator of poetry), an incisive journalist, and a very courageous man.

Actually, the question had already been raised by Belinsky and in Herzen's novel 'Who is Guilty?' But theirs were as yet solitary voices.

16. The marriage of Pyotr Bokov, an active member of the underground revolutionary group *Zemlya i Volya* (Land and Freedom), to Mariya Obrucheva, a very remarkable person and the first woman doctor in Russia—a marriage to which the physiologist Sechenov was a third party—

is a case in point. So is the marriage of Nikolai Shelgunov, whose wife, a very much less remarkable woman, had a *liaison* with Mikhailov and, after Mikhailov's deportation to Siberia, with Alexander Serno-Solov'evich. Mikhailov, as has been noted, was condemned to twelve years penal servitude for his authorship of a proclamation (printed in London and smuggled into Russia) against the university measures introduced by Putyatin. In fact, the proclamation was written by Shelgunov or, rather, jointly by Shelgunov and Mikhailov. Mikhailov was also charged with the writing of another proclamation composed by Shelgunov and addressed to the soldiers. He confessed to all the charges in order to save his friend and his mistress. See G. Bogdanovich, *Lyubov' lyudei shestidesyatykh godov* (Love among the People of the Sixties), L., 1923; also Shelgunov, *Vospominaniya* (Reminiscences), M.–L., 1923, p. 33. Shelgunov was a personal friend of Chernyshevsky, and his memoirs, together with those of Antonovich (see below, Note 27), are an important source for the study of Chernyshevsky's life and thought.

17. A recent study by J. M. Meijer, *Knowledge and Revolution. The Russian Colony in Zürich (1870–1873)*, Assen, Holland, 1958, though dealing chiefly with a later period, contains an excellent account of groups of emancipated Russians living abroad. The women flocked to Zurich, where they were not debarred, as in Russia, from higher education. Apart from academic pursuits and the practice of 'free love', they took part in various revolutionary activities, particularly those associated with the names of Lavrov and Bakunin.

18. The quotation is from a biographical essay which appeared in the *Bell* (15 October 1864). Though attributed to Pypin, the essay bears all the marks of Herzen's style. In fact, the author was A. Voronov, a pupil of Chernyshevsky in Saratov and later his secretary. I am indebted to Prof. Oksman for drawing my attention to this recently established fact.

19. Shelgunov, op. cit., pp. 136 f; and the biographical essay in *Bell*, quoted in the preceding Note. The Rector was not opposed to admitting Chernyshevsky to the Degree. But admissions did not depend on him or on anyone else within the University. They were the prerogative of the Minister of Education (Norov, at the time). As a rule, the Minister did not interfere in matters of technical academic procedure, but the Degree required his signature, which he could withhold. This he did in Chernyshevsky's case on the advice of a certain Davydov, an advocate of extreme political conformity in university life. See *Works*, vol. xiv, p. 370; and vol. ii, pp. 83 ff. for the thesis itself. It is interesting that Chernyshevsky's original intention was to write a dissertation on Hegel, but Hegel was a prohibited author at the time and Fischer, the professor of philosophy, warned him of the dangers involved in studying a subject that was so much out of favour. See *Works.*, vol xiv, p. 185.

20. See *Pis'ma russkikh literaturno-obshchestvennykh deyatelei k N. Y. Nikoladze* (Letters to N. Y. Nikoladze by Representatives of Russian Literary and Social Life), Tbilisi, 1949, p. 13.

21. See V. Evgeniev-Maksimov, *Ocherki po istorii sotsialisticheskoi zhurnalistiki v Rossii XIX veka* (Essays in the History of Socialist Journalism in Nineteenth-Century Russia), M.–L., 1936; also his *Sovremennik pri*

Chernyshevskom i Dobrolyubove ('The Contemporary' under Chernyshevsky and Dobrolyubov), L., 1936. For the earlier period, see A. Dementiev, *Ocherki po istorii russkoi zhurnalistiki 1840–1850 gg.* (Essays in the History of Russian Journalism between 1840 and 1850), M.–L., 1951. After Chernyshevsky's arrest the 'Contemporary' was edited by G. Eliseev, Antonovich, Saltykov-Shchedrin, Pypin, and Nekrasov.

22. Among the authors whose writings appeared in the 'Contemporary' were Tyutchev, Turgenev, Goncharov, Dostoevsky, Lev and Aleksey Tolstoy, Ostrovsky, Saltykov-Shchedrin, Herzen, Granovsky, Soloviev (the historian), and others.

The reasons for the suspension and eventual suppression of the review are well summarized in a memorandum prepared by one of the chief censors, A. Berte, as early as 1861. Berte lists seven such reasons: (1) the review's 'lack of all Christian import'; (2) its pervasive materialism; (3) its 'active incompatibility with the existing order'; (4) 'its approval of revolution and rejection even of . . . liberalism, as represented by Cavour and Tocqueville'; (5) its 'contempt for the upper classes of society'; (6) its 'strange idealization of woman'; (7) its 'affection for the lower class'. 'According to the reports of the chief censorship administration', Berte explains, 'there was such a number of articles rejected by the censors . . . that the editors could not claim ignorance of the demands of the Government in regard to the review.' The document is quoted by Evgeniev-Maksimov, 'Essays . . .', pp. 98 f. (see also ch. 14 *passim*). According to Evgeniev-Maksimov's calculations, the censorship cuts during the sixties (1857–65) amounted to almost 66 pages per issue of the review (not counting, of course, the material which was rejected by the editors for fear of attracting even more drastic measures).

23. On Nekrasov, see Charles Corbet, *Nekrasov: l'homme et le poète*, Paris, 1948. One of the most brilliant studies is K. Chukovsky's *Rasskazy o Nekrasove* (Essays on Nekrasov), M., 1930. See also E. Evgeniev-Maksimov, *Nekrasov kak chelovek, zhurnalist i poet* (Nekrasov, the Man, the Journalist and the Poet), M.–L., 1936.

24. Avdotiya Panaeva's notoriety was not confined to her role in Nekrasov's life or to her beauty. She was a prominent figure in St. Petersburg literary society, and her memoirs (*Vospominaniya*, L., 1927 [also M., 1956]) are an important if unreliable source for the study of literary life in the capital. Shortly before his death, Chernyshevsky planned to produce these memoirs in a new edition and to write a preface to them.

25. H., vol. xiv, p. 327. See also Y. Chernyak, *Ogarev, Nekrasov, Gertsen i Chernyshevsky v spore ob ogarevskom nasledstve* (Ogarev, Nekrasov, Herzen and Chernyshevsky in the Dispute about Ogarev's Inheritance), M.–L., 1938.

26. The almost insuperable difficulties under which Nekrasov laboured are well illustrated by his correspondence during the forties and early fifties. See Nekrasov's *Works*, 12 vols., M., 1949–52, vol. x.

27. The story has been told by a number of Chernyshevsky's contemporaries who were directly or indirectly involved in it. See, for example, M. Antonovich, *Reminiscences* in *Shestidesyatye gody* (The Sixties), ed. by Evgeniev-Maksimov, M.–L., 1933; and Panaeva's memoirs, mentioned

above, which provide the gossip; also Chernyshevsky's own *Polemicheskie krasoty* (Polemical Beauties), *Works*, vol. vii, pp. 707, 775 ff. For a detailed account of the controversy, see G. Berliner, *N. G. Chernyshevsky i ego literaturnye vragi* (N. G. Chernyshevsky and His Literary Enemies), M.–L., 1930.

28. This, by the way, was not Turgenev's final verdict, for some eighteen months later, when the 'sons' began to outvie the 'fathers', he beat a temporary retreat and wrote to the same correspondent: 'I do not find any "lifelessness" in him [Chernyshevsky]; on the contrary, I feel a living current in him . . . . He understands the needs of contemporary life, and in him this is not a sign of biliousness, as our splendid Grigorovich used to say, but the very root of his existence. . . . I consider Chernyshevsky to be useful. Time will show if I am right or wrong.' *Pervoe sobranie pisem, 1840–1883* (First Collection of Letters, 1840–1883), P., 1884, pp. 25 f. For the quotation in the text, see p. 14.

29. L. N. Tolstoy, *Perepiska s russkimi pisatelyami* (Correspondence with Russian Writers), M., 1962, p. 32. This did not, however, prevent Tolstoy from referring to Chernyshevsky in his Diary as a 'very intelligent and ardent man'.

30. 'Nekrasov', Antonovich writes in his memoirs, 'drew Chernyshevsky into the "Contemporary" when he [Chernyshevsky] was still a very modest contributor to Kraevsky's "Annals of the Fatherland", where Chernyshevsky was not admitted beyond the review's bibliographical section. Outside journalism Chernyshevsky appeared to be an academic failure, a man who had ignominiously come to grief with his magisterial thesis on "The Aesthetic Relations of Art to Reality" and who had not succeeded in obtaining a university degree. But Nekrasov was not put out. Having invited him to his review and having made closer acquaintance with this "academic misfit", he came to value him highly and put him in charge of the review's critical section.' Op. cit., p. 188. It should be noted that Antonovich was one of the few radicals who disliked and mistrusted Nekrasov.

31. See the interesting comments on Chernyshevsky by Vasilii Rozanov in *Solitaria* (*Uedinennoe*), Engl. transl., London, 1927, pp. 62 ff.

32. Of these, two must be singled out: A. Suvorin, *Vsyakie. Nechto v rode povesti* (All Kinds of People. A Tale of Sorts). It is a talented book, published originally in 1866 when the author, who eventually became the editor of the famous reactionary 'New Time', was still a liberal. Although he did not mention Chernyshevsky by name, the book was seized and all copies were burnt. It was republished only in 1909. The other is Korolenko (see below, Note 57).

33. See 'Novye materialy o revolyutsionnoy situatsii v Rossii (1859–1861 gg.)' (New Documents on the Revolutionary Situation in Russia [1859–1861]) in *LH.*, vol. 61. An interesting, if somewhat sensational and not very reliable, personal account of these revolutionary beginnings is *Shturmany gryadushchei buri* (The *Avant-Garde* of the Coming Storm) by M. Sleptsova (*Zveniya* [Links], 1933, vol. ii). The title is an adaptation of Herzen's description of the young revolutionaries.

34. See Longin Panteleev, *Iz vospominanii proshlogo* (From Memories of the Past), M., 1934, chapters xxiv, xxv, and especially xxix; and Alexander

Sleptsov, whose fragmentary reminiscences (*Zametki iz tetradi* [Notes from the Notebook]) exist, as far as I know, only as part of Lemke's commentaries to his edition of the works of Herzen, vol. x, pp. 425 f., and vol. xvi, pp. 72 ff. Panteleev and Sleptsov disagree in some important respects, but their estimate of Chernyshevsky's part in revolutionary work is the same. See also the similar account by Pyotr Ballod, quoted by Cheshikhin-Vetrinsky, op. cit., p. 157. Despite Chernyshevsky's pronounced sympathies with the Petersburg revolutionary activites, there is no evidence to prove Baskakov's contention that Chernyshevsky 'had created a secret revolutionary centre' or that 'he stood at its head' (V. Baskakov, *Mirovozrenie Chernyshevskogo* [Chernyshevsky's View of the World], M., 1956, pp. 148, 150, 154, and elsewhere). Although Baskakov gives a detailed analysis of the whole question, he omits the testimony of Panteleev and Sleptsov.

35. See, for example, Baskakov, op. cit., p. 152, or V. Shulgin, *Ocherki zhizni i tvorchestva N. G. Chernyshevskogo* (Essays on N. G. Chernyhevsky's Life and Work), M., 1956, *passim*. It is surprising that even such a trust-worthy scholar as M. Nechkina should ascribe to Chernyshevsky's wife an 'important part in revolutionary conspiracy'. To prove this Nechkina refers to Chernyshevsky's remark in a letter to Olga Sokratovna that her 'name belongs to history' (*LH.*, vol. 61, p. 460; also 'N. G. Chernyshevsky v gody revolyutsionnoi situatsii' [N. G. Chernyshevsky during the Years of the Revolutionary Situation], *IZ.*, 1941, vol. x). Surely, such claims by Cherny-shevsky on behalf of his wife, unsupported as they are by more tangible evidence, mean no more and no less than his similar remarks about her being 'a genius', 'the most wonderful woman in the world', 'a Russian Madame de Staël', &c.: they merely provide another chance for examining their relationship from the psychological angle, and fresh evidence of Chernyshevsky's love fantasy. The most plausible account of the whole matter, particularly of the central question of Chernyshevsky's own part in the incipient revolutionary movement, will be found in *Politicheskie protsessy 60-kh godov* (The Political Trials of the Sixties), P.–M., 1923, edited by B. Koz'min; in the Notes to the *Complete Works* of Chernyshevsky, and in N. Alekseev's *Protsess Chernyshevskogo. Arkhivnye dokumenty* (The Trial of Chernyshevsky. Archival Documents), Saratov, 1939 (hereafter cited as *The Trial*). See also Y. Steklov's monograph on Chernyshevsky (Note 65 below), vol. ii, p. 248 (2nd ed.).

36. Herzen's *Works* (Lemke), vol. x, p. 426.

37. Pypina, op. cit., pp. 32 f.

38. Ibid., p. 35. Pypina's account of Chernyshevsky's married life is based partly on family archives and partly on Chernyshevsky's own testimony in his unfinished novel 'Prologue'. Of this two parts exist—'Prolog k prologu' (Prologue to the Prologue) and 'Dnevnik Levitskogo' (The Diary of Levitsky)—and it is dedicated 'to her in whom Volgina [the heroine] will be recognized'. 'Volgin's [the hero's] whole manner of speech', Pypina observes, 'is unmistakably Chernyshevsky's and the speech of Olga Sokra-tovna is also reproduced with amazing accuracy' (ibid., p. 35).

39. Ibid., p. 105.

40. Ibid., op. 37. See also 'Prologue', *Works*, vol. xiii, pp. 70 f.

41. See S. Ashevsky, 'Russkoe studenchestvo v epokhu shestidesyatykh godov' (The Russian Students during the Sixties) in *Sovremennyi mir* (Contemporary World), 1907, nos. 6–7; also in Herzen's *Bell*, 'Materiyaly dlya istorii goneniya studentov pri Alexandre II' ('Documents for the History of the Persecution of Students during the Reign of Alexander II'), 1 December 1851–22 June 1862; and the more recent study by S. Gessen, *Studencheskoe dvizhenie v nachale shestidesyatykh godov* (The Student Movement at the Beginning of the Sixties), M., 1932. Among the series of restrictive measures was a drastic reduction of scholarships. In 1861 only twelve non-paying students were admitted to the University of St. Petersburg, whereas in 1859 of the 1,019 students only 369 were paying any fees at all. In this respect conditions were even worse than at the height of the régime of Nicholas I.

42. Only three issues appeared (30 June, 7 September, 20 October). They are reproduced in Lemke's *Essays on the Liberation Movement* . . . , cited above, pp. 359 ff. Significantly, it was printed on the press of the General Staff in the capital. The editors spoke in the name of a 'Committee', which may have included Dobrolyubov as well as some of the students and officers mentioned above (p. 121). Their programme consisted in the establishment of a constitutional Government, the emancipation of the peasants with land and without redemption fees, 'the unconditional liberation of Poland', and the right for the Ukraine 'to decide its fate according to its own wishes'. While willing to give the Tsar a last chance, the 'Committee' expressed its conviction, 'shared by all progressive patriots', 'that legality and the dynasty of today are incompatible', and that 'should we see that the liberals fail to act, we shall have no choice but to speak another language and talk of other things.' Chernyshevsky was not a member of the group, although he was aware of and in sympathy with its activities. See N. Novikova, 'Komitet "Velikorussa" i bor'ba za sozdanie revolyutsionnoi organizatsii v epokhu padeniya krepostnogo prava' (The Committee of the 'Great Russian' and the Struggle for the Establishment of a Revolutionary Organization at the Time of the Abolition of Serfdom), *VI.*, 1957, no. 5; also Venturi, op. cit., vol. i, ch. x.

43. 'Russia is entering the revolutionary stage of its existence', the proclamation began. An irreconcilable contradiction exists between the interests of the people and those of the 'imperial party', i.e. the landowners, the State functionaries, and the Tsar. 'There is but one solution for this oppressive, terrible state of affairs', it continued, '—a revolution, a bloody and implacable revolution, a revolution that will radically transform everything, all the foundations of society today, and destroy the upholders of the existing order.' This revolution, emanating from the peasants and headed by 'our youth', would establish 'a federal republican league' based on the peasant commune, to which all land was to be assigned. Other proposed measures included the nationalization of industry, the emancipation of women, the abolition of inheritance and even of the legal institution of marriage, and the closing of monastic establishments, 'the main cesspool of corruption'. 'Soon, soon, the day will come', the proclamation concluded, 'when we will unfurl the great flag of the future, the red flag. . . . We will attack the imperial party with no more mercy than they show us: we will kill them in

the squares . . . in the houses . . . in the narrow town lanes, in the broad avenues of the capitals, kill them in the villages and hamlets. . . . If our cause fails, if we have to pay with our lives for the daring venture to give man human rights, then we shall go to the scaffold. We shall put our heads on the block or in the noose, and we shall repeat the great cry: "Long live the Russian social and democratic republic!".' For the full text, see Koz'min, op. cit., pp. 259 ff.; also his *P. G. Zaichnevsky i 'Molodaya Rossiya'* (P. G. Zaichnevsky and 'Young Russia'), M., 1932; and Venturi, op. cit., vol. i, ch. xi. The impression created by the proclamation is described by N. Nikoladze, a friend of Chernyshevsky and later a prominent journalist in Georgia, who spent a term of imprisonment in the Peter and Paul Fortress in connexion with the student disturbances: 'Vospominaniya o shestide-syatykh godakh' (Recollections of the Sixties), *KS.*, 1927, no. 5 (34).

44. H., vol. xviii, p. 287.

45. See S. Reiser, 'Peterburgskie pozhary 1862 g.' (The Petersburg Fires of 1862), *KS.*, 1932, no. 10.

46. A valuable bibliography about this and other trials, as well as about many other measures taken by the Government against every kind of opposition, will be found in *Tsentralnyi gosudarstvennyi istoricheskii arkhiv SSSR v Leningrade* (The Central Historical State Archive of the USSR in Leningrad), ed. by S. Valka and V. Bedina, L., 1956. It contains a description of the archives of the tsarist State Council and the Senate. A detailed index makes this a most convenient work of reference. See also Lemke, op. cit.

47. *The Trial*, pp. 24 ff. See also A. Shilov, 'N. G. Chernyshevsky v doneseniyakh agentov III Otdeleniya' (N. G. Chernyshevsky in the Reports of the Third Section), *KA.*, 1926, no. 1.

48. *The Trial*, p. 54.

49. *The Trial*, pp. 40, 80; and the eye-witness account of the arrest by Antonovich, op. cit., pp. 125 ff. See also *LH.*, vol. 67, pp. 685 f. Since the case against Chernyshevsky rested at first largely on the sentence quoted above it is important to stress that the words did *not* mean what the deliberately travestied version of them by the Senate implied: 'We intend [*sic*] to publish the "Contemporary" with Chernyshevsky . . .', &c., i.e. that Chernyshevsky had come to some kind of understanding with Herzen. In fact, the latter merely repeated what had been previously announced by him in public, namely, that the editors of the *Bell* were ready to publish in London any and every journal suppressed in Russia 'as a result of political terror' (H., vol. xvi, pp. 214, 420). At no point did Chernyshevsky correspond with Herzen on this or any other matter.

Serno-Solov'evich was, of course, also arrested and eventually condemned to twelve years penal servitude, but died in Siberia soon after deportation.

50. *The Trial*, pp. 85 ff.; and V. Shulgin, op. cit., p. 14.

51. All written material found in Chernyshevsky's cell was subject to the supervision of the prison authorities; all letters and communications with the outside world had to be approved by the commission. Having examined the manuscript of the novel (addressed to Pypin), it did not find anything in it bearing on the case and let it pass. It was then submitted to the press censorship in the normal way. As the censor knew that the sheets, covered

as they were with innumerable official seals and stamps, had passed through a State Senate commission he did not venture to raise any objections and the novel was approved for publication. Before reaching the editorial office of the 'Contemporary', however, Nekrasov lost the manuscript in a cab, but eventually recovered it in somewhat dramatic circumstances. When the novel appeared in the 'Contemporary' the authorities realized what they had let themselves in for. It was banned and did not reappear in Russia until after the revolution of 1905. See Shulgin, op. cit., pp. 88 ff.

52. *The Trial*, pp. 327 ff. The appeal in question (*Barskim krest'yanam* [To the Landlords' Peasants]), written in simple peasant language, explained to the peasants that the freedom of the Emancipation statutes was bound to bring about their complete impoverishment, that nothing more could be expected from the autocracy, and that there was no other choice but to rise against their oppressors, making common cause with the soldiers and the revolutionary leaders on whom the peasant could rely for support (for full text, see *Works*, vol. viii, pp. 523 f.). The authorship of the proclamation is still disputed. It may have originated in the circle close to Chernyshevsky, but Shelgunov attributes it (or another similar proclamation) to Chernyshevsky himself (op. cit., p. 33; see also Sleptsov's testimony, Lemke, op. cit., p. 318), and Nechkina has made a fairly strong if not foolproof case in favour of Chernyshevsky's authorship (*IZ.*, 1941, vol. x, pp. 19 ff.). Yet Chernyshevsky categorically denied this at his trial and the commission had nothing to substantiate its indictment except an unmistakably forged document produced by Vsevolod Kostomarov, a young protégé of Chernyshevsky who had become a police informer. See Lemke, op. cit., pp. 471 ff.; and *KA.*, 1927, vol. 25, pp. 152 ff.

53. Quoted by Lemke, op. cit., p. 487.

54. See Suvorin, op. cit., p. 221, and other accounts with minor variations in *Ch.*, vol. ii, pp. 19 ff.; also the official report in *The Trial*, p. 355.

The Chernyshevsky affair produced an unfavourable impression even in some conservative and liberal circles, both in Russia and abroad. Nikitenko noted in his *Zapiski i dnevnik* (Notes and Diary) that 'there is widespread indignation against the Government on account of Chernyshevsky. How could one condemn him in the absence of any legal proof? Such is the opinion of almost everyone, even of those who are not reds. The Government has won a considerable number of enemies' (new ed., 2 vols. M., 1955, vol. ii, pp. 441 f.). There were, however, two striking exceptions: the Slavophil Samarin, who expressed his indirect approval of the Government action in his correspondence with Herzen (see my *Studies in Rebellion*, pp. 220 f.), and, still more surprisingly, the liberal Kavelin. Kavelin wrote to Herzen after the arrest of Chernyshevsky and others that 'the news from Russia is, in my opinion, not bad. . . . The arrests do not surprise me and, to be quite frank, they do not shock me either. This is a life and death struggle. The revolutionary party considers all means to be good for overthrowing the Government, and the Government defends itself with its own means' ('Letters . . .', p. 82). For a survey of foreign press reactions to the Chernyshevsky affair, see *LN.*, vols. 25–26, pp. 545 f.; and vol. 63, pp. 71 ff.

55. H., vol. xviii, pp. 221 f.

56. This account was recorded by Vladimir Kokosov, a doctor, a folklorist, and the author of a number of Siberian travelogues. See *Russkoe Bogatstvo* (Russian Wealth), 1905, nos. 11–12, pp. 162 ff.; and *Ch.*, vol. ii, pp. 187 ff.

57. Extracts from many of these will be found in *Ch.*, vol. ii. But three memoirs claim particular notice. (1) *Nikolai Gavrilovich Chernyshevsky na katorge i ssylke* (Nikolai Gavrilovich Chernyshevsky in Penal Servitude and Deportation), P., 1907, by Vyacheslav Shaganov. Shaganov (1829–1902) was condemned to twelve years' forced labour in connexion with the Karakozov affair and an attempt 'to rescue the political criminal Chernyshevsky from penal servitude'. He spent several years with Chernyshevsky in Aleksandrovsk and later met him in Vilyuisk. (2) *Lichnye vospominaniya o prebyvanii N. G. Chernyshevskogo na katorge* (Personal Recollections of N. G. Chernyshevsky's Life in Penal Servitude), M., 1906, by Pyotr Nikolaev. Nikolaev (1844–1910) was condemned to eight years forced labour also in connexion with the Karakozov affair and spent five years in Aleksandrovsk. (3) *Vospominaniya o Chernyshevskom* (Recollections of Chernyshevsky) by Vladimir Korolenko. These appeared in a number of versions (in the first place, without the author's permission, in London in 1894) and are included in his *Collected Works*, 10 vols., M., 1956, vol. viii. Korolenko (1853–1921), a talented short-story writer and poet, also spent several years in Siberia as a political exile, but not as a convict. His memoir is based on a number of eye-witness accounts and on his own impressions of Chernyshevsky whom he met briefly in Saratov in 1889. Additional mention must be made of the record of a complete stranger, Alexander Koksharsky, who as a young man held the post of Assistant District Police Officer in Vilyuisk. He and his wife were very kind to Chernyshevsky. His reminiscences, reproduced in full in *Ch.*, vol. ii, though badly written, give a moving account of Chernyshevsky's daily life in Vilyuisk jail. Of Chernyshevsky's term of deportation in Astrakhan, see the account by an English correspondent of the *Daily News*, 11 December 1883 (Cheshikhin-Vetrinsky, op. cit., pp. 186 ff.).

58. It appeared, of all places, in Meshchersky's weekly 'Citizen' (5 January 1873). A similar tribute is contained in the *Diary of a Writer* (1873) and 1876. Tolstoy, on the other hand, remained strangely silent.

59. *Ch.*, vol. ii, pp. 195 f.

60. Ibid., p. 218.

61. Her income, it is true, was considerably reduced. The horses and carriages had to be sold. But until the suppression of the 'Contemporary' Nekrasov continued to pay her 150 roubles a month, and the Pypins provided most of the rest. There was also an income from Chernyshevsky's house in Saratov. It is a puzzle why Olga Sokratovna did not in fact remarry. There are two possible explanations: either nobody asked her, or she was at bottom too conventional and too conscious of other people's opinion of herself to face the inevitable opprobrium if she had done so while her husband was a political convict in Siberia. Shulgin's determined effort to prove that she was absorbed in plans to liberate her husband is so tenuous and out of character as to evoke suspicion in the most credulous of students. He himself feels bound to admit that some aspects of the question allow only of 'guesses' (op. cit., ch. ii, *passim*).

62. *Ch.*, vol. ii, p. 370.

63. Shulgin, op. cit., pp. 361 ff.

64. Quoted from *Ch.*, vol. ii, p. 300.

65. There is a great number of works on Chernyshevsky's thought. A full bibliography of pre-revolutionary publications (up to 1909) will be found in M. Antonov's *N. Chernyshevsky*, M., 1910, pp. 279 ff. In addition to Antonov's own book, written from a populist point of view and interesting only in the chapters on Chernyshevsky's economic ideas, three must be mentioned as particularly valuable; Plekhanov's essays, originally published in *Sotsial-Demokrat* (The Social Democrat), nos. 1–4, London–Geneva, 1890–2 (they exist.in a separate German version, *N. G. Tschernischewsky. Eine literatur-historische Studie*, Stuttgart, 1894); his full-length study *N. G. Chernyshevsky*, P., 1910 (all these are included in Plekhanov's *Collected Works*, vols. v and vi); and Y. Steklov's already cited *N. G. Chernyshevsky, ego zhizn' i deyatelnost'*, *1828–1889* (N. G. Chernyshevsky, His Life and Work, 1828–1889), 2 vols., P., 1909 (2nd ed., M.–L., 1928; and an abridged German version, *N. Tschernischewski, ein Lebensbild*, 1913). For a fairly full bibliography of post-revolutionary works (up to 1947), see A. Skaftymov, *Zhizn' i deyatelnost' N. G. Chernyshevskogo* (The Life and Work of N. G. Chernyshevsky), Saratov, 1947, pp. 96 ff.; also M. Rozental, *Filosofskie vzglyady N. G. Chernyshevskogo* (The Philosophical Views of N. G. Chernyshevsky), M., 1948; and the most recent and largest work by V. Baskakov, mentioned above. The latter provides some painful reading: despite the formidable length and display of scholarship, it is unreliable; it is abusive of everything and everybody not in conformity with received dogma; it is written in a cast-iron, pedestrian jargon; and it fails completely to bring to life either Chernyshevsky or his thought. It has, however, been subjected to criticism by Soviet scholars (e.g. in *Novyi mir* [The New World], 1957, no. 2), who at their best, and contrary to a belief held widely in the West, are perfectly capable of discussing movements and people on their own merits. Indeed, the important work on Chernyshevsky has been done in post-revolutionary Russia. The foreign literature on Chernyshevsky's thought is scanty, and even the most valuable work—Venturi's *Il populismo russo*—deals with Chernyshevsky mainly in the context of populism. See also the chapter on Chernyshevsky in T. Masaryk's *The Spirit of Russia*, 2 vols., London, 1919, vol. ii; and in Richard Hare's *Pioneers of Russian Social Thought*, London, 1951. For Chernyshevsky's own writings in English translation, see *Select Philosophical Essays*, Foreign Languages Publishing House, M., 1953.

66. See *Works*, vol. iv, pp. 206 f.; vol. iii, pp. 770 f.

67. *Works*, vol. vii, p. 223; cf. pp. 222, 224.

68. Ibid., p. 223; see also vol. xiv, p. 651, for similar references to Kant.

69. See *Works*, vol. iv, p. 6; vol. vii, p. 645; vol. x, p. 925.

70. *Works*, vol. i, p. 230.

71. See *Works*, vol. iii, pp. 207 ff. See also E. Lyatsky, ' N. G. Chernyshevsky i uchitelya ego mysli: Gegel, Belinsky, Feuerbach' (N. G. Chernyshevsky and the Teachers of His Thought: Hegel, Belinsky, Feuerbach') in *Sovremennyi mir* (Contemporary World), 1910, nos. x–xi. Of Herzen Chernyshevsky said: 'I admire him more than any other Russian' (*Works*, vol. i, p. 241).

72. *Works*, vol. i, pp. 231 f.

73. See *Works*, vol. ii, pp. 169.

74. *Works*, vol. xv, p. 23; cf. vol. ii, pp. 121, 124 f.

75. The most outspoken of these was G. Shpet, who had such a low opinion of Chernyshevsky's philosophical mind as to consider him incapable of influence by any philosopher worthy of the name, let alone Feuerbach (see Shpet's otherwise illuminating essay in the symposium on 'P. L. Lavrov', P., 1922, especially pp. 93 f.). His arguments are, on the whole, as opinionated and perverse as the opposite contention that Chernyshevsky had completely outstripped Feuerbach or that he was a philosopher of genius (see, for example, Baskakov, op. cit., ch. 3, *passim*).

76. See *Works*, vol. ii, pp. 53 f.; vol. xv, p. 23; also *Ch.*, vol. ii, p. 344. More will be said on Chernyshevsky's affinities with Feuerbach in the section on 'Beauty, Art, and Reality'.

77. *Literaturnye vospominaniya i sovremennaya smuta* (Literary Reminiscences and the Contemporary Upheaval), 2 vols., P., 1900, vol. i, p. 307.

78. *Works*, vol. v, p. 391; vol. iii, pp. 207 f.

79. See *Works*, vol. iv, pp. 229 f.; vol. xi, p. 119; vol. x, pp. 62, 954 f.

80. See, for example, *Works*, vol. xiv, p. 667.

81. See, for example, *Works*, vol. vi, pp. 198 ff.; vol. xiv, p. 660.

82. *Works*, vol. xi, p. 448; also p. 120.

83. *Works*, vol. vii, pp. 248 ff., 275 ff., 364 f.; vol. v, pp. 230, 253 f.

84. *Works*, vol. ii, p. 165.

85. *Works*, vol. vii, p. 242.

86. *Works*, vol. ix, p. 161.

87. See, for example, *Works*, vol. vii, p. 251; vol. xv, p. 265.

88. Plekhanov, *Works*, vol. v, p. 208; Chernyshevsky, *Works*, vol. vi, p. 197; vol. ix, p. 161.

89. See, for example, *Works*, vol. vi, pp. 198 ff., 220; vol. vii, p. 248.

90. Steklov, op. cit., vol. i, p. 234.

91. *Works*, vol. ii, p. 125.

92. *Works*, vol. x, pp. 720 ff.; see also vol. xv, pp. 274 f. It is significant of Chernyshevsky's occasional inconsequence that these views went hand in hand with admiring reference to Auguste Comte, who explicitly denied the possibility of knowing 'things in themselves': Comte, he says, 'the originator of the positive philosophy, the only philosophical system in France that is true to the scientific spirit', is 'one of the greatest men of genius in our time' (*Works*, vol. vii, p. 166). Later, however, he spoke of Comte as 'that poor wretch . . . who fancied himself a genius' ' and spread over six volumes two or three little pages which, from time immemorial, used to be copied by every writer of handbooks on natural philosophy—copied mainly from Locke. . . . To this Auguste Comte added some snippets from Saint-Simon and, from his own inventory, the formula about the three stages of human thought (the theological, the metaphysical, the positive)—a completely absurd formula. . . .' 'Thus', Chernyshevsky concludes with some justification, 'there emerged six volumes, very fat and very boring' (*Works*, vol. xiv, p. 651).

93. *Works*, vol. vii, pp. 185, 291.

94. Ibid. As has been noted in the previous section, similar ideas are expressed throughout Chernyshevsky's novel *What Is To Be Done?*

95. While waiting for his trial in the Peter and Paul Fortress, Chernyshevsky began to translate Rousseau's *Confessions* and also composed a few biographical notes on him. He was impressed neither by Rousseau's romantic morality nor by his romantic politics, but by his personality and by his experience as a commonplace man without background and without roots who 'wished to reveal man in all the truth of nature' (see *Works*, vol. iii, p. 640).

96. *Works*, vol. vii, p. 260; also p. 264. Exactly the same idea was somewhat later expressed by J. S. Mill: 'All phenomena without exception', he wrote, 'are governed by invariable laws, with which no volitions, either natural or supernatural, interfere' (*Auguste Comte and Positivism*, London, 1865, pp. 12 f.). And Comte's 'positive philosophy' is nothing but a vast attempt to establish natural laws that would account for the unaccountable vagaries of man, whether in solitude or in society.

97. *The Theory of Legislation*, London, 1931, 'Principles of Legislation', iv; and Leslie Stephen, *The English Utilitarians*, 3 vols., London, 1900, vol. i, pp. 310 ff.

98. *Capital*, Engl. translation by Cedar Paul, 2 vols., London, 1930, vol. ii, p. 671. See Chernyshevsky's own remarks to this effect (*Works*, vol. i, p. 385); but he thought that Helvétius, too, had a very limited view of human behaviour.

99. *Works*, vol. vii, p. 288.

100. See, for example, his account of Lermontov's Pechorin as an 'egotist' who 'lives disinterestedly for his passions', and of Turgenev's 'enthusiastic' Rudin who does the same for his ideas (*Works*, vol. iv, p. 699); or his tribute to the Italian revolutionaries and their 'disinterested self-sacrifice' (*Works*, vol. vi, p. 261).

101. *Works*, vol. vii, pp. 240, 293; vol. viii, p. 245. Shpet (op. cit., p. 93) contends that such or similar statements by Chernyshevsky are either irrelevant or trivial, since the only philosopher against whom they could possibly be quoted was Empedocles! But if Empedocles, why not Plato, whose famous image of the world below as a cave, in which we see only shadows of the realities above, is known to have come straight from Empedocles? It is even more surprising that Shpet, a competent philosopher, should have completely forgotten Cartesian dualism and the whole 'ghost-in-the-machine' tradition in European philosophy.

102. *Works*, vol. iii, p. 289; cf. vol. ii, p. 131.

103. *Works*, vol. ii, pp. 616, 132, 111; vol. iii, p. 230; see also vol. ii, p. 148; vol. v, p. 597.

104. See N. Kotlyarevsky, *Kanun osvobozhdeniya* (The Eve of Liberation), P., 1916, pp. 295 ff.

105. *Works*, vol. ii, p. 64.

106. Ibid., pp. 66, 68; cf. p. 131.

107. *Works*, vol. ii, p. 103.

108. See, for example, *Works*, vol. viii, p. 222.

109. See *Works*, vol. ii, p. 103; vol. iii, p. 102; vol. iv, p. 229; vol. xi, p. 119.

110. See Ivanov-Razumnik, *Istoriya russkoi obshchestvennoi mysli* (History of Russian Social Thought), 2 vols., P., 1907, vol. ii, pp. 18, 33. Razumnik even believes that the contradiction between Chernyshevsky's 'sociological individualism' and 'ethical anti-individualism' lies at the root of the decline of Russian radicalism after the sixties.

111. See *Filosofskoe nasledstvo P. D. Yurkevicha* (The Philosophical Heritage of P. D. Yurkevich,) M., 1915, by G. Shpet, p. 42. Yurkevich's output was insignificant in quantity and consists mainly of articles and public lectures. The monograph by Shpet is the best available critical account of his thought; but there is also a substantial article by Vladimir Soloviev who was a pupil of Yurkevich at the University of Moscow (Soloviev's *Works*, vol. i, pp. 162 ff.) and a chapter in Zenkovsky's *History of Russian Philosophy* (vol. i, pp. 318 ff.), quoted above.

112. It is something of an irony that Yurkevich should be complaining that 'our epoch differs *toto coelo* from the Middle Ages: very often today a man is persecuted and tortured in the name of perfectly innocuous natural science for his love of spiritual truth, as in the past he was tortured and persecuted in the name of Christ by esteemed inquisitors for his love of the truths of natural science'. Shpet, op. cit., p. 10.

113. *Works*, vol. vii, pp. 762 f., 769 f.

114. An active and somewhat unsavoury role in this connexion was played by the ex-censor Alexander Nikitenko who was otherwise known for his enlightened liberalism. See G. Berliner, op. cit., p. 138.

115. Dostoevsky, *Works* (ed. 'Prosveshchenie'), vol. x, pp. 118 f. See also V. Dorovatskaya-Lyubimova, 'Dostoevsky i shestidesyatniki' (Dostoevsky and the Men of the Sixties) in the symposium *Dostoevsky*, M., 1928; and the excellent work by S. Borshchevsky, *Shchedrin i Dostoevsky* (Shchedrin and Dostoevsky), M., 1956, ch. 1. The author has used much unpublished material and throws new light on the whole controversy and Dostoevsky's rather wayward part in it.

116. See 'On Orthodoxy . . .', e.g., pp. 20, 45, 64, 66 f., 209; also Bukharev's *O sovremennykh dukhovnykh potrebnostyakh mysli i slova* (On Contemporary Spiritual Needs in Thought and Word), M., 1865, in which he discussed Chernyshevsky's novel *What Is to Be Done?*

117. See Askochensky's article in his own paper, 'Home Conversation' 1861, no. 11, quoted in H., vol. xv, p. 372.

118. This view is adopted by a number of Russian writers with a Christian bias, among them Berdyaev, Bulgakov, and Zenkovsky. But even Cheshikhin-Vetrinsky thought that 'when Chernyshevsky's outlook on life changed another object was merely substituted for the religious spirit inherited from his home' (op. cit., p. 55). See also the unexpected testimony to this effect by Panteleev, one of Chernyshevsky's collaborators, *Ch.*, vol. i, pp. 268 f.

119. This is Baskakov's contention. By the curious method of collocating some of Chernyshevsky's early fragments and sentences and of omitting others, Baskakov tries to convey the impression that Chernyshevsky professed materialism at the age of sixteen (op. cit., pp. 330 ff.).

120. *Ch.*, vol. i, p. 171.

121. See, for example, *Works*, vol. iv, p. 270; also the sympathetic account

of the 'fools in Christ' (*yurodivye*), whom Chernyshevsky used to meet in Saratov, in the already mentioned unfinished autobiography which he began writing in the Peter and Paul Fortress in 1863. I could find no references to Chernyshevsky's personal views on religion in later life, except for a remark in the reminiscences of Melikov, an attorney in Yakutsk: 'Once, in the course of a conversation,' Melikov reports, 'Nikolai Gavrilovich asked me suddenly if I believed in God. I said that I did. "I don't", Nikolai Gavrilovich retorted. He never reverted to the subject' (*Ch.*, vol. ii, p. 254). Elsewhere it is reported that when the Archbishop of Yakutsk expressed a wish to meet Chernyshevsky he declined to see him: 'I have no juicy pies to offer him', Chernyshevsky said. 'Let him hasten to the Rural Dean where the pies are getting cold' (*Ch.*, vol. ii, p. 217). Olga Sokratovna wished her husband to take Holy Communion before his death. She sent for a priest when Chernyshevsky was already unconscious: he died before the priest arrived.

122. See, for example, the essay on 'The Origins of the Fall of Rome', quoted above, where he says that the development of knowledge and science constitutes 'the operative force of human progress' (*Works*, vol. vii, p. 645). Elsewhere he even states that 'although politics and industry figure so prominently in the forefront of history, the basic force in history is, none the less, science, to which politics, industry and everything else is subordinated' (vol. iv, p. 6). This has prompted some students of Chernyshevsky's thought to regard him as pre-eminently a scientific rationalist intoxicated with the ever-widening prospects of human advance as a result of enlightenment. Korolenko is a case in point. Others have adopted Plekhanov's formula, to the effect that Chernyshevsky was 'a materialist in philosophy and an idealist in history'. This has become something of a shibboleth among a few of the older and now discarded Soviet writers (Steklov, Deborin, Kamenev, and others).

123. See, for example, his excellent discussion of Herodotus and Thucydides: *Works*, vol. ii, pp. 276 f.; vol. iii, p. 356. But he acquits Aristotle of this charge: vol. ii, p. 277.

124. *Works*, vol. iii, p. 592; see also vol. i, p. 232.

125. *Works*, vol. xiv, pp. 47 f.

126. *Works*, vol. iv, p. 329.

127. *Works*, vol. iii, p. 286; vol. iv, p. 727.

128. *Works*, vol. ii, p. 294.

129. *Works*, vol. xiii, p. 197.

130. *Works*, vol. xiv, p. 551.

131. The extent of Chernyshevsky's acquaintance with the work of Marx is uncertain. He may have been indirectly acquainted (through articles in the 'Contemporary' and in the 'Annals of the Fatherland') with the *Communist Manifesto* and possibly with the *Critique of Political Economy*. But among Chernyshevsky's books in Siberia there was a copy of *Capital* in Danielson's translation, which appeared in St. Petersburg in 1872. It is interesting that Nikolaev, the already mentioned fellow prisoner of Chernyshevsky in Alexandrovsk, claims to have seen this note made by Chernyshevsky on the title-page of Marx's work: 'Revolution in rose-water.' 'To an advocate of

the interests of the whole proletariat and the proletarianized peasantry such as Chernyshevsky was', Nikolaev comments, 'the evolution and peaceful development of capitalism, inevitably leading to a *Zusammenbruch*, seemed indeed like the rose-water of revolution' (*Ch.*, vol. ii, p. 164). Elsewhere, however, Chernyshevsky spoke very highly of Marx as an economic historian (ibid., p. 214). Marx, for his part, paid high tribute to Chernyshevsky as one of the 'most original contemporary economists'; he said that 'the Russians should be ashamed of not having bothered . . . to acquaint Europe with such a remarkable thinker', and that 'Chernyshevsky's political death is a loss not to Russia alone but to the whole of Europe'. *Complete Works* of Marx and Engels (in Russian), 29 vols., 1928–, vols. xii, p. 354; xvii, p. 13; xxv, p. 306; xxvi, pp. 87 f.; and the symposium on *G. A. Lopatin* (P., 1922, pp. 65 f.), who was a friend of Marx and took an active part in the abortive attempts to arrange Chernyshevsky's escape from Siberia.

Lenin, according to recently published evidence, said that, though, owing to the censorship, 'one has to guess many of his [Chernyshevsky's] views . . . a perceptive reader of his articles will soon find the infallible key for deciphering his political ideas, even where these are expressed obliquely, by allusion. There are musicians who are said to possess absolute pitch; there are other people of whom it might be said that they possess an absolute revolutionary sense. Such was Marx, and such was also Chernyshevsky.' See N. Valentinov, *Vstrechi s V. I. Leninym* (Meetings with V. I. Lenin), New York, 1953, pp. 103, 106, 117.

132. *Works*, vol. x, p. 981; vol. v, p. 391.

133. *Works*, vol. x, pp. 745 ff.

134. See, for example, *Works*, vol. i, p. 194; vol. ii, p. 122.

135. *Works*, vol. i, p. 356; cf. vol. v, p. 491; vol. vi, p. 91; vol. vii, p. 631.

136. 'Let there be oppression of one class by another, for it will lead to a struggle, and then the oppressed will realize that they are oppressed in the present order of things, but that there can be another order in which oppression will cease; they will realize that it is not God but men who oppress them; that they can expect no justice . . . from others. . . . They will realize that they are surrounded by scoundrels, grafters, extortioners, cruel oppressors, leeches, profligates . . . and that none of them would ever exchange their state for yours, or take your side . . . with sincerity, conviction and without ulterior purpose. . . .' *Works*, vol. i, p. 356. See also similar ideas expressed later in 'Prologue', *Works*, vol. xiii, pp. 187 f.

137. *Works*, vol. ii, p. 111.

138. *Works*, vol. xvi, p. 493; vol. xiv, p. 643. See also the unpublished essay 'Po povodu smesheniya v nauke terminov "razvitie" i "protsess" ' (Apropos of the Confusion in Science between the Terms 'Development' and 'Process'), quoted by Baskakov, op. cit., p. 589.

139. See *Works*, vol. ix, pp. 254, 315, 741. The quotation from Malthus belongs to Chernyshevsky. It will be recalled that, to Chernyshevsky's horror, Kavelin, though not apparently a Malthusian, also assumed that social inequality belongs to the natural order, beyond the sphere of conscious political or social action.

140. *Works*, vol. vii, pp. 157 ff.; vol. xi, p. 672. See, however, the quota-

tion in Note 122 where the same force is assigned to the development of knowledge and science.

141. *Works*, vol. i, pp. 372 f.

142. *Works*, vol. i, pp. 356 f., 478; vol. iv, pp. 313 f.

143. *Works*, vol. i, p. 395.

144. *Ch.*, vol. ii, p. 91. Reporting his London meeting with Herzen, Chernyshevsky wrote to Dobrolyubov that 'the visit has, naturally, served a useful purpose . . . but, by God, there is something to discuss! . . . Kavelin squared—that's all' (*Works*, vol. xiv, p. 378). The meeting in question was an important landmark in the relations between Herzen and the young radicals in Russia. A heated controversy ensued among Soviet historians as to its meaning and implications. See Koz'min's and Nechkina's conflicting statements about the matter in *Izvestiya Akademii nauk SSSR. Otdelenie yazyka i literatury* (Reports of the Academy of Sciences of the USSR. Department of Language and Literature), 1953, vol. xii, Issue 2; 1954, vol. xiii, Issue 1; vol. xiv, Issue 2. The most satisfactory summary and interpretation of the question will be found in *Gertsen i Chernyshevsky* (Herzen and Chernyshevsky) by I. Porokh, Saratov, 1963 (ch. 3).

145. *Works*, vol. i, pp. 356 f.

146. How Chernyshevsky applied this indirect method of stating the idea of revolution can be seen in such articles as 'Bor'ba partii vo Frantsii pri Lyudovike XVIII i Karle X' (The Party Struggle in France at the Time of Louis XVIII and Charles X), in 'Cavignac', in 'Russky chelovek na rendez-vous' (The Russian at a rendezvous), and in nearly all that he wrote about contemporary events in Italy.

147. *Works*, vol. vi, p. 114; vol. vii, p. 923; see also vol. v, p. 590; vol. vi, pp. 13, 417 f.; vol. xiii, p. 197.

148. *Works*, vol. x, pp. 93 f.

149. Ibid., p. 92; see also pp. 100 f.

150. 'N. G. Chernyshevsky i Rossiya 60-kh godov' (N. G. Chernyshevsky and the Russia of the Sixties) in *Russkoe Bogatstvo* (Russian Wealth), 1905, no. 3, pp. 181 f. A similar estimate of Chernyshevsky's position was formed by Shaganov and by Bervi-Flerovsky, whose acquaintance with Chernyshevsky dated from 1861. Other interesting evidence is contained in the curious viva voce dispute between Chernyshevsky and the liberal journalist Arkady Evald. Evald attacked Chernyshevsky for his defence of the students and of academic freedom in general (see Chernyshevsky's article entitled 'Nauchilis' li?' [Have They Learned?']), following the new Government measures against the universities. The dispute took place in the spring of 1862 in Evald's Petersburg flat, in circumstances that seem almost like a parody of the nineteenth-century Russian intelligentsia. Antonovich was one of the appointed witnesses of the proceedings and he preserved a verbatim report of the conversation, which was subsequently signed by the disputants. Both Antonovich and Evald left records of the occasion, which are reproduced in *Ch.*, vol. i, pp. 363 ff. For the relevant evidence, see ibid., p. 370.

151. It is impossible not to agree with Shulgin's verdict that 'no other work of fiction [in Russian literature] had brought out so clearly the idea

of revolution as the only solution for the people', and that 'no other work of fiction (with the exception of *What Is to Be Done?*) presents such a forceful appeal to revolution' (op. cit., p. 205, and the whole section [2] which gives a close analysis of the work from this point of view). The novel was smuggled abroad and published by Lavrov in Switzerland. Chernyshevsky's cousin Pypin was so alarmed at the possible effects of the publication that he did his best to suppress it. Shulgin is very hard on Pypin on that account, but he fails to appreciate that Pypin was primarily moved by a concern for Chernyshevsky's safety and the prospects of his return from deportation.

152. For Chernyshevsky's indebtedness to Blanqui, see *Works*, vol. i, pp. 61, 174, 297, 358. Later he became more critical of the Blanquist cult of isolated conspiratorial *élites* and of attempts to start a revolution before the time was ripe for it. See, for example, *Works*, vol. xiii, p. 54.

The appeal to Herzen is contained in the anonymous 'Letter from the Provinces' (by 'A Russian'), which was published in the *Bell* in the spring of 1860 (see my *Studies in Rebellion*, p. 253). Chernyshevsky's authorship has been disputed by some scholars, notably by Koz'min. See the latest discussion of 'The Question of the Authorship of the Letter from "A Russian"' (*K voprosu ob avtore pis'ma 'russkogo cheloveka'*), *Izvestiya Akademii nauk. Seriya istorii i filosofii* (Reports of the Academy of Sciences. Historical and Philosophical Series), 1951, vol. 2. The Letter appears to have emanated from the circle of Chernyshevsky's close friends, possibly from Dobrolyubov. Chernyshevsky himself admitted much later to having often found it necessary 'to remind people of the axes' (*Ch.*, vol. ii, p. 89).

153. Even this welcoming article evoked the displeasure of the authorities. Chernyshevsky's correspondence shows that the 'welcome' was only apparent. See the evidence in N. Sladkevich, *Ocherki istorii obshchestvennoi mysli Rossii v kontse 50 — nachala 60-kh godov XIX veka* (Essays in the History of Russian Social Thought at the End of the Nineteen-Fifties to the Beginning of the Sixties), L. 1962, pp. 71 ff.

154. *Works*, vol. x, p. 99; vol. xiii, pp. 187 f.; cf. vol. v, pp. 360 f. It is interesting to compare Chernyshevsky's attitude to redemption payments with that of Chicherin, one of his chief opponents, for whom they were basic to the whole economic development of Russia: 'What a just payment is', Chicherin wrote, 'can be established only on the basis of the gross value of the economic gains which the landowner derives from the land alienated from him as a result of the emancipation of the serfs' ('Of the Present and Future Position of the Landowner's Peasants' [see above, Note 79], pp. 497 f.)

155. See, for example, *Works*, vol. ix, p. 1003. It is this ambiguity of Mill which seems to have moved Chernyshevsky to take him as a point of departure for expounding his own economic views. Mill was interesting to Chernyshevsky not because he had solved the dilemmas of economics, but because he epitomized them, because he reflected the tension between individualism and collectivism, between freedom and morality, between the rights of the *élite* and popular rule, and so on.

156. *Works*, vol. ix, pp. 537 ff.

157. *Works*, vol. ix, p. 627. For an analysis of capitalist tendencies in contemporary Russian economy, see, for example, vol. iv, pp. 303 f., 744 f.

158. *Works*, vol. iv, p. 740.

159. This idea seems to have a following even among some modern western European economists. See, for example, Richard Law, *Return from Utopia*, London, 1950; or F. Hayek, *Essays on Individuality*, London, 1958.

160. *Works*, vol. vii, p. 49. To this was added the precept that 'while there is a shortage in the supply of goods for ordinary needs, articles of comfort should be treated as of no value; and while these are in short supply luxury goods should be treated as of no value'. Vol. ix, p. 550.

161. *Works*, vol. iv, p. 322. See also p. 331; and vol. v, p. 379. As is well known, even Marx conceded, as late as 1881, that, given certain conditions, of which the 'free development' of the peasant commune and the coincidence of a proletarian socialist revolution in western Europe were the most important, the commune might provide the basis for a future Russian socialism and save Russia from the torments of full capitalist development. Actually, the idea that the conversion of communalism into socialism is contingent in some way on these conditions was also expressed by Chernyshevsky who, while relying on the peasantry as far as Russia was concerned, did not share Herzen's scepticism about the revolutionary possibilities of the western proletariat. Marx's concession, however, was later withdrawn by Engels, partly under the influence of Plekhanov and partly because by the end of the century Russia was already too far involved in that development

It has been claimed that Chernyshevsky's case for peasant socialism and his critique of capitalist development was largely derived from the early nineteenth-century Franco-Swiss economist Simonde de Sismondi, especially from his later work *Nouveaux Principes d'économie politique*. It is difficult to sustain the claim. Quite apart from the fact that Chernyshevsky's idea of peasant revolution was a wholly indigenous Russian product, he set independent communal land tenure against all forms of capitalist enterprise as well as against feudal economic relations. Sismondi, on the contrary, advocated small individual farming and a petty *bourgeois* economy against large-scale capitalist production. The distinction between 'national wealth' and the 'well-being of the people', which Chernyshevsky, admittedly, shared with Sismondi, was also fairly widespread among the early English socialists; and Fourier believed that wealth creates poverty and that economic crises have a plethoric character.

162. See *Works*, vol. iv, pp. 345, 740, 744 f.; vol. vii, p. 54. For the Slavophil views, see A. Koshelev, *Ob obshchinnom vladenii* (On Communal Ownership), Berlin, 1875, pp. 16 f., 39, 54. See also Sladkevich, op. cit., pp. 67, 74, 86.

163. The most important of these articles are an examination of August Haxthausen's *Studien über die inneren Zustände, das Volksleben und insbesondere die ländlichen Einrichtungen Rußlands*; an essay 'On the Possession of Land' (*O pozemelnoi sobstvennosti*); and especially the already mentioned 'Critique of the Philosophical Prejudices against Communal Ownership' (*Kritika filosofskikh predubezhdenii protiv obshchinnogo vladeniya*).

164. In his Reminiscences Shelgunov states that 'Chernyshevsky's controversy with Vernadsky . . . and the other economists has helped to clarify many things to the commission entrusted with the editing [of the Emancipation statutes]. I even think that Russia owes it to Chernyshevsky that the

Statute of 19 February did not destroy the commune' (op. cit., p. 93). But there is more evidence to show that the Government had its own reasons for preserving the commune which had nothing to do with Chernyshevsky: it was, as has been noted earlier, enabled by this means to keep a tighter control over the peasantry and to guarantee the payment of dues and taxes. For an analysis of the contemporary economic problems and the controversies occasioned by them see N. Tsagolov, op. cit.

165. See the essay on Turgot, *Works*, vol. v, pp. 292 ff.; also vol. vii, pp. 38, 468; vol. ix, p. 30.

166. *Ch.*, vol. i, p. 270. This must have been said in the late seventies or early eighties. Similar charges of destroying the 'smooth process' of economic and political growth were made by other contemporary and later spokesmen of Russian liberalism. As has been noted, it is also the burden of Leontovich's estimate of the revolutionary movement in Russia.

167. See, for example, *Works*, vol. v, pp. 336, 404; vol. vii, p. 415, and the passages cited in Note 140; also Sladkevich, op. cit., pp. 75 ff.

168. *Works*, vol. v, pp. 106, 217; see also pp. 302 f., 599; vol. i, p. 121.

169. *Ch.*, vol. ii, p. 73.

170. This explains also Chernyshevsky's attitude to most of the reforms introduced after his deportation to Siberia. He viewed them all in the light of what he called 'the fundamental nature of the existing social order' (*Works*, vol. xiii, p. 242). 'The highly unfavourable estimate made by Nikolai Gavrilovich of our *zemstvo* institutions', writes Stakhevich, 'showed that he did not find in them the slightest sign of constitutional possibilities, or even the smallest step that could lead us to true political freedom. I don't remember . . . a single occasion on which he mentioned the *zemstvo* institutions, except once, when we drew him into a conversation on the topic; and this is, roughly, what he said: 'You have seen many times how sucking pigs are fed in our farmyards: they cluster round the trough full of rotten potatoes and all sorts of rubbish, stamp on each other, push and bite each other, grunt and screech—that's our man of the *zemstva*'" (*Ch.*, vol. ii, p. 74).

171. See the incisive essay 'The Russian at a rendezvous', cited above, about Turgenev's story *Asya*.

172. *Works*, vol. i, p. 90; vol. xiv, p. 333.

173. See *Works*, vol. vi, p. 374. Baskakov quotes an unpublished document dated 1861, issued by the Central Censorship Department and reprimanding the censors for passing Chernyshevsky's articles which deal with the events in Italy. 'The enthusiastic descriptions of the Italian rising' were taken to be a camouflaged appeal for 'a political uprising in Russia.' Op.cit., p. 110.

174. *Works*, vol. v, p. 38.

175. Venturi, op. cit., vol. i, p. 274. See also *Works*, vol. vi, pp. 281 f., 323 f.

176. *Ch.*, vol. ii, p. 135.

177. *Works*, vol. ix, p. 828.

178. It is interesting that even Marx found a good word for 'the co-operative movement and especially the co-operative factories', even while stressing their limitations (Inaugural Address to the First International, 1864).

179. *Ch.*, vol. ii, p. 139.

180. On Mazzini, see *Works*, vol. viii, pp. 305 ff.

181. *Works*, vol. ix, pp. 346 f.

182. Herzen, *Works*, vol. xvii, p. 106, and vol. vii, pp. 122 f.

183. See V. Semevsky, *M. V. Butashevich-Petrashevsky i petrashevtsy* (M. V. Butashevich-Petrashevsky and the Petrashevskists), M., 1922, p. 171. This is still the most important monograph on Petrashevsky and his group. The main sources are contained in *Petrashevtsy v vospominaniyakh sovremennikov* (The Petrashevskists in the Recollections of Contemporaries), ed. by P. Shchegolev, 3 vols., M.-L., 1926-8; *Filosofskie i obshchestvenno-politicheskie proizvedeniya petrashevtsev* (The Philosophical and Socio-Political Works of the Petrashevskists), ed. by V. Evgrafova, M., 1953; and the complete records of their trial, *Delo petrashevtsev* (The Case of the Petrashevskists), ed. by V. Leykina, E. Korolshuk, and V. Desnitsky, 3 vols., M.-L., 1937-51. There is a fairly detailed but jaundiced account in P. Scheibert's *Von Bakunin zu Lenin*, Leiden, 1956, vol. iii of *Studien zur Geschichte Osteuropas*.

184. *Works*, vol. i, p. 274.

185. Ibid., pp. 178, 181 f., 196; and *Russkaya Mysl'* (Russian Thought) 1913, no. 1, p. 141.

186. See *Works*, vol. xi, pp. 197, 303, 72 f.

187. It is known that Speshnev was one of the prime movers of the famous *pyaterki* ('Groups of Five'), the revolutionary and conspiratorial cells which came into being in the sixties. They are commonly associated with Slepstov, the already mentioned leading member of 'Land and Freedom' and, in a more sinister context, with Nechaev. Chernyshevsky knew of their existence and, according to the extremely unreliable testimony of Sleptsov's wife, took part in initiating them (see Sleptsova's memoirs, op. cit., p. 404).

188. Whatever modifications may be found in the development of Chernyshevsky's treatment of art, he remained throughout essentially faithful to the views expressed in this early work. As late as 1888 he had plans to republish the book in its original form and even wrote a new preface to it; but the censorship prevented the publication.

Apart from sections dealing with Chernyshevsky's aesthetics in most of the previously mentioned works on him, there are a few special monographs of which the most important are by George Lukacs, *Einführung in die Ästhetik Tschernyschewskys*, Berlin, 1954; and by M. Kagan, *Esteticheskoe uchenie Chernyshevskogo* (Chernyshevsky's Teaching on Aesthetics), L.-M., 1958. The latter work is especially interesting, for the author succeeds in combining his Marxist presuppositions with a refreshing freedom, in manner and matter, from the jarring echoes of decreed propositions, and he never misses an opportunity of approaching his subject from a fresh angle. It also contains a useful bibliography of all Chernyshevsky's writings on art. For Chernyshevsky's treatment of literature, see A. Lavretsky, *Belinsky, Chernyshevsky, Dobrolyubov v bor'be za realizm* (Belinsky, Chernyshevsky, Dobrolyubov in the Struggle for Realism), M., 1941; and especially A. Karaganov, *Chernyshevsky i Dobrolyubov o realizme* (Chernyshevsky and Dobrolyubov on Realism), M., 1955.

189. See Soloviev's essay in appreciation of Chernyshevsky, 'Pervyi shag v polozhitelnoi estetike' (First Step in Positive Aesthetics), *Collected Works*, vol. vi, pp. 424 ff.

190. Unless otherwise stated, all quotations are from Chernyshevsky's treatise on aesthetics.

191. See Chernyshevsky's appraisal of Tolstoy's early work, *Works*, vol. iii, pp. 428, 431.

192. Op. cit., p. 89.

193. See *Works*, vol. ii, p. 263.

194. See, for example, *Works*, vol. ii, p. 278.

195. Ibid., pp. 234, 109.

196. See the italicized remarks in the preface to the third edition of the treatise (*Works*, vol. ii, p. 278).

197. *Works*, vol. ii, p. 278; vol. iv, p. 152; vol. ii, p. 111.

198. On Chernyshevsky's view of the relations between science and art, see the observations by Kagan, op. cit., p. 91.

199. See the remarks to this effect in 'Essays on the Gogolian Period . . .', *Works*, vol. iii, pp. 299 ff.; also vol. iv, p. 536.

200. See, for example, *Works*, vol. ii, pp. 116, 117, 273. One might mention in this connexion Chernyshevsky's interesting treatment of tragedy. He opposed the traditional 'sensational' interpretation, according to which a character passing from prosperity to adversity must be endowed with special distinction, superiority, or grandeur in order to be tragic. But, Chernyshevsky says, 'the greatness of suffering' is no less significant than 'the greatness of the sufferer'; and the little man is as much entitled to his tragedy as the big man of old. *Works*, vol. ii, pp. 28, 184; see also the article 'Ne nachalo li peremeny?' (When Will the Change Begin?), published in the 'Contemporary' (1861), about N. Uspensky's peasant tales, which he praised for a refreshingly unsentimental approach to 'the people'.

201. See *Works*, vol. ii, p. 64; vol. iii, p. 303; vol. iv, pp. 535, 562; cf. my *Studies in Rebellion*, p. 106.

202. *Works*, vol. iii, pp. 426 ff.; vol. iv, p. 514.

203. It is significant—or perhaps ironical—that Chernyshevsky condemned Tolstoy's later, post-conversion work on the grounds of its lack of literary value. Korolenko records an otherwise not very remarkable conversation with Chernyshevsky about this, in the course of which Chernyshevsky took out his handkerchief and blew his nose with particular deliberation.

' "It's a good thing, isn't it?", he asked, to our [Korolenko's and his wife's] astonishment. "Don't I blow my nose well? . . . If someone were to ask you whether Chernyshevsky blows his nose well, you could have replied: 'No manners at all; and where, if you please, could a seminarist get his manners from?' But what if I were to present incontrovertible proof that I am not a seminarist but a duke, and that I have received, not a seminary but a ducal education? Surely, you would then consider immediately: 'Yes, nothing doing, it must be admitted, his nose-blowing isn't bad at all—a genuine, a rare ducal gesture.' Isn't it so, eh?"

' "Perhaps."

' "That's it. It's the same with Tolstoy. If someone had written a little tale about Ivan-the-fool, no publisher would look at it. But it's signed by Count Tolstoy, and everybody stands agog. Oh yes, the great novelist! It can't be rubbish. It's just unusual, a piece of genius! Only a count could blow his nose like this." ' *Ch.*, vol. ii, p. 314.

204. I. Repin, *Dalekoe i blizkoe* (The Distant and the Near), M., 1937, p. 181. Similar accounts are given by Shaganov, Shelgunov, Stasov, and others.

205. Repin, op. cit., p. 430.

206. *Selected Works*, 2 vols., M., vol. ii. p. 384.

207. *Works*, vol. xi, p. 11. He goes on to say in the same letter that his tale 'cannot stand comparison with the works of any writer of real talent', although 'it could easily compete with those who have gained the favour' of some sections of the Russian reading public.

208. The principal mouthpiece of the former was the well-known journal 'Library for Reading'. To run down the novel was also *de rigueur* during the aesthetic revival in Russia at the beginning of the present century. Herzen found 'immense merit' in it, but, he wrote to Ogarev, 'by God, what a language, what prosiness . . .—a seminarist from Vasily Island [the 'academic' part of St. Petersburg, where the Academy of Sciences, the University and other learned institutions were situated]!' For the controversy over *What Is to Be Done?*, see Berliner, op. cit., chapters x, xi, xii.

Of the latter, the most important were Pisarev and, later, the majority of Soviet critics. Of these the most interesting is Lunacharsky (see his *Russkaya literatura* [Russian Literature], M., 1947). An exception is A. Skaftymov (*N. G. Chernyshevsky*, Saratov, 1926), whose trenchant if by no means unsympathetic discussion of the novel is probably the best that has been written on it.

CHAPTER IV

1. Chernyshevsky's *Materiyaly dlya biografii N. A. Dobrolyubova* (Documents for a Biography of N. A. Dobrolyubov), hereafter referred to as *Documents*, were published separately in 1890 (2 vols., M., of which only vol. i is available). Dobrolyubov's next important biographer, A. Skabichevsky (*N. A. Dobrolyubov. Ego zhizn' i literaturnaya deyatelnost'* [N. A. Dobrolyubov. His Life and Literary Work], P., 1902), continued to propagate the legend. For a biographical account, see *Letopis' zhizni i deyatelnosti N. A. Dobrolyubova* (A Chronicle of N. A. Dobrolyubov's Life and Work), ed. by S. Reisner, M., 1953; and the best monograph on Dobrolyubov's life and thought is still Polyansky's (P. Lebedev) *N. A. Dobrolyubov. Mirovozrenie i literaturno-kriticheskaya deyatelnost'* (N. A. Dobrolyubov. His Outlook and Work of Literary Criticism), M., 1933. The two later substantial studies by V. Kruzhkov (*Mirovozrenie N. A. Dobrolyubova* [The Outlook of N. A. Dobrolyubov], M., 1952) and by M. Naumova (*Sotsiologicheskie, filosofskie i esteticheskie vzglyady N. A. Dobrolyubova* [The Sociological, Philosophical and Aesthetic Views of N. A. Dobrolyubov], M., 1960) compare unfavourably with Polyansky's work: A book on Dobrolyubov by V. Zhdanov, the best recent work on him, was unfortunately not available at the time of writing. Of great biographical

interest are the memoirs of Antonovich, Shelgunov, and Panaeva, quoted in the sections on Chernyshevsky, and, for the earlier period, N. Zlatovratsky's 'Iz vospominanii o N. A. Dobrolyubove' (Some Recollections about N. A. Dobrolyubov), reproduced in his *Vospominaniya* (Reminiscences), M., 1956. See also Chernyshevsky's *biographie romancée* which forms part of the novel 'Prologue' and is entitled *Dnevnik Levitskogo* (The Diary of Levitsky); and the material published in *LN.*, vols. 25–26; 67, and in *KA.*, 1936, ii, pp. 145 ff. A good bibliography (up to 1939) will be found in the valuable Notes to Dobrolyubov's *Complete Works*, 6 vols., ed. by Lebedev-Polyansky, Y. Oksman, and B. Koz′min, L., 1934–9, hereafter referred to as *Works*. This edition is more complete than Anichkov's (1912–13), but it does not include Dobrolyubov's letters. Many of these are included in Chernyshevsky's *Documents*; others are quoted or reproduced in full in various Soviet publications, particularly in the volumes of *LN.* mentioned above. A new complete edition of Dobrolyubov's works in 9 vols., of which three are already available (1961–2), has started coming out since the completion of this section. There is a more easily available edition of Dobrolyubov's *Selected Philosophical Works*, 2 vols., M., 1948, quoted hereafter as *Selected Works*, and a shortened English version of this (*Selected Philosophical Essays*, Foreign Languages Publishing House, M., 1956).

2. The Diary or Diaries were published by Polyansky in a separate edition (M., 1932) and are quoted hereafter as *Diaries*. They appeared, in part, for the first time in the 'Contemporary' in 1862.

3. *Works*, vol. vi, pp. 375, 382.

4. *Diaries*, p. 105; cf. *Documents*, vol. i, pp. 120 f., 204.

5. *Documents*, vol. i, p. 325.

6. See Dobrolyubov's own complaints to this effect in a reference to Lavrsky, an older fellow pupil at the seminary—one of the few with whom he was able to establish some personal relations: 'he [Lavrsky] taught me to laugh at everything that caught my eye, although I was by nature serious-minded. He induced me, despite my fairly temperate and scrupulous disposition, to rush to conclusions, to judge matters from outside, without considering them in themselves; he helped to turn understanding into ready wit, contempt for many things into mockery, insight into mere ingenuity.' *Diaries*, p. 83.

7. N. Tatarina (Ostrovskaya), 'Moi vospominaniya o N. A. Dobrolyubove' (My Recollections of N. A. Dobrolyubov), *Volzhskii vestnik* (Volga Messenger), 1893, no. 296 (quoted in *Diaries*, p. 201).

8. *Documents*, vol. i, p. 492.

9. See, for example, Naumova's quotations from unpublished material, op. cit., p. 27.

10. Quoted by S. Borshchevsky, *Shchedrin i* [and] *Dostoevsky*, M., 1956, pp. 55 f.

11. *Diaries*, p. 230.

12. See *Works*, vol. iv, pp. 429 ff.

13. In a speech at the meeting held in London to commemorate the revolution of 1848. See H., vol. xii, pp. 241 ff., 247 f. For Stsiborsky's testimony, see 'Vospominaniya o N. A. Dobrolyubove' (My Recollections

of N. A. Dobrolyubov), *LH.*, vols. 25–26, pp. 300 ff., which contain additional evidence about the 'Dobrolyubov gang'.

14. *Literaturnye vospominaniya* (Literary Reminiscences), separate (2nd) edition, M., 1950, pp. 322 f.

15. 'N. G. Chernyshevsky, Literary Heritage' [Ch. III, Note 1], vol. iii, p. 468.

16. See V. Evgeniev-Maksmov, 'Essays in the History of Socialist Journalism . . .', p. 71. The author found this note among Nekrasov's unpublished papers. The italicized words were underlined by Turgenev.

17. Antonovich, op. cit., pp. 140 f.

18. 'The Whistle' was at first planned as a separate magazine, but permission for this was refused by the authorities. Nekrasov, Panaev, Chernyshevsky, Mikhailov, Eliseev, and others contributed to the supplement. It was suppressed in 1863, and only nine issues appeared. Of Dobrolyubov's plans in connexion with the publication, see *Works*, vol. vi, pp. 692 ff. The only other contemporary satirical journal of any interest was the weekly *Iskra* (Spark). Edited by V. Kurochkin, it appeared with interruptions between 1859 and 1873, but became very tame after 1864 when Kurochkin was removed from the editorship.

19. *Ch.*, vol. ii, p. 213.

20. *LH.*, no. 25–26, p. 314; *Documents*, vol. i, pp. 495, 510 f.; *Works*, vol. iv, p. 397. See also some of Dobrolyubov's poems, for example, *Works*, vol. vi, pp. 11, 266 f., 759. Kruzhkov's strained attempt (op. cit., pp. 245 f.), however, to infer from such and similar uncertain evidence the existence of, and Dobrolyubov's part in, a revolutionary organization gives the impression of wishful thinking rather than of genuine historical reconstruction.

21. *LH.*, ibid., p. 150.

22. Op. cit., pp. 156 f. See also Dobrolyubov's letter to Turgenev (1 August 1856), quoted by Naumova, op. cit., p. 113; and Chernyshevsky's *Works*, vol. x, pp. 117 ff.

23. There remain a few fragments which contain Dobrolyubov's translations from Feuerbach for the edification of the members of his 'gang'. Feuerbach helped him to work for the solution of 'the great questions' about 'the great future of Russia'. See *Diaries*, 18 December 1855; and *LH.*, ibid., pp. 243 ff.

24. *Works*, vol. ii, p. 489; vol. i, pp. 206 f., 432; vol. iii, p. 95; vol. ii, pp. 498 f. For other evidence of Dobrolyubov's materialism or anti-dualism, see vol. i, p. 432; vol. iii, pp. 94, 97, 345: vol. iv, pp. 309 f.

25. *Works*, vol. iii, p. 92.

26. See, for example, the witty but somewhat crude critique of transcendentalism and agnosticism in a review of A. Kuskov's essay, itself rather flat, 'Ob istinnosti ponyatii ili o dostovernosti chelovecheskikh znanii' (On the Veracity of Concepts or the Trustworthiness of Human Knowledge), *Works*, vol. iii, pp. 361 ff.

27. Ibid., pp. 94 ff.

28. See *Works*, vol. iii, pp. 71, 93; also vol. i, p. 206. There is a striking similarity between these fragmentary epistemological statements and Herzen's treatment of the theory of knowledge: see, for example, 'Letters on the Study of Nature', Letter ii, H., vol. iii; cf. my *Studies in Rebellion*, pp. 202 f.

29. *Works*, vol. iv, pp. 58 f., 308; see also vol. ii, p. 273; vol. iv, p. 62.

30. *Works*, vol. i, p. 432. See also the attack on the 'triviality' (*krokho-borstvo*) of certain scientific procedures in the essay on Peter the Great, *Works*, vol. iii, p. 115.

31. *Works*, vol. iv, p. 60.

32. An exception to this is the essay on Buddha (*Works*, vol. iii) in which Dobrolyubov gives a highly individualized picture of the man, deliberately dwelling on his human peculiarities as far as these are known. It was intended as a retort to the conventional and allegorical treatment of the subject.

33. *Works*, vol. i, p. 278. See also Antonovich's testimony about Dobrolyubov's distaste for dogmatic finality and unquestioned beliefs (op. cit., p. 138).

34. See, for example, the essay 'Organicheskoe razvitie cheloveka v svyazi s ego umstvennoi i nravstvennoi deyatelnostiyu' (The Organic Development of Man in Relation to His Intellectual and Moral Activity), *Works*, vol. iii; also *Selected Works*, vol. ii, p. 325.

35. See, for example, *Works*, vol. i, p. 215.

36. *Works*, vol. i, p. 440.

37. The essay, it should be noted, appeared before 1859, when Dobrolyubov's attitude to the older generation became less sympathetic than might be inferred from this article.

38. See *Works*, vol. vi, pp. 37 f.; and 'Literaturnye melochi proshlogo goda' (Last Year's Literary Miscellanea), *Works*, vol. iv, pp. 41 ff.

39. *Works*, vol. iii, pp. 13 f.

40. *Works*, vol. iii, p. 253; vol. i, pp. 206 f. See also Dobrolyubov's objections to any idea of the 'logical', 'rectilinear movement' of history which he expressed in the travelogue 'Ot Moskvy do Leiptsiga' (From Moscow to Leipzig), *Works*, vol. iv, especially pp. 391 ff.

41. See, for example, *Works*, vol. iii, pp. 65 f., and statements to the same effect in 'Reign of Darkness'.

42. *Works*, vol. iii, p. 120. See also Dobrolyubov's earlier statements concerning the 'inconsistency' and 'suddenness' of historical trends in Russia: vol. i, pp. 183 ff.

43. See *Works*, vol. iii, pp. 66, 210 f., 334 f.

44. *Works*, vol. ii, p. 183; vol. iii, pp. 241, 268.

45. *Works*, vol. ii, p. 388.

46. *Works*, vol. iv, pp. 107, 395. See also his account of Robert Owen's 'noble' but 'day-dreaming', 'childish' reliance on the goodness of human nature: vol. iv, pp. 22 f.; and *Selected Works*, vol. i, p. 343.

47. See, for example, his letter to Slavutinsky, a fellow student, *Ogni* (Fires), i, P., 1916, pp. 67 f.

48. See *Works*, vol. ii, p. 110; and Antonovich, op. cit., p. 142.

49. See, for example, the already quoted essays 'Last Year's Literary Miscellanea', which appeared in the 'Contemporary' in January and April 1859, and 'Novye obrazchiki russkoi glasnosti' (New Specimens of Russian Publicity) in the second issue of 'The Whistle'; also 'Po povodu odnoi ochen' obyknovennoi istorii' (Apropos of A Very Ordinary Affair) and 'Zhizn' i smert' grafa Kamillo Benso Kavura' (The Life and Death of Count Camillo

Benso Cavour). The last two essays are ostensibly devoted to foreign affairs (of which, unlike Chernyshevsky, Dobrolyubov had an inadequate notion) but, in fact, deal largely with Russian social and political problems.

Saltykov-Shchedrin, who also satirized the current reformist trends in Russia, published an imaginary dialogue between a general called Postepennikov ('Gradualist') and a minor civil servant, Kolobrodnikov ('Skylark'). 'No, sir, I am not prepared to hop', the General repeats, without listening to the other's assurances that no such unbridled movements are expected of him. 'To my mind', the General insists, 'we ought to proceed in a proper fashion. If you want reforms, begin at the beginning and take each district in turn. Having reformed one district, go on to the next, and so on. That's the way—shock-proof, imperceptible. I refuse to leap!' At the end Kolobrodnikov sums up the process: 'In Russia', he says, 'there are more than 600 districts, and to make the result satisfactory each district would require one year of reforming treatment . . ., so that the last district will have to wait 600 years for its turn.' The prospect meets with General Gradualist's approval, which he accompanies by repeated exclamations 'Surely, you do not expect me to hop!'

50. *Works*, vol. i, p. 206; vol. ii, pp. 139, 211; vol. iv, pp. 400 f.

51. See also *Documents*, vol. i, p. 439. The Diary entry was occasioned by Herzen's celebrated article 'Very Dangerous!', in which he complained about the 'Contemporary's' and notably Dobrolyubov's systematic strictures on the 'denunciatory tendency' and on the social and literary cult of the 'superfluous men'. Dobrolyubov was pained by some of Herzen's imputations, especially by his veiled suggestion that Dobrolyubov's 'whistling' might land him straight in the lap of the tsarist Establishment (*dosvistat'sya do Stanislava na sheyu*). But, on the whole, he inclined to view the matter as largely a misunderstanding. Chernyshevsky, as has been noted, went to London to clarify the position, while Nekrasov nearly had a nervous breakdown. To put the conflict and Herzen's own inhibitions in their proper perspective it is necessary to emphasize once more the rejection by Herzen himself of 'half-measures', of 'reasonable freedom' and 'moderate progress' which he expressed unequivocally in his controversy with Chicherin (see my *Studies in Rebellion*, p. 252), in his attitude to Russian developments after Panin's appointment to the commission on peasant reforms, and, finally, in his remarkable 'Ends and Beginnings', which is, in the main, a decisive *Auseinandersetzung* with Turgenev (H., vol. xvi). On the other hand, Dobrolyubov, too, was not as intransigent towards the 'Herzen line' as is frequently suggested. 'We are accused', he wrote, 'of mocking denunciatory literature and even publicity (*glasnost'*). And yet we yield to none in our ardent love of criticism and free speech, and there is scarcely anyone who desires as much as we do to extend these as far as possible. We seek more integral and thoroughgoing forms of action, and still we are blamed for indulging in childish pranks' (*Works*, vol. ii, p. 484). A fuller account of the relations between Herzen and Dobrolyubov will be found in S. Reiser's *Dobrolyubov i* [and] *Herzen, Izvestiya AN SSSR. Otdel obshchestvennykh nauk* (Reports of the Academy of Sciences of the USSR. Department of Social Sciences), 1936, nos. 1–2; also *LN.*, vol 67, pp. 277 f.

52. *Works*, vol. ii, pp. 232, 334.

53. *Works*, vol. iv, pp. 398.

54. *Works*, vol. ii, p. 132; vol. iii, p. 268; also vol. ii, p. 187; vol. iv, pp. 109, 292, 434, and elsewhere in this essay entitled *Narodnoe delo* (The People's Cause).

55. *Works*, vol. iv, pp. 138 f., 157.

56. See also the distinction which, following Chernyshevsky, Dobrolyubov made between 'national wealth' and the 'well-being of the people' (*Works*, vol. i, p. 211). For Dobrolyubov's other populist ideas, see vol. i, pp. 117, 465; vol. ii, p. 262; vol. iii, p. 65; vol. iv, pp. 262, 402, 434. Three essays are especially relevant in this connexion: 'The People's Cause', quoted above; a review article on Marko-Vovchok's tales, entitled 'Cherty dlya kharakteristiki russkogo prostonarodiya' (Elements towards a Characterization of the Simple Russian People), *Works*, vol. ii; and 'O stepeni narodnosti v razvitii russkoi literatury' (On the Extent of Popular Trends in the Development of Russian Literature), *Works*, vol. i. A more detailed assessment of Dobrolyubov's populist tendencies will be found in an essay by Zaitsev, Pisarev's collaborator in the 'Russian Word' ('Belinsky i [and] Dobrolyubov', 'Russian Word', 1864, no. 1); in Polyansky, op. cit., pp. 229 f.; and Venturi, op. cit., vol. i, ch. vi. On Dobrolyubov's political views, see the monograph by F. Burlatsky, *Politicheskie vzglyady N. A. Dobrolyubova* (N. A. Dobrolyubov's Political Views), M., 1954. The author tends to ignore or to deny populist elements in Dobrolyubov's political outlook.

57. Works, vol. iii, p. 283.

58. See Zaitsev's article quoted above; and Ivanov-Razumnik, op. cit., vol. ii, p. 55.

59. Druzhinin's *Works*, 8 vols., P., 1865–6, vol. vii, p. 214. In a sense, it would be more relevant to regard Druzhinin's trend as a danger to the Russian literature of his time, for it was his own 'Library for Reading,' not the 'Contemporary', which extolled such cheap and sentimental playwrights as Polevoy, Rosen, and Kukolnik whose patriotic plays enjoyed a considerable success in Russia. Kukolnik was described by the 'Library for Reading as 'more intelligent, more learned and more to the point than Pushkin' and 'superior as a prose writer to Gogol' (quoted by Kagan, op. cit. [Ch. III, Note 188], p. 40).

60. See, for example, *Works*, vol. i, p. 540; also the work by A. Karaganov, 'Chernyshevsky and Dobrolyubov on Realism', cited in the chapter on Chernyshevsky.

61. *Selected Works*, vol. ii, p. 331.

62. Ibid., pp. 15, 331.

63. *Works*, vol. i, p. 199.

64. *Selected Works*, vol. ii, pp. 20, 328.

65. See ibid., vol. i, p. 91.

66. Chernyshevsky's *Works*, vol. iii, p. 17. The writers whom he had particularly in mind were A. Kantemir (1708–44), A. Sumarokov (1717–74), and D. Fonvizin (1744–92) whose 'realistic' tendencies and satiric attacks on Russian conditions anticipated to some extent the two salient features of later Russian literature.

67. *Works*, vol. ii, p. 139. See also S. Abakumov, *N. A. Dobrolyubov kak satirik* (N. A. Dobrolyubov as a Satirist), Kazan, 1922.

68. Ostrovsky grew up in the *Zamoskvorechie*, the merchant quarter of Moscow and, like his father, worked at first as a civil service clerk. Towards the end of his life he became a director of the Imperial Theatres of Moscow and the Head of the Imperial School of Dramatic Art.

69. *Selected Works*, vol. ii, p. 21.

70. e.g. *Ne v svoi sani ne sadis'* (Know Your Place) and notably *Bednost' ne porok* (Poverty is no Vice), with its vaguely *pochvennik* hero Lyubim Tortsov—a large-hearted bibacious merchant in adversity. For Grigoriev's estimate, see his *Works*, M., 1915, Issue 1, pp. 263 ff.

71. Druzhinin, it may be noted, attacked Ostrovsky for his 'gloom' and demanded of him the creation of characters who 'look at life from a bright, comforting and reasonable standpoint' (Druzhinin's *Works*, vol. iv, p. 640).

72. *Works*, vol. ii, pp. 5 ff. Goncharov seems to have been much impressed by Dobrolyubov's analysis of his novel: see his letters to P. Annenkov and I. Lkhovsky (Goncharov's *Works*, 8 vols., M., 1955, vol. viii, p. 320 f.)

73. *F. M. Dostoevsky v russkoi kritike* (F. M. Dostoevski in Russian Criticism), M., 1956, p. 69.

CHAPTER V

1. The quotation is from Saltykov-Shchedrin, whose work represents to a large extent an elaboration of this, applied to Russia as a whole. A similar picture of Russian life will be found in some of the plays of the 'Russian Zola', Aleksey Pisemsky (1821–81), which describe the dizzy pursuits of money-making characteristic of the post-Reform decades.

2. The most important biographies of Pisarev are: E. Soloviev, *D. I. Pisarev*, 3rd ed., Berlin-P.-M., 1922, which contains important and otherwise not easily accessible material; E. Kazanovich, *D. Pisarev (1840–1856)*, P., 1922, which covers, in greater detail, Pisarev's early years; V. Kirpotin's works on Pisarev, of which the most important is *Radikalnyi raznochinets D. I. Pisarev* (The Radical *Raznochinets* D. I. Pisarev), 3rd ed., M., 1934; L. Plotkin, *Pisarev i literaturno-obshchestvennoe dvizhenie shestidesyatykh godov* (Pisarev and the Literary and Social Movement in the Sixties), M., 1945; and the best monograph in other than the Russian language, by A. Coquart, *Dimitri Pisarev (1840–1868) et l'idéologie du nihilisme russe*, Paris, 1946, vol. xxi of the series *Bibliothèque russe de l'Institut d'études slaves*. See also Coquart's 'La Sage Enfance du nihiliste Pisarev', *Revue des études slaves*, 1945, vol. xxii. First-hand biographical evidence, including letters, will be found in *Shestidesyatye gody. Materiyaly po istorii literatury i obshchestvennosti* (The Sixties. Documents Regarding Literary and Social History), M.-L., 1940, pp. 107 ff.; in the previously mentioned memoirs of Shelgunov, and in *Literaturnye vospominaniya* (Literary Reminiscences), M.-L., 1928, by A. Skabichevsky, who was a fellow student of Pisarev. See also *LN.*, 1936, no. 25–26.

3. For evidence about this, see *Zapiski otdela rukopisei (Biblioteka Lenina)* (Notes of the Manuscript Department [Lenin Library]), Issue 9, 1940, pp. 19 ff.

4. *Collected Works* by Pisarev, 4 vols., M., 1955–6, vol. ii, p. 179. This most up-to-date if incomplete edition of Pisarev's essays by Y. Sorokin will

be quoted as *CW* (*2*). A previous edition in 2 vols., M., 1934–35, by Kirpotin will be quoted as *CW* (*1*). No other Russian radical enjoyed so many editions of his works in pre-revolutionary times. Apart from the first edition in ten parts in Pisarev's lifetime (P., 1866–9), there are five more, in 6 vols., with a seventh supplementary volume (1907). The dates are: 1894, 1897, 1900–1, 1904–7, 1909–13. Though more complete than the post-revolutionary editions, the text is more or less heavily censored and therefore not always reliable. I have consulted the 1894, the 1897, the 1900, and the 1909 editions, and these are quoted as *Works* (*2*), *Works* (*3*), *Works* (*4*), and *Works* (*6*) respectively.

5. Skabichevsky, op. cit., pp. 118, 112 f.

6. *CW* (*2*), vol. ii, p. 175.

7. Ibid., p. 180.

8. See, for example, the letter to his parents, dated 15 December 1851: 'Tonight', he wrote, 'I was reading *Les Méditations réligieuses* to Auntie. Oh, how beautiful, how lofty, how deep and yet how simple it all is!'

9. *CW* (*2*), vol. ii, pp. 180 ff.

10. See I. Ivanov, *Istoriya russkoi kritiki* (The History of Russian Criticism), P., 1905, p. 605; also A. Volynsky, *Russkie kritiki* (Russian Critics), P., 1896, p. 383.

11. See V. P. Soloviev, *Zhurnal 'Russkoe slovo'. Publitsistika D. I. Pisareva* (The Review 'Russian Word'. D. I. Pisarev's Journalism), M., 1955, especially pp. 44 ff.; also B. Koz'min, 'G. E. Blagosvetlov i "Russkoe slovo"' (G. E. Blagosvetlov and the 'Russian Word'), *Sovremennik* (Contemporary [not, of course, Nekrasov's journal of the same name]), 1922, no. 1, pp. 192 ff.

When this book was written no comparative study of Nekrasov's 'Contemporary' and the 'Russian Word' existed. Accounts of Russian journalism as a rule confine themselves to a straightforward history of these and other journals, to the political vicissitudes which they underwent, to the controversies in which they engaged and to the various writers who contributed to them. But the most important Russian reviews were in themselves distinct cultural or literary phenomena with clearly recognizable characteristics, which cannot be reduced either to individual contributors or to political 'tendencies'. The only work which deals with this wider aspect is, as far as I know, V. Kuleshov's *'Otechestvennye zapiski' i literatura 40 godov XIX v.* (The 'Annals of the Fatherland' and the Literature of the Eighteen-Forties), M., 1958. But he is concerned with another journal and another period. What follows is but a rough and tentative attempt at comparative characterization.

12. *LN.*, no. 25–26, p. 403. It should be noted that Shelgunov's attempt to represent Dobrolyubov and Pisarev as a Boerne and Heine respectively is only partly justified, for later on Pisarev took the side of the former against the latter's 'political faithlessness' and vacillating attitude towards revolution. See *Works* (*6*), vol. ii, p. 296: the essay in question ('Heinrich Heine') was written not in 1862, as this and other editions of Pisarev's works state, but in 1866 or even later, for he quotes the seventh and eleventh volumes of Heine's works in Russian translation which appeared only in 1866.

13. 'Mr. Shchedrin or the Schism among the Nihilists' (*'Gospodin Shchedrin ili raskol v nigilistakh'*) was the title of an article published by Dostoevsky in 'Epoch', 1864, no. 5.

14. On Shchedrin, see the monographs by Ivanov-Razumnik, *M. E. Saltykov-Shchedrin, zhizn' i tvorchestvo* (M. E. Saltykov-Shchedrin, Life and Work), M., 1930 (unfinished: only vol. i appeared); by Y. Elsberg, *Saltykov-Shchedrin, zhizn' i tvorchestvo* (Saltykov-Shchedrin, Life and Work), M., 1953; and by Kyra Sanine, *Saltykov-Chtchédrine: sa vie et ses œuvres*, Paris, 1955, vol. xxiv of the *Bibliothèque russe de l'Institut d'études slaves*.

15. It should be noted that this partnership was not entirely harmonious. From 1863 the 'Contemporary' was run by an editorial board consisting of five men: Eliseev, Antonovich, Pypin, Shchedrin, and Nekrasov. The last two, however, stood somewhat apart by reason of their seniority and more cultured background. The other three were ex-seminarists who had not shed their seminarist roughness, and Shchedrin, a nobleman with a distinguished career in the civil service behind him, suffered especially from what he called 'the dictatorship of the Consistory'.

On Antonovich, see the introductory essay by G. Tamarchenko to a selection of his 'Literary and Critical Articles' (*Literaturno-kriticheskie stat'i*) M.–L., 1961; *Mirovozrenie M. A. Antonovicha* (M. A. Antonovich's View of the World), M., 1960, by M. Peunova; and the first-rate critical appreciation of this work by A. Lebedev, 'Chernyshevsky ili [or] Antonovich?' in *Novyi mir* (New World), 1962, no. 3.

16. The best account is still B. Koz'min's 'Raskol v nigilistakh' (The Schism among the Nihilists), originally published in *Literatura i marksizm* (Literature and Marxism), 1928, no. 2, and reproduced in a collection of Koz'min's essays entitled *Iz istorii revolyutsionnoi mysli v Rossii* (Essays on the History of Revolutionary Thought in Russia), M., 1961. At the time Koz'min shared the strong anti-populist bias of early Soviet historiography. He is also not quite fair to Shchedrin. In his later works (especially in the important study 'Narodnichestvo na burzhuazno-demokraticheskom etape osvoboditelnogo dvizheniya' [Populism at the Bourgeois-Democratic Stage of the Liberation Movement], *IZ.*, 1952, vol. 56), Koz'min revised his estimate of populism. See also V. Evgeniev-Maksimov, *Poslednie gody 'Sovremennika'* (The Last Years of the 'Contemporary'), L., 1939. Another excellent account will be found in the Appendix to S. Borshchevsky's 'Shchedrin and Dostoevsky', quoted in the section on Chernyshevsky.

17. More precisely, the quarrel was started by Zaitsev in 1863, in the April issue of the 'Russian Word'. In an article entitled 'Perly i adamanty nashey zhurnalistiki' (The Pearls and Diamonds of Our Journalism) he reproached the 'Contemporary' with having 'spent its wits'. Ironically, Zaitsev was particularly incensed by the negative reaction of the 'Contemporary' to Dostoevsky's *Notes from the House of the Dead*. 'Such works', Zaitsev wrote of this book, 'are written with one's blood, not with the ink from a Vice-Governor's table' (this was aimed at Shchedrin who for a time held the post of Assistant Governor-General in Ryazan). He advised the 'Contemporary' 'to drop the tone of Vice-Generalship'.

18. Shchedrin's later, more positive estimate of nihilism can be inferred

from his *Blagonamerennye rechi* (Well-meaning Discourses) (7) and from *Kruglyi god—1-oe maya* (The Whole Year—1st of May), Shchedrin's *Works*, 20 vols., M., 1933–41, vols. x and xii.

19. *Works* (2), vol. iii, p. 306; pp. 276 f.; and vol. iv, p. 33. When Antonovich accused Pisarev of betraying Dobrolyubov's heritage Pisarev replied: 'I have never been a very ardent or even just an ardent adept of Dobrolyubov. . . . I disagreed with him on a great number of points. . . . I always considered him, and still consider him, a very intelligent and honest man, but I do not share many of his views' (vol. v, pp. 154 f.). Elsewhere Pisarev was even more outspoken (e.g. vol. iv, p. 33). But he also emphasized that his disagreement with the 'Contemporary' was about 'aberrations', not about essentials (*Works* (3), vol. iv, p. 146).

20. *CW* (2), vol. i, pp. 113 f.

21. The fact that Pisarev chose this subject could be significant of his attitude to religion. Although the thesis is mainly concerned with the historical and social background, Pisarev attaches considerable importance to Apollonius's legendary life-story by Philostratus which was regarded as a pagan counterblast to the New Testament.

22. E. Soloviev, op. cit., p. 143.

23. See Lemke, *Political Trials* . . . , pp. 557 f.

24. For an account of the rather unsavoury activities of Shedo-Ferroti, see *LN.*, vol. 63, pp. 677 ff.; also P. Valesklan, *Revolyutsionnyi demokrat Pyotr Davidovich Ballod* (The Revolutionary Democrat Pyotr Davidovich Ballod), Riga, 1957.

25. It was published for the first time by Lemke in 1907 (op. cit., pp. 539 ff.), but the censorship prevented its inclusion even in the last pre-revolutionary edition of Pisarev's works.

26. *LN.*, no. 25–26, p. 402.

27. See, for example, the curious letter, in impeccable French, to Suvorov, Governor-General of St. Petersburg, who, incidentally, did his very best to alleviate Pisarev's position. The letter is reproduced by Coquart, op. cit., pp. 198 f.

28. They are extensively quoted by E. Soloviev, op. cit. See also Koz'min, 'Pis'ma D. I. Pisareva iz kreposti' (D. I. Pisarev's Letters from the Fortress), *KA.*, 1924, no. 5, pp. 248 ff.; and N. Bykhovsky, 'Pisarev v petro-pavlovskoi kreposti' ('Pisarev in the Peter and Paul Fortress'), *LN.*, no. 25–26, pp. 655 ff.

29. See E. Soloviev, op. cit., p. 163.

30. See ibid., pp. 181 f.

31. See ibid., pp. 171 f.

32. An account of Pisarev's move to and work for the 'Annals of the Fatherland' will be found in Skabichevsky, op. cit., pp. 167 ff., 204 ff. On the review itself (after 1868), see Evgeniev-Maksimov, *Essays in the History of Socialist Journalism* . . . , part iii.

33. Quoted by Coquart, op. cit., pp. 361.

34. Skabichevsky's view of her was very scathing: he describes her as 'some sort of female of vulgar appearance, with colourless, hideous eyes, tow-haired eyebrows, a flat figure, and no conversation. Her sole replies were "yes" and "no"'. Blagosvetlov was equally negative. One of the

reasons why Pisarev finally broke with Blagosvetlov was the latter's refusal to help Maria Markovich in the publication of her writings.

35. The circumstantial evidence points to suicide. Pisarev, who was an excellent swimmer, chose a quiet morning and a deserted part of the shore; the place where his body was recovered showed that he must have swum out as far as he could and then, in the words of Coquart, 'se laissa couler'. Coquart suggests that the suicide might have been due to Pisarev's sexual incapacity, which left his passion for Maria unconsummated. Only the lady herself could have enlightened us on this not unduly important point, but she left no clue whatever, although she lived to the advanced age of 72. Blagosvetlov was in no doubt that Pisarev had drowned himself. His testimony is indirectly confirmed by Pavlenkov, a friend of Pisarev's family and the indefatigable editor of his works. But Skabichevsky denies the suicide theory. So do a number of other contemporaries. For the full evidence, see Coquart, op. cit., pp. 382 ff.

36. Quoted by Evgeniev-Maksimov, 'D. I. Pisarev i okhraniteli' (D. I. Pisarev and the Custodians), *Golos minuvshego* (The Voice of the Past), 1919, no. 1–4, p. 158.

37. See, for example, *CW* (*1*), vol. i, p. 60.

38. *CW* (*2*), vol. i, p. 77.

39. Ibid., p. 80.

40. Herzen's philosophical culture was, needless to say, deeper and more extensive than Pisarev's. Although Pisarev wrote about Plato, it is not certain if he ever read him: the essay in question was a review-article on a book about Plato. He also wrote about Kant and Hegel, and it is almost certain that he never read them, because he said so himself.

41. *CW* (*2*), vol. i, p. 86; also pp. 120 f.

42. Ibid., p. 130.

43. It should be noted that Büchner at least explicitly repudiated the appellation 'materialist'. Science, he stated in the preface to the 1867 edition of *Kraft und Stoff*, was not to be regarded as either materialist or idealist: it is 'realist' and concerns itself with 'existing facts' and their relations. Pisarev similarly preferred this kind of language.

44. In his comments on the celebrated controversy between Pouchet and Pasteur, Pisarev resolutely took the side of Pouchet. Although he found himself in fairly respectable company, his own reasons for doing so had no scientific basis, for he had no access to the relevant evidence. He opposed Pasteur because Pasteur's demonstration that there was no known instance of the derivation of living from non-living matter did not accord with Pisarev's philosophical assumptions.

45. *Works* (*2*), vol. iii, p. 315.

46. See ibid., vol. v, pp. 439 f.

47. *CW* (*1*), vol. i, p. 550; *Works* (*2*), vol. v, p. 579.

48. *CW* (*1*), p. 139; see also *Works* (*2*), vol. i, pp. 311 ff.; *CW* (*1*), vol. i, p. 534; and the article on Dostoevsky's *Crime and Punishment*, *CW* (*2*), vol. iv.

49. *CW* (*2*), vol. i, p. 308.

50. *CW* (*1*), vol. i, pp. 50, 60.

51. *CW* (*2*), vol. i, p. 12.

52. Ibid., pp. 124 ff.

53. *CW* (*2*), vol. i, pp. 82 ff.

54. E. Soloviev, op. cit., p. 144.

55. *CW* (*1*), vol. i, p. 109; also pp. 39, 50, 52.

56. For the *locus classicus* of Pisarev's utilitarianism, see *CW* (*1*), vol. i, p. 460, where a frank pursuit of one's interests is derived not from any impulse of benevolence which demands to be satisfied, but from the realization that a world in which all 'succeed in escaping the yoke of material necessity' is more expedient for each of us. Elsewhere he speaks of a co-incidence of 'reasonable egotism' and 'the true love of other men' (*CW* (*1*), vol. ii, pp. 52 f.). See also *Works* (*3*), vol. iv, pp. 128 ff., 132.

57. See also *CW* (*1*), vol. i, p. 542.

58. See *CW* (*1*), vol. i, p. 264.

59. *Works* (*3*), vol. vi, pp. 39 f. This statement coincides with Pisarev's early views: 'The main cause [of man's conduct]', he said, 'resides in man himself and depends on his own volition', rather than on outward circumstances (see *The Sixties. Documents* . . . , p. 138).

60. *Works* (*2*), vol. i, pp. 310 f.

61. *CW* (*1*), vol. i, p. 460; also p. 534.

62. See also *Works* (*3*), vol. ii, p. 385; *CW* (*1*), vol. i, p. 492. Pisarev extolled the frog-dissecting Bazarov for his preoccupation with 'facts and particular phenomena' and for his refusal to admit 'any general methods and general laws'.

63. *Works* (*3*), vol. iv, pp. 319, 389, 393, 409; *CW* (*1*), vol. ii, p. 455. The decline of Pisarev's faith in the omnipotence of natural science became more pronounced towards the end of his life (see, for example, his introductory essay to Huxley's *Lessons in Elementary Physiology*, *Works* (*3*), vol. v, pp. 381 ff.).

64. For a history of the term 'nihilism', see M. Alekseev, 'K istorii slova nigilizm' (Note on the History of the Word 'Nihilism') in *Sbornik statei v chest' Alekseya Ivanovicha Sobolevskogo* (A Collection of Articles in Honour of Aleksey Ivanovich Sobolevsky), ed. by V. Perets, L., 1928; also Benoît P. Hepner, 'Nihilisme — mot et idée' in *Synthèses*, Brussels, January 1949.

65. H., vol. xx (2), p. 791.

66. Ibid., (1), pp. 349 f. (italics in the original).

67. *CW* (*1*), vol. i, p. 66.

68. Ibid., pp. 223, 199.

69. *Works* (*3*), vol. ii, p. 385.

70. For the above quotations and other evidence of Pisarev's nihilism, see *CW* (*1*), vol. i, pp. 228, 234, 255, 284.

71. Ibid., p. 185.

72. Ibid., pp. 185, 228.

73. *CW* (*2*), vol. i, pp. 320 f. Elsewhere Pisarev wrote: 'It should at last be realized that an ideal is not even an abstract concept, but simply a semblance of another person. Every ideal has its author. . . . To discover its name is always very difficult and, in most cases, impossible. But when a moral portrait is made of a certain person—be it flattering or disparaging—an ideal is suited only to its originator, or to those who fully resemble him in temperament, situation, and inner force. It is hard to find two persons with complete facial resemblance. Complete moral similarity between two

people . . . is even rarer. There are many colourless and depersonalized individuals: those who have been crushed by circumstances, moulded to one pattern by social discipline or polished to a single likeness by the despotism of fashion and etiquette. At first glance, they all seem alike in face, voice, manners. In such a society the least originality in the way of life . . . will seem an affront to the law and a challenge to morals. But a real human person will look with contempt upon this kind of society. He will wonder why men surrender freely to laws, designed to smother man's individual character.' *CW* (*2*), vol. i, p. 84.

74. *CW* (*1*), vol. ii, p. 11.

75. *Works* (*2*), vol. iii, pp. 358, 360; vol. v, p. 490.

76. See, for example, *CW* (*1*), vol. i, p. 144.

77. A contemporary observed that Pisarev stubbornly denied the balance and harmony which, at other times, he claimed to detect in life: 'What chaos, what contradictions!', Pisarev exclaimed. 'But are these not symptoms of abundant life, of new ideas, of vigour and variety?' (*The Sixties*. Documents . . . , pp. 228 f.)

78. *Works* (*2*), vol. v, p. 171.

79. *CW* (*1*), vol. ii, p. 17; also vol. i, p. 244.

80. *Works* (*4*), vol. vii (Suppl.), p. 14.

81. See *Works* (*4*), ibid., pp. 13 ff.; *CW* (*1*), vol. i, pp. 319, 457. It is interesting that Zaitsev, Pisarev's principal associate in the 'Russian Word', on leaving Russia, joined the anarchists in Switzerland. According to Vera Zasultich, Pisarev was the most widely read author in the Nechaev circle (see her *Vospominaniya* [Reminiscences], M., 1931, p. 58).

Coquart ascribes the anarchistic tendencies in Pisarev, and even his mixture of individualism and nihilism, to Proudhon. In point of fact, although Pisarev undoubtedly read Proudhon, as he read Fourier and the other 'utopian' socialists, the ideas to which Coquart refers were the stock-in-trade of Russian political and social thought since Radishchev. Proudhon's influence was quite incidental. Nothing could be further from Pisarev than Proudhonian 'mutualism', the cult of the family as the essential basis of society, and the hostility to women's rights as destructive of the patriarchal pattern of life.

82. *CW* (*1*), vol. i, p. 422; see also *Works* (*4*), vol. iii, pp. 305 f.

83. See *CW* (*1*), vol. i, pp. 264, 256.

84. *CW* (*2*), vol. ii, p. 104.

85. The evidence is too extensive to be cited in full: see, for example, *Works* (*3*), vol. ii, p. 394; *Works* (*2*), vol. v, pp. 317, 412, 577; *CW* (*1*), vol. i, pp. 54, 460, 527.

86. *CW* (*1*), vol. ii, pp. 417 f.

87. *Works* (*4*), vol. iii, pp. 144, 158, 232; see also *CW* (*1*), vol. i, p. 289. An examination of the 'Russian Word' shows that, among the contributors to the review, Pisarev was almost alone in his tributes to the French Revolution, and especially to Jacobinism, and that Blagosvetlov disliked such tributes. In the prevailing censorship conditions they were always an indication of a writer's attitude to revolution as such.

88. *CW* (*1*), vol. i, p. 282; *CW* (*2*), vol. iv, p. 50.

89. For the above quotations, see *Works* (*4*), vol. iii, p. 171; *Works* (*2*), vol. ii, p. 2; and *CW* (*1*), vol. i, p. 459.

90. *Works* (*3*), vol. iii, pp. 64 f.; *CW* (*1*), vol. i, pp. 496 f., 527.

91. *Works* (*3*), vol. iv, pp. 190 ff., also vol. i, pp. 225 f.; vol. ii, p. 234; vol. iii, pp. 276 f., 306.

92. *Works* (*3*), vol. ii, p. 234.

93. See Koz'min's observations about this in *Essays on the History of Revolutionary Thought* . . . , p. 44.

94. It is noteworthy that in the essay on Rakhmetov he ignores Chernyshevsky's plea for 'communal associations'.

95. See, for example, *Works* (*2*), vol. ii, pp. 583, 588, 597; vol. iv, p. 578. See also the interesting essay by V. Pereverzev, 'Nigilizm Pisareva v sotsiologicheskom osveshchenii' (Pisarev's Nihilism in the Light of Sociology) in *Krasnaya nov*' (Red Virgin Soil), 1926, no. 6. The author describes Pisarev as 'an ideologue of industrial culture.'

96. See, for example, *CW* (*1*), vol. i, pp. 479 f., 496 f.; vol. ii, pp. 526 f.; *Works* (*3*), vol. iv, p. 132.

97. Quoted by Koz'min, op. cit., pp. 50 f.

98. This is evident even in his early, most individualistic essays, such as 'The Scholasticism of the Nineteenth Century' (see *CW* (*2*), vol. i, p. 124; but also *Works* (*3*), vol. vi, p. 69).

99. See, for example, *Works* (*3*), vol. iii, pp. 113 f.; and the already quoted references, however qualified, to popular revolutions. Some of Pisarev's last utterances about 'the voice of the people' have even given occasion for ascribing populist tendencies to him. See especially the essay on 'The French Peasant in 1789' (*Frantsuzskii krest'yanin v 1789 g.*), published already in the 'Annals of the Fatherland' (1868, no. 6), where populism became an increasingly dominant theme. Pisarev was either compelled or chose to change his language.

100. *CW* (*1*), vol. ii, p. 88; also p. 466; *Works* (*3*), vol. i, p. 304; vol. iv, p. 578. Later, departing from his idea of the leading role of enlightened *entrepreneurs*, Pisarev came to hold that, in the last resort, it is 'the hungry and the disinherited' themselves who will have to solve the question (*Works* (*2*), vol. v, pp. 408 f).

101. See *CW* (*1*), vol. i. p. 460.

102. These ideas are mainly expounded in two essays: '*Realisty*' (The Realists) and '*Ocherki iz istorii truda*' (Essays in the History of Labour), written in 1864 and 1863 respectively. For the above quotation, see *Works* (*3*), vol. iv, p. 4. The ideas were to some extent derived from the American economist Henry Carey, whose most important work (*The Principles of Social Science* [1858]) represents a restatement of classical economics in terms of the expanding economy, particularly the expanding agricultural economy, in North America. Pisarev, who did not possess Chernyshevsky's profound understanding of economic problems, tried to apply somewhat indiscriminately Carey's ideas to Russian conditions.

103. The other two are: 'The Realists' and 'A Promenade through the Gardens of Russian Literature' (*Progulka po sadam rossiiskoi slovesnosti*); to this must be added the already quoted article against Antonovich, 'We Will See!'

104. See *CW* (*1*), vol. ii, pp. 51, 308 f; *CW* (*2*), vol. i, pp. 80, 115 f.

105. See, for example, Volynsky, op. cit., p. 383.

106. For the evidence of Pisarev's iconoclastic attitudes, see, for example, *CW* (*1*), vol. ii, pp. 75, 78 f., 308 f.; also vol. i, p. 492; *Works* (*4*), vol. iv, p. 115.

107. *Works* (*4*), vol. iv, p. 63.

108. A literary lady, Countess Elizaveta Sailhas de Tournemir, who wrote under the name Eugénie Tour and was herself responsible for a number of glutinously sentimental publications, declined his collaboration on the grounds that 'the young man', as she said, was 'too much addicted to the cult of beauty and pure art' (quoted by E. Soloviev, op. cit., p. 120). See also *Works* (*4*), vol. i, pp. 226 f.

109. See A. Mazon, 'L'élaboration d'un roman de Turgenev: Terres Vierges', *Revue des études slaves*, 1925, no. 5, p. 92. But, unlike Pisarev, Nezhdanov was a populist—'the bastard aristocrat aspiring to be a peasant-loving democrat, the poet *manqué* aspiring equally ineffectually to be a practical revolutionary' (Richard Freeborn, *Turgenev: The Novelist's Novelist*, Oxford, 1960, p. 171, and the whole chapter (7) which contains an excellent discussion of the novel and its hero).

110. See, for example, *Works* (*4*), vol. iv, p. 115.

111. Ibid., pp. 120 f.; *CW* (*2*), vol. ii, p. 115.

112. *CW* (*1*), vol. ii, pp. 75 f.

113. *CW* (*2*), vol. iii, pp. 73, 109, 232, 294 f., and elsewhere. Some of the strongest attacks on Pushkin were made by Pisarev in an essay entitled 'Pushkin and Belinsky', written like the rest in this vein from prison in 1865. See his similar views on Fet and Polonsky, whom he called 'microscopic poetasters', producing verse that is 'as beautiful as Brussels lace and as useless'. *CW* (*1*), vol. i, pp. 119, 123, 125.

114. See, for example, *CW* (*1*), vol. i, p. 209; vol. ii, pp. 75, 220.

115. Ibid., vol. i, p. 87.

116. Ibid., p. 124; vol. ii, p. 192.

117. See ibid., vol. ii, pp. 189, 261.

118. It is interesting that he rudely refused to recommend any works, even those which appeared in his own journal, if they were worthless from the artistic point of view, however much they may have conformed to the standards of 'usefulness'.

119. *CW* (*1*), vol. i, p. 259. Later, in the article on Dostoevsky's *Crime and Punishment*, Pisarev wrote that he is 'not in the least concerned either with the personal views of the author . . . or with the nature of his public activities', however much he may condemn both. Ibid., vol. ii, p. 497.

120. He describes Heine as a 'Hellenic type': 'There are two types of people—those who passionately and obstinately concentrate their energy on one idea which they worship. . . . These represent the Jewish type. The others, who disperse their efforts on all sides and seek enjoyment for themselves everywhere, represent the Hellenic type. . . . The two types are wonderfully personified in the two nations to whom they owe their origin, although they are often intermingled, so that someone who is essentially

a Jew may be Hellenic by inclination, and the purest Hellene may be
Jewish in some of his attitudes . . . .' *CW* (*2*), vol. IV, p. 238.

121. It should be noted that the Leskov Pisarev abused was the Leskov
of the early and largely trivial political novels (such as 'Nekuda' [No Way
Out]), not of the later Stories, which earned him his great reputation.

122. See *Works* (*4*), vol. i, pp. 213 f.; *CW* (*1*), vol. ii, p. 118; and the
unfinished essay on the first parts of *War and Peace*, ibid., p. 543.

123. Another essay on Dostoevsky ('Pogibshie i pogibayushchie' [The
Perished and the Perishing]) is even more concerned with externals. Its
subject-matter is Dostoevsky's *House of the Dead*, which Pisarev discusses
side by side with a study of Pomyalovsky's *Seminary Essays*.

INDEX

References to Notes are shown by italicized roman figures followed by italicized arabic figures, indicating chapter and number of Note respectively. Under N. Chernyshevsky, N. Dobrolyubov, and D. Pisarev will be found only those references which occur outside the chapters dealing specifically with these men.